MOUNT MARY COLLEGE LIBRARY
Milwaukee, Wisconsin 53222

Castro's Cuba in the 1970s

MOUNT MARY COLLEGE LIBRARY
Milwaukee, Wisconsin 53222

Castro's Cuba in the 1970s

Edited by Lester A. Sobel

Contributing writers: Joanne Edgar, Christopher Hunt, John Miner

Indexer: Grace M. Ferrara

78- 717

Facts On File
119 West 57th Street, New York, N.Y. 10019

Castro's Cuba in the 1970s

© Copyright, 1978, by Facts on File, Inc.

All rights reserved. No part of this book may be reproduced in any form without the permission of the publisher except for reasonably brief extracts used in reviews or scholarly works.

Published by Facts on File, Inc.,
119 West 57th Street, New York, N.Y. 10019.

Library of Congress Cataloging in Publication Data
Main entry under title:
Castro's Cuba in the 1970s.
   (Checkmark books)
   Includes index.
    1. Cuba—History—1959-   2. Cuba—Relations
(general) with foreign countries.   I. Sobel, Lester A.
II. Facts on File, Inc., New York.
F1788.C29   972.91′064   77-87241
ISBN 0-87196-151-2

9 8 7 6 5 4 3 2 1
PRINTED IN THE UNITED STATES OF AMERICA

Contents

INTRODUCTION	1
Cuba & Its People	3
Brief History of Cuba	5
Fidel Castro Ruz' Leadership	9
1970–73: A TIME OF RESTRAINT	13
Agreement with U.S. on Curbing Hijackings	13
Hijacking Incidents	17
Exile Actions & Castro Regime's Response	23
Confrontations at Sea	28
Terrorists & Prisoners Win Haven in Cuba	31
Relations With the U.S.S.R. & Other Communist Nations	33
Soviet Arms Aid & Soviet Submarine Base Warning	41
Relations With the U.S.	44
Export of Revolution	51
Western Hemisphere Relations	54
Other Foreign Affairs	62
Sugar & the Economy	64
Government & Communism	68
Other Developments	69
1973–75: A PERIOD OF ACCOMMODATION	73
Barriers Against Cuba Crumble	73
Both Sides Soften, But Sanctions Remain	80
Bars Keep Falling, Sanctions Finally End	86
CIA Plots Vs. Castro	91

Relations With Communist & Third World Nations	101
Other Foreign Affairs	105
Government & Politics	108
Other Developments	110
1975–77: CONFLICTING OBJECTIVES	**113**
Relations With U.S. Develop	113
Cuban Troops in Angola & Other African Countries	115
Cuba's Version of Angola Affair	123
Further African Developments	125
U.S.-Cuban Relations Under Jimmy Carter	131
Terrorism Hampers Detente, Castro Cancels Hijack Pact	148
Prisoners & Human Rights	156
Other Foreign Developments	157
Domestic Events	163
DOCUMENTS	**167**
1976 Constitution	167
Cuban Situation: U.S. Overview	185
Repression & Political Prisoners	211
The Church in Castro's Cuba	219
INDEX	**229**

Introduction

Fidel Castro Ruz has been the undisputed *jefe maximo* (supreme chief) of Cuba almost since Jan. 1, 1959, when the Cuban dictator Fulgencio Batista fled into exile from Castro's guerrilla force and the widespread civil resistance movement it inspired.

In the nineteen years that followed Batista's downfall, Castro's Cuba has played a role in international affairs far more significant than would appear to be justified by its size (slightly less than Pennsylvania's) or population (probably a bit more than Michigan's).

Castro's Cuba was the focal point of the 1962 "missile crisis," which brought the United States and the Soviet Union into one of the most threatening confrontations of the long Cold War. Castro's Cuba is described by some of its foes as the most disruptive force to arise in Latin America in this century. And in 1975-76, the Cuban military intervention in Angola, with Cuba said to be acting as the Soviet Union's unacknowledged agent, again cast Castro's tiny Cuba in a superpower's international role.

In the meantime, the country was being transformed by "Fidelismo," which has been described as a distinctively Latin American mutation of Marxism-Leninism. Supporters of Castro claim that his policies have brought great economic and educational blessings to Cuba's poor. Critics denounce the Castro regime as the masters of a slave state in which human rights are ignored and democratic freedoms denied.

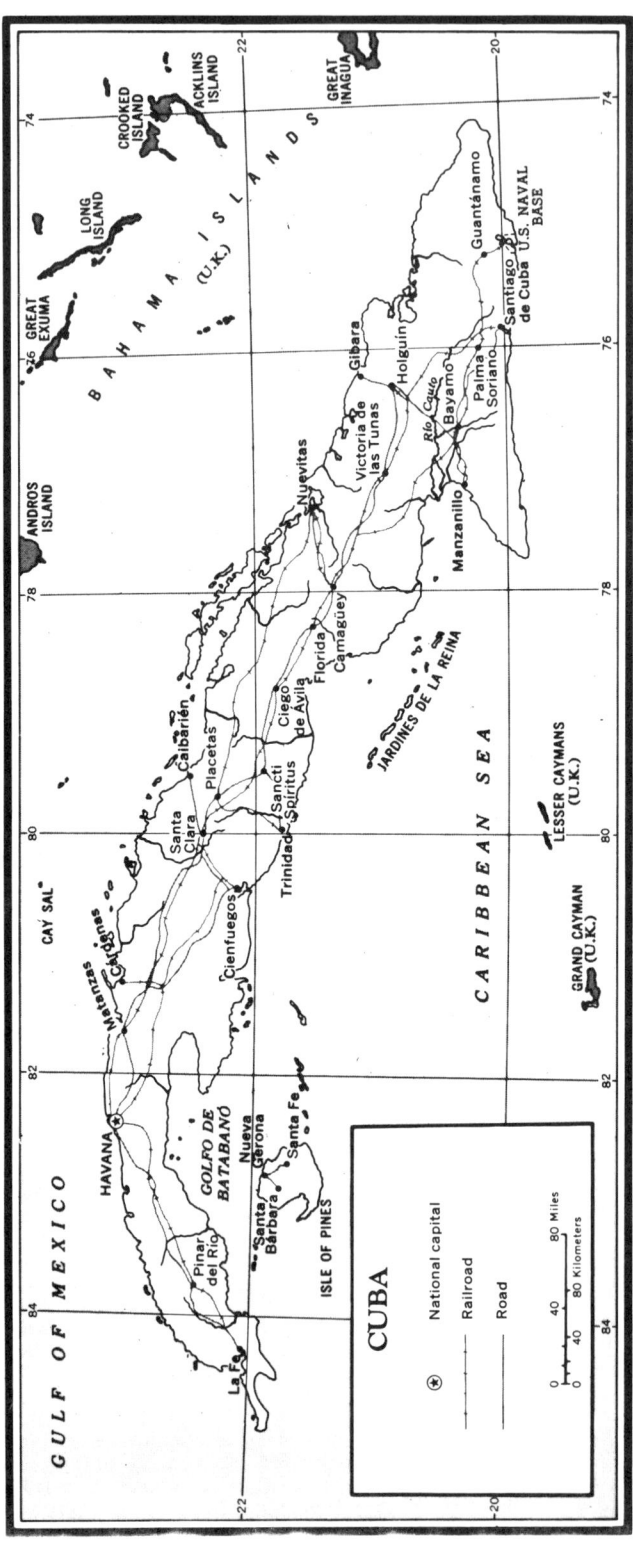

INTRODUCTION

In recent years there has been a growing movement in the United States to resume normal relations with Cuba, and there are indications that the Cuban leadership would welcome such a development.

Cuba & Its People

The land ruled by Fidel Castro is a little country consisting of the main island of Cuba, the smaller Isla de Pinos (Isle of Pines) and about 1,600 lesser keys and islets. Situated strategically at the entrance to the Gulf of Mexico, between the Atlantic Ocean to the north and the Caribbean Sea to the south, Cuba is only 90 miles (145 kilometers) south of Key West, Fla. It comprises 44,218 square miles (114,524 square kilometers) and stretches about 745 miles from east to west. Its width averages 60 miles and ranges from 22 miles to a maximum of 124 miles. The 2,175 miles of coastline provide numerous excellent harbors, among them such internationally renowned ones as the ports of Havana, Guantanamo, Bahia Honda, Matanzas, Cardenas, Nuevitas, Cienfuegos and Santiago de Cuba.

Mountains and hills account for about 40% of the countryside. There are three major mountain regions. The highest and wildest mountains constitute the Sierra Maestra in the east; its Pico Turquino has an altitude of 6,560 feet (2,000 meters). It was in the Sierra Maestra that Castro found a haven to gather strength and launch his revolution. The western range, the Sierra de los Organos, is lower and less wild. Central Cuba's hilly Sierra de Trinidad is the third range.

Although Cuba is in the tropics, the trade winds cool the air down to an average year-round temperature of 77° Fahrenheit (25° Celsius), with a summer average of about 81° F. and a winter low of about 70° F. There are two seasons—dry from November to April and wet from May through October.

More than half of Cuba consists of flat countryside or gently rolling plains and wide valleys.

The population of Cuba was estimated in mid-1976 at 9,470,000.

Most Cubans are of Spanish, African or mixed Spanish-African ancestry. Persons of mixed white-black heritage are usually called *mestizos* in Cuba. The term *criollo* was once used to identify persons who were born in Cuba, who were considered Cuban by nationality and who were frequently (but not always) of mixed race. More recently the term *criollo* appears to have lost its racial connotation and

Fidel Castro Ruz

to refer instead both to those of Cuban birth and to members of the white Cuban leadership who have formulated the *criollo* nationalist ideology.

It had been thought that Cuba's Indian population had died out or assimilated completely, but in the 1960s a few presumably Indian families were found in remote areas of Oriente Province. The Chinese minority is considered to number far less than 1% of the population, including some of "mixed" ancestry who identify themselves with the Chinese community. The Jewish population is even smaller. Both the Chinese and Jewish communities have lost many of their members through emigration since the Castro regime came to power.

The language of Cuba is Spanish with a distinctive Cuban accent. Some African language—especially Yoruba, Fon and Efik—is still used, but largely for religious ritual.

Perhaps 85% of Cubans are thought to be Roman Catholics.

Brief History of Cuba

Cuba was discovered by Christopher Columbus Oct. 28, 1492 on his first voyage to the New World. He claimed the island for Spain, but Spain did not colonize Cuba until 1511.

The conquest of Cuba was ordered in 1511 by Columbus' son, Diego, who was then governor of Hispaniola. Acting on these orders, Diego de Velazquez seized the island and founded Cuba's first white settlements.

Initially, Spain regarded Cuba as valuable because of its position at the entrance to the Gulf of Mexico. The island was viewed as a useful barrier to protect Spain's Caribbean and mainland interests from the competing Portuguese, French and English.

Stockraising became the first major industry. African slaves were imported to replace the declining numbers of Arawak Indians. The demand for slaves increased with the growing need for labor on sugar and tobacco plantations that the Spanish colonists began to create in the Eighteenth Century as the early years of strife and piracy ended.

Spain supported France in the Seven Years' War (of 1756-63) between Great Britain and France. As a consequence, in 1762 the British captured Havana. The ten months of British rule led to enormous changes in Cuba as the colony suddenly gained access to North American markets. It was a different and potentially more prosperous Cuba that was returned to Spain by the Treaty of Paris in 1763.

The defeat of the Spanish crown and the revolutionary changes in Europe and the Americas during the following 60 years had a strong effect on Cuba's economy and society. Trade increased, and immigration from Europe and other Latin American areas helped inspire innovation. The sugar industry continued to expand, especially after the introduction of steam-powered sugar mills in 1819, and the demand for slaves grew for both sugar and coffee production. In 1817, a year of record slave importation by Cuba, Spain signed a treaty with Great Britain in which it agreed to prohibit the slave trade after 1820. The number of slaves imported by Cuba declined thereafter although the treaty was not enforced.

During the three decades that followed there were several unsuccessful slave revolts. Autonomist and separatist movements arose, the former seeking more freedom under Spanish rule and the latter seeking independence from Spain. In the late 1840s and early 1850s there were several unsuccessful uprisings by Cubans who sought to win freedom from Spain through annexation by the U.S. while maintaining slavery in Cuba.

The *criollo* opposition to repressive Spanish rule erupted in 1868 in what became known as the Ten Years' War. The Cuban leader in this struggle was Carlos Manuel de Cespedes, whom Cubans consider the "father" of their country. Cespedes opened the struggle in Yara Oct. 10, 1868 by reading a Declaration of Independence from Spain. The revolutionary movement won important victories at first, forming a government, adopting a constitution and achieving military control of half of the island. But as Spain reinforced its military strength in Cuba, the rebels were forced back into what ultimately became only a guerrilla campaign. The end came in 1878 with the Treaty of Zanjon, in which Spain promised many political reforms, of which only a few actually took effect. Spain, however, did enact an emancipation law in 1880, and slavery in Cuba came to an end in 1886.

Another unsuccessful uprising—the Little War—was led by Maximo Gomez in 1880. Thereafter the leadership of the revolutionary movement shifted to New York.

The charismatic Jose Marti, a Cuban writer, launched a new revolt with a landing led by himself and Gomez in eastern Cuba in April 1895. Marti, known as the "apostle of Cuban liberty" and considered his country's paramount national hero, was killed the following month. For about a year, however, the rebels made gains. But in

INTRODUCTION

1896, after rebel leader Antonio Maceo was killed and Spain had strengthened its forces on the island, the revolutionists began to lose ground.

Strong pressure, meanwhile, had been growing in the U.S. for the American government to intervene, especially against the brutal Spanish military commander, Gen. Valeriano Weyler, widely denounced as "the butcher." The U.S. administration firmly resisted the pressure even though Congress adopted a resolution favoring intervention. The change came with the controversial sinking of the U.S. warship the *Maine* in Havana harbor Feb. 15, 1898. U.S. President William McKinley April 11, 1898 asked for a declaration of war. Congress quickly authorized the administration to use American forces to end the fighting in Cuba, but the Teller Amendment stated that the U.S. must then "leave the governmnet and control of the island to its people."

Thus began the Spanish-American War, which ended in August 1898, less than four months later, with U.S. victory. An armistice was followed by the Treaty of Paris, signed Dec. 10, 1898 and effective April 11, 1899, under which Cuba became an independent republic and Spain ceded Puerto Rico, the Philippines and Guam to the U.S.

The U.S. continued to occupy Cuba until May 20, 1902, under a military government headed first by Gen. John R. Brooke and then by Gen. Leonard E. Wood. The military administration helped rebuild wartorn Cuba under Wood's administration, and yellow fever was conquered through a binational effort under the leadership of an American, Walter Reed, and a Cuban, Carlos J. Finlay.

During Wood's administration, the Cubans held their first elections for municipal officials in June 1900 and elected 31 delegates to a Constituent Assembly in September 1900. The Assembly, meeting from November 1900 to February 1901, framed and adopted a constitution providing for a presidential system of government similar to the U.S.' The Assembly also accepted, but only under pressure, the U.S. Platt Amendment to the U.S. Army Appropriation Bill of 1901. The Cuban constitution became law June 12, 1901 with the Platt Amendment as an appendix. The Platt Amendment was then incorporated into the permanent treaty between the U.S. and Cuba July 2, 1903.

The Platt Amendment gave the U.S. "the right to intervene for the preservation of Cuban independence, the maintenance of a government adequate for the protection of life, property and individual liberty. . . ." It provided that "the Isle of Pines shall be omitted from the proposed constitutional boundaries of Cuba, the title thereto being left to future adjustment by treaty." It also provided that "the government of Cuba will sell or lease to the United States lands necessary for coaling or naval stations at certain specified points, to be agreed upon with the President of the United States." The 1903 treaty implemented the third of these provisions by Cuban cession of some territory at Guantanamo Bay and Honda Bay for U.S. naval use. The U.S. relinquished its Honda Bay territory in 1912 in return for additional Guantanamo territory. The U.S. never exercised any control over the Isle of Pines, and by a 1904 treaty (ratified in 1925), the U.S. recognized Cuban sovereignty over the island.

Cuba began its career as an independent republic May 20, 1902 under the presidency of Tomas Estrada Palma, who had won the endorsement of both the Nationalist and Republican parties after Maximo Gomez refused to run.

Estrada Palma won a controversial reelection in 1905 but, faced with possible insurrection, called on the U.S. to intervene under the Platt Amendment. The U.S. finally did so Sept. 29, 1906. William Howard Taft and then the controversial Charles E. Magoon served as provisional governor. New elections were held in 1908, and the U.S. withdrew Jan. 28, 1909. Thereafter the U.S. invoked the Platt Amendment only for brief interventions to protect lives and property, and the U.S. discarded the Platt Amendment in 1934.

World War I, by nearly destroying the European sugar beet industry, brought unprecedented prosperity to Cuba's sugar producers. This prosperous period, ending in late 1920 with a break in sugar prices, is known in Cuba as "the dance of the millions," in which speculators and sugar dealers made great fortunes.

Gerardo Machado, elected president in 1924, began his term in 1925 with attempts at economic reform but ended it with repressive actions to reinforce his power. In 1927 and 1928 he pushed through constitutional amendments to lengthen the president's term to six years and to abolish the vice presidency. Opposition voices were silenced with repressive tactics that included deportation and even assassination. Opposition became so dangerous that Machado was the only candidate when he was reelected for a six-year term in November 1928.

Repression was heightened during Machado's second term, and his *porristas* (toughs) were accused of hundreds of murders. Underground opposition to Machado increased under this type of treatment, and by Aug. 11, 1933 the army commanders abandoned Machado, who fled into exile.

Carlos Manuel de Cespedes was chosen as president, but his administration failed to restore order and endured less than a month.

A group of army sergeants at Camp Colombia then seized the initiative under Sgt. Fulgencio Batista y Zaldivar. Joined by Prof. Ramon Grau San Martin and his radical Directorio Estudentiantil (Student Directorate), the sergeants took command of the army Sept. 4, 1933. Grau San Martin was put in charge of a commission whose task was to form a new government. But the government thus produced also was unable to curb the growing disorders.

Meantime Batista had become a colonel and the country's most powerful figure as the head of an army officered largely by the former sergeants who supported him. Batista forced Grau San Martin to resign Jan. 15, 1934 and secured the appointment of Carlos Mendieta Jan. 17 as provisional president. The U.S. recognized this new government Jan. 24.

From then until he fled into exile Jan. 1, 1959, Batista was the outstanding political figure in Cuba. He served as army chief of staff during 1934-40 but throughout this time was always more powerful than the president. Batista was president during most of the World War II years—from 1940 to 1944, and he returned to power through a bloodless *coup d'etat* in 1952. The presidency was held during 1945-48 by Grau San Martin, who was followed in office by Carlos Prio Socarras, his chosen successor. Batista, supported by the army, engineered the *coup d'etat* March 10, 1952 when it became clear that he could not win another presidential election.

Fidel Castro Ruz' Leadership

The leader of the first Communist-bloc nation in the Western Hemisphere, Fidel Castro Ruz was born Aug. 13, 1926 on his father's sugar plantation near Biran in Oriente Province. Angel Castro y Argis, Fidel Castro's father, had come to Cuba as a Spanish-born laborer and had ultimately put together an estate of more than 23,000 acres.

Fidel Castro was a son of Angel Castro's second wife, Lina Ruz Gonzalez, who had originally been the Castro family's cook. He worked on his father's sugar cane fields as a boy but persuaded his parents to give him an education. After attending three Jesuit institutions (in 1944 his fellow students named him the best athlete at the Colegio Belen, a Jesuit preparatory school in Havana), Castro in 1945 enrolled in the Faculty of Law at the University of Havana, where he was chosen president of the University Students' Federation.

While still a student, Castro participated in an unsuccessful effort to overthrow the Dominican Republic's Trujillo dictatorship in September 1947 and took part in the Bogotazo student uprising in Bogota, Colombia in April 1948. During his student activist days, however, Castro's political orientation could probably be described as liberal, and he was involved in several clashes with Communists. Castro was married Oct. 12, 1948 to Mirta Diaz-Balart, a fellow student. They had one son, Fidel (known as Fidelito), before their divorce in 1955. (Castro was reported to have married Isabel Coto in 1962.)

Castro graduated with a doctorate in law in 1950 and started a law practice in Havana. He largely represented the poor. He became a Partido Ortodoxo candidate for parliament in the scheduled June 1952 election, which was aborted by the Batista *coup d'etat*. Castro appealed to the Court of Constitutional Guarantees on the ground that Batista's action was unconstitutional, but the court rejected his petition. Castro then joined in the formation of a group of young rebels in opposition to the Batista dictatorship.

The rebels, numbering about 165 men led by Castro, struck July 26, 1953 with an attack on the Moncada Barracks in Santiago de Cuba. An attack was also mounted against the Bayamo garrison. The rebels hoped to spark a popular uprising in Oriente, but they were defeated easily. The government forces killed about half of the rebels and jailed most of the survivors, including Castro and his younger brother Raul. At his trial, Castro delivered an impassioned speech ending with the declaration *"La historia me absolvera"* (History will absolve me). But he was found guilty and sentenced to 15 years in prison on the Isle of Pines.

Batista on May 15, 1955 issued a general amnesty under which the Castros were freed. In July 1955 Castro shifted his activities to Mexico City, where he and other Cubans formed a rebel force that was later named the 26th of July Movement to memorialize the attack on the Moncado Barracks. It was in Mexico City that Castro met Ernesto "Che" Guevara, a young Argentine doctor who later became an important figure in the Castro revolution.

Castro and his group bought the yacht *Granma* with money contributed by former President Carlos Prio Socarras and used the vessel for a landing by Fidel and Raul Castro, Guevara and 79 fellow rebels

Dec. 2, 1956 on the north coast of Oriente Province. Government forces easily defeated the invaders, of whom only 12, including the Castros and Guevara, escaped to the Sierra Maestra mountains.

In the mountains, Castro and his growing force began an ultimately victorious guerrilla war against the Batista dictatorship. Although Castro's guerrillas probably never numbered more than 800, their example inspired a widespread resistance movement that finally brought down a dictatorship supported by a 30,000-man army.

Batista fled Jan. 1, 1959 to exile in the Dominican Republic.

In the new government created by the rebels, Castro assumed the position of commander-in-chief of the armed forces, and the presidency went to Dr. Manuel Urrutia Lleo, a former judge. But then and since there has been no doubt that Castro was the unquestioned leader of the country and had the decisive voice in any government decision. The new provisional government was recognized by the U.S. Jan. 7, 1959.

Jose Miro Cardona, a law professor who had been installed as the revolutionary government's first premier, resigned Feb. 16, 1959. Castro took his place as premier, and Raul Castro became armed forces commander-in-chief. Urrutia was forced out as president July 17, 1959, and the post was turned over to Osvaldo Dorticos.

Early in the Castro regime the revolutionary government was subjected to criticism for massive arrests and executions of alleged war criminals (Batista supporters). Trials and death sentences were often decided by the crowds who filled stadiums in which captives were paraded and accused. Verdicts were shouted by the spectators, and the death sentences were executed by firing squads.

The Castro regime's expropriation of U.S. property caused an early deterioration in relations between the two countries. At the same time, Cuba was cementing ever closer links with the Soviet Union and other Communist countries. The U.S. finally broke relations with Cuba Jan. 3, 1961. (A detailed account of Cuba's relations with the U.S. and the Soviet Union as well as of events in Cuba during the years 1960-63—including the 1961 Bay of Pigs invasion and the 1962 Cuban missile crisis—can be found in the FACTS ON FILE book *Cuba, the U.S. & Russia 1960-63.*)

Castro, who had previously denied that he was a Communist, announced in a May Day TV speech in 1961 that Cuba was now a Socialist country. He said in a Dec. 2 TV address that he was leading Cuba to communism—through socialism to "a people's democracy, or the dictatorship of the proletariat." "I am a Marxist-Leninist and will be one until the day I die," he declared. He said he had concealed his Communist beliefs from Cubans and U.S. friends for years "because otherwise we might have alienated the bourgeoisie and other forces which we knew we would eventually have to fight." But he added that he had become a Communist only after he had achieved power.

The Organization of American States, reacting to Castro's assertion that he planned to export communism throughout Latin America, formally excluded Cuba in February 1962. By September 1964, all Latin American countries except Mexico had broken relations with Cuba.

Well over a quarter of a million Cubans have fled Cuba for voluntary exile since Castro came to power. In November 1965, the Cuban and U.S. governments agreed to a plan under which 3,000 to 4,000 Cubans would be permitted to leave each month for asylum in the U.S., and an airlift was started in December 1965 to handle the flights. A major source of U.S.-Cuban friction has been attempted anti-Castro invasions of Cuba by Cuban exiles based in the U.S. and, at least in the early 1960s, often supported by U.S. sources.

THIS BOOK IS INTENDED TO SERVE as a record of major domestic events in Castro's Cuba as well as of developments involving Cuba's relations with the United States, the Soviet Union, Latin America and the rest of the world during the period beginning in 1970 and continuing on through 1977. The material that follows consists principally of the record compiled by FACTS ON FILE in its ongoing examination of world affairs. A conscientious effort was made to record all events without bias and to make this volume a balanced and accurate reference work.

LESTER A. SOBEL

New York, N.Y.
December, 1977

1970-73: A Time of Restraint

Agreement with U.S. on Curbing Hijackings

It has been noted that Cuban foreign policy, like the foreign policies of other countries, does not follow a straight line but shifts and veers as circumstances or changing views of its leader(s) dictate. Cuba's international initiatives have seemed to alternate from actions based on extreme revolutionary fervor to more moderate behavior that appears to indicate a pragmatic effort to accommodate to a world in which revolution is often fiercely opposed. Sometimes both types of conduct were followed simultaneously. On balance, the period 1970-73 seems to have been one in which restraint on the part of Cuba predominated. A major indication of this is the series of moves that culminated Feb. 15, 1973 in a Cuban agreement with the United States to curb the hijacking of planes and ships between the two countries.

U.S. seeks anti-hijack accord. A U.S. State Department official disclosed March 9, 1970 that the U.S. government had contacted Cuba regarding the possibility of negotiation of a bilateral agreement on hijackers. In a law announced in September 1969, Cuba had offered to negotiate bilateral treaties on the extradition of hijackers but had rejected adherence to multilateral treaties.

Carlos Rafael Rodriguez, the chairman of the Cuban National Commission for Economic, Scientific and Technological Cooperation, told members of the U.N. Correspondents Association March 24 that Cuba was studying the U.S. proposals.

Mexico to cancel aviation pact. Mexico announced July 29, 1970 that it had notified Cuba of its desire to cancel the 1954 air agreement providing for twice weekly air service between Mexico City and Havana. Under the agreement, air service was to cease one year after either country gave formal notice of its desire to cancel it or earlier if both parties agreed to an earlier date.

In its official communique to the Cuban government, Mexico termed the agreement "out of date" and urged negotiations on a new pact "based on present day requirements," a Mexican spokesman said.

Mexican officials declined to comment on speculation that the action was taken because of Mexico's anger over Cuba's refusal to extradite hijackers of Mexican planes, but said that hijackings "might" be discussed if negotiations on a new treaty were opened.

Cuba offers U.S. pact. Cuban Foreign Minister Raul Roa asserted Sept. 26, 1970 that Cuba would enter into an agreement with the U.S. for the joint extradition of all sea and air hijackers if no exceptions to the accord were made.

In a speech broadcast on Radio Havana, Roa said: "If the U.S. government really wishes to discuss in a serious and definitive way that problem [hijacking], the Cuba government is willing to subscribe right away." He added: "We also wish to express in a final and categorical way that we do not accept and we do not respect any international agreement about the hijacking of planes, unless it concretely includes all piracy forms and violations without any exception."

In an address before the U.N. General Assembly Oct. 2, Cuban representative Ricardo Alarcon de Quesada repeated Roa's offer to negotiate agreements with individual countries. "We reject any multilateral accord but reiterate our willingness to conclude bilateral treaties that provide strict reciprocity" on the joint return of hijackers, Alarcon said.

Cuba returns hijacker—Cuba, for the first time, directly returned a hijacker to the U.S. Sept. 24. Cuban authorities allowed U.S. officials to fly to Varadero, Cuba and pick up Robert Labadie, an Army private who had hijacked a Trans World Airlines jet to Havana Aug. 24. He was flown to Miami on one of the two daily flights carrying refugees to the U.S. from Cuba.

Labadie, 27, who was absent without official leave from an Army psychiatric clinic in Pennsylvania, was ordered held in $500,000 bond. He had been indicted by a federal district court in South Bend, Ind. Sept. 10 for air piracy and kidnaping.

In his Sept. 26 radio statement, Roa had pointed out that Labadie's return was negotiated through secret diplomatic channels and was initiated by the U.S. Aug. 27. U.S. officials had said Sept. 24, however, that Labadie's return was unexpected.

Cuba abstains in U.N. anti-hijack vote. Cuba abstained in November 1970 when the U.N. assailed air hijackings.

The General Assembly Nov. 25 unanimously condemned "without exception whatsoever all acts of hijacking or other interference with civil air travel." The resolution called on all nations to prosecute or extradite hijackers. Eight countries abstained in the 105–0 vote, including Cuba and some Arab delegations. Egypt, Jordan and Lebanon supported the resolution.

The International Air Transport Association, representing 106 world airlines, expressed approval of the vote Nov. 26.

Talks follow diplomatic moves. The U.S. and Cuba Nov. 15–16, 1972 began a series of diplomatic moves that within 10 days produced actual negotiations on the anti-hijacking accord.

In statements Nov. 15, both governments said such talks should be conducted with the Swiss government acting as a go-between in the absence of diplomatic relations between the U.S. and Cuba. But the U.S. officially confirmed Nov. 16 that it would be willing to conduct direct negotiations with Cuba to expedite an agreement.

In an announcement over Havana radio, the Cuban government said it was "ready to take such steps which might lead to the adoption of a broad agreement" on the hijacking problem if the U.S. "shows an equal willingness and interest."

The broadcast said the agreement should also cover what it described as the hijacking of Cuban ships, armed attacks against Cuba by exiles and the "illegal" departure of Cubans to the U.S.

The Cuban statement reiterated previous charges that Washington had arranged such departures and condoned attacks on Cuban ships and territory by Cuban exiles.

After studying the statement, State Department officials said it was noteworthy that it did not include any reference for the return of Cuban exiles in the U.S. wanted by Castro's government. That demand had proved to be a major stumbling block at earlier attempts to initiate U.S.-Cuban talks on a hijacking treaty.

The State Department said Nov. 15 that the broadcast "would seem to confirm" the impression that Cuba was ready to open discussions "and to the extent it does so, we are gratified."

Secretary of State William P. Rogers said Nov. 16 that the U.S. was ready to meet face-to-face with Cuba to discuss an agreement on hijacking.

Rogers' remarks about direct talks were made during his meeting with the Swiss ambassador, Felix Schnyder. Following the Rogers-Schnyder meeting, Charles W. Bray 3rd, State Department spokesman, said the U.S. wanted an agreement "in the most expeditious and effective manner possible" and was "prepared to engage in any process which will produce results."

U.S.-Cuban talks begin—The U.S. State Department announced Nov. 27, 1972 that bilateral talks on an accord to halt the hijacking of airliners to Cuba had begun in Havana Nov. 25. The Swiss ambassador to Cuba was representing the U.S. The talks followed announcement by Cuba Nov. 20 that a local court would try three U.S. hijackers who recently extorted a $2 million ransom and forced

Text of U.S.-Cuban Agreement Signed Feb. 15, 1973

The government of the United States of America and the Government of the Republic of Cuba, on the basis of equality and strict reciprocity, agree:

FIRST: Any person who hereafter seizes, removes, appropriates or diverts from its normal route or activities an aircraft or vessel registered under the laws of one of the parties and brings it to the territory of the other party shall be considered to have committed an offense and therefore shall either be returned to the party of registry of the aircraft or vessel to be tried by the courts of that party in conformity with its laws or be brought before the courts of the party whose territory he reached for trial in conformity with its laws for the offense punishable by the most severe penalty according to the circumstances and the seriousness of the acts to which this article refers. In addition, the party whose territory is reached by the aircraft or vessel shall take all necessary steps to facilitate without delay the continuation of the journey of the passengers and crew innocent of the hijacking of the aircraft or vessel in question, with their belongings, as well as the journey of the aircraft or vessel itself with all goods carried with it, including any funds obtained by extortion or other illegal means, or the return of the foregoing to the territory of the first party; likewise, it shall take all steps to protect the physical integrity of the aircraft or vessel and all goods carried with it, including any funds obtained by extortion or other illegal means, and the physical integrity of the passengers and crew innocent of the hijacking, and their belongings while they are in its territory as a consequence of or in connection with the acts to which this article refers.

In the event that the offenses referred to above are not punishable under the laws existing in the country to which the persons committing them arrived, the party in question shall be obligated, except in the case of minor offenses, to return the persons who have committed such acts, in accordance with the applicable legal procedures, to the territory of the other party to be tried by its courts in conformity with its laws.

SECOND: Each party shall try with a view to serve punishment in accordance with its laws any person who, within its territory, hereafter conspires to promote, or promotes, or prepares, or directs, or forms part of an expedition which from its territory or any other place carries out acts of violence or depredation against aircraft or vessels of any kind or registration coming or going to the territory of the other party or who, within its territory, hereafter conspires to promote or promotes, or prepares, or directs, or forms part of an expedition which from its territory or any other place carries out such acts or other similar unlawful acts in the territory of the other party.

THIRD: Each party shall apply strictly its own laws to any national of the other party who, coming from the territory of the other party, enters its territory, violating its laws as well as national and international requirements pertaining to immigration, health, customs and the like.

FOURTH: The party in whose territory the perpetrators of the acts described in Article First arrive may take into consideration any extenuating or mitigating circumstances in those cases in which the persons responsible for the acts were being sought for strictly political reasons and were in real and imminent danger of death without a viable alternative for leaving the country, provided there was no financial extortion or physical injury to the members of the crew, passengers, or other persons in connection with the hijacking.

Final provisions:

This agreement may be amended or expanded by decision of the parties.

This agreement shall be in force for five years and may be renewed for an equal term by express decision of the parties.

Either party may inform the other of its decision to terminate this agreement at any time while it is in force by written denunciation submitted six months in advance.

This agreement shall enter into force on the date agreed by the parties.

Done in English and Spanish texts, which are equally authentic.

a Southern Airways jet to land in Havana.

Swiss Ambassador Silvio Masnata, whose government normally represented U.S. interests in Havana, sent a report to the State Department after meeting Nov. 25 with Cuban Foreign Minister Raul Roa. State Department officials said the report contained Cuban proposals on hijacking, some of which appeared to be "fairly reasonable."

U.S. State Secretary Rogers said Dec. 3 that Cuba and the U.S. had agreed in principle that their proposed accord to curb hijackings should cover ships as well as airplanes.

U.S. State Department spokesman Charles W. Bray 3rd revealed Feb. 13, 1973 that an agreement between the two countries was virtually concluded. Bray said details of the pact would not be disclosed pending consultation with Congress, but asserted that agreement had been reached on all substantive issues.

This official confirmation followed a disclosure by President Richard M. Nixon Feb. 13 that three months of indirect negotiations between Cuba and the U.S. on a hijacking agreement had been successfully concluded.

U.S. & Cuba sign anti-hijacking pact. Representatives of the U.S. and Cuba Feb. 15, 1973 signed a five-year agreement, effective immediately, to curb the hijacking of aircraft and ships between the two countries. The U.S. insisted, however, that the accord did not foreshadow any improvement in its relations with the Cuban government.

The agreement, officially a "memorandum of understanding" rather than a formal treaty requiring Senate confirmation, was signed simultaneously by U.S. Secretary of State William P. Rogers in Washington and Cuban Foreign Minister Raul Roa in Havana. It committed both countries to either try hijackers "for the offense punishable by the most severe penalty" or extradite them.

The accord also permitted both nations to grant political asylum to hijackers under carefully defined terms, but committed each to punish anyone who used its territory to organize attacks against the other. The latter provision was of particular importance to Cuba because U.S.-based Cuban exile groups had conducted raids against their former homeland, and had committed random violence against Cuban citizens.

The agreement stated that each country would promptly return stolen airplanes or vessels and protect innocent persons and goods on board, and would send back "without delay" any ransom collected by the hijackers. Cuba previously had not returned hijacking ransom money, and was still holding $2 million, taken by hijackers from Southern Airways in November 1972, for use as evidence in the trial of the hijackers in Havana.

Rogers told a news conference after he signed the accord that "nothing in this agreement is inconsistent with the traditional and strongly felt American view of the right to emigrate freely nor does it constitute a change in our overall policy toward Cuba." He said the U.S. would not ease its diplomatic and trade boycott of Cuba until "the policies and attitudes of the Cuban government" changed.

Mexico anti-hijack pact. Cuba and Mexico signed an agreement June 7, 1973 to curb the hijacking of airliners and ships between their borders.

The treaty, signed in Havana by Foreign Minister Raul Roa Garcia and Mexican Ambassador Victor Alfonso Maldonado, obligated countries to which planes or ships were hijacked to either prosecute the hijackers or return them to the country of departure. However, it allowed both countries to grant asylum to hijackers when they appeared "in real and imminent danger of death or of being deprived of their liberty for clearly political reasons, and had had no other way of gaining safety."

The agreement also required each country to "punish severely according to its laws" any person who, from its territory, conspired or took part in an attack on ships or planes traveling to or from the other country.

1970-73: A TIME OF RESTRAINT

Venezuelan pact. Venezuela and Cuba July 6, 1973 signed a five-year treaty to bar the hijacking of planes and ships between the two countries.

The pact, signed simultaneously in Havana and Caracas, required each country to prosecute or extradite persons who hijacked vessels to it from the other. Hijacked vessels and their passengers would be protected and returned to the country of origin, as would any ransom money obtained by the hijackers.

The signatories were allowed to "take into consideration purely political motives and the circumstances under which the [hijackings] were perpetrated, in order to abstain from returning or prosecuting [hijackers], save when there has been economic extortion or damage to the crew members, passengers, or other persons."

The signing followed an incident June 28 in which a Venezuelan air force pilot, reportedly angered by a charge of reckless flying, flew a jet bomber to Havana and asked political asylum. The plane was returned to Venezuela June 30, but no decision on the asylum request was reported.

Relations between Venezuela and Cuba were improving steadily. Negotiations for the sale of Venezuelan oil to Cuba were reported under way June 8, and a Cuban education mission was reported visiting Venezuela June 7.

Hijacking Incidents

Skyjackings in 1970. The first hijacking of 1970 took place Jan. 1, but the plane failed to reach Cuba until Jan. 3 due to fuel stops and mechanical problems. The plane, a Brazilian Cruzeiro Do Sul Caravelle on a flight from Montevideo, Uruguay to Rio de Janeiro, was taken over by five Brazilians, including a woman, who identified themselves as members of the Palmares Armed Revolutionary Vanguard.

Following fuel stops in Buenos Aires, where two elderly passengers were allowed to leave the plane, and Antofagasta, Chile, the plane was stranded for 27 hours in Lima, Peru while a special battery was flown in from Chile. The plane was again held up in Panama Jan. 3 until automobile batteries could be hooked up to get the engines started again. The hijackers, along with 21 passengers and six crewmen, finally landed in Cuba Jan. 3.

In an impromptu press conference in Lima Jan. 2, the hijackers explained that they were going to Cuba to "pay homage" to guerrilla leader Ernesto 'Che' Guevara, killed in Bolivia in 1967.

An attempted hijacking was foiled Jan. 9 in Panama, when National Guardsmen shot and killed the would-be hijacker. Identified as Jorge Tulio Medrano Caballero, 20, the hijacker took control of the Rutas Aereas Panamenas S.A. plane with 28 passengers aboard on a regular flight from David to Bocas del Toro. Upon returning to David for refueling, the plane was surrounded by National Guardsmen who had been ordered by Brig. Gen. Omar Torrijos to prevent the hijacking. A flight mechanic, who had been held as hostage by Medrano, was also wounded in the shooting.

A Dutch Antilles Airways plane with 37 persons aboard was diverted over Haiti and forced to fly to Santiago, Cuba Jan. 24. The flight was en route from Santo Domingo to Curacao.

Lawrence M. Rhodes, 30, who identified himself as the hijacker of a Delta Air Lines jet to Cuba in 1968, turned himself in to U.S. military authorities in Spain Feb. 9. Rhodes, who said that he had been intoxicated at the time of the hijacking, had left Cuba Feb. 2. He returned to the U.S. Feb. 11 accompanied by two U.S. marshals.

An Eastern Air Lines Newark-to-Miami jet with 104 persons aboard was hijacked to Cuba Feb. 16 by a man with a revolver and a homemade bomb. It was the first Eastern flight to be hijacked since the airline instituted an anti-hijacking detection system in October 1969. An Eastern spokesman said the system was not in operation at the Newark gate through which the hijacker boarded.

A Cleveland-to-Florida United Air Lines jet with 106 persons aboard was commandeered by a gunman March 11 and forced to fly to Havana. The hijacker, later identified by the Federal Bureau of Investigation as Clemmie Stubbs of Cleveland, remained in Cuba with his wife and four children.

A Colombian Avianca jet, carrying 78 persons from Bogota to Baranquilla, was diverted to Cuba the same day by four armed men.

A Brazilian Varig Airline jet, en route from Santiago, Chile, to Buenos Aires, Argentina, was hijacked March 12 and ordered to Cuba; the plane, with 42 persons aboard, landed in Havana March 13.

An Aerolineas Argentina jet with 61 persons aboard was commandeered by two armed hijackers March 24 and ordered to fly to Cuba. The plane arrived in Havana March 25.

Three chartered flights were also hijacked to Cuba March 26–April 27: A twin-engine British tourist plane on its way from British Honduras to Mexico was ordered to fly to Cuba March 26 by two armed men. Two persons who paid $6 for a private sightseeing flight in North Carolina hijacked the plane to Cuba April 22. A twin engine plane with one passenger was hijacked over Florida April 27 and ordered to fly to Cuba.

A Brazilian Viacao Aerea de Sao Paulo (VASP) airliner on a flight from Brasilia to Manaus was ordered to fly to Havana April 26 by an armed hijacker. The plane landed in Cuba April 26, after a refueling stop in Guyana, where the hijacker allowed the 37 passengers to disembark. The French newspaper Le Monde reported April 29 that the hijacker had been identified as Joaquim Camara Ferreira, considered the successor of the left-wing Brazilian urban guerrilla leader Carlos Marighela, killed in November 1969.

Two blacks from the U.S. abandoned their plans to hijack a British West Indian Airways flight to Africa after being "talked out of it" by Cuban authorities and British embassy representatives. The Boeing 727 flight from Jamaica to Miami was brought down in Havana May 1 when the two men demanded to be flown to Senegal. Cuban officials refused to re-fuel the plane. The two men remained in Cuban police custody while the plane with its 60 passengers and crew of eight continued on to Miami May 3.

Eight armed Dominicans took over a KLM Dutch Antillean Airways airliner on route from the Dominican Republic to Curacao and forced the pilot to land in Cuba, according to a May 13 report.

Thomas James Boynton, 33, who had hijacked a chartered plane to Cuba in February 1968, pleaded guilty to a charge of kidnaping May 14 and was sentenced by a federal judge in Miami June 4 to 20 years in prison.

A Colombian Avianca DC-3 airliner making a domestic flight was seized and forced to Cuba May 21; 26 persons were reported aboard.

A Mexicana de Aviacion plane, on a domestic flight from Merida to Mexico City, was commandeered to Cuba May 24, reportedly by three Brazilians and one Mexican.

A Delta Airlines jet, flying from Chicago to Miami with 102 persons aboard, was hijacked near Atlanta May 25. Havana Radio reported that the hijacker was a woman, accompanied by her 12-year-old son.

An American Airlines jet with 96 persons on a Chicago–New York flight was also hijacked to Cuba May 25; the hijacker allowed the passengers to debark during a refueling stop in New York.

A Colombian Avianca airliner with 45 persons aboard was hijacked by two armed men and flown to Cuba May 31.

Another Colombian Avianca plane, on a domestic flight from Cucuta to Bogota, was hijacked to Cuba June 26; 92 persons were reported aboard.

A National Airlines jet with 39 persons aboard a San Francisco–Miami, Fla. flight was diverted to Cuba July 1.

Lorenzo Edward Ervin Jr., 25, was convicted June 5 in a federal court in Newnan, Ga. on charges of aircraft piracy and kidnaping. He had hijacked an Eastern Airlines plane to Cuba Feb.

1970–73: A TIME OF RESTRAINT

25, 1969. Ervin was sentenced to life imprisonment July 6 in what was reported to be the first life sentence for a skyjacker.

Four hijackers were thwarted in their attempt to hijack a Brazilian Cruzeiro do Sul plane with 41 persons aboard July 1. The plane, hijacked after takeoff from Rio de Janeiro, returned to the Rio airport and was attacked by military police who shot out the tires of the plane and forced passengers and hijackers off the plane with tear gas; three men and one woman were reported arrested.

A Brazilian Cruzeiro do Sul plane with 60 persons aboard was hijacked to Cuba July 4 and landed in Santiago, Cuba July 5. The hijackers allowed 37 passengers to disembark during a refueling stop in French Guiana.

In a later hijacking, one Mexican and three Dominican men hijacked an Aeronaves de Mexico jet to Cuba July 25. The plane, with 27 passengers aboard, was on a domestic flight from Acapulco to Mexico City.

A Trans Caribbean Airways jet, with 154 persons aboard, making a flight from Newark, N.J. to Puerto Rico, was diverted to Cuba Aug. 19 by three young Spanish-speaking men with a gun and hand grenades.

A man who said he had a bomb hijacked a Delta Air Lines jet to Cuba Aug. 20; the plane, with 81 persons aboard, was hijacked after takeoff from Atlanta, Ga. on a flight to Savannah.

A Trans World Airlines jet, with 86 persons aboard a scheduled flight from Las Vegas, Nev. to Philadelphia, was forced to Cuba Aug. 24 by a man who claimed there was a bomb aboard.

A hijacked Allegheny Airlines aircraft was diverted to Havana, Cuba Sept. 19 after the hijacker, who had originally demanded to be flown to Cairo, was persuaded to go to Havana instead. The flight, en route from Pittsburgh to Boston, made a scheduled stop in Philadelphia, where the hijacker allowed 90 passengers to debark, and continued to Cuba with eight crew members.

A National Airlines plane, on a scheduled flight from Miami to San Francisco with 49 passengers aboard, was hijacked and flown to Cuba Oct. 30. The plane, its crew and passengers were held in Havana 20 hours before being allowed to return to Miami.

A United Air Lines commuter flight from San Diego to Los Angeles was commandeered by a Mexican-American Nov. 1 and ordered to Cuba. The plane, with 73 persons aboard, was diverted to Havana and returned to Miami early Nov. 2.

An Eastern Air Lines plane, on a flight from Richmond, Va. to Dallas, was hijacked to Cuba Nov. 13. There were 83 persons aboard. Eastern Airlines officials identified the armed hijacker as Gilbert Jones who had boarded during a stop at Raleigh-Durham, N.C.

Castro visits hijacked 747—A Pan American Airways 747 jumbo jet, hijacked to Cuba Aug. 2, was met by Premier Castro after landing at Jose Marti Airport near Havana. The jet, the first 747 to be hijacked to Cuba, was on a New York-Puerto Rico flight with 379 persons aboard.

The pilot, Augustus Watkins, said he left the plane to meet Castro and "took him for a tour of the outside of the airplane. He [Castro] asked all manner of questions related to the plane's capacity and speed. He was particularly interested in whether the plane would be able to take off from the Cuban airfield." The plane left Cuba and arrived safely in San Juan, Puerto Rico later Aug. 2. The hijacker, who was armed and carried a bag he said was full of explosives, remained in Cuba.

Nicaraguan guerrillas get Mexican asylum after hijack to Cuba—Mexico granted political asylum Oct. 22, 1970 to four Nicaraguan guerrillas who had been released by the Costa Rican government following the hijacking to Cuba of a Costa Rican plane.

The Costa Rican LACSA airliner with about 30 passengers aboard a flight from Puerto Limon, Costa Rica to San Andres Island, a possession of Colombia, was commandeered Oct. 21 and ordered to fly to Cuba. While waiting for refueling in San Andres, the hijackers radioed the Costa Rican government that four American passengers (or, according to some reports, four crewmen) would be killed unless the Costa Rican government released four Nicaraguan guerrillas, imprisoned in Costa Rica. The Costa Rican government, under the interim presidency of Manuel Aguilar since President Jose Figueres was in the U.S. attending anniversary celebrations of the United Nations, agreed to the plan and released the four prisoners, who were flown to Mexico Oct. 22.

The four Nicaraguans—Fonseca Amador, Plutarco Hernandez, Humberto Ortega and Rufo Marin—had fled Nicaraguan national guardsmen in 1969 and entered Costa Rica where they were subsequently arrested and imprisoned. They were members of the Nicaraguan Sandinist National Liberation Front, a terrorist organization aimed at the overthrow of President Anastasio Somoza. Havana radio reported Oct. 27 that the four prisoners had arrived in Cuba.

The passengers and crew of the plane were released and returned to Costa Rica Oct. 28.

(Costa Rican President Jose Figueres had warned in Washington, D.C. Oct. 24 that he would invoke the Rio de Janeiro mutual security treaty against Cuba if the plane and its occupants were not released. The Rio Treaty, which went into force in 1948, stated that an attack against one member nation of the Organization of American States was considered an attack against all members.)

■ Ten political prisoners released in Bolivia following the kidnaping of two West German technicians in Teoponte were reported to have arrived in Cuba Aug. 30.

Hijackers not welcome in Cuba. Additional confirmation was made public in early 1971 that the Castro regime was embarrassed and annoyed by the airliner hijackings.

Outgoing Swiss Ambassador to Cuba Alfred Fischle said Jan. 29 that plane hijackers in Cuba were not well received. He said that they were "sent to prison or to mental hospitals." Fischle, who was recently reassigned to Mexico, made the comments at the Mexico City airport.

Hijackings during 1971. A National Airlines plane with 96 persons aboard a flight from Los Angeles to Miami was diverted to Havana Jan. 3; it was the first hijacking of the year. The two gunmen who hijacked the plane remained in Cuba with their wives and four children.

A jet aircraft of Northwest Airlines flying 61 persons from Milwaukee to Washington was hijacked Jan. 22. The hijacker, who claimed he had a bomb and a hatchet, originally demanded to be flown to Algeria, but agreed on Cuba when he was told the Boeing 727 was incapable of flying that far. The hijacker, tentatively identified as Gerald Grant, remained in Havana.

A Delta Airlines jet with 27 persons aboard was diverted to Cuba Feb. 4 by a man who said he was carrying explosives; the plane was on a scheduled run from Chicago to Nashville, Tenn.

An Eastern Airlines jet with 82 persons aboard a flight from New York to San Juan, Puerto Rico, was hijacked March 31 and flown to Havana.

A Pan American Airways aircraft, hijacked to Havana May 29 during a flight from Caracas, Venezuela to Miami, was released by Cuban officials four days later. The 59 passengers and 9 crew members aboard the Boeing 707 were held in Havana longer than any previous group of hijack victims. There was no official explanation from Cuba, but observers believed that the action was in retaliation for the seizure May 27 of four boats and eight Cuban fishermen inside U.S. territorial waters near the Dry Tortugas off Florida. Four of the fishermen were released on May 31, but four others remained jailed on charges of fishing illegally in U.S. waters.

The hijacker was identified by Radio Havana as Ivan Gustavo Garcia Landaetta, 22, of Venezuela.

A Radio Havana announcement said July 12 that a Communist party official, Reynaldo Naranjo Leiva, was killed by a hand grenade when two men tried to hijack a Cubana Airlines domestic flight July 11. The two hijackers and another person were wounded in the blast. The government said that the two hijackers would be tried by revolutionary tribunals. The attempted hijacking was the first reported involving a Cuban airliner in more than five years.

A National Airlines jet was hijacked to Cuba July 24 and released the same day. The jet with 83 persons aboard was hijacked shortly after leaving Miami International Airport en route to Houston by a man brandishing a gun and a stick of dynamite. One stewardess and a passenger were wounded when the hijacker panicked and fired the gun.

A potential passenger, stopped for questioning before boarding an Eastern Air Lines flight at Detroit, pulled a gun and ordered the jet, which was loading, to fly to Havana Oct. 9.

On board the jet, the hijacker, identified as Richard Frederick Dixon, an ex-convict, reportedly held a cocked revolver against the head of a stewardess. An airline spokesman said 39 passengers and a crew of seven were aboard when the plane took off. The flight had been scheduled to stop at Miami and San Juan.

The plane's captain, E. W. Buchanan, was the pilot of the first Eastern Air Lines plane hijacked to Cuba in July 1961.

An American Airlines 747 jet, carrying 221 passengers and a crew of 15 on a flight from New York to San Juan, was hijacked to Cuba Oct. 25 by a man who held a gun to the head of a stewardess.

The jumbo jet refueled in Miami before heading for Havana. The 747 was detained in Havana, but two smaller planes arrived at Jose Marti airport Oct. 27 to return the passengers to the U.S.

A Trans World Airlines jet was hijacked to Cuba Nov. 27 by three armed men wanted as suspects in the slaying of a New Mexico state policeman. The plane was returned to Miami the following day.

The three men, who identified themselves as members of a black militant group called the Republic of New Africa, hijacked the plane in Albuquerque, New Mexico Nov. 27 and ordered it to Cuba after they were told the plane could not make it to Africa. The 43 passengers aboard were left behind during a fueling stop at Tampa (Fla.) International Airport the same day.

A State Department spokesman said the U.S. had delivered a message in Havana Nov. 28 asking for the return of the men, identified as Robert L. Goodwin, 24; Michael R. Finney, 20, and Charles Hill, 21.

Hijackings blamed on Cuban 'school'— A British aviation expert charged Nov. 29 that the upsurge in airline hijackings could be blamed on a Cuban-based Communist conspiracy.

John Masefield, chairman of the government board which controls major British airports, told an international conference on airport security that the Castro regime organized a school for hijackers in Havana in 1966.

He said between 1930 and 1966 hijackings throughout the world totaled only 55. In the next three years, he said, the total was 220.

Hijackings of 1972. Among airplane hijackings involving Cuba during 1972:

An unidentified couple with an infant hijacked a Pacific Southwest Airlines jet over California Jan. 7, forcing it to fly to Havana when they found the plane did not have the range to reach Africa.

The couple took over the plane on a flight between San Francisco and Los Angeles, permitting the 132 passengers to disembark at Los Angeles before beginning their cross-country flight.

Cuba released the jet to return to Miami with the three-man flight crew and seven stewardesses who had been kept as hostages. The hijackers and infant remained in Havana.

A gunman used a banker as a hostage to collect $290,000 ransom from a San Juan, P.R. bank, then hijacked a plane April 7 to take him and his hostage to Cuba.

The State Department said the U.S. had asked Cuban authorities through intermediaries to return the banker, the plane and its crew and the money.

The hijacker was later identified as Jose Luis Lugo. His hostage was Jose Luis Carrion, executive vice president of a San Juan bank.

A young gunman hijacked a Western Airlines aircraft to Cuba May 5 after taking control of the plane en route to Los Angeles.

The plane landed in Havana with 70 passengers and six crewmen aboard May 6. Four hours later the plane was flown back to Miami.

The hijacker was identified as Michael Lynn Hansen, 21, of Salt Lake City, Utah. When Hansen first took over the Salt Lake City-to-Los Angeles jet, he demanded that the plane be flown to Hanoi. But he changed his mind and settled on Havana when he was told that the plane, a Boeing 737, could not travel that far.

Charles A. Tuller, a former Commerce Department employe, his sons Bryce and Jonathan, and a third youth, William Graham, hijacked an Eastern Airlines jet Oct. 29 and forced it to Cuba.

Japanese police Nov. 6 seized a hijacker who tried to force a plane with three hostages from Tokyo to Cuba. The seized air pirate was identified as Tatsuji Nakaoka, 47, a Japanese who had been living in Los Angeles since 1948.

Nakaoka, who had arrived in Japan Oct. 31, commandeered a Japanese Airlines Boeing 727 with 126 persons aboard 40 minutes out of Tokyo on a flight to Fukuoka in western Japan. He forced the pilot at gunpoint to fly back to Tokyo and then held the plane hostage for seven hours while authorities were preparing to meet his demands for $2 million and a larger jet for a flght to Cuba via Vancouver and Mexico City. After releasing the passengers and three stewardesses, Nakaoka left the plane and marched the pilot, co-pilot and flight engineer to a waiting DC-8. As they entered the cabin, the co-pilot broke away and five policemen hiding inside disarmed the hijacker.

Four Mexican leftists, all members of the Armed Communist League, a small guerrilla group, hijacked a Mexican airliner with 75 passengers in Monterrey Nov. 8. They flew the plane to Havana after obtaining arms, release of five imprisoned comrades, a government promise to drop charges against two fugitive comrades, and a ransom of about $330,-000. Cuba returned the plane and passengers Nov. 9, but kept the 11 guerrillas and the ransom. Mexico asked for extradition of seven of the guerrillas Nov. 16, but Cuba refused Nov. 30 on grounds that their action was "political."

Long-distance hijack ends in Cuba—Three hijackers, armed with pistols and hand grenades, took over Southern Airways Flight 49 after it departed Birmingham, Ala. Nov. 10. On board the DC-9, destined for Memphis, were 27 passengers and a crew of four.

The three hijackers were positively identified as Henry D. Jackson, 25; Melvin C. Cale, 21; and Lewis D. Moore, all of Detroit.

(Jackson and Moore were described by Detroit officials Nov. 12 as suspected rapists. Cale, a half-brother of Moore, was an escapee from a Tennessee penitentiary.)

Under the hijackers' control, the DC-9 was diverted to Jackson, Miss., where it was refueled. As it flew north to Detroit, the hijackers radioed ahead for officials to meet them to negotiate demands for a $10 million ransom. But the plane never landed in Detroit, instead flying to Cleveland. Landing there shortly after midnight, it was refueled and loaded with supplies.

Shortly before 2:00 a.m. Nov. 11 the plane took off for Toronto, Canada. After circling the airport three hours, the plane landed in Toronto where the hijackers turned down an offer of $500,-000, demanding $10 million.

The hijackers took the plane south and while the plane circled Knoxville, Tenn., the hijackers demanded an official document stating that the $10 million would be a "U.S. government grant."

The hijackers then ordered the plane flown to Lexington, Ky., where it was refueled at 9:35 a.m. The plane returned to its circling pattern over Knoxville. At 1 p.m. the plane headed for Chattanooga, 100 miles southwest, where the hijackers took aboard $2 million in cash as a ransom. They also received bulletproof vests, medical supplies and food.

The gunmen ordered the jet to Havana, where it arrived in the late afternoon. But after negotiations broke down between the hijackers and Cuban authorities—Premier Fidel Castro was at the airport but did not take part in the discussions—the plane took for Key West, Fla.

After landing in Key West the DC-9 was refueled a fourth time and flew to McCoy Air Force Base in Orlando, Fla. Base personnel serviced the DC-9. During the stopover, one of the hijackers shot co-pilot Billy H. Johnson in the shoulder.

As the plane taxied out for takeoff, Federal Bureau of Investigation (FBI) agents shot out the plane's tires in hopes of keeping the DC-9 at the base, a move that later stirred debate.

Despite the punctured tires, the pilot, Capt. William R. Haas, successfully took the jet south to Key West where the plane circled while the hijackers demanded unsuccessfully to talk to President Nixon, who was at his Key Biscayne home.

The gunmen then ordered the plane back to Havana where Haas circled the plane over Jose Marti airport to burn off fuel and safely landed the disabled plane on a foam-covered runway.

Moore, Jackson, and Cale were seized by Cuban authorities, who also took the ransom.

The passengers and crew of the hijacked jet returned to Miami Nov. 12 aboard another Southern Airways plane.

Cuban authorities were reported Nov. 13 to have told U.S. officials the three hijackers would be jailed as criminals and not regarded as political refugees.

Exile Actions & Castro Regime's Response

Infiltration attempts. A group of 15 Cuban exiles tried to infiltrate Cuba Jan. 9, 1970 but failed when one of their two boats capsized off Oriente Province. One of the group drowned and the others sought sanctuary at the U.S. Navy base at Guantanamo, from which they were flown to Miami. After inquiry by U.S. authorities, 13 of the exiles, representatives of the militant anti-Castro group Alpha 66, were released Jan. 14; the other, Jesus Dominguez Benitez, was held in custody for violating bond on a 1968 bombing conviction.

Radio Havana announced Feb. 23 that Jose Antonio Quesada Fernandez, leader of the Miami-based exile group the Second Front of the Escambray, had been executed by a firing squad; Quesada Fernandez had led a small military expedition to Cuba in September 1969 to establish contact with the Cuban anti-Castro underground.

Thirteen Cuban exiles reportedly landed clandestinely in eastern Oriente Province April 17, the ninth anniversary of the Bay of Pigs invasion. After clashes with government forces, during which four exiles and five Cuban soldiers were reported killed, the last four invaders were captured April 24 and 26, according to an April 27 announcement of the Armed Forces Ministry.

In announcing the invasion attempt April 19, Premier Fidel Castro described "a group of mercenaries coming from the United States, equipped with modern automatic arms of the Yankee Army." The U.S. State Department stressed April 19 that no government agency had any knowledge of the incident.

The Alpha 66 exile group April 20 took credit for the April 17 landing. Alpha 66's statement said that "various guerrilla groups are at this moment fighting in different parts of Cuba." Explaining that its exile groups were operating on "two basic fronts," Alpha 66 stressed: "Our men are not of the CIA [Central Intelligence Agency], nor of the North American government, nor are they reactionaries or mercenaries." The secretary general of the organization, Andres Nazario Sargen, declined, "for obvious reasons" to disclose the size of the force in Cuba, but he added that the group had made "several" landings in the area.

The U.S. State Department April 15 had told Cuban exile groups that guerrilla raids on Cuba must be stopped.

Alpha 66 announced in Miami May 18 that it had released 11 Cuban fishermen whom it had held as hostages for about two weeks. An Alpha 66 spokesman said the fishermen had been left on the island of William Key in the Bahamas. The spokesman said the fishermen had been captured off the port of Caibarien in central Cuba when men from Alpha 66 sank two Cuban fishing boats there.

Alpha 66 had offered May 14 to trade the 11 captives to Cuban premier Fidel Castro for four prisoners jailed in Cuba. Castro refused.

About 25,000 demonstrators besieged the former U.S. embassy in Havana May 15, virtually imprisoning a Swiss official and a Cuban night watchman who remained inside. Cuban authorities released the two men May 18.

The anti-American demonstration was in protest against the capture of the fishermen by the anti-Castro exiles. The protesters contended that the building, which had been used by Swiss diplomats representing U.S. interests in Cuba since 1961, was illegally occupied.

Ambassador Alfred Fitchli of Switzerland led his staff out of the building May 15, leaving behind his colleague, Karl Hunziker, 36, and the watchman.

The 11 fishermen were flown back to Havana from Nassau in the Bahamas May 19, but the incident resulted in a deterioration of Swiss-Cuban relations. Castro announced May 21 that the Cuban ambassador in Switzerland had been recalled to Havana.

In response to a Swiss complaint about Cuban demonstrations in front of the Swiss embassy in Havana, Cuban Foreign Minister Raul Roa May 22 accused Swiss Foreign Minister Pierre Graber of "assuming the same attitude and speaking the same language as the imperialists and their agents."

In a message to Roa May 23, Foreign Minister Graber said: "It is perfectly unjust to identify Switzerland with the U.S. because she represents the American interests in Cuba. Switzerland is totally uninvolved in the kidnaping of the fishermen. She disapproves of all acts of piracy, especially when it involves innocent people. Besides, she intervened in order to get the fishermen repatriated."

After a Sept. 14 landing, the Armed Forces Ministry said Sept. 23 that its troops had crushed a nine-man invasion party launched from the U.S. Eight of the invaders were reported captured and one killed, while three Cubans were reported killed. The ministry said the group had trained in Florida for five months and had left Miami Sept. 1 for the Bahamas, from which they launched the invasion. In Miami, Alpha 66 confirmed that the invaders were Alpha 66 members.

Alpha 66 asserted Sept. 28 that there had been landings by two separate groups of its forces. It added Nov. 5 that one of the two groups had reached its destination in Oriente Province.

The Voice of Cuba broadcast a report Oct. 28 that "mercenary military bases" existed in Nicaragua and Costa Rica in preparation for an invasion of Cuba. The radio was echoing a charge made by Carlos Fonseca Amador, a political prisoner in Costa Rica released following the hijacking of a Costa Rican airliner to Cuba. Radio Havana Jan. 20, 1971 reiterated the charge that Nicaragua and Costa Rica were planning a new invasion of Cuba "with the implicit complicity of the United States." The broadcast reported that Nicaraguan President Anastasio Somoza had frequently visited his Costa Rican farm on which Cuban counter-revolutionaries were reportedly being trained for a new invasion. "Costa Rican and Cuban mercenaries are being trained in this territory, even though [Costa Rican] President Jose Figueres has denied that military bases of aggression are installed in his country," the broadcast charged.

A Cuban TV program said March 7, 1971 that government forces had killed exile leader Vicente Mendez and eliminated two invading commando units in Oriente Province in April and September of 1970. The broadcast said that five members of the April invasion led by Mendez were killed and 16 captured, while four members of the September group were killed and nine captured. A spokesman for Alpha 66 in Miami said March 8 that he had indirect reports that Mendez and other members of the invasion teams were still fighting, although "four or five" of the men had been killed.

1970–73: A TIME OF RESTRAINT

The Castro regime said Oct. 14 that U.S-backed commando "mercenaries" had attacked a small fishing village on the northern coast Oct. 12, killing two persons and injuring four others.

Radio Havana, in a broadcast monitored in Miami, said the night attack was carried out by two boats and blamed it on "the government of the U.S. and its accomplices." The broadcast said a border patrol guard and an Interior Ministry policeman were killed in the raid. Havana Radio said the "mercenaries" immediately fled out to sea, heading north" after machine-gunning the town.

In New York, Guillermo Martinez Marquez, a spokesman for a Miami-based exile organization headed by Jose de la Torriente, claimed responsibility for the raid, called it a success and said it was the beginning of a series of actions by the group "to free Cuba from its Communist yoke."

(The Miami Herald reported Oct. 20 that the Cuban exile group had claimed that it had seized the small fishing village for more than an hour during the raid. The head of the Cuban Liberation Front claimed its goal had been a military installation outside the town and that the commandoes had torn down telephone lines and sabotaged the village electrical plant.)

Anti-Castro plot thwarted. U.S. Justice Department officials in New Orleans July 1, 1972 arrested nine men and seized seven tons of ammunition allegedly intended for use to overthrow Castro.

The arms were reportedly taken at an airport near Shreveport, La., and the suspects, who included two Mexicans and a former U.S. immigration official, Michael B. Pollack, were arrested in Louisiana and Texas. According to one official, the ammunition was to have been shipped clandestinely to Veracruz, Mexico, from where it would have gone to Cuba to be used by anti-Castro insurgents.

A U.S. magistrate in Shreveport ordered two pilots and a third man held for grand jury action in connection with the plot, the Miami Herald reported July 23.

The men, Joseph Mazzuka and James M. Miller, both of Baton Rouge, La., and Arthur Lussier of Fort Lauderdale, Fla., were among those arrested July 1.

Two others arrested in the case, Murray Kessler of New York and Barry Seal of Baton Rouge, were bound over for grand jury action at a preliminary hearing in New Orleans July 10.

Overseas targets bombed. Two plastic bombs exploded April 4, 1972 at the Cuban Trade Commission offices in Montreal, killing a Cuban security guard and badly damaging the building.

Authorities arrested seven Cuban officials and charged six of them with possessing weapons and interfering with the police investigation. (But the Washington Post reported April 12 that charges against six of them had been dropped.)

The Post reported the day after the explosion that an anonymous phone caller had informed United Press International in Miami that the bombings had been carried out by a group called the Young Cubans "in the name of Alejandro Del Valle, who died in the [1961] Bay of Pigs invasion."

Cuban Premier Fidel Castro alleged April 5 that Montreal police had used "brutal and fascist methods" in their handling of the incident and that the blast had been a "sad event" engineered by the U.S. Central Intelligence Agency (CIA).

In Ottawa, the Canadian External Affairs Department said it "understood" Castro's feelings and hoped the "regrettable" explosion would "not prejudice the good relations between Canada and Cuba."

C. M. Drury, serving as Canada's acting minister of external affairs, apologized April 6 to Cuban Ambassador Jose Fernandez de Cossio for the "intrusion of the police" after the bombing.

Drury said the commission, which had previously been "assimilated to a consulate and as such enjoyed diplomatic immunity," should not have been entered by the police.

An anti-Communist organization calling itself the Cuban Secret Government

Dec. 12, 1972 admitted placing bombs that destroyed a travel agency and three office handling packages for Cuba in Miami, New York and Montreal. No persons were injured by the explosions, but the group warned of further attacks against persons and concerns doing business with Cuba.

About six weeks thereafter a bomb explosion in San Juan, Puerto Rico Jan. 22 destroyed two automobiles belonging to Cuban exile leader Alberto Rodriguez and damaged his residence.

Anti-Castro aid sought. A group of prominent Cuban exiles headed by ex-President Carlos Prio Socarras and former Sen. Eduardo Suarez Rivas asked U.S. President Richard M. Nixon May 10, 1972 to provide them with economic and military aid to overthrow the Castro regime.

The request, presented in writing, was also signed by Andres Rivero Aguero, president-elect at the time Castro seized power, and Juanita Castro, the premier's exiled sister. Eduardo Boza Masdival, former bishop of Havana living in exile in Venezuela, also supported the petition.

The signatories cited a 1966 report by the security commission of the Organization of American States, which claimed meetings of the Organization of Latin American Solidarity in Havana sought to "institutionalize the practice of subversion in the Americas."

Meeting of Castro foes—A meeting of 80 Cuban exiles convened Nov. 23 in San Jose, Costa Rica to plan "the strategy of the first phase of the overthrow of the tyranny of Fidel Castro."

The group, calling itself the Latin American Democratic Left, consisted mainly of Cubans residing in the U.S. Leaders thanked Costa Rican President Jose Figueres for cooperating in the organization of the meeting. They also claimed the support of prominent former Cuban officials, and of two important Venezuelan politicians, ex-President Romulo Betancourt and current presidential candidate Carlos Andres Perez.

Exile & repatriation flights. The monthly airlift flying U.S. citizens of Cuban descent and their relatives from Cuba to Matamoros, Mexico was apparently canceled by the Cuban government, the Miami Herald reported March 4, 1971. The last such flight took place in August 1970 and carried only five passengers, compared with the previous average of 60–70.

About 2,000 Cuban-Americans and their relatives reportedly left Cuba on the 33 flights which had covered a period of nearly four years. About 819 American citizens and 1,400 relatives of Americans were reportedly still in Cuba and had applied to leave the island on the repatriation flights.

The apparent cancellation of the repatriation flights, which had begun in December 1966 after arrangements were made by Cuba and Mexico, did not affect the daily refugee flights from Cuba to Miami, on which only Cuban citizens were allowed.

The U.S. State Department said Aug. 10 that Cuba had ordered a suspension for at least one week beginning Aug. 9 of the airlift bringing refugees to Miami. Cuba was reported to have informed the Swiss embassy in Havana (which represented the U.S.) that the daily flights were suspended due to administrative delays in the joint processing of names. The airlift was resumed Aug. 16.

But Cuba then informed the U.S. Aug. 31 that it intended to terminate the airlift, which by then had brought 246,000 Cuban refugees to Florida since December 1965.

The flights were halted by the Cuban government Sept. 1.

U.S. State Department spokesman Robert McCloskey said the U.S. had been notified by the Swiss embassy in Havana, which represented American interests in Cuba, that the airlift would be suspended for several weeks. It would then resume until Cuban authorities had processed the names of the last group of refugees permitted to leave. McCloskey said the Cuban government would submit for U.S. approval a final list of 1,000 Cubans eligible for the airlift.

Officials said a "master list" of Cubans registered to leave and approved by both the U.S. and Cuba for the flights contained 33,000 names. The U.S. had also approved the entry of 94,000 Cubans whose names were registered by their relatives in the U.S.

The State Department said the Cuban government had given no reason for its decision to terminate the airlift which flew twice a day, five days a week. McCloskey said the U.S. "urged the Cuban government to continue until all of those Cubans who have asked to be reunited with their families in the U.S. have left."

U.S. Secretary of State William P. Rogers said Sept. 3 that he regretted the Cuban decision and hoped the government of Premier Fidel Castro would resume the flights.

According to the New York Times Sept. 1, U.S. officials believed that the Cuban government, which had previously decided that all those who were hostile to the Cuban regime except those of military age could leave the country, reversed its decision due to the emigration of greatly needed skilled workers.

Sporadic resumptions and suspensions of the airlift continued thereafter.

In a related development, the State Department expressed "deep concern" Sept. 28 over a threat by Cuban Premier Fidel Castro to encourage the hijacking of U.S. planes if the U.S. promoted illegal escapes from Cuba once the airlift ended. Castro had made the threat in a radio speech earlier that day.

Route through Canada cut. The New York Times reported May 7, 1972 that 61 Cubans who had arrived at Toronto airport April 25 had been turned back by immigration officials after the Cubans admitted their actual destination was the U.S.

According to the officials, the travelers may have been an advance party testing a route by which some 30,000 Cubans living in Spain could come to the U.S. via Costa Rica, Jamaica and Canada. The 61 Cubans remained overnight in Toronto and were flown back to Kingston, Jamaica.

Suarez defects. Refugees from Cuba occasionally included former leaders of the Castro revolution.

Ismael Suarez de la Paz, friend of Castro and former provisional national coordinator of the 26th of July Movement, defected to the U.S., the Miami Herald reported July 31, 1970. Suarez, who represented the Cuban trading firm Cubalse on the island of Martinique, had fled to Puerto Rico in late June. He and his family were admitted into the U.S. as refugees in late July. Explaining that he had lost faith in the Cuban revolution over the past two years, Suarez said the "present leadership" was unable to meet the economic problems of the country.

Flight by sea. Thirty-three Cuban refugees arrived in Miami Feb. 19, 1970 after being picked up by a U.S. Coast Guard cutter. The group, which had left Cuba 20 days before, had spent 18 days on a small island trying to repair its motor boat.

Fifty-five refugees arrived July 1, 1971 at La Ceiba in Honduras after fleeing Cuba in a fishing boat. The group included 30 men, 13 women and 12 children, all reportedly in good health.

A group of 44 Cubans had hijacked a boat in Cuba and forced it to Mexico, where they asked political asylum, Mexican immigration authorities disclosed Oct. 18, 1972.

A U.S. immigration official had ruled that three Cuban fishermen who had hijacked a Cuban boat to Florida Dec. 6, 1972 and sought asylum in the U.S. had entered the U.S. without proper documentation and were therefore excludable, the State Department announced Dec. 21. Officials said, however, that the men would not necessarily be sent back to Cuba.

Confrontations at Sea

Cuba seizes U.S. boat. An American treasure-hunting boat with sophisticated electronic equipment aboard was seized by a Cuban patrol boat about 20 miles off Cuba's northern coast March 1, 1970 and escorted into the Cuban port of Caibarien. The vessel, the Jocelyn C, reportedly carried a crew of five, including the skipper, Sten Carlson of Chatham, Mass.; it was detained for about 24 hours before being released March 2.

David Shamp, an official of Submare, Inc. of Washington D. C. to which the vessel was leased, explained March 1 that the Jocelyn C was searching for sunken Spanish treasure in the Caribbean with the aid of sonar and metal detection devices. He added that the boat "was definitely on a peaceful mission and is not connected in any way with a governmental activity."

(The U.S. had made inquiries about the incident through the Swiss embassy in Havana, which served as an intermediary in U.S. negotiations with Cuba. The Swiss embassy reported March 2 that the Cubans had seized the vessel under the apparent assumption that it had intruded into Cuban territorial waters.)

U.S. seizes 4 Cuban fishing boats. Four Cuban fishing boats were seized off the southern Florida coast Feb. 24 and 25, 1971 for fishing within U.S. and Florida territorial waters. The boats were released March 2 after their captains had been fined a total of $25,500.

The U.S. Coast Guard took into custody one of the vessels south of the Dry Tortugas islands Feb. 24 after it had been observed fishing within the 12-mile fishing limit recognized by the U.S. Three other Cuban vessels, which were inside the U.S. limit but were not observed fishing, were escorted into international waters by the U.S. Coast Guard. However, the Florida Marine Patrol intercepted the party Feb. 25, seized the three boats and took them to Key West; Florida authorities claimed that an American fishing boat captain had seen all four boats fishing within the U.S. limits.

(Florida then claimed as its territorial fishing waters all the area between the mainland and the Florida Keys, which at some points extended well beyond 12 miles. A federal injunction, issued in late 1970, prevented Florida from seizing Cuban boats operating anywhere in Florida Bay, which lies north of the Keys; the injunction had been issued after Florida announced that it would seize Cuban shrimp boats in that area even if they were beyond the U.S.-recognized 12-mile limit.)

The state of Florida Feb. 26 dropped charges against the three captains of the boats it had seized after the U.S. government said it would prosecute under federal law on the basis of a sworn affidavit by the American fishing captain who saw all four boats fishing. The U.S. district court in Miami fined the four captains a total of $13,500 March 2 and charged the Cuban government another $12,000 in civil penalties. The U.S. government said that it had received the payment from the Cuban government. The four boats, their captains and crew, returned to international waters March 3.

Havana Radio had announced March 1 that it was sending two fleets of fishing boats to fish in the waters where the four were picked up. "Those two fleets that have left are a symbol of the courage of our people" the broadcast said.

Cubans & Americans freed. Cuba released 12 Americans July 7, 1971, one day after four Cuban fishermen held for violating U.S. waters, were released from a federal prison. A thirteenth American, Fritz Sprandel, had been freed by Cuba July 6.

Four of the Americans detained by Cuba, one of whom was wanted as a material witness in a draft fraud case, were reported July 11 to have been permitted to leave aboard their yacht.

The State Department maintained that the exchange "was not a deal, not a swap." Premier Fidel Castro, however, said in a radio broadcast July 7 that the arrest of the fishermen and the detention of the Americans were closely connected.

The Cuban government had announced June 10 that it was holding 13 Americans (those later released July 6 and 7), who had been taken from three vessels, and would try at least five in "revolutionary tribunals." The announcement came a day after the four Cuban fishermen, who had been arrested May 27, were found guilty of violating U.S. waters in a federal court in Key West and were sentenced to fines of $10,000 each and six months in jail. (The U.S. judge also said he would consider a motion within the next 120 days to ease the sentence and would take into consideration whether the Cuban government paid the fines.)

Sprandel had been forced ashore by bad weather in his canoe en route to Mexico. Four people were on a 58-foot yacht and eight were on a disabled tugboat.

State Department officials declined to speculate whether the Cuban action was in retaliation for the sentencing of the Cuban fishermen. The department said June 11 that it had asked the Swiss embassy in Havana to seek access to the 13 Americans and to discover the reasons for their detention.

The Cuban newspaper Granma reported June 15 that five of the Americans had been fined $20,000 each after trials by revolutionary tribunal. The paper reported that all the accused admitted having entered Cuban territorial waters and landing illegally on Cuban soil. The U.S. State Department announced that the Cuban government had agreed to release the eight crewmen of the tugboat.

Radio Havana announced that the government was holding three Americans on charges of transporting $2 million worth of marijuana aboard a sailboat captured in Cuban waters en route from Jamaica to Florida in February, according to a July 16 report.

Cuba attacks U.S.-based freighter. A Cuban gunboat attacked a Miami-based freighter and wounded its captain in international waters 100 miles off Cuba's east coast Dec. 15, 1971. The vessel was said by the Cubans to be used for counter-revolutionary activities against Cuba.

The Johnny Express, a Panamanian-registered ship operated by the Bahama Lines of Miami, was taken to Cuba after being strafed with machine gun fire and rammed while en route to Miami from Haiti where it had reportedly delivered foodstuffs.

The 235-foot vessel was the sister ship of the freighter Lyla Express, seized by the Cuban Navy Dec. 5 on charges that some of its crew members were counter-revolutionaries. (Cuba announced Dec. 17 that it would bring criminal charges against at least some of the Lyla Express' 14 crew members.)

In a call for help Dec. 15, Jose Villa, captain of the Johnny Express, radioed: "The deck is covered with blood . . . tell the Coast Guard to come quickly. Tell them there are dead and wounded here."

The U.S. Coast Guard ordered planes to the scene to provide medical assistance, but by the time they arrived the ship was out of sight.

In acknowledging the attack, the Cuban government Dec. 16 called the Johnny Express "a pirate ship" in the service of the U.S. Central Intelligence Agency. Cuba said, "This ship, like the Lyla Express, was flying the Panamanian flag to facilitate its activities of transporting arms and men to Cuba."

(Premier Fidel Castro said Dec. 22 that Villa had confessed to being an agent for the CIA and would be submitted to "revolutionary justice.")

Cuba also accused the Babun family, operators of the Express vessels, and prominent anti-Castro exiles in Miami, of being "well-known counter-revolutionary agents in the service of the U.S. government."

Teofilo Babun, president of Bahama Lines, and one of four brothers who own the line, denied any connections with the CIA Dec. 16 and claimed that the attack on the Johnny Express was part of a personal vendetta against the Babun family by Premier Castro.

The Miami Herald reported Dec. 16 that Santiago Babun Sr., a brother of

Teofilo, had participated in numerous anti-Castro activities after coming to Miami in 1960. It was also reported that Teofilo Babun and his nephew, Santiago Babun Jr., a veteran of the Bay of Pigs invasion, were arrested in 1968 by police who seized a large quantity of explosives from their Miami shipyard.

U.S. protests to Cuba—The U.S. protested to Cuba Dec. 16 for its seizure of the Johnny Express, and demanded the immediate return of Villa, a Cuban exile and naturalized U.S. citizen, "as soon as his physical condition permits."

White House Press Secretary Ronald L. Ziegler said Dec. 16 that the Administration deplored the attack as "inexcusable" and "unconscionable" and said it was "an act that cannot be tolerated within the international community."

(A report Dec. 19 in Cuba's official Communist newspaper, Granma, said Villa had only received slight wounds, and was "the only crew member to be wounded.")

State Department vows to take measures—The U.S. State Department issued a warning to Cuba Dec. 17 that it would take "all measures under international law" to protect American and other ships in the Caribbean from any new attacks by the Cubans.

Unidentified Pentagon sources reported the same day that orders had been issued to naval and air units in the Caribbean to provide armed assistance to any vessel that might be attacked by Cubans.

Ricardo Alarcon, Cuba's ambassador to the United Nations, announced Dec. 18 that Cuba was putting its air and naval forces on alert in support of Cuba's policy of "proceeding against any ships engaged in piracy against Cuba."

Russia scores U.S. on military alert—The Soviet Union charged Dec. 20 that the U.S. military alert in the Caribbean was "completely groundless," and said that the Lyla Express and the Johnny Express "were widely used by the U.S. Central Intelligence Agency for criminal actions."

The Soviet press agency Tass reported Dec. 20 that the U.S had intensified tensions with Cuba without justification as part of an effort to prevent Latin American nations from restoring normal diplomatic relations with Havana. Responding to Russia's charges, the U.S. State Department Dec. 21 renewed denials that the U.S. was involved in any plans to attack Cuba. State Dept. spokesman Robert J. McCloskey said there was no reason to believe that either the Lyla Express or the Johnny Express were engaged in anything but commercial pursuits, nor was either ship carrying arms or agents to Cuba.

(Granma Dec. 22 called the U.S. denial "a shameful lie" comparable to Washington's original denial of involvement in the 1961 Bay of Pigs invasion.")

Cuba frees 27, holds Villa—Cuba Dec. 27, 1971 released 26 crewmen of the Lyla Express and Johnny Express.

The 26 men returned to Panama Dec. 27 with a three-man Panamanian commission that had been sent to Cuba to investigate the boat seizures. The commission reported Dec. 30 that the ships' logs revealed they had participated in armed attacks on eastern Cuba in 1968 and 1969.

Pablo Gari Camany, first mate of the Johnny Express, returned to Panama Sept. 5, 1972 after he also had been given his liberty by Cuban authorities. He was accompanied by a Panamanian delegation headed by Romulo Escobar, rector of the University of Panama, who said Gari Camany's release had been requested "by the revolutionary government of Panama."

Gari Camany, a Spanish-born Cuban citizen, was to be held in Panama for questioning by authorities to see if he had violated Panamanian law.

Cuba was said to be holding Villa and two crew members of the Lyla Express.

Ships sent to Panama—The two seized ships were finally handed over to Panama in April 1973.

The Johnny Express arrived in Panamanian waters April 23 and the Lyla Express the next day. The ships, which had flown the Panamanian flag when captured, were entrusted to the Panamanian government on the condition that they not be returned to their owners, Cuban exiles opposed to the Communist regime.

The captain of the Johnny Express, Jose Villa, was reported in custody in Panama April 29.

U.S. orders warships to resist seizures. In a change of policy, the U.S. had ordered its military command in the Caribbean to protect merchant ships of friendly nations against harassment by the Cuban navy, the Wall Street Journal reported April 13, 1972.

The new instructions reversed nonintervention directives in effect in December 1971 after Cuba had seized the Lyla Express and Johnny Express.

According to the Journal, the new directives authorized military commanders in the area, without instructions from Washington or even a request from the country whose ship seemed threatened, to "interpose" U.S. warships between Cuban attackers and endangered merchant ships to block the Cuban line of fire and thwart any boarding attempts.

Such action could be ordered, the Journal said, if the following conditions seemed present:

■ The merchant ship facing seizure must be sailing in international waters at least three miles from the Cuban shore.

■ The commander of U.S. warships moving to the rescue must have "no knowledge" that the threatened ship had been engaging in illegal activities against Cuba.

■ The U.S. commander must have reason to believe some U.S. citizens were aboard the threatened ship.

The Journal noted that the instructions did not require the commander to make certain the ship had not engaged in illegal activites, and allowed room for error about whether U.S. lives were in danger. The orders stated that "in the absence of other certification" that a U.S. citizen was aboard the ship, the U.S. commander could "take the word" of the ship's captain.

Fishing boats sunk near Bahamas. Two Cuban fishing boats were burned and sunk Oct. 11, 1972 south of Andros Island in the Bahamas, but their 11 crewmen were rescued. Cuban authorities had demanded that the British government investigate the incident, Havana radio reported Oct. 14.

One rescued fisherman claimed "pirates operating from U.S. territory" had boarded the boats and sunk them with dynamite, according to a radio broadcast reported Oct. 17. However, none of the Miami-based Cuban exile groups claimed credit for the action. Observers said the incident might be linked to a continuing dispute over fishing rights in Bahama waters.

In the past, Bahamian patrol boats had hauled in fishing boats from both the U.S. and Cuba for allegedly fishing in Bahama waters.

Cuban boat attacked—A Havana radio broadcast said a Cuban fisherman was wounded in a machinegun and hand grenade attack on his boat by "counterrevolutionaries" operating from the U.S., the Washington Post reported Feb. 2, 1973. The attack was said to have taken place in Bahamian waters.

Terrorists & Prisoners Win Haven in Cuba

Terrorists and political prisoners in several countries were granted asylum in Cuba in exchange for the release of captured hostages.

Cross freed; 7 fly to Cuba. British Trade Commissioner James R. Cross was released unharmed in Montreal, Canada Dec. 3, 1970, 59 days after he had been kidnapped from his home by Quebec separatists.

Three of the kidnappers and four of their relatives were flown to Cuba aboard a Canadian military plane in accordance with the terms of an agreement worked out earlier in the day by representatives of the Quebec government and the abductors, members of the terrorist Front de Liberation du Quebec (FLQ).

Police spokesmen for the Royal Canadian Mounted Police (RCMP), the Quebec Provincial Police (QPP) and the Montreal police had announced Dec. 2 that investigators were "making headway" in the case of the kidnaped British diplomat. At that time, the police were involved in a stakeout around 10949 Des Recollets Street in a Montreal working-class suburb.

Police then sealed off a six-block area in Montreal North around the house.

In the early hours of Dec. 3, the kidnappers sent a message that they were willing to negotiate. After preliminary talks at the hideaway house, the kidnappers drove Cross to the site of Man and His World on St. Helen's Island.

Cross was delivered to Ricardo Escartin, Cuba's acting consul in Montreal, at the Canadian Pavilion, which had been declared Cuban territory for the exchange.

A helicopter took the kidnappers and their relatives, who had joined them at St. Helen's Island, to Montreal's Dorval airport, where an RCMP plane took them to Cuba. Cross was held by Cuban officials in the Pavilion until the plane arrived in Cuba.

The seven persons on the military transport to Cuba were identified as Marc Carbonneau, 37, a Montreal taxi driver, sought by police in the kidnappings of both Cross and Quebec Labor Minister Pierre Laporte; Jacques Lanctot, 25, also a suspect; Lanctot's wife, Suzanne, and child; Pierre Seguin, another alleged kidnapper; Jacques Cossette-Trudel, and Louise Cossette-Trudel. The seven arrived in Havana Dec. 4 and were greeted by Foreign Ministry officials.

The Cuban government emphasized that it had agreed to take the seven only at the request of Ottawa and for "humanitarian reasons." The official newspaper Granma stated: "The transfer of these people to our country happened following a formal request from the Canadian government to which the Cuban government agreed with a view to realizing the rescue of the British official."

Trelew hijackers reach Cuba. Ten Argentine guerrillas who had hijacked an airliner Aug. 15, 1972 from the Patagonian town of Trelew to Santiago, Chile were sent to Cuba by the Chilean government Aug. 25. The hijacking was by alleged terrorists involved in a jail break at the prison in the naval air base near Trelew.

The Argentine government, which had demanded extradition of the guerrillas, angrily recalled its ambassador from Santiago Aug. 26 and delivered what it called a "very severe" protest to Chile Aug. 27.

In a nationwide radio and television message Aug. 25, Chilean President Salvador Allende said his government's decision to grant the guerrillas political asylum and then sent them to Cuba was motivated by "profound humanity and morality" and followed "international conventions and principles and the dispositions of our internal laws."

Mexican prisoners released. The Mexican government agreed Nov. 28, 1971 to exchange a group of political prisoners for the life of a kidnap victim, Dr. Jaime Castrejon Diez, rector of the State University of Guerrero who was kidnapped on his way to work Nov. 19.

Castrejon Diez, millionaire owner of the Coca-Cola bottling concession in Guerrero, was released Dec. 1, two days after his family paid a $200,000 ransom and nine political prisoners (eight men and one woman) were flown to Cuba, where they were accepted by the Castro government for "humanitarian reasons," according to a Nov. 30 Havana Radio broadcast.

The kidnapping was believed to be the work of a group of leftist rural guerrillas active in the mountains near Acapulco under command of a former schoolteacher, Genaro Vazquez Rojas. Five of the prisoners exchanged were said to be close associates of Vazquez Rojas and the woman was said to be his sister-in-law.

Bolivian escapees reach Cuba. Sixty-seven Bolivian political prisoners, who escaped from the jail on Coati island in Lake Titicaca, were flown to Havana Nov. 6, 1972 after the Peruvian regime refused to grant them political asylum. Six others were returned to Bolivia at their own request, according to the Peruvian Foreign Ministry.

The prisoners, who reportedly included trade unionists, student leaders and members of opposition parties and revolutionary groups, broke out of Coati Nov. 2. According to one escapee, they overpowered prison guards at the end of a soccer match between guards and inmates. Four were recaptured, but the rest crossed the border into Peru, where they were held by police until the government responded to their request for political asylum.

Relations With the U.S.S.R. & Other Communist Nations

Soviet trade & economic assistance. Cuban Deputy Foreign Trade Minister German Amado Blanco left Moscow Feb. 17, 1970 after signing a trade pact with the U.S.S.R. providing for exchanges in 1970 totaling 1.2 billion rubles ($1.3 billion at the official exchange rate), an increase of almost 50% over their trade in 1968. The protocol was signed within the framework of the six-year Soviet-Cuban trade agreement expiring in 1970. The overall agreement covered Soviet importation of Cuban sugar and Cuban importation of Soviet oil and oil products, machinery and some foodstuffs.

Cuban Minister without Portfolio Carlos Rafael Rodriguez and Vladimir Novikov, deputy chairman of the Soviet Union Council of Ministers, signed an agreement Dec. 9 in Moscow creating an intergovernmental Soviet-Cuban commission to handle economic, scientific and technical cooperation. The commission's duties included a study of Soviet-Cuban economic relations and drafting of proposals for increased trade based on a greater variety of goods.

Under a recent agreement between the Soviet Union and Canada, Soviet-purchased Canadian flour was to be shipped directly to Cuba, it was reported Jan. 15, 1971. Russia bought about $25 million of Canadian flour for 1971 shipment. Canada had been supplying Cuba with Soviet-purchased flour for several years.

The annual Soviet-Cuban trade pact was signed in Moscow Feb. 22, 1971. This followed three months of talks in which a joint commission was set up to study Cuba's "economic management and ways to increase the efficiency of the national economy."

A brief communique announcing the signing did not reveal the estimated amount of Soviet-Cuban trade in 1971, but the Soviet press agency Tass quoted Soviet Deputy Foreign Trade Minister Mikhail Kuzmin who said at the signing ceremony that "in 1971 we must send Cuba a broad and varied range of Soviet goods worth 100 million rubles [$110 million] more than last year."

Cuban Foreign Minister Raul Roa June 11–21, 1971 paid an 11-day visit to the Soviet Union which included meetings with Communist party General Secretary Leonid Brezhnev and Premier Aleksei Kosygin. A communique made public June 22 stated that "the parties expressed their disposition to continue efforts to strengthen the unbreakable and fraternal Soviet-Cuban relations."

In a message commemorating the 18th anniversary of Castro's revolutionary 26th of July Movement, Soviet leaders pledged to "spare no effort and no energy" in aiding the development of Cuba, according to a July 27, 1971 report.

The message said the Soviet Union and Cuba "are united by common aims in the struggle for the future of mankind, for freedom and for successful development along the road of social progress."

A Soviet delegation, headed by Vladimir Novikov, vice president of the council of ministers, arrived in Havana Sept. 3 to discuss mechanization of sugar production and exploitation of new sources of electric energy.

Radio Havana said Sept. 10, 1971 that Cuba and the Soviet Union had signed a comprehensive agreement under which Soviet participation in the planning and execution of Cuban economic and technical projects would be greatly increased.

The signing of the agreement Sept. 9 in Havana was preceded by a week's discussion between officials of Cuba and the Soviet Union. It was also reported that Premier Castro and President Osvaldo Dorticos had taken part in the talks.

It was reported Dec. 28 by the Soviet news agency Tass that Cuba and the Soviet Union had agreed to strengthen future economic and trade ties following a meeting in Moscow between Dorticos and Soviet Premier Alexei N. Kosygin.

Soviet goals political, not economic. Leon Goure and Julian Weinkle of the University of Miami's Center for Advanced International Studies asserted in the March–April 1972 issue of Problems of Communism that the Soviet Union was seeking political rather than economic rewards in its economic relations with Cuba. They wrote:

In its steady expansion of economic relations with Cuba over the past decade, the Soviet Union has been motivated primarily by political rather than financial or humanitarian considerations. Basically, Soviet aid and trade do not reflect any major economic need or even any commercial interest in Cuba on the part of Moscow, for the island has little to offer the USSR economy. In fact, Cuba has turned out to be a growing economic liability,[1] for which the Soviet Union has attempted to compensate itself by such measures as the resale of imported Cuban cane sugar. However, the more important compensation has been in the political realm. Moscow views the Cuban Revolution as a triumphant "national liberation movement" which promises to weaken US prestige in Latin America and has given communism a foothold in the Western Hemisphere.

Thus it is not surprising that the USSR came to Cuba's assistance when the Castro regime seemed to face economic crisis. As the Soviets have observed, "world socialism helps the national emancipation of oppressed peoples," and conversely, the latter's "liberation struggle contributes to the struggle for socialism. . . ."[2]

But if indeed Fidel Castro's 1959 victory can be said to have contributed to the "struggle for socialism," it also injected a discordant note into relations within the international socialist community. The Cuban leader has sought from the outset to maintain a wide sphere of independence in his dealings with the Soviet bloc, while promoting Castroism as the appropriate political model for both Latin America and the Third World in general. Proudly asserting that "we [Cuba] are not anyone's satellite and never shall be,"[3] he attempted to export his own brand of revolution, much to the chagrin of the USSR. Predictably, serious disputes arose between Moscow and Havana. As Carlos Rafael Rodriguez, Castro's Minister without Portfolio and one of the most influential of Cuba's old-line Communists, was later to acknowledge, "there have been inevitable differences which on some occasions became acute."[4] . . .

INITIAL SOVIET INVOLVEMENT

Soviet economic involvement in Cuba began essentially as a rescue operation in which Moscow came to Castro's assistance after the latter found himself first threatened with a reduction in US sugar purchases and then, in early 1962, cut off entirely from the US market.[5]

---

[1] Soviet aid to Cuba is presently believed to exceed one million dollars a day. In the past decade, according to Norman Gall, Cuba has received more foreign economic aid per capita than any nation on earth. See Norman Gall, "How Castro Failed," *Commentary* (New York), Vol. 52, No. 5, November 1971, p. 56.
[2] *The USSR and Developing Countries*, Moscow, Novosti Press Agency Publishing House, n.d., p. 17.
[3] *Bohemia* (Havana), March 19, 1965.
[4] Prensa Latina (English), June 12, 1969.
[5] All trade between Cuba and the United States was suspended in February 1962, one month after the Organization of American States (OAS) foreign ministers had voted at Punta del Este, Uruguay, to exclude Cuba from participation in the inter-American system because of its "incompatible" ties with a Marxist-Leninist government *i.e.*, the USSR). The OAS subsequently voted, in July 1964, to condemn Cuban aggression and intervention against Venezuela and called on member states to "suspend all their trade, whether direct or indirect with Cuba, except in foodstuffs, medicines, and medical equip-

1970–73: A TIME OF RESTRAINT

TABLE 1.—VOLUME OF CUBAN TRADE WITH THE SOVIET UNION

[In millions of rubles and percentages]

	1960	1961	1962	1963	1964	1965	1966	1967	1968	1969	1970
Turnover	160.6	539.0	540.7	507.8	588.6	645.9	689.2	842.2	811.8	770.1	1,045.0
Imports	67.2	258.3	330.1	359.8	329.4	337.9	431.9	506.7	561.8	561.6	580.0
Exports	93.4	280.7	210.6	148.0	259.2	308.0	257.3	335.5	250.0	208.5	465.0
Balance	+26.2	+22.4	−119.5	−211.8	−70.2	−29.9	−174.6	−171.2	−311.8	−353.1	−115.0
Cuba's share of Soviet trade (percent)	1.6	5.1	4.5	3.9	4.2	4.4	4.5	5.1	4.5	3.9	4.7
U.S.S.R. share of Cuban imports (percent)	13.8	41.1	54.2	53.1	40.2	49.5	56.3	58.3			
U.S.S.R. share of Cuban exports (percent)	16.7	48.2	42.3	30.2	38.5	47.0	46.2	52.1			

Sources: Vneshniaia torgovlia S.S.S.R: statisticheskii sbornik 1918–66, (U.S.S.R. Foreign Trade: Statistical Handobok 1918–66), Moscow, Mezhdunardonie Otnosheniia, 1967, p. 69; Vneshniaia orgovlia S.S.S.R. za 1968 god, (U.S.S.R. Foreign Trade in 1968), Moscow, Mezhdunarodnie Otnosheniia, 1969, p. 15; Foreign Trade (Moscow), No. 6, 1970, p. 55, and No. 5, 1971, p. 48; Compendio estadistico de Cuba, 1967 (Statistical Handbook of Cuba 1967), Havana, Juceplan, 1967, p. 27.

Moscow initially remained aloof from Castro and his problems, and it was not until February 1960, during a visit to Havana, by Soviet Deputy Premier Anastas Mikoyan, that the USSR signed a trade agreement providing for the Soviet purchase of 425,000 metric tons [9] of sugar that year and one million tons a year in each of the following four years. (Prior to 1960, Soviet purchases of sugar from Cuba had been more modest—205,600 tons in 1955; 214,300 tons in 1956; 350,000 tons in 1957; 197,900 tons in 1958, and 132,500 tons in 1959.[10]) In addition, the Soviet Union granted Cuba a credit of $100 million, at low interest, for the purchase of Soviet machinery and materials required in the "construction of plants and factories."[11] The agreement also called for the resumption of diplomatic relations, which occurred in May 1960.

When the United States in July 1960 cut its annual Cuba sugar quota by 700,000 tons,[12] the Soviet Union agreed not only to increase its own purchases for that year by one million tons but also to take the 700,000 tons left by the United States. (Actual Soviet purchases, however, reached only 1,467,800 tons for the year.) Following an exchange of views in Moscow between Raul Castro and Premier Nikita Khrushchev, the USSR also agreed to supply Cuba with petroleum and other strategic products "in amounts full meeting" Cuba's needs.[13]

The Soviet Union further expanded its economic commitments to Cuba in December 1960, perhaps in part as a response to the signing in October of a Sino-Cuban trade agreement providing for the purchase by the People's Republic of China of one million tons of sugar in 1961 and granting Cuba credits totaling $60 million. Moscow then pledged to buy 2.7 million tons of sugar from Cuba in 1961 at a fixed price of four cents per pound (1.25 cents a pound below the US-subsidized price) "if the United States carries out its

---

ment that may be sent to Cuba for humanitarian reasons." See *Final Act. Ninth Meeting Consultation of Ministers of Foreign Affairs Serving as Organ of Consultation in Application of the Inter-American Treaty of Reciprocal Assistance,* Pan American Union, OEA/Ser. C/11.9 (English), Washington, D.C., 1964, p. 6.

[9] In this paper, all tonnage figures are in metric tons, except where otherwise noted.

[10] *Vneshniaia torgovlia SSSR: statistichekii sbornik 1918–1966* (USSR Foreign Trade: Statistical Handbook 1918–1966), Moscow, Mezhdunarodnie Otnosheniia, 1967, pp. 227–28.

[11] *Pravda* (Moscow), Feb. 15, 1960.

[12] In the five years preceding the Cuban revolution of 1959, the United States purchased about 50 percent of Cuba's average annual sugar production of 5.1 million tons. See International Sugar Organization, *Sugar Year Book 1960*, London, 1961, p. 38.

[13] *Pravda*, July 21, 1960.

threat not to buy Cuban sugar."[14] Under the new commitment, Soviet payments for Cuban products were to be 80 percent in goods and 20 percent in convertible currency.

The 1960 accord also committed the Soviet Union to assist Cuba in its newly-initiated industrialization program—especially in the construction of an iron and steel mill and an oil refinery, and in the development of Cuban petroleum and ore deposits and electric power resources. As US-Cuban trade continued to constrict, the Soviet Union in 1961 bought 3,345,000 tons of sugar, greatly exceeding the commitments made in December 1960. At the same time, Soviet exports to Cuba, including petroleum products and machinery, increased dramatically from 67.3 million rubles ($74.6 million)[15] in 1960 to 258.3 million rubles in 1961, but Cuba still maintained a favorable trade balance with the USSR through 1961 (See Table 1).[16] Clearly, the new relationship with Moscow involved a major reorientation of Cuba's foreign trade. Whereas the island's trade with the Soviet bloc in 1959 amounted to only $16 million, or roughly 2 percent of total Cuban trade, the figures rose to $905 million and 72 percent in 1961 and $1,056 million and 82 percent in 1962. For the same years, the United States' share dropped from 68 percent to zero.[17]

THE FAILURE OF INDUSTRIALIZATION

The Soviet decision to channel significant trade and aid resources into Cuba's industrial development proved ill-conceived. As one foreign observer remarked, "when the Russians came to the rescue of the Cuban Revolution, their sense of solidarity was in direct proportion to their total ignorance of the situation and problems in that country."[18] The Cuban leaders were equally naive, both in assuming that the Soviet Union would finance their industrialization effort without hesitation and in anticipating immediate success for the program. Ernesto "Che" Guevara, then Minister of Industries in the Castro government, predicted that ". . . within a year, industrialization will have eradicated unemployment throughout the country."[19] Regino Boti, President of JUCEPLAN (Junta Central de Planificación—Central Planning Board) and Castro's economic minister, similarly asserted in August 1961 that Cuba's economic growth rate would rise to a level of 10–15 percent in each of the next four years and that Cuba "would be the most industrialized country in Latin America."[20]

Despite such optimism, the Cuban industrialization program soon faltered, and by the end of 1963 the experiment was patently a costly failure which the Soviet Union was no longer willing to underwrite. This experience demonstrated the inadequacies of Moscow's simplistic doctrine stressing rapid industrialization after the Soviet model as the *sine qua non* of economic progress in underdeveloped countries. The failure also generated considerable disappointment and frustration in both Havana and Moscow. As K. S. Karol reports, "much of the obsolete Russian equipment neither met their [the Cubans'] need nor enabled them to get out of their economic difficulties."[21] The Soviet Union, on the other hand, learned the hard way how ill-prepared Cuba had been for diversified industrial development. A 1968 Soviet study frankly recognized this fact:

Between 1960 and 1963, with the assistance of the socialist countries, a significant number of old enterprises were reconstructed in Cuba, and new plants and factories were built in various branches of industry. However, such a rate of construction inevitably resulted in the dissipation and exhaustion of Cuba's internal savings. Some enterprises were constructed without sufficiently accurate economic calculation. They turned out to be unprofitable since they worked on expensive raw material imported for hard currency

---

[14] *Hoy* (Havana), Dec. 20, 1960.
[15] For the purposes of this paper, the Soviet ruble is considered equal to $1.11 (US), and the Cuban peso at part with the US dollar.
[16] A word of caution is in order concerning data on Soviet and Cuban economic activities. Both governments, as well as the various bureaus within them, publish "official" statistics on these operations. They are not always in agreement, which tends to cast a measure of doubt on their overall reliability. For a discussion of the problems arising in connection with the use of Soviet and Cuban economic and trade data, see Carmelo Mesa Lago, "Availability and Reliability of Statistics in Socialist Cuba," *Latin American Research Review* (Austin, Texas), Vol. 4, No. 1, Spring 1969, pp. 53–91, and No. 2, Summer 1969, pp. 47–81. Also see Vassili Vassilev, *Policy in the Soviet Bloc on Aid to Developing Countries*, Paris, Development Center of the Organization for Economic Cooperation and Development, 1969, pp. 61–74. Similarly, statistics from Western sources—such as the International Sugar Organization, the United Nations and the US Department of Agriculture—do not always agree. However, these various sources are sufficiently close to reflect the general trends, as well as the critical points, in Soviet-Cuban relations. For the purpose of consistency in this discussion, Soviet sources will be used insofar as is possible, with other sources being cited only where Soviet information is not readily available.
[17] Republic of Cuba, *Boletin estadistico 1966* (Statistical Bulletin 1966), Havana, JUCEPLAN, 1966, p. 124; *Compendio estadistico de Cuba 1967* (Statistical Handbook of Cuba 1967), JUCEPLAN, Havana, 1967, p. 27 (Original figures in pesos).
[18] K. S. Karol, *Guerrillas in Power*, New York, Hill and Wang, 1970, p. 209.
[19] *Ibid*, p. 49.
[20] *Ibid*, p. 218.
[21] *Ibid*, p. 282.

and with the insufficiently high labor productivity of poorly qualified Cuban labor.[22]

An important consequence of the disastrous industrialization experiment was the creation of an unfavorable balance in Cuba's trade with the USSR. This came about because of several interrelated developments. First, Havana came to rely on high-priced capital goods and raw materials imported principally from the Soviet Union. Second, in the interest of diversification of the economy, Cuba had cut back sugar production. The result was that, in 1962, Cuba's exports to the USSR declined in value to a point where they failed to balance the growing Soviet shipments to Cuba (see Table 1).

Although Havana's debt to Moscow was beginning to rise, Soviet-Cuban ties deteriorated markedly in the aftermath of what Castro viewed as a Soviet "sell-out" to the U.S. during the 1962 missile crisis. Moscow therefore felt obliged to pacify Castro with further economic concessions. A trade agreement signed in February 1963 raised the Soviet purchase price for Cuban sugar to bring it into line with rising world market prices. A joint communique issued on May 23, 1963, at the end of Castro's visit to Moscow, noted that the Soviet government had proposed the price change "on its own initiative."[23] The agreement also allowed Cuba to withhold delivery of one million tons of sugar due the Soviet Union under the previously designated quota of some two million tons for 1963. While this step doubtless was a response to the sharp decline in Cuban sugar production in that year, the concession ostensibly enabled Cuba to obtain hard currency through sales on the world market.[24] Such currency may have been necessary, particularly, in order to import certain required machinery and equipment which the Soviet Union was unable to provide. In any case, Cuba's trade with non-Communist countries increased to 25.7 percent of her total trade volume in 1963, as compared with 17.6 percent in 1962.[25] But the ultimate result was a further sharp decline in Cuban sugar deliveries to the U.S.S.R. and a marked rise in Cuba's trade deficit with that country. . . .

CASTRO'S MOUNTING DEBT

It sems useful at this point to attempt to assess the overall dimension of Castro's mounting indebtedness to Moscow. According to available Soviet statistics (see Table 1), the cumulative Cuban trade deficit with the USSR for 1960–70 amounted to 1,508 million rubles. It appears likely that the trade deficit for 1971 will amount to approximately another 400 million rubles, which indicates that the cumulative trade deficit will have surpassed 1,900 million rubles, or $2,000 million, by 1972. The trade deficit, however, represents only part of Cuba's total debt to the Soviet Union. Not included in this figure are the cost of maintaining Soviet technical and military advisors in Cuba (in addition to their ruble salaries, they receive substantial monthly living allowances in pesos); the cumulative interest charged on credits since 1968; Soviet loans of hard currency for Cuban purchases in non-Communist countries; military aid; and other forms of assistance. A recent Cuban defector who formerly occupied a responsible position Cuba's central planning agency claims that Havana's total economic indebtedness to the USSR officially stood at $2,200 million in January 1971. Consequently, the total debt—excluding the cost of Soviet arms assistance—is likely to approach $3,000 million by 1972.

It is difficult, of course, to make an accurate assessment of the true cost of Soviet assistance to Cuba. This is particularly so because the prices charged by the Soviet Union for its exports to Cuba appear in many instances to have been inflated over world market prices. An estimate by the National Bank of Cuba places the total cost of the Soviet goods supplied to Cuba at about 50 percent above what Cuba would have had to pay if it had been able to purchase the same quality and types of goods from non-Communist countries. To pay for these goods, Cuba is required to deliver sugar—the only medium it has for generating urgently needed dollar exchange. In effect, Castro is "forced to make dollar investments for ruble sales."[45]

There are other factors, however, which are to Cuba's advantage. In the first place, the Soviet price paid for Cuban sugar has remained above the prevailing world market price since 1964. Furthermore, Moscow has shown considerable leniency in relaxing Cuba's quota for sugar deliveries to the USSR, apparently in order to allow Havana to make hard-currency sales on the world market. (It might be noted in this regard that in May 1971 Cuba's annual quota under the International Sugar Agreement for sales on the world market was set at 2.3 million tons.[46])

---

[22] V. V. Volskii, Ed., *Kuba: 10 let revoliutsii* (Cuba: Ten Years of the Revolution), Moscow, Nauka, 1968, p. 226.

[23] Stephen Clissold, Ed., *Soviet Relations with Latin America, 1918–1968: A Documentary Survey*, New York, Oxford University Press, 1970, p. 285.

[24] *Ibid.* In May 1963, sugar prices on the world market stood at nine cents (US) per pound.

[25] *Compendio estadistico de Cuba 1967*, p. 27.

[45] Karol, *op. cit.*, p. 424.

[46] Cuba's 1972 quota for sugar sales on the world market, as established at the Seventh Session of the International Sugar Council meeting in London last November, is 2,257,500 tons. This compares with a 1972 quota of

Another measure of Soviet aid to Cuba is the volume of Soviet shipping engaged in traffic between the two countries. According to a 1969 Moscow shipping report, 400 Soviet vessels called at Cuban ports on 1,600 occasions that year.[47] This same source stated that "an average of 60–65 large vessels are daily sailing between Cuba and the USSR or are in the ports of both countries," and that more ships would be placed in service "in the next few years." It was also reported that besides the Black Sea ports of Odessa, Novorossiisk, Tuapse, and Batumi—the main shipping points for trade with Cuba—the port of Feodosiya in the Crimea was added at the end of 1968, and a special oil jetty was built there to facilitate the loading of tankers destined for Cuba.[48] According to a Moscow radio broadcast, Soviet ships in 1969 carried 7.8 million tons of cargo to Cuba, including 5.6 million tons of oil, but brought back only 1.3 million tons of cargo from Cuba.[49] This indicates that the Soviet Union bears the additional cost of a highly uneconomical use of its ships in the Cuban trade—a factor further compounded by the long delays in loading and unloading in Cuban ports.

Kosygin's 4-day Cuban tour. Soviet Premier Aleksei N. Kosygin arrived in Havana Oct. 26, 1971 for a four-day tour of Cuba. His visit ended with a reaffirmation by Kosygin of Soviet readiness to continue support of Premier Fidel Castro's regime.

Kosygin was welcomed on his arrival by Castro, Cuban President Osvaldo Dorticos Torrado and an estimated 500,000 persons, including workers and students given time off for the occasion. The visit was the first to Cuba by a top Soviet leader since 1967, when Kosygin came to Havana following his meeting with former President Lyndon B. Johnson at Glassboro, N.J.

Details of the substantive discussions by the two leaders were not disclosed. Castro and Kosygin spent much of the four-day visit touring factories, schools and construction projects.

1,175,000 tons set for the USSR. See International Sugar Organization Press Release (71) 17, London, Nov. 19, 1971.
[47] Moscow Maritime Press Service, July 4, 1969.
[48] Radio Moscow, Feb. 14, 1969.
[49] Moscow Maritime Press Service, March 25, 1970.

In a joint communique released Nov. 1, one day after Kosygin's departure, both leaders expressed their support for leftist regimes in Chile and Peru as well as non-Communist Latin regimes that asserted their political and economic independence from the U.S.

The Soviet premier assured Cuba that it would support the Castro government "in the struggle for strengthening socialist gains and against provocations by the forces of imperialism." The communique stressed Soviet condemnation of "the U.S. imperialistic blockade against Cuba and U.S.-encouraged hostile actions."

The Washington Post Nov. 2 cited Western diplomats as indicating that Kosygin had attempted to allay Cuban concern over a scheduled visit by U.S. President Richard M. Nixon to the Soviet Union.

The communique also condemned U.S. violations of Cuban airspace and the "unlawful presence of the North American military base of Guantanamo in Cuban territory." It "reaffirmed" Cuban and Soviet "conviction that in conditions marked by unceasing attempts by international reaction to undermine the unity of the socialist countries, unity which is a decisive force in the anti-imperialist struggle and a guarantee of the success of the world revolutionary process, an imperative need is to strengthen the unity of the socialist countries and all the revolutionary forces."

The communique also expressed Cuban and Soviet "resolute support for the struggle of the Arab peoples for the elimination of the consequences of Israel's aggression, for an immediate withdrawal of Israeli troops from all Arab lands occupied in June 1967, for the recognition of the legitimate and inalienable rights of the people of Palestine and for the establishment of a lasting and fair peace in the Middle East."

Soviet visit highlights 10-nation Castro tour. During an unprecedented two-month absence from Cuba, Fidel Castro visited 10 African and East European nations May 3–July 6, 1972, capping his tour with a 10-day visit to the Soviet Union, where he received assurances of continued economic assistance and support for Cuba's foreign policy.

Castro's itinerary: Guinea May 3-8, Sierra Leone May 8, Algeria May 8-17, Bulgaria May 17-26, Rumania May 26-30, Hungary May 30-June 6, Poland June 6-13, East Germany June 13-21, Czechoslovakia June 21-26, and the Soviet Union June 26-July 6.

Castro held long talks with leaders of each country he visited except in Sierra Leone, where he remained only a few hours. He spoke in public frequently, asserting Cuba's support for socialist and revolutionary governments and making constant references to the war in Vietnam.

In Guinea, Castro conferred with President Sekou Toure; in Sierra Leone, with President Siaka Stevens; in Algeria, with President Houari Boumedienne; in Bulgaria, with Communist party First Secretary Todor Zhivkov; in Rumania, with party Secretary General Nicolae Ceausescu; in Hungary, with party First Secretary Janos Kadar; in Poland, with party chief Edward Gierek; in East Germany, with party First Secretary Erich Honecker; in Czechoslovakia, with party First Secretary Gustav Husak; and in the Soviet Union, with party leader Leonid Brezhnev, Premier Alexei Kosygin and President Nikolai Podgorny.

According to the London newsletter Latin America June 23, the trip gave Cuba a forum in which to express solidarity with revolutionary regimes such as those in Algeria and Guinea, and gave Communist bloc countries the opportunity to showcase Castro, whose vitality and unconventionality caused a sensation among Eastern Europeans.

The Cuban press agency Prensa Latina repeatedly stressed the length of the journey, saying it showed the strength and unity of Cuban leadership and disproved the frequent charge that the government could not make day-to-day decisions without Castro.

The highlight of the trip, according to most reports, was Castro's stay in the Soviet Union, emphasizing the favorable relations currently existing between the two countries. Some significance was also attached to Castro's visit to Algeria, with which Cuba had had strained relations since the overthrow of Ahmed Ben Bella in 1965.

At a Kremlin dinner in his honor June 27, Castro noted the aid of the Communist countries to Cuba in its struggles against "the economic blockade... which remains in force to this very day, the most diverse forms of subversive activities, mercenaries' attacks and threats of military aggression." He continued:

"The Soviet Union... as well as other socialist countries, acting to the best of their abilities, supplied us with weapons and rendered us technical and economic assistance necessary to prevent the imperialists from achieving their aim—break the will of the Cuban people through hunger. Today the prestige of revolutionary ideas is growing, and they are spreading not only among the peoples of Latin America, but also in the American society itself...

"The increased might of the USSR has created a stupendous obstacle in the way of imperialism's adventuristic, bellicose aggressive policy. This was a decisive factor in the struggle for peace, a factor facilitating the achievement of considerable successes in the past few years, recognition of the existing European borders, renunciation of the use of force and the weakening of the threat of war in this region, a factor promoting the efforts aimed at holding an all-European conference on security. Imperialism was forced to make major concessions...."

Soviet-Cuban communique—In a joint communique issued July 6, at the end of Castro's visit to the Soviet Union, the Soviet government expressed continued support for Cuba. It also mentioned a further expansion of economic and technical cooperation, but gave no indication of any specific new aid agreement.

In an extensive section on international affairs, the communique described the resolution of the Vietnam war as "one of the most pressing tasks of our time." It called for the removal of the U.S. naval base at Guantanamo and an end to the alleged "economic and political blockade" of Cuba by the U.S.

The document avoided mention of the problem of Cuban sugar deliveries, which had been irregular and generally below planned amounts.

(According to the New York Times July 7, during Castro's visit the Soviet government issued a high-level decree calling for greater domestic output of sugar, which the Soviet Union produced from beets. However, the decree reportedly was omitted from the principal newspapers in deference to the Cuban leader.

(In Cuba, President Osvaldo Dorticos announced that all commitments to sell sugar on world markets in 1972 would be met, but deliveries to the Soviet Union would be lower than originally contracted, according to the newsletter Latin America July 7. Cuba reportedly faced a very low harvest in 1972—somewhere between 3.5–4.5 million tons—but world sugar prices were higher than usual and expected to offset the poor crop.)

(During his visit to Poland, reports circulated that Castro was suffering from heart trouble. According to the Associated Press June 6, a change in Castro's activities had been ordered because he was "in a state prior to a heart infarct." However, Castro denied the reports June 7, asserting he had "a heart of steel." He showed no evidence of illness during the rest of the trip.)

The communique asserted that "the Cuban Revolution, its achievements in the building of the foundations of socialism, the successful struggle of the Cuban people, led by the Communist Party of Cuba, for the solution of radical social and national-economic tasks play a great role in deepening the liberation process in Latin America."

Castro again in U.S.S.R. Fidel Castro departed for the Soviet Union Dec. 18, 1972 to participate in ceremonies commemorating the 50th anniversary of the founding of the U.S.S.R. He stopped over in Morocco Dec. 19, conferring briefly with King Hassan. During a speech in Moscow Dec. 22, Castro praised the Soviet Union for its aid to Cuba, and attacked President Nixon for his latest escalation of the bombing of North Vietnam. He ended his trip and returned to Cuba Dec. 25 with a new Soviet aid agreement, according to a Havana radio report.

Castro Jan. 4, 1973 gave details of five agreements through which the Soviet Union would provide "extraordinary" new economic aid to Cuba. The pacts, signed by Castro and Soviet officials in Moscow Dec. 23, included these provisions:

■ The combined Cuban debt to the Soviet Union through 1972, including trade deficits and unpaid credits, would be deferred until 1986, and then repaid in Cuban products over the next 25 years. Interest charges would be frozen as of Jan. 1.

■ The Soviet Union would provide new credits to cover Cuba's 1973–75 trade deficits, to be repaid in Cuban goods and services over 25 years beginning in 1986.

■ The two countries agreed on the amount of goods to be exchanged in 1973–75.

■ The Soviet Union would provide up to $390 million worth of economic and technical aid to Cuba for capital development in 1973–75, the total to be repaid as of 1976 at a "low" interest rate.

The aid would help finance development of textile and nickel production, oil refining, electric power, transportation, communications, electronic computers, mechanization of the sugar harvest, irrigation, hydraulic resources, auto repair plants and factories to produce transistor radio and television sets.

■ From then until 1980 the Soviet Union would pay 11¢ a pound for Cuban sugar—reportedly 2¢ more than the current high world market price—and $5,000 a ton for Cuban nickel, compared with the recent world price of $2,000–$3,000 a ton.

Castro said the initiative for the agreements had come from the Soviet Union, which he called "a true friend, who has acted toward us with a high degree of generosity, unselfishness and fraternity." He termed the pacts "a clear response" by a rich nation to the problems of a poor and underdeveloped country, adding: "I believe it is unprecedented in the history of [Latin American] countries."

According to the London newsletter Latin America Jan. 12, the agreements would assure Soviet industry of vital nickel supplies for the foreseeable future from Cuba, which held 40% of the world's known reserves. They might also make Cuba economically viable, and thus a showcase for the Soviet version of communism in the Third World, the newsletter commented.

Communist communications net. An international space communications organization named Intersputnik was created in Moscow Nov. 15, 1971 under an agreement signed by Cuba, the U.S.S.R. and seven other Communist countries: Bulgaria, Hungary, East Germany, Mongolia, Poland, Rumania and Czechoslovakia.

The agreement asserted that "all states of the world," Communist or otherwise, could join. Intersputnik was to "coordinate its activities with the International Telecommunications Union as well as with other organizations whose activities are related to the use of communications satellites."

Radio Havana had announced Jan. 9, 1970 that Cuba and the Soviet Union had signed a technical assistance agreement the previous day for installation of a satellite communications station in Cuba. The agreement provided for establishment of radio, telephone and television links between the two nations.

Contacts with other Communist countries. Among developments involving Cuba with other Communist countries:

A Bulgarian delegation, led by Todor Zhivkov, first secretary of the Bulgarian Communist Party and chairman of the Bulgarian Council of Ministers, paid an official visit to Cuba July 25–Aug. 2, 1970.

Chinese Ambassador Chang Te-hsun arrived in Havana Dec. 3, 1970. Communist China had been represented in Cuba by a charge d'affaires since 1966.

A Cuban government trade delegation arrived in Peking Feb. 10, 1971. Under Ismail Bello Rios, a director of the Cuban Foreign Trade Ministry, the mission's role was to handle Chinese-Cuban trade negotiations.

Radio Havana announced signing of a commercial and economic aid pact between Cuba and North Vietnam, it was reported Jan. 22, 1971. The accord provided for a regular interchange of products during 1971 and for Cuban non-repayable aid to North Vietnam of unspecified nature.

Cuba and Czechoslovakia in Prague Jan. 6, 1973 signed a pact for Czechoslovakia to supply Cuba with credits for an electric power plant, sugar refinery machinery, and equipment for constructing pipe and tube fittings.

Soviet Arms Aid & Soviet Submarine Base Warning

U.S. warns Russia on Cuban sub base. The Nixon Administration warned Sept. 25, 1970 against Soviet construction of a strategic submarine base in Cuba. The warning was issued in Washington after Defense Department reports the same day that the Soviet Union could be in the process of constructing a Cuban support base capable of servicing its missile-carrying, Polaris-type submarines.

Jerry W. Freidheim, deputy assistant secretary of defense for public affairs, told newsmen Sept. 25 that intelligence reports had indicated that Soviet ships had moved three heavy barges and other equipment into the harbor at Cienfuegos on the southern coast of Cuba. The nature of the equipment, he said, "makes us feel they [the Soviets] may be seeking sustained capabilities in the area." He added, however, that the U.S. was "not sure that they are building a submarine support facility," and said: "There are some new naval facilities in the Cienfuegos area within the past several months. Some of the Soviet support ships have visited there. There are no submarines there at present."

A senior White House official, who declined to be identified, told newsmen later that day that "the development of Soviet naval activity and of possible construction" in Cuba was being watched "very closely." "The Soviet Union can be under no doubt that we would view the establishment of a strategic base in the Caribbean with the utmost seriousness," he added, but noted that "nothing very rapid and dramatic is likely to occur."

The Administration official cited as current U.S. policy a statement made by President John F. Kennedy at the conclusion of the Cuban missile crisis in 1962: "If all offensive weapons are removed from Cuba and kept out of the hemisphere in the future, under adequate verification and safeguards, and if Cuba is not used for the export of aggressive Communist purposes, there will be peace in the Caribbean."

Sen. J. William Fulbright (D, Ark.) Sept. 27 described the reports as "inconclusive" and stressed that U.S. reaction should be based on "diplomacy, not bluff." Fulbright suggested that the matter be taken to the U.S.-Soviet arms limitation talks in Vienna.

Rep. L. Mendel Rivers (D, S.C.), however, called the construction of a base "a crisis of the same gravity" as the 1962 missile crisis and called on the U.S. to use every measure, including military force if necessary, to remove it. Speaking on the House floor Sept. 28, Rivers added that the U.S. had to act "quickly and decisively if we are to maintain some shred of credibility as a world power."

The New York Times Sept. 30 reported that U.S. officials had expressed surprise at the timing and the substance of the Administration's warning to the Soviet Union. The officials, who included members of the intelligence community, noted that the U.S. had only dubious and unconfirmed reports of base construction at Cienfuegos and said most of the information had been available since early 1970. The Times reported that almost all the information on the base had been presented in testimony to the House Subcommittee on Inter-American Affairs between July 8 and Aug. 3.

Recent Soviet activity in Cuba included the arrival of a Soviet naval squadron in Cienfuegos Sept. 9. The squadron, including two anti-submarine ships, a submarine tender, a supply ship, a hydrographic vessel, an oiler and a tug, was the third to visit the Caribbean in 14 months. A Soviet naval task force had sailed into Havana in 1969 for the July 26 celebrations of the anniversary of the Castro revolution.

Another squadron had arrived in Cienfuegos May 14. (A Tass news agency report, cited in the Miami Herald May 14, said that the squadron was visiting Cienfuegos "on a courtesy visit and a short rest for personnel, as well as to refuel, to replenish water supplies and for repairs." Tass said the ships included "anti-submarine ships, submarines and auxiliary ships from among those that participated in naval exercises in the Atlantic."

Among earlier 1970 developments concerning increased Soviet military activity in Cuba:

■ The Miami Herald reported May 24 that a Miami television station had shown pictures of missiles in Cuba that were published in the Spanish magazine Gaceta Ilustrada. WTVJ in Miami said the missiles, reportedly "ground-to-ground missiles that can be launched from a boat," were said by Gaceta Ilustrada to be capable of hitting the Florida coast.

■ Robert A. Hurwitch, deputy assistant secretary of state for inter-American affairs, testified July 8 at a hearing of the House Subcommittee on Inter-American Affairs that the Soviet hold over Cuba had increased, but insisted that the U.S. "would rate as 'low' the chances of renewed Soviet military adventures involving Cuba." He added that the U.S. was "confident" that no offensive missiles had been reintroduced into Cuba.

■ In testimony to the same subcommittee, Assistant Defense Secretary G. Warren Nutter was reported July 15 to have predicted increased Soviet naval presence and reconnaissance flights in the Caribbean, and to have added that the increased activity could "challenge our security interests."

■ A Defense Department spokesman July 20 denied reports in Time Magazine that the U.S. had increased reconnaissance flights over Cuba.

■ State Department spokesman Carl Bartch said July 20 that "on the basis of our investigations, which include the evaluation of information from all available sources, we believe that there are no offensive weapons systems in Cuba."

Russians deny sub base charge. The Soviet Union Sept. 30 derided the U.S. warnings against building a submarine missile base in Cuba.

The Communist party newspaper Pravda called the warning an attempt to stir up a "war psychosis" and said: "It is clear to anyone that the furor about preparations in Cuba that supposedly threaten U.S. security has been raised for a definite purpose."

According to the New York Times Oct. 3, the Soviet Union had been reguarly operating missile-carrying submarines off the east coast of the U.S. and possibly in the Caribbean since April.

The Soviet news agency Tass said Oct. 13 that it "has been authorized to state that the Soviet Union has not built and is not building its military base on Cuba and is not doing anything that would contradict the understanding reached between the governments of the U.S.S.R. and the United States in 1962. ... The U.S.S.R. has always strictly adhered to this understanding [and] will adhere to it in the future, too. ..." Tass denounced "a propaganda campaign [that] has of late been conducted in the United States concerning an imaginary 'Soviet threat' to the Western Hemisphere." It charged that "the American press is spreading concoctions that the Soviet Union allegedly began building on Cuba 'a permanent strategic naval base for nuclear submarines.'"

Although U.S. State Department spokesman Robert J. McCloskey termed the Tass statement "positive" Oct. 13, observers noted that its wording clearly left open the possibility that the Soviet Union was constructing a base for Cuban use.

Pentagon sources disclosed Oct. 13 that the submarine tender and the ocean-going tug—two of the four ships that entered the harbor at Cienfuegos in September—had left Cuba Oct. 10. The two ships were reported Oct. 15 to have put in at the Cuban port of Mariel.

Cuban base agreement reported. U.S. officials Oct. 18 refused to confirm or deny reports that the U.S. and the Soviet Union had reached secret agreement on the removal from Cienfuegos, Cuba, of Soviet equipment for constructing a base to serve missile-carrying submarines.

But State Department officials said Nov. 17 that the Soviet Union had given private assurances it would refrain from introducing "offensive weapons" anywhere in the Western Hemisphere.

The officials, who said the term "offensive weapons" could be taken as synonomous with nuclear weapons, declined to reveal the form and manner in which Soviet assurances had been received. They did not dispute reports that Henry A. Kissinger, President Nixon's advisor on national security affairs, had discussed the matter Oct. 22 in New York with Soviet Foreign Minister Andrei A. Gromyko and Anatoly F. Dobrynin, the Soviet ambassador to the U.S.

In return for the Soviet promise, the U.S. was understood to have pledged not to invade Cuba. State Department spokesman Robert J. McCloskey said Nov. 17 that the continued presence in Cienfuegos of a Soviet submarine tender and tug, which had returned there Nov. 10, was not considered a violation of the understanding.

Exiles report on Soviet subs & arms. The reports of Soviet submarines, warships, armaments and military personnel in Cuba have often originated with Cuban exiles in the U.S. who manage to maintain clandestine communications with anti-Castro countrymen in Cuba. Dr. Manolo Reyes, a Cuban exile and Latin American news editor for the Miami TV station WTVJ, gave some of this background to the Platform Committee of the Democratic National Committee in Atlanta June 9, 1972. Reyes said:

"On Aug. 7th, 1962, I disclosed that there were 5,000 Russian soldiers in Cuba. The story was officially denied saying they were not soldiers, but technicians. Twelve weeks later we had the missile crisis of October 1962. On April 28, 1969 I denounced on television and other news media that there was the beginning of a new Soviet military buildup in Cuba. Again, the story was denied, but three months later, July 26, for the first time in the history of my country and the Americas, a Soviet naval squadron anchored in Cuba. On July 27, 1971, testifying before the Interamerican Affairs Subcommittee of the House in Washington, chaired by Congressman Dante B. Fascell, I disclosed that there was a Soviet naval facility for nuclear submarines in Cienfuegos, Cuba. Two months later the Pentagon and the White House disclosed the same.

"Three years have gone by since my first denouncement in April 1968, and the Soviets have sent to Cuba eight naval squadrons, the last one in May of this year. In the last visit to Nipe Bay, Oriente Province, there was a submarine called Golf Two, that carried three 'Serb' missiles with a range of 750 miles. Prior to this recent visit, 11 Soviet submarines of three types have visited Cuba since July 1969 along with 30 surface vessels, including submarine tenders. Four of these submarines were Echo 2 type and each carried eight missiles called 'Shaddock' with a range of 500 miles.

"In a recent visit to Miami, Sen. Hubert Humphrey pointed out that Soviet naval units have been making maneuvers on the Caribbean, with Castro naval units, just 30 miles from American soil, and that the Soviet military presence in Cuba is a real threat not only to the Continent but to the United States.

"On May 22 it was announced that the Soviet naval units had left the Cuban ports. But the naval facilities for their ships and submarines remained there. There also remained some 30,000 Russian troops, an international Communist brigade of several thousand hard-core international Communist agents and the Soviet arsenal of tanks, weapons, artillery and MiG 15, 17, 19, 21 and the most advanced model of the MiG 21. Three major airports of Cuba are in Soviet military hands, and many caves throughout Cuba have been excavated and now only house Russian military personnel...."

Soviet fighters delivered. U.S. Defense Department sources said Oct. 30, 1971 that the first deliveries in four years of new MiG-21 Soviet jets arrived in Cuba Oct. 24.

Soviet missile boats supplied. U.S. Defense Department sources quoted in the New York Times Feb. 1, 1972 said that the Soviet Union had begun sending Cuba bigger and more heavily armed missile-firing patrol boats. The first two boats, each carrying four missiles with a range of 15 miles, allegedly reached Havana in mid-January.

Soviet planes patrol U.S. coast. The Pentagon said Sept. 12, 1972 that two Soviet aircraft operating from Cuba had carried out a 12-hour reconnaissance flight Sept. 11 off the east coast of the U.S. No official concern was expressed over the mission, reportedly the first of its kind.

Pentagon officials said the planes, reconnaissance versions of the Soviet TU-95 Bear bomber, had been tracked by land-based radar and Navy jets. They reportedly flew 50–60 miles offshore along the U.S. coast to a point just north of Norfolk, Va. before returning to Cuba.

Relations With the U.S.

Export curbs eased. The U.S. April 29, 1970 lifted restrictions on 222 items for export to almost all Communist countries, although licenses would still be necessary before the goods could be exported to Cuba, Communist China, North Vietnam and North Korea. The Associated Press reported the action April 29. Included on the list were textile fabrics, chemicals, iron and steel products, office machines, telephone and telegraph equipment, agricultural machines, some radio and television equipment, hand and power tool parts and electrical apparatus.

1970–73: A TIME OF RESTRAINT

U.S. dissidents aid Cuba sugar crop. Starting in late 1969, hundreds of dissident Americans had been sailing to Cuba as the Venceremos (We Shall Win) Brigade to help Cuba with its sugar crop. The dissidents, largely young, included representatives of the Black Panthers, Students for a Democratic Society and Mexican and Puerto Rican minority groups.

U.S. Sen. James O. Eastland (D, Miss.) asserted March 16 that the American cane cutters "are being indoctrinated and trained to attack and destroy our institutions and government." In a speech on the Senate floor, Eastland, chairman of the Senate Subcommittee on Internal Security, described the youths as "missiles in human form." Noting that his subcommittee planned hearings to "examine the leadership and membership" of the Venceremos Brigade, he warned: "It is not only a likelihood but a very clear and present danger that these militant revolutionaries will return to implement the Communist purpose of causing chaos, confusion and outright revolution."

Travel to Cuba remained illegal under U.S. law. The State Department announced Sept. 15, 1970 that restrictions on travel by U.S. citizens to Cuba, Communist China, North Korea and North Vietnam would be extended for another six months. The regulations, which had been extended for six months in March, restricted travel in the four countries to persons with specially validated passports.

Castro rules out rapprochement. In a speech marking the 18th anniversary of his revolutionary movement July 26, 1971, Premier Castro ruled out any possibility of rapprochement with the U.S. and declared "we are not seeking conciliation of any kind with Yankee imperialism. There will be no concessions of any kind with the imperialists." He added that "the revolution will not retreat, will not waiver."

Castro spoke optimistically of the international situation as it reflected his "Socialist" policy, although he recognized the difficulties Cuba faced. The premier indicated that he would consider renewing relations with other countries of the Western Hemisphere, while repeating his "intransigent position" against the U.S. He said the "revolutionary process in Chile, the Peruvian revolutionary process, the Bolivian revolution, are all in full swing, although they have different characteristics, different methods."

The major portion of his speech concerned internal affairs. In a comprehensive analysis of the economic situation, Castro mentioned some improvements in the economic sphere, although he said a severe drought had affected agricultural production adversely. Castro devoted nearly an hour of his $2\frac{1}{2}$-hour speech to the need for "the rigor and importance of sanitary measures" in daily life.

U.S. volleyball team to visit Cuba. The U.S. State Department confirmed reports Aug. 5, 1971 that a U.S. volleyball team had been given official clearance to travel to Cuba Aug. 12 to participate in a pre-Olympic tournament, the North American Zone Volleyball Championship. The 12-man team, three coaches and other officials would constitute the largest delegation of U.S. athletes to visit Cuba since Premier Fidel Castro came to power.

The State Department emphasized that the decision was "not a departure from previous policy" and added that it was the policy of the U.S. "to permit U.S. teams to go to Cuba and participate in international competition."

The State Department announced Aug. 6 that a Cuban volleyball team participating in the Pan-American games in Colombia was told it would be permitted to play in the U.S.

U.S. scientists in Havana. The State Department confirmed July 10, 1972 that a seven-man U.S. delegation had attended an oceanographic conference in Havana June 19–24, marking the first time the U.S. had been represented at an international meeting in Cuba in nearly 12 years.

However, a department spokesman emphasized that the previously unpublicized visit did not imply any change in U.S. policy nor a political overture toward the Castro government. The delegation, from the Commerce Department's National Oceanic and Atmospheric Administration, reportedly attended the meeting because it was sponsored by a United Nations agency, the Intergovernmental Oceanographic Commission.

Dr. Harris B. Stewart, who headed the delegation, said July 10 that the conference was part of a 15-nation project begun two years ago. Its purpose, he said, was to study currents and plankton drift in the Caribbean and how they affect fish.

U.S. Presbyterians for Cuban ties. The Presbyterian Church of the U.S. (Southern) June 16, 1972 urged the establishment of diplomatic relations with Cuba and an end to the economic boycott against that country.

U.S. party platforms. Both U.S. political parties mentioned the issue of Cuba in their national political platforms during 1972. The Democratic platform said that "the next Democratic Administration should":

■ Recognize that, while Cuba must not be permitted to become a foreign military base, after 13 years of boycott, crisis and hostility, the time has come to re-examine our relations with Cuba and to seek a way to resolve this cold war confrontation on mutually acceptable terms....

The Republican platform said:
We believe the continuing campaign by Cuba to foment violence and support subversion in other countries makes it ineligible for readmission to the community of American states. We look forward to the day when changes in Cuba's policies will justify its re-entry into the American community and to the day when the Cuban people achieve again their freedom and their true independence.

Castro assails U.S., lauds Soviets. Premier Castro July 26, 1972 praised Cuba's close ties with the Soviet Union while asserting that relations with the U.S. could not improve until Washington substantially changed its policies in Latin America.

In a three-hour speech commemorating the 19th anniversary of the revolutionary assault on the Moncada Barracks, Castro said Cuba was prepared for "five, 15 or even 30 years without relations with the U.S." Before ties could be re-established, the U.S. must give up its role of "policeman" in Latin America, unconditionally withdraw from Guantanamo, and end its economic and trade embargo of Cuba, Castro said.

Stressing the need for Latin American solidarity against U.S. imperialism, Castro said Cuba was not interested in being readmitted to the Organization of American States or in resuming relations with countries which were "vassals of the North American government." He praised the re-establishment of ties with Chile and Peru, and expressed solidarity with "the struggle of the Panamanian people to reconquer the Canal."

Celebrating the "eternal friendship" between Cuba and the Soviet Union, Castro said "Cuba would not have been able to resist the blockades imposed by the United States without the support, given in all domains, by the Soviet Union." The Soviets, Castro said, had not come to Cuba to take its mines or its lands, exploit its people, or to bring vice and prostitution, as the U.S. had. Furthermore, all military assistance given by the Soviet Union was free, Castro asserted.

(On the dais with Castro was Mrs. Nguyen Thi Binh, foreign minister of the Provisional Revolutionary Government of South Vietnam [PRG] and head of its delegation to the Paris Peace Talks. Mrs. Binh visited Cuba July 22-29. A joint Cuban-PRG communique issued July 31 said the only way to reach a political solution to the Vietnam war was for the U.S. to "put an end to its unjust and immoral intervention and accept the PRG's seven-point peace plan.")

Castro & Angela Davis call for socialism in U.S. Castro and U.S. black militant Angela Davis Sept. 23, 1972 made a joint appeal to their "American brothers" for solidarity in attempts to create a Socialist U.S.

Speaking to a crowd of thousands in Havana's Revolutionary Plaza, Castro asked, "if socialism emerged 90 miles from the U.S., why shouldn't it emerge one day ... 90 miles from Cuba?" Davis, who was guest of honor at the rally commemorating the 12th anniversary of the Committees for the Defense of the Revolution, then exhorted "American Negroes, Puerto Ricans, Latin Americans, Chicanos, Indians, progressive intellectuals and laborers" to join in the construction of U.S. socialism and the "struggle against imperialism, racism and the war in Vietnam."

U.S. Congressmen for resumption of relations. Twelve members of the U.S. House of Representatives urged President Nixon and Congress Jan. 29, 1973 to take early steps to normalize U.S. relations with Cuba. They said such action "would eliminate an apparent policy contradiction which strives for friendship with Russia while concurrently condemning Cuba for harboring Soviet presence."

The representatives, all Republicans, proposed at a Washington news conference that Nixon make every effort to reach an agreement with Cuba on airliner hijacking and use talks on that subject as a starting point for discussion of other issues. The anti-hijacking accord was achieved Feb. 15.)

The congressmen also urged Nixon to support a recent Peruvian proposal to the Organization of American States (OAS) that would permit any member state to resume normal relations with Cuba. They further recommended that the House Foreign Affairs Committee and the Senate Foreign Relations Committee hold hearings on U.S. policy toward Cuba.

The congressmen said Premier Castro had indicated a new attitude toward the U.S. by agreeing to negotiate a hijacking pact, and Cuba had reduced its aid to local insurgents throughout Latin America. They added that Cuban leaders had privately indicated the U.S. naval presence in Guantanamo Bay would not be a major issue in any effort to normalize relations.

The 12 Congressmen were Charles W. Whalen Jr. (Ohio), Alphonzo Bell (Calif.), Edward G. Biester (Pa.), John Dellenback (Ore.), Marvin Esch (Mich.), William Frenzel (Minn.), Orval Hansen (Idaho), John H. Heinz III (Pa.), Paul McCloskey (Calif.), Stewart B. McKinney (Conn.), Charles S. Mosher (Ohio), Frank Horton (N.Y.).

The Congressmen's statement, entitled "A Detente With Cuba," said in part:

United States-Cuba relations have been marked by over a decade of mutual distrust, hostility and recriminations. Political and strategic considerations suggest that it may be in our national interest to initiate a dialogue with Cuba that might lead to an eventual normalization of relations between the two countries.

The United States severed commercial and diplomatic ties with Cuba in 1961, as a result of a threatening Soviet military presence on the island, Cuba's subversive activities against Latin American countries and the expropriation of U.S. owned properties in Cuba. In subsequent actions the U.S. halted economic and military aid, eliminated the Cuban sugar quota and placed an embargo on exports to Cuba. The Bay of Pigs invasion and the missile crisis further exacerbated the deep cleavages and hostilities between the two governments.

Relations between other Latin American countries and Cuba were equally bad. In 1964, the Organization of American States (OAS) voted to cut off diplomatic and commercial ties with Cuba. The ban proved relatively effective until several years ago when some OAS countries began to defy the ban and to establish diplomatic relations with Cuba.

American isolation of Cuba has continued to this day. Administration officials have publicly indicated that to date two factors have dictated our present hardline policy and impede any kind of policy review: (1) the Soviet military presence in Cuba, and (2) Cuba's export of subversive revolution to the rest of Latin America.

But action which was understandable, and even right, at one time and under one set of circumstances may no longer be right or even wise at another date and under another set of circumstances.

THE POLITICAL PENALTIES OF 1973: THREE DEVELOPMENTS INDICATING A NEED FOR A POLICY REVIEW

The political realities of 1973 indicate to us the need for a review of United States-Cuba relations. Specifically, during the past several months three developments have occurred which make the normalizing of relations between the two countries desirable and potentially attainable.

First, President Nixon is pursuing a pragmatic policy designed to deal realistically with all governments. This approach has resulted in relaxation of tensions between the United States and respectively, the People's Republic of China and the Soviet Union.

Our rapprochement with the Soviet Union has brought about the SALT agreements, established medical, environmental and space research contacts and increased trade and commercial ties.

The President's China visit renewed communications after more than twenty years of hostility. The recent announcement of a multi-million dollar grain sale to China further improves the favorable climate brought about by the President's initiative. Increased trade contacts with East European socialist countries have also materialized as a result of the President's policy.

In light of the Administration's efforts to negotiate and cooperate with Russia and China, a dialogue with Cuba would represent an extension of this philosophy. It would eliminate an apparent policy contradiction which strives for friendship and an increasing dialogue with Russia while concurrently condemning Cuba for harboring a Soviet presence.

Second, there has been a growing trend among Latin American countries to normalize relations with Cuba. In the past two years, an increasing number of Latin American States either have recognized the Government of Cuba or have strongly indicated a desire to do so. This development represents a significant change from the policy of isolation of Cuba followed by the nations of the OAS since 1964 when Cuba was excluded from participation in the Inter-American system and member states collectively severed diplomatic and economic relations with Fidel Castro's government.

Mexico was the only Latin American country that did not sever relations with Cuba, holding that the OAS measures against Cuba were in violation of the principles guiding the Inter-American system. In November, 1970, Chile, under the newly elected government of Salvador Allende also recognized Cuba.

Even prior to the Chilean move, Peruvian leaders indicated a disposition to change their country's policy toward Cuba. Fidel Castro on occasions had praised the Peruvian military government for its reformist policies and it can be assumed that the Peruvians were grateful for the massive earthquake relief effort extended by Cuba during the 1970 disaster.

Peruvian initiatives brought the matter of Cuban hemispheric relations to the surface and were responsible for the first OAS consideration of the issue since the 1964 ban. On May 31, 1972, the Permanent Council of the OAS held a special session to consider the draft resolution submitted by Peru which would permit any member state to normalize its relations with Cuba. The Peruvian resolution said:

"Some member states for different reasons maintain official relations with the Republic of Cuba and . . . others have expressed, on the basis of their own appreciation of the changes that are taking place in the world and inter-American circumstances, the convenience of re-establishing relations with the Republic."

By a vote of 14 to 1 with 8 abstentions, the matter was referred to the general committee of the Permanent Council for consideration. The Peruvian representative saw the agreement to debate the proposal as ". . . a representation of the current spirit of the Americas, a spirit that precisely indicates that Inter-American policies are aimed at the future."

At the conclusion of the meeting to consider the Cuba question on June 9, 1972, the OAS decided against the Peruvian resolution by a vote of 13 against, 7 for, and 8 abstaining. The Central American bloc, Brazil and the United States, voted against the resolution, as did Bolivia, Colombia, Dominican Republic, Haiti, Uruguay, and Paraguay. In favor of the resolution were Chile, Ecuador, Jamaica, Mexico, Panama, Peru, Trinidad and Tobago. Argentina, Barbados and Venezuela abstained.

In July, 1972 Peru recognized Cuba. In December, 1972, Guyana, Trinidad and Tobago and Barbados announced the resumption of diplomatic relations with the Castro government. Panama and Ecuador have indicated their willingness to re-open relations. Venezuela has hinted that a change in her policy is possible.

Several factors are responsible for the trend toward recognition of Cuba. Many Latin American governments believe Castro's revolutionary fervor has waned and no longer see Cuba as a subversive threat. Furthermore, many of the states feel change toward Cuba is very much in line with the changing world situation as illustrated by the U.S. rapprochement with China and the Soviet Union.

Whether or not the United States makes overtures to Cuba, indications are that the number of Latin American governments re-establishing relations with Cuba will continue to increase.

The third reason for reviewing our Cuba policy is that Cuba itself seems to be softening its formerly intransigent foreign policy position. There is growing evidence to support this contention. . . .

In 1970–1971, there has been increased evidence that Cuba's revolutionary activities and the Soviet interest in Cuba are diminishing: subversive activities throughout Latin America have reduced significantly since the Che Guevara effort in Bolivia in 1967. Both State and Defense Department officials have testified that Cuba has reduced its aid to local insurgents throughout Latin America and no longer shows the revolutionary fervor of earlier days.

During 1971 in Castro's visit to Chile, it was significant that he stated that his methods of revolution were not to be prescribed for all other nations. This is considered an acknowledgment by Castro of his unsuccessful efforts to establish his own brand of revolution throughout the hemisphere. The victorious election of Salvador Allende in Chile through a coalition of leftist parties represented a victory for the "via pacifica," a policy earlier scorned by Castro.

American officials continually have asserted that the Russian missiles in Cuba are defensive in nature and pose no offense threat to the United States. However, some authorities contend that the Russian presence does present a security threat which could be minimized by our establishing relations with Cuba.

There have been several indications that the Soviets would welcome a detente or at least a warming of relations between the United States and Cuba. On February 13, 1969, the *Wall Street Journal* reported that a secret message was sent from the Soviet Union to a Western nation that might mediate a United States—Cuban settlement. The note reportedly stated that the Russians would "look favorably on anything the mediating country could do to normalize relations between Cuba and the United States."

An American reporter who recently visited Cuba reported that Soviet diplomats told him that Russia would reduce its military presence in exchange for an American withdrawal from Guantanamo. The economic burden of Cuba upon the Soviet Union, coupled with the lack of any tangible political benefits, could be motivating factors for their alleged interest in reducing their presence....

BENEFITS OF NORMALIZATION

If renewed dialogue with the Castro government eventually leads to more normalized relations between Cuba and the United States, it is our opinion that at least three significant benefits will accrue.

The first and clearly a major benefit is a probable reduction of plane hijackings to Cuba. Obviously the United States and the Cuban government are equally disturbed by this problem and are willing to cooperate in an effort to curb these criminal acts.

Almost eighty percent of planes hijacked since 1963 have gone to Cuba. In general, the Cubans have been cooperative about returning these planes. Hijackers who have sought asylum in Cuba are clearly not welcome there as has been made obvious by the punitive treatment they receive from the Cuban government.

The president of the American Air-Line Pilots Association has called for a resumption of relations between the two countries to curb hijacking. American pilots are threatening to strike unless stronger anti-hijacking measures are implemented and enforced. A normalization of relations would result in cooperation between the two nations for the return and conviction of hijackers.

It is hoped that the Swiss-moderated negotiations will produce an agreement that will discourage further hijacking. These talks should serve as a point of departure for a broader discussion of issues of mutual concern. They are clearly a first step toward normal ties between the two countries.

Second, with normalization Cuba once again could be an important trading partner for the United States. In 1958, the year before Castro came to power, the U.S. imported $527.8 million worth of goods from Cuba and exported $546.9 million worth of goods to Cuba. Cuba supplied sugar and sugar-byproducts, and some minerals, principally nickel. The United States exported finished goods, grain, and automobile parts, as well as the machinery for the sugar industry. The re-opening of the Cuban market to American products could again lead to healthy and productive commercial relations between the two countries.

Now, some of our closest allies maintain strong trade ties with Cuba. Cuba presently imports British and Japanese busses and trucks, Spanish fishing boats and many other Japanese and European products. Canada and Mexico still maintain consular and diplomatic relations and have been exporting foodstuffs to Cuba. There are strong indications that the Chilean trade agreement with Cuba is just the beginning of a movement among some Latin American States to resume trade if not diplomatic relations. Trinidad and Tobago's resumption of relations is based largely on their interest in Cuba as a lucrative oil market.

Cuba has recently made two major trade commitments in an effort to improve its economic position. In November 1971, Cuba was admitted to membership in the "Group of 77", the organization of developing nations within UNCTAD (United Nations Commission for Trade and Development), with strong backing from the Latin American bloc. In 1972, Cuba joined COMECON, the Communist counterpart of the European Common Market organization, allegedly to expand its commercial ties and obtain development and technical assistance.

It seems inconsistent that we impose commercial restrictions and limitations on our OAS allies for trading with Cuba while at the same time we sell millions of tons of grain to the U.S.S.R. and China and encourage commercial relations with other Communist nations.

Third, a warmer political atmosphere and improved hemispheric relations are bound to occur if relations between the United States and Cuba normalize. Nearly every year the Cuban matter severely cripples the OAS and makes it appear ineffective, besides becoming an extremely divisive issue among Latin

American countries. Any further defiance of the OAS ban by Latin American countries would continue to strain relations of member countries. Unless changes are made in view of present realities, the Cuban issue will continue to impair relations between Western Hemisphere nations.

For over a decade, American isolation of Cuba has given substance to much anti-American rhetoric and ill feeling towards the United States among various groups in Latin America. Removing this vestige of the Cold War would significantly reduce tensions and redirect hemispheric policy, focusing attention on more urgent priorities such as trade economic development, foreign investment and regional integration.

Normalization of relations and a relaxation of tensions might provide an impetus for a regional economic integration program in the Caribbean which would involve Cuba. Although such a development is not imminent, the potential is there and should be explored further. . . .

Cuba raises Puerto Rico issue at U.N. Cuba's chief delegate to the U.N., Ricardo Alarcon Quesada, said July 23, 1971 that he would ask the U.N. General Assembly to take up the issue of Puerto Rican independence in the fall as an unsolved "colonial" problem. The statement came at a press conference in New York with the secretary general of the Puerto Rican Independence Movement, Juan Mari Bras, at Alarcon's side. The Cuban delegate said he was acting on the petition of the movement.

(The General Assembly had gone on record in November 1953 as approving the way Puerto Ricans, "expressing their will in a free and democratic way" had achieved self-government in association with the U.S.)

Mari Bras accused the U.S. of "impeding the [U.N. Committee on Colonialism] from sending a mission to examine the situation and the desires of the population." He demanded that the Committee of the 24 make an inquiry into the possibility of a plebiscite "free of all constraint and pressure from the American administration" to register the peoples' decision regarding self-determination.

Gov. Luis A. Ferre of Puerto Rico, harshly deploring what he termed "unwarranted intrusion" into his island's relationship with the U.S., denounced Cuba's proposal to bring the question of Puerto Rican independence to the U.N.

In a letter to Cuban U.N. Ambassador Ricardo Alarcon, Ferre wrote that "Cuba has no right to represent Puerto Rico before the U.N." He added that "the people of Puerto Rico have expressed through voting their categorical rejection of independence and have reiterated their aspiration to continue enjoying American citizenship."

The General Assembly's 25-nation General Committee voted Sept. 23 not to put on the agenda an item described by Cuba as the "colonial case of Puerto Rico."

Mari Bras in Havana Jan. 7, 1972 addressed a "student rally of solidarity with the independence struggle of Puerto Rico."

During the rally, organized by the Cuban Federation of University Students (FEU), Mari Bras, said, "Thanks to the existence of the Cuban revolution, the will for nationhood of the Puerto Rican people has not been isolated."

He reaffirmed the decision of the Boricua (Puerto Rican) people to achieve their independence despite the fact that "North American imperialism has tried through every means to silence the struggle of the Puerto Rican people for their freedom and independence."

The U.N. Special Committee on Colonization met at U.N. headquarters in New York Aug. 18, 1972 to consider the Cuban proposal that Puerto Rico be classified as a "colony" of the United States. No vote was taken on the motion, which was opposed by the U.S. as interference in its internal affairs.

Representatives of Ecuador, China and the Soviet Union spoke in favor of the proposal. The Soviet delegate, Ambassador Vasili Safronchuk, charged Puerto Ricans were "subjected to ruthless colonial exploitation" by the U.S.

Outside the U.N. buildings, a group of Puerto Ricans demonstrated in favor of independence from the U.S.

The committee Aug. 28 approved a resolution recognizing the "inalienable right of the people of Puerto Rico to self-determination and independence." The vote was 12-0, with 10 abstentions. Alarcon Quesada hailed this as a victory although the committee had not clearly classified

Puerto Rico as a colony of the U.S. A U.S. spokesman said after the vote that Puerto Rico had enjoyed the right of self-determination since 1952 and freely chose to be associated with the U.S. in commonwealth status.

In Puerto Rico, groups advocating independence from the U.S. reportedly reacted jubilantly to news of the U.N. vote. However, the decision was dismissed by Gov. Luis Ferre, an advocate of statehood for the island, who said "Russia, China and Cuba have missed the point. What they should have sought at the United Nations is Cuba's freedom."

Mrs. Julia Rivera de Vicenti, an alternate U.S. delegate to the General Assembly, angrily asserted before the Assembly Oct. 11 that Puerto Ricans were tired of Cuban interference in the affairs of that island and the U.S.

Mrs. Vincenti's denunciation followed an address by Alarcon, who had said Puerto Rico was the last Latin American country subject to colonialism, but the island would "be free one day." He had added that Cuba would "continue to do its duty regarding Puerto Rico, both within and without the U.N."

Speaking in Spanish, Mrs. Vincenti asserted "we in Puerto Rico know the meaning of self-determination, which we have enjoyed and continue to enjoy, and we know from experience the true meaning of freedom." She said "perhaps the representative of Cuba, whose people have not seen ballot boxes in their country in more than a decade, simply does not understand the meaning of the free electoral process and other democratic institutions which mean so much to Puerto Ricans."

Export of Revolution

Latin guerrillas score Castro. Venezuelan revolutionary leader Douglas Bravo, in a manifesto received by Caracas newspapers Jan. 13, 1970, accused Fidel Castro and Cuba of "betraying proletarian internationalism" and accepting "the comfortable position of a Soviet satellite." Bravo, head of the Armed Forces of National Liberation (FALN), charged that Castro had "suspended all aid to Latin American revolutionary movements" in order to concentrate solely on reinforcing the Cuban economy. Castro was also accused of favoring the Movement of the Revolutionary Left (MIR) and the Venezuelan Communist Party.

Four MIR leaders issued a communique Jan. 16 denouncing Bravo's manifesto. The MIR communique was signed by Simon Saez Merida, national MIR coordinator, Moises Moleiro, MIR secretary general, Hector Perez Marcano and Americo Martin.

The London publication Latin America Feb. 13 cited a Bogota newspaper report that Colombia's guerrilla National Liberation Army (ELN), led by Fabio Castano, had broken ties with Cuba because of decreasing aid from the Castro government.

Complicity in D.R. attack? Cuba was accused of complicity in a mini-invasion by nine Dominican guerrillas who landed in Azua Province, Dominican Republic Feb. 4, 1973.

Seven guerrillas were reported killed, the last two in a clash with soldiers near Bonao March 22, and one was reported captured March 25.

The captive guerrilla was identified as Hamlet Herman Perez, 39, a former university professor. He was reported March 28 to have confirmed the death of the insurgents' leader, former Col. Francisco Caamano.

Herman Perez also told authorities the insurgents had arrived in the Dominican Republic by a circuitous route from Cuba, where they had been trained in guerrilla warfare, the Herald reported.

Five soldiers had been killed and seven wounded in clashes with the guerrillas, according to El Nacional of Caracas March 28.

Claudio Caamano, nephew of the late Francisco Caamano and a survivor of the guerrilla invasion, said in Mexico City that the invasion had been launched from the Caribbean island of Guadeloupe after the insurgents picked up arms "somewhere in Venezuela," the London newsletter Latin America reported June 1. Caamano's return to Cuba was reported June 8.

Herman Perez also had been allowed to move to Cuba, according to Latin America June 15. The third surviving guerrilla, Toribio Pena Jaquez, had left the Dominican Republic with safe-conduct to Chile, it was reported July 6.

Castro pledges support for rebels. In a speech honoring the centennial of Lenin's birth, Castro April 23, 1970 denied accusations that Cuba had stopped aiding revolutionaries. "Cuba has not denied, Cuba will never deny support to revolutionary movements," he asserted. "Our position on the revolutionary movement is that while there is imperialism, while there are fighters ready to fight imperialism, our people will give them help." However, Castro denounced "pseudo-revolutionaries who had the chance to make the revolution and sabotaged it."

Castro also denounced the Organization of American States as a "whorehouse" and affirmed that Cuba would not re-enter the institution until "the day they expel the United States . . ." However, he added that "Cuba is prepared to establish relations with countries breaking the economic blockade against her and attempting to lift themselves out of underdevelopment."

Bolivian relations change. Relations between Cuba and Bolivia began to improve after Alfredo Ovando Candia was overthrown as president of Bolivia Oct. 6, 1970 and leftist Gen. Juan Jose Torres appointed himself president the following day. But the improvement stopped Aug. 22, 1971 with the overthrow of Torres and the installation of a rightist regime headed by Col. Hugo Banzer Suarez.

In a speech marking the 18th anniversary of his revolutionary movement Castro July 26, 1971 had said that he would extend diplomatic relations to Bolivia. Bolivia had recently made an overture to Cuba on the matter of diplomatic ties. The premier also added that he was optimistic over the possibility of a "popular government" taking power in Uruguay during the elections in November.

Cuba Aug. 23 called the overthrow of Gen. Torres a "fascist coup" and attributed it to machinations of "Yankee imperialism."

Assailing Banzer, Castro told a group of Bolivian students in Havana Aug. 28 that the new Banzer government would not be capable of retaining power and the Bolivian people would not stop until they regained lost ground and took power through revolutionary means.

The Bolivian government believed that hundreds of exiled citizens were being trained as guerrilla fighters in Chile, the Miami Herald reported Feb. 17, 1972.

Bolivian Interior Minister Mario Adett Zamora said that "Bolivian exiles in Chile are receiving military and subversive instruction with the consent of the [Chilean] government and with the support of Cuba and . . . the countries behind the Iron Curtain." Officials were said to believe the guerrillas would return to Bolivia to commit acts of urban terror and to foment labor uprisings in the nation's economically vital tin-mining regions.

'Export of revolution' charged. Repeated charges that Castro continued to advocate and practice the "export of revolution" from Cuba were summarized in the U.S. Senate Feb. 8, 1973 by Sen. Edward J. Gurney (R, Fla.). Gurney's statement, as recorded in the Congressional Record, said:

" . . . Ever since consolidating power in 1960, Castro has tried to impose his style of revolutionary government on a number of unwilling Latin American nations. These efforts have not had popular support, but they have caused nations like Venezuela, Colombia, Brazil, Uruguay, and Bolivia untold trouble and expense.

" For example, Venezuela has been a primary target of Communist subversion since 1960. From 1960 to 1962, guerril-

1970–73: A TIME OF RESTRAINT

las supported by the Castro regime, resorted to urban terrorism and sabotage of oil installations in an effort to create enough turmoil to discredit the democratically elected Betancourt government and provoke a military coup. Bombings and killings became daily events in Caracas and elsewhere....

"... Despite a lack of popular support, the rebels persevered. In June 1963, an unsuccessful attempt was made on the life of President Betancourt. Then, in November 1963, the Venezuelan authorities discovered a 3-ton arms cache together with a plan for using the smuggled weapons to help Communist guerrillas capture Caracus while Venezuelan troops were guarding polling places during a national election. The plot failed, but subsequent evidence that Castro had supplied the weapons, led the OAS to condemn Cuba for aggression. The OAS also called on Latin American nations to impose sanctions including the severence of diplomatic relations and the suspension of all trade. Three of the four Latin American countries which had not previously broken relations with Cuba then did so, and the policy of economic sanctions was implemented more fully.

"However, Castro was not to be deterred. Instead, he supported guerrillas, like Douglas Bravo, who simply shifted their operations from the urban areas to the rural areas of Venezuela and continued their policy of assassination and sabotage. By 1966, pro-Communist terrorists had also infiltrated the university system, which they turned into a series of armed revolutionary camps.

"Despite all these efforts Venezuela remained strong and free. But, nonetheless, Castro persisted. In June 1967, the OAS Council appointed a five-man committee to investigate Venezuelan charges that Castro was promoting revolutionary activity in Venezuela. The committee report substantiated these charges by stating that early in May 1967 a motorship, sailing from Santiago, Chile and manned by a Cuban crew, transported seven Cuban and nine Venezuelan guerrillas to the coast of Venezuela. After two of these armed Cuban interlopers were captured, it was learned that the Cubans involved were members of the Cuban Armed Forces.

"Another case in point is Bolivia, which is, perhaps, the best known example of Castro's efforts to export revolution to Latin America. As early as 1960 Fidelistas, in collusion with leftist Juan Lechin, tried to topple the government of Paz Estenssoro. That failed but, in 1967, Ernesto "Che" Guevara turned up as a guerrilla leader, after having disappeared from Cuba in 1965. After months of guerrilla activity in the back country—activity that did not attract popular support—Guevara was killed by the Bolivian Army on October 9, 1967. Even so, the remaining guerrillas have not given up the struggle.

"Guatemala, also, has been the scene of considerable revolutionary activity dating as far back as 1960. Ever since then two guerrilla groups—the FAR of Turcios Lima and the Trotskyite MR-13 of Yon Sosa—have carried out repeated attacks against the government. These groups carried out the sporadic raids against government installations and army convoys that took place in the eastern part of the country in 1966. And, reunited, under the FAR banner, they were responsible for the killing of two U.S. Army officers and U.S. Ambassador John Gordon Mein in 1968.

"Turcios Lima, Yon Sosa and a number of the older guerrilla leaders are now dead but their successors fight on. And a number of them have been trained by the forces of Fidel Castro.

"In Colombia, where guerrilla warfare had become a way of life during La Violencia, Castro's influence was felt not long after he came to power. The first Fidelista group to be formed was the workers, students, and peasants movement—MOEC—started by Antonio Larotta in January 1960. Then came other pro-Castro guerrilla groups—the United Front of Revolutionary Action—FUAR—the Army of National Liberation—ELN— and, still later, the Revolutionary Armed Forces of Colombia—FARC. The army was able to clean out the Communist 'Republics' of Marquetalica, Sumapaz and El Pato in 1964 and 1965 but guerrilla activity continued, spurred by the propagandistic activities of Father Camilo Torres. In April and May of 1967, rebels were responsible for the killing of 50 security officers and in January 1968 a pro-Peking guerrilla group—the People's Liberation Army—took to the field. Insurgency continues to this day, and according to reliable sources, Cuban money and Cuban agents are still being funneled into Colombia—and elsewhere—to foment revolution.

"In Brazil, after Leftist Joao Goulart was thwarted in his attempts to take the country into the Communist orbit in 1964, Cuban trained revolutionaries turned to urban terrorism in their efforts to overthrow the Brazilian Government. Evidence indicates that they were involved in the recent kidnaping of the United States and Swiss Ambassadors.

"The same kind of activity—on an even wider scale—had been going on in Uruguay. Here the Tupamarus, founded by Raúl Sendic in 1962, have been robbing, kidnaping, killing, and terrorizing the people of Montevideo since mid-1969—with Castro's support. In 3 years, under Tupamaru auspices, many policemen were assassinated and over a dozen prominent Uruguayans and foreign diplomats were kidnaped....

"Last April, after failing miserably in the national elections, the Tupamarus launched an all out attack in an effort to impose a Castro-style dictatorship on Uruguay. This effort failed, but there was considerable bloodshed and enough Tupamarus are still left to see that it continues. Castro, of course, is doing nothing to discourage them.

"In spite of this record, there are some people who believe that Castro has reduced his efforts to export revolution to Latin America. What in fact has happened is that, instead of a reduction, there has been a shift in tactics from rural guerrilla warfare, like that which took place in Colombia and Venezuela, to urban terrorism, such as practiced by the Tupamarus.

"On a philosophical level, this shift has manifested itself in the replacement of the Guevara's 'guerrilla warfare' by Carlos Marighella's 'Mini Manual of the Urban Guerrilla' as the bible for revolutionary subversion; on a practical level it has meant changes in the guerrilla training programs being conducted by Castro. Instead of training a large number of revolutionaries as in the past, Castro gives a limited number of them specialized training in urban terrorism at one of the dozen or more Cuban-run training camps.

"The reduction that some have perceived is, therefore, deliberate; Castro has concluded that there is more to be gained by sending a smaller number of better trained guerrillas to certain selected Latin American countries. According to recent estimates, there are about 2,000 of these revolutionaries now operating in Latin America.

"Time and time again Castro has restated his intention to revolutionize the hemisphere. On April 19, 1971, he said that, before a truly inter-American system can function:

There first must be revolution in each of the Latin American countries.

"And that:

American revolutionary peoples can depend on Cuba for support.

"On July 26, 1971, he said that:

Revolutionaries shall not make a single concession to imperialism and that they shall stand here firmly erect, raising our banner until the last Latin American nation is liberated.

"In August 1971, he said:

We have not repented one whit and the path we have followed up to today is the path we will follow in the future.

"And following the visit of Soviet Premier Kosygin in October 1971, Castro hailed: 'An upsurge of revolutionary movement in Latin America.' ..."

Western Hemisphere Relations

Arms aid offered to Honduras? United Press International reported May 17, 1970 that Cuba had offered to supply Honduras with planes, arms and men during the 1969 war with El Salvador.

According to the information obtained by UPI, the offer, made by two persons in Washington, D.C. July 23, 1969 and repeated in Tegucigalpa, was rejected by Honduras President Osvaldo Lopez Arellano.

Quake aid to Peru. Joining other countries in aiding Peru after a devastating May 31, 1970 earthquake, Cuba June 6 announced its first relief program for a non-

Communist nation. According to a June 14 report, Cuba's contribution to air relief operations was substantial and second only to the U.S.'

The first Cuban medical team to go to Peru, consisting of 40 doctors, nurses and other medical personnel, left Havana June 9. In a statement at the Havana airport, Premier Fidel Castro expressed Cuba's willingness to send Peru more personnel, "as many as necessary." Cuba had also sent planes, first aid supplies and vaccines and plasma.

Economic conferees discuss Cuban return. The issue of Cuba's possible reintegration in the inter-American system was discussed at length by delegates to the eighth ministerial-level Inter-American Economic & Social Council conference, held Feb. 3-6, 1970 in Caracas.

Speaking at the opening session of the ministerial-level meeting Feb. 3, Venezuelan President Rafael Caldera said: "It is not possible that any of us fail to feel the absence of Cuba strongly in our family." Trinidad & Tobago Prime Minister Eric Williams stressed that "in the 1970s we should have learned the lesson that economic boycott is not the most realistic nor indeed the most productive attitude to be adopted toward a country whose economic and social system we do not share." However, Williams added that Cuba's reintegration should be conditional on "the strict adherence on the part of that country to a basic tenet of the Organization of American States—namely, nonintervention in the internal affairs of any other country." U.S. Assistant Secretary of State Charles Meyer, head of the U.S. delegation, asserted that the U.S. "has no objection whatsoever to Cuba's returning to the inter-American system so long as its government respects the principle of nonintervention in the internal affairs of neighboring countries." (OAS Secretary General Galo Plaza explained Feb. 5 that consent of 16 OAS nations—two-thirds of the members—was required to bring Cuba back into the organization, and that any member could initiate action on the matter at any time.)

Cuba wins games amid controversy. Cuba swept the 11th Central American and Caribbean Games held in Panama Feb. 28–March 14, 1970, but Cuban participation was fraught with controversy.

Cuba won 101 gold, 59 silver and 52 bronze medals. Mexico placed a distant second with 124 medals (38 gold), while Colombia, Puerto Rico and Venezuela finished third, fourth and fifth respectively.

Among the incidents involving Cuba:

A group of Cubans was reported to have distributed pro-Castro propaganda and made political speeches in defiance of orders by games officials prohibiting such action; Rafael Arguelles, a member of the Cuban soccer team, defected March 6 and sought political asylum at a Latin American embassy; the defection of Jorge Wilson, a Cuban high-jumper, was reported after he sought asylum in the U.S. embassy March 9; a brawl erupted when a U.S. referee disqualified a Cuban long-distance walker; and numerous charges of professionalism were leveled at the Cuban delegation.

(Three Cuban athletes taking part in the 1971 Pan-American games in Cali, Colombia asked for asylum in Panama, according to a report Aug. 5 from the Panamanian embassy in Colombia.)

Relations with Chile. Salvador Allende Gossens, an avowed Marxist, became president of Chile Nov. 3, 1970. But even before the pro-Castro Allende government took control, Chile had been considering a normalization of relations with Cuba.

Gabriel Valdes, pre-Allende foreign minister of Chile had confirmed Jan. 27, 1970 that Chile was discussing with other hemispheric governments renewal of diplomatic and trade relations with Cuba. "Whether Cuba belongs or does not belong to the Organization of American States is its own affair," he said, "but we believe that the widest possible continental unity is worthwhile." He added that even Venezuela, formerly a strict anti-Cuba adherent, was participating in the discussions. La Nacion, a Santiago newspaper which usually reflects the views of the Chilean government, had published an editorial Jan. 25 calling for a resumption of relations between Chile and Cuba.

Rafael Moreno, vice president of the Chilean Agrarian Reform Corp., announced Feb. 20 that Chile had agreed to sell $11 million worth of foodstuffs to Cuba. Moreno explained that $3 million worth of garlic, beans and onions would be delivered in 1970 and another $8 million worth of foodstuffs in 1971.

The Chilean action presumably ruptured the trade embargo imposed against Cuba by the Organization of American States in 1964. All OAS members except Mexico were reported to have complied with the embargo, which stipulated that "the governments of the American States suspend all their trade whether direct or indirect with Cuba excepting foodstuffs, medicines and medical equipment that may be sent to Cuba for humanitarian reasons." (Chilean officials had recently called for an end to the embargo on trade with Cuba.)

Chilean and Cuban TV officials in Havana signed an agreement to exchange TV news programs between the Cuban Broadcasting Institute and the television channel of the Catholic University of Chile, the New York Times reported Aug. 8.

A Cuban trade delegation visited Chile July 10-17; the group was invited by a subdivision of the Chilean agrarian reform organization.

After winning a plurality of votes in the Chilean presidential election Sept. 4, Allende said at a press conference Sept. 5 that he intended to establish diplomatic and trade relations with all nations, including Cuba. An unofficial delegation from Cuba attended Allende's inauguration.

After a week in office, he reiterated Nov. 12 that he had "decided to re-establish diplomatic, consular, commercial and cultural relations with the Republic of Cuba."

In a six-minute nationwide speech, Allende explained that the action would contribute "to ending a situation which we consider unjust towards a sister nation that is struggling to shape its own destiny according to the sovereign will of its people." Allende added that documents resuming relations between the two countries had already been signed by Chilean Foreign Minister Clodomiro Almeyda and Cuban Minister without Portfolio Carlos Rafael Rodriguez, who had headed the Cuban delegation to Allende's inauguration Nov. 3.

Allende asserted that the 1964 Organization of American States resolution which called on hemispheric nations to sever ties with Cuba lacked "juridical and moral basis" and that the measures adopted by the OAS did not "serve the interests of peace and friendship between the countries in the way stipulated by the charter of the United Nations."

The U.S. State Department Nov. 13 strongly criticized Chile's decision to resume relations with Cuba. State Department spokesman Robert J. McCloskey said "we deplore the fact that Chile has acted outside the consultative framework decided in 1964 by OAS foreign ministers for collective consideration of the question of Cuba by OAS member states." He added that the U.S. planned "to continue to support the existing OAS decision and recommendations on Cuba and we hope other OAS members will continue to do likewise."

Jaime Gazmuri was appointed Chilean ambassador to Cuba (reported Dec. 10). His appointment also had to be confirmed by the Senate, but in the meantime, Jorge Edwards had arrived in Havana to set up the embassy and serve as charge d'affaires.

The Chilean government announced Jan. 15, 1971 that its national airline, LAN, would begin regular flights to Cuba in March. The service would begin by adding a Havana stop on LAN's European flight, which also included a stop in Lima, Peru. Radio Havana said June 20 that the state-owned Cubana Airlines would inaugurate regular flights from Havana to Santiago, Chile beginning June 26. Actual air service between the two countries began July 18 when the first LAN flight arrived in Havana.

Cuba and Chile signed a trade agreement Feb. 12 totaling about $20 million. The terms included sale of Cuban sugar to Chile and Cuban purchase of Chilean agricultural products, cellulose, wood, and copper and steel.

Cuba and Chile signed a communications agreement Feb. 15 in Santiago. The pact included establishment of a Santiago-Havana radio network which could later be transformed into a telex system.

The Soviet news agency Tass reported from Havana Aug. 2, 1971 that Cuba and Chile had signed a five-year pact for scientific and technical cooperation. The agreement provided for the mutual exchange of specialists, data, scientific and technical documentation and experience. A standing mixed inter-governmental commission would implement the agreement, according to the report.

Cuban Foreign Affairs Minister Raul Roa Garcia arrived in Santiago, Chile Aug. 16 for a six-day visit where details of a future trip by Cuban Premier Fidel Castro to Chile were discussed. Roa said his meeting with Chilean President Salvador Allende Aug. 17 had been "very cordial and friendly."

On his return to Cuba Aug. 22, Roa stopped at the Lima, Peru, airport where he met with Peruvian Foreign Minister Edgardo Mercado Jarrin. In a statement at the airport, Roa said "it was probable" that Castro would stop in Lima on his planned trip to Chile.

The Miami Herald reported Oct. 8 that Cuban and Chilean women signed a public document calling on the women of Latin America to "join the liberation battles of their people." A Cuban women's delegation had been in Santiago to attend the Women's Political Committee of President Allende's Popular Unity government.

Castro visits Chile—Fidel Castro paid a 25-day visit to Chile Nov. 10–Dec. 4, 1971. His return to Cuba Dec. 4 included airport stopovers for meetings with the presidents of Peru and Ecuador. He called his trip a "triumphant success" and "proof that we are not as alone as we once were."

It was the Cuban leader's first trip to South America since 1959. It indicated a breach in the united policy of diplomatic and economic boycott of Cuba begun when the Organization of American States (OAS) expelled Cuba in 1962.

The government of Chilean President Salvador Allende, a long-time friend of Castro, had resumed diplomatic relations with Cuba shortly after his election in 1970.

From his arrival in Chile Nov. 10, Castro received an enthusiastic reception, mainly among organized students and workers. Despite a heavy cold, he made two or three speeches a day the length of the country. Castro made appearances in the cities of Santiago and Concepcion and in fishing towns and mining camps from Antofagasta in the extreme north to Punta Arenas, Chile's southernmost city.

The only denunciation of his visit came from right-wing nationalists. According to a Nov. 17 report, the opposition Santiago newspaper Tribuna called Castro's visit—which had been extended from 10 to 24 days—"marathonic." Right-wing congressmen introduced a motion Nov. 29 that the visiting Cuban premier end his trip "as soon as possible."

In Santiago Nov. 11, Castro indicated an end to the Cuban dogma that guerrilla violence was the only means to revolution. Asked if he believed that armed struggle was the only way to achieve power, Castro said Cuba had never excluded elections as a means of attaining that goal. His comments were seen by observers as a veiled criticism of the Chilean terrorist group Revolutionary Left Movement (MIR), which had criticized Allende for not being radical enough.

In a speech Nov. 16, Castro said the Cuban revolution was not "a model for export" and added, "it's up to each country to find its own solutions."

"Our revolution solved problems particular to Cuba," he said. "Today we have eradicated gambling, prostitution, begging and illiteracy... but we don't intend to prescribe solutions to any other country."

Castro's low-key approach during his appearances was interpreted as an effort not to make unnecessary domestic difficulties for President Allende or interfere in Chile's internal affairs. However, a demonstration Dec. 1 by 5,000 women protesting his visit and food shortages produced a new level of violence in relations between the Allende regime and its anti-Marxist opposition.

Castro Dec. 4 called these clashes "an escalation of fascist sedition" and said that "perhaps our visit has served as a stimulus for those who want to create difficulties for the popular government."

Castro had touched on Chilean internal politics for the first time Nov. 14 at Chuquicamata, the world's largest open pit copper mine, nationalized in July. The visit by the Cuban coincided with a dispute between militant mineworkers and the government over pay. Castro told the workers that they should put the state's interest before their own.

In appearances before peasants, workers and students Castro often repeated his call for the people to work harder under socialism. He said that the Allende government would bring socialism to Chile if the left-wing parties were united and if the workers increased production, two of the Allende government's most persistent problems.

The Cuban premier also noted Nov. 18 that Soviet aid had been crucial to the survival of his government in the early 1960s, when the U.S. applied economic sanctions against Cuba.

Castro Nov. 24 dropped the discretion which had marked his tour and charged the U.S. with keeping the Latin American continent weak and divided.

However, he said Nov. 25 that he was "a great admirer" of the American people, whom he described as "very idealistic." He added that President Nixon "does not respond to the realities now and to the new spirit of the people of the U.S." The Cuban leader predicted an era of "true friendship between the U.S. and Latin America, but "not while Nixon is in the White House." He said "when the United States has a government that does not represent reaction, and does not act as a gendarme, then there can be peace with Cuba." Castro Nov. 11 had reiterated his position that Cuba would never rejoin the OAS.

In Punta Arenas Nov. 22, where Castro arrived with President Allende after a two-day boat trip south from Concepcion, he told students that Cuba would eventually force the U.S. Navy out of its Guantanamo (Cuba) base without firing a shot. "We can't get them out now because they're stronger than we are," he said.

Stressing his unity with the Latin nations, Castro said Nov. 16 that "we in the Caribbean don't want to join the United States, we want to join Latin America." He urged Latins "to fight for the union of all our countries." In a speech at the Santiago headquarters of the Economic Commission for Latin America (ECLA) Nov. 29, Castro urged Latin nations to integrate their economies to counter the "taxes and economic discrimination" of the U.S. government.

In Concepcion Nov. 18 the Cuban premier called the Peruvian government's expropriation of the U.S. owned International Petroleum Co. the emergence of an "anti-imperialist conscience" among Roman Catholic priests, and the organization of the left-wing Broad Front in Uruguay "evidence that imperialism is deteriorating in Latin America."

On the eve of his departure from Chile Dec. 3 Castro said his government was prepared to establish diplomatic relations with any Latin country that was willing to defy the U.S.

Uruguay rejects Castro declaration—The Buenos Aires newspaper La Prensa reported Dec. 2 that the Uruguayan government had rejected "with maximum force" declarations made by Castro in Chile that "armed violence is the only revolutionary road for Uruguay." Castro had refused to comment further on the results of Uruguay's Nov. 28 presidential elections.

Castro denies criticizing Allende—Fidel Castro Sept. 10, 1972 denounced as "base, gross, truculent lies" an assertion by Washington newspaper columnist Jack Anderson that Castro had privately criticized President Allende during his visit to Chile in 1971.

Anderson's report, allegedly based on a Central Intelligence Agency (CIA) document, appeared in U.S. newspapers

Sept. 8. It claimed that before his departure from Chile, Castro had told local Communist leaders that Allende had not imposed Marxism on Chile forcefully enough, and was "physically spent." Castro had reportedly added that other Chilean leaders lived "too well," and were "not under sufficient tension."

According to the alleged CIA document, "Castro said the [government] does not have a solid front to face the opposition, which he claimed is growing rapidly. Castro added that the situation in Chile is rapidly approaching a critical stage . . ." Among factors which could precipitate a crisis and confrontation with the opposition, Castro allegedly cited a breakdown of public order, which could come about "at any time because the opposition, especially the middle class, has lost its fear of the government."

Allende visits Cuba—Salvador Allende visited Cuba in December 1972 on the way home after a trip to the U.S.S.R.

Allende arrived in Havana Dec. 10 to an enthusiastic welcome from Premier Fidel Castro, President Osvaldo Dorticos and a large crowd. A joint Cuban-Chilean communique issued at the end of Allende's visit Dec. 14 called for Latin American unity against "foreign economic exploitation and oppression," which it said were aimed at crushing Latin America's "struggle for emancipation." It attacked large international consortiums which had "exploited for years the national wealth of our peoples, obtaining exorbitant profits," and denounced "imperialist maneuvers" designed to punish economically those countries that did not share U.S. social and ideological policies.

Ties with OAS & hemisphere nations. The question of Cuban relations with the Organization of American States (OAS) and the individual nations of the hemisphere came up again when the OAS General Assembly met in Washington June 25–July 8, 1970.

Peru and Bolivia urged June 27 that OAS members consider renewing diplomatic and trade relations with Cuba. Bolivian Foreign Minister Edgardo Camacho Omiste noted that the "inter-American system has spent a great part of its strength and prestige in the attempt to isolate one government and consequently, one American people." He then questioned whether, in light of "the practical results achieved, it would not be opportune to begin asking whether it is really worthwhile to pursue this policy indefinitely."

U.S. diplomats said that Secretary of State William P. Rogers had issued a 25-page telegram to all U.S. hemispheric ambassadors urging them to warn Latin foreign ministers against resuming relations with Cuba. Rogers' action was reported by Tad Szulc in the New York Times Dec. 20.

Rogers' message, apparently sent on White House orders, included detailed information on the U.S.' conviction that Soviet and Cuban subversive activities existed in Latin America. The telegram was reported to have concluded that the new Chilean government was playing into Cuban and Soviet hands in its resumption of diplomatic ties with Havana in November.

In a radio speech April 19, 1970 on the 10th anniversary of the Bay of Pigs battle, Castro said the Organization of American States (OAS) must disappear and be replaced by a union of all Latin American nations "when each has made its revolution."

Castro rejected any possibility that Cuba would rejoin the OAS. He also maintained that Cuba would never change its hostility toward the U.S. as long as its policies remained "imperialistic."

Cuba and Chile signed a joint declaration in Havana attacking the OAS accords through which Latin American nations had broken diplomatic relations with Cuba, according to an Aug. 4 report.

The joint declaration said "both parties believe that the OAS agreements that brought the rupture of diplomatic, consular and commercial relations between the countries of Latin America and Cuba are without juridical and moral value." It added that both countries "believe that the policy of economic isolation constitutes a violation of the right of self-determination of the Cuban people on the pretext of damaging their course of economic development."

OAS Secretary General Galo Plaza Aug. 12 began probes to determine whether the differing attitudes some Latin nations had adopted toward Cuba could be resolved harmoniously within the framework of the OAS.

According to an Aug. 18 report, Plaza feared that President Nixon's policy of a "new focus" towards Communist China could cause a "disbanding" of Latin American solidarity and that several Latin countries would soon establish relations with Cuba. Many Latin officials were felt to believe that the U.S. policy of rapprochement with China was inconsistent with the continued isolation of Cuba from the rest of the hemisphere.

(Peru and Uruguay, as well as other countries, had recently begun a re-evaluation of their policies with Cuba.)

Plaza began quiet consultations over the Cuba issue in November 1970—according to an Aug. 14 report—in Mexico City with diplomats from Mexico, Peru, Chile, Ecuador, Colombia, Uruguay, Bolivia and Costa Rica. All of these countries reportedly favored steps to normalize relations with Cuba.

Plaza had reportedly believed that reestablishment of relations with Cuba on a country-by-country basis would deal such a severe blow to the inter-American system that it would destroy its political and juridical framework. He believed that differences of opinions over Cuba would lead to the loss of prestige for the OAS.

Plaza's argument, according to the Aug. 18 report, was that the Latin countries should not act on their own but should discuss their differing opinions within the inter-American forum.

It was reported Aug. 13 that the U.S., Brazil, Argentina, Guatemala and the Dominican Republic were strongly opposed to easing sanctions against Cuba.

The Dominican position was announced by President Joaquin Balaguer Aug. 11 when he said the OAS must maintain without any modification the diplomatic and economic blockade it imposed in 1961. He added that Cuba had not been expelled from the OAS for its Communist ideology, but for its policy of intervention in the internal affairs of other nations.

The Venezuelan ambassador to the Dominican Republic, Gloria Stolk, said in a television broadcast reported Aug. 12 that Castro had not changed his policy of interference in Latin America, and that Cuba had been subsidizing guerrilla extremist groups in Venezuela. Argentina and Brazil reportedly held similar positions.

Cuban Foreign Minister Raul Roa said Aug. 13 that his regime had no intention of returning to the OAS. Roa attacked the organization as an "entity in an accelerated process of corruption and impudence . . . historically, a ministry of the colonies of the American State Department."

Roa added that Cuba was disposed to maintain relations "with those Latin American governments which, in utilizing their sovereignty, assume an independent position in defense of their national dignity and international actions."

U.S. Sen. J. William Fulbright (D, Ark.), chairman of the Senate Foreign Relations Committee, had offered July 30 a resolution that, if adopted, would indicate Senate sentiment that U.S. policy toward Cuba should be reviewed "with the objective of beginning a process that would lead to the reestablishment of normal relations between the U.S. and Cuba."

Sen. Stuart Symington (D, Mo.) said, according to an Aug. 20 report, that "of all things that make the U.S. look silly from a diplomatic standpoint, nothing can beat our relationship with Cuba."

Chilean Foreign Minister Clodomiro Almeyda said the Chilean government had no plans to ask for the suspension of diplomatic and political sanctions imposed by Latin nations against Cuba. He said the "necessary conditions" did not yet exist for Cuba's return to the OAS "because Cuba is not interested in it." These remarks were reported in Chile by La Prensa Oct. 8, 1971.

Peru asked the OAS Dec. 6 to allow nations that so desired to "remain free to renew relations with Cuba." Both Peru and Ecuador were understood to want to be the first nation to ask the OAS to remove the economic and diplomatic sanctions imposed on Cuba in 1964 by the OAS.

The OAS announced Dec. 8 that it was appointing a committee to consider lifting the sanctions against Cuba. Plaza said the plan would allow OAS member nations to establish individual diplomatic and trade relations with Cuba if they wished. However, he added: "We will not ask Cuba into the OAS."

Cuba not readmitted—The readmission of Cuba to the OAS was postponed indefinitely April 21, 1972 after the failure of a Peruvian resolution calling for an end to OAS sanctions against Cuba. The rejection took place in Washington at the General Assembly of the OAS. Cuban Foreign Minister Raul Roa said in Lima that his country would never return to the OAS, the Miami Herald reported April 22.

In a speech to the assembly April 12, Secretary of State William P. Rogers had recommended continuation of the sanctions, saying "Cuba's continued interventionist behavior and its support for revolution—even though on a different scale than in the past—still constitute a threat to the peace and security of the Hemisphere."

The assembly passed a weak condemnation of Premier Fidel Castro for interfering in Uruguayan internal affairs by saying that leftists could reach power in that country only through violence, El Nacional of Caracas reported April 22.

Galo Plaza, secretary general of the OAS, declared later that the current isolation of Cuba was "not constructive," and that OAS member states should "examine, coolly and calmly, the possibility of lifting the sanctions imposed on Cuba" in 1964, the newsletter Latin America reported Jan. 13, 1973.

Puerto Rico's ex-governor, Luis Ferre, had urged the U.S. to "find a formula that leads to the normalization of its relations with Cuba... [and] that would make possible [Cuba's] return to the Organization of American States," the Miami Herald reported Jan. 28. Carlos Sanz de Santamaria, president of the Inter-American Committee of the Alliance for Progress, said Feb. 5 that "any hemispheric movement to be prepared for the future must include Cuba" and "other countries that are going to have political liberty in the coming years."

Relations with Mexico. Cuba and Mexico were reported Dec. 2, 1971 to have signed an accord for direct trade between the countries for the first time since 1959.

Previously, trade between Cuba and Mexico had been conducted through Canada and payments for goods made through Canadian banks.

Cuba and Mexico were reported Aug. 3, 1971 to have agreed on a new aviation pact to replace one that had expired July 30. The agreement was reached after months of negotiations between the countries' foreign ministers. The old pact had been renounced by Mexico in 1970 over an extradition dispute involving hijackers.

The new agreement called for the continuation of the twice-weekly flights between Mexico City and Havana by Cubana Airlines. A Mexican Foreign Ministry press release said the new pact would "update the conditions under which air communication between the two countries will develop."

The Miami Herald reported Feb. 6, 1972 that the Cuban government's news agency, Prensa Latina, had closed down its office in Mexico City, discharging all but one of its 15 local employes. Jose Carlos Ferreyra, a Mexican journalist who had been the operation's bureau chief, remained as Prensa Latina's correspondent in Mexico.

According to the Herald, the Cuban government had spent over $80,000 a year for the past 10 years to maintain the service. Although the Prensa Latina news and feature services had been provided free to Mexican newspapers and magazines, its material had been used regularly by only a limited number of leftist publications sympathetic to the Cuban regime.

Castro effigy burned. Guatemalans burned an effigy of Cuban Premier Fidel

Castro in front of headquarters of the governing National Liberation Movement Party on Guatemala's annual Burning of the Devil Day, it was reported Dec. 10, 1971.

Peruvian ties. Peru and Cuba agreed July 8, 1972 to reestablish diplomatic relations, suspended by Peru in 1964 at the request of the U.S.

Joaquin Heredia Cabieses, a retired army major and former ambassador to Czechoslovakia, was named Peruvian ambassador to Cuba, while Antonio Nunez Jimenez, a former guerrilla leader and past president of the Cuban Academy of Sciences, was to represent Cuba in Lima.

Peru had formally proposed the lifting of sanctions against Cuba by the Organization of American States at a meeting in Washington in May, but the proposal had been defeated.

The newsletter Latin America reported Jan. 12, 1973 that Cuba had bought 110 fishing vessels worth about $30 million from Peru.

Caribbean nations set ties. Jamaica, Barbados, Guyana and Trinidad & Tobago had established diplomatic relations with Cuba, it was announced Dec. 12, 1972. The U.S. called the move "unfortunate" Dec. 13. All but Guyana belonged to the Organization of American States, which maintained diplomatic and economic sanctions against Cuba.

Costa Rican view. Costa Rican President Jose Figueres told a group of Cuban exiles in Puerto Rico Jan. 29, 1973 that they should begin a "dialogue" with Premier Fidel Castro, and offered himself as an intermediary. His proposal reportedly outraged the exiles, but received the support of Puerto Rico Gov. Rafael Hernandez Colon, who called it "very realistic."

Despite his offer to mediate between Castro and Cuban exiles, Figueres said Costa Rica could not re-establish relations with Cuba, "at least not until the current Cuban regime meets two conditions: freedom for political prisoners and freedom for Cubans to return to their homes and leave them whenever they wish." During a visit to Panama Jan. 30, Figueres evaded questions from newsmen concerning his ability, as a long-standing opponent of communism in Cuba, to mediate successfully with Castro.

Colombians for ties. Sixty-eight Colombian senators, representing all political groups, issued an appeal Feb. 1, 1973 for their country to agree to establish diplomatic relations with Cuba, China, East Germany, North Korea, North Vietnam "and all other nations with which Colombia does not have relations."

IAPA press freedom report. The board of directors of the Inter-American Press Association (IAPA) had approved a report by the organization's freedom of the press committee on press liberties in Latin America, the Miami Herald reported March 25, 1972.

The report charged that there was no freedom of the press in Cuba, Haiti, Panama and Paraguay, and only limited freedom in Bolivia, Brazil, Ecuador, Guyana, Nicaragua and Peru.

At its 28th annual assembly, held in Santiago, Chile Oct. 9–13, IAPA designated Castro as "public enemy No. 1 of press freedom in the Americas" for the 12th consecutive year.

In a report issued Jan. 2, 1973, the IAPA board of directors said that there was no press freedom in Cuba, Brazil, Haiti, Panama and Paraguay.

Other Foreign Affairs

British trade. It was reported Jan. 30, 1970 that a $7.2 million deal had been negotiated between the Leyland Motor Corp. of Great Britain and Cuba. The contract, signed in London in May 1969, included the sale of 300 15-ton British-made trucks to Cuba. British Leyland was also reported to have sold more than 1,200 buses to Cuba.

An $840,000 order of rails and steel joints for Cuba was announced by the British Steel Corp., according to an Aug. 14, 1971 Washington Post report.

The Times of the Americas reported March 1, 1972 that National Westminister, one of Britain's largest banks, had agreed to provide Cuba with $7 million in credit. Cuba was to use the credit to buy British equipment and services during the following year.

Cuba buys shipping from various nations. Havana radio reported Feb. 15, 1970 that Cuba had recently taken possession of the first of 30 shrimp boats under construction in France, bringing its shrimp fleet to more than 150 vessels. Seventy-three had been built in Spain. A New York Times report Feb. 17 stated that three 20,000-ton tankers were under construction by the Soviet Union, and that Cuba was to take possession of the last two of three Swedish 15,000-ton ships in 1970, bringing the Cuban merchant marine to 49 freighters with 376,600 tons displacement; this compared with 14 ships totaling 57,900 tons in 1959.

Japanese-Cuban trade expands. A wide expansion of trade between Japan and Cuba began in the early 1970s.

Hino Motors of Japan, an affiliate of Toyota, was reported Aug. 11, 1970 to have arranged for the delivery of 550 buses to Cuba.

The Cuban government said that imports from Japan in 1972 would be 10 times above the annual average pre-1969 figure, the Miami Herald reported Nov. 11, 1972. Japan had become the top non-Communist buyer of Cuban sugar since 1969, providing in return machinery, trucks, buses, fishing boats and other products.

U.S. ousts 2 Cuban U.N. aides. The U.S. government Oct. 9, 1970 named two Cuban diplomats to the U.N. persona non grata and ordered their expulsion from the country within 48 hours. The two were charged with relaying intelligence collected for them by a "female employe of a friendly foreign embassy." An Oct. 22 report identified the girl as Jennifer Miles, 26, of South Africa, who had worked as a receptionist at the South African embassy in Washington.

The two Cubans, Rogelio Rodriguez Lopez, 28, counselor to the Cuban mission to the U.N., and Orlando Prendes Gutierrez, 29, a first secretary at the mission, were reportedly charged on evidence provided by Miss Miles after she was taken into custody Oct. 3. U.S. officials denied her actions had harmed American security. She was reported to have returned to South Africa Oct. 29.

Portugal jails captain. A military court in Lisbon, Portugal April 26, 1971 sentenced Cuban Army Capt. Pedro Rodriguez Peralta to 26 months in prison for serving as a training instructor and adviser to the African Party for the Independence of Guinea and Cape Verde, a nationalist organization based in Conakry, Guinea. Half of the 524 days he had already spent in prison would be counted toward fulfillment of the sentence.

The prosecutor had introduced documents that allegedly linked Rodriguez to the anti-Portuguese guerrilla movement, but he failed to prove that Rodriquez had taken up arms against Portugal or that he had acted on orders of the Cuban government.

Rodriguez had been wounded and captured by the Portuguese army in Portuguese Guinea in November 1969 during a clash with nationalist guerrillas.

New Africa ties set. Cuba had established diplomatic relations with the African states of Zambia and Somalia, the official press agency announced July 20, 1972.

Problems with Spain surface. The 15-man Cuban diplomatic mission in Madrid left Spain abruptly with their families Aug. 2, 1971, leaving only a first secretary in the embassy. No immediate explanation was given for the departure. A Spanish Foreign Ministry spokesman, admitting that the action was "drastic," said "there are minor problems, but there is no crisis" in Spanish-Cuban relations.

Informed sources attributed the Cuban departure to Spanish demands that Cuba reduce the number of diplomats in Madrid to six or seven, the same number Spain retained in Havana. The Spanish government had also threatened to impose restrictions on the Cubans similar to those Cuba had imposed on the movements of Spanish diplomats in Havana, according to an Aug. 3 report.

The departure came as Spain and Cuba reached a deadlock on current negotiations dealing with trade and payment by Cuba for the property of Spanish citizens nationalized when Cuban Premier Fidel Castro came to power. It was reported Aug. 8 that, while Cuba was "disposed" to provide compensation for the confiscated property, Spain had been pressing for "favorable conditions" and short-term payment. Another problem was the long-standing and growing trade debt owed by Cuba to Spain. Madrid had also pressed for resolution of the issue of Spaniards imprisoned in Cuba for political activity.

It was said in Madrid Sept. 22 that Cuba had suspended tobacco shipments to Spain as a result of a "cooling" of relations between the two countries. The Cuban action was believed to be in retaliation over unsuccessful negotiations in extending a trade agreement in August.

The Miami Herald reported Sept. 30 that Spain's Commerce Ministry had announced that Cuba had reneged on a bilateral commercial agreement by suspending the export of tobacco, sugar, coffee and cigars to Spain until the Spanish government agreed to pay for the commodities in convertible currency.

As 1971 neared its end, Cuba signed a four-year trade pact with Spain Dec. 18 guaranteeing repayment of Cuban debts to Spain and providing mutual recognition for trade purposes as "most favored nations."

The Spanish Government was holding down domestic sugar production in order to give Cuban sugar access to the Spanish market and ease the island's chronic trade deficit with Spain, the London newsletter Latin America reported Sept. 22, 1972.

ROK lifts ship ban. The South Korean government announced March 17, 1972 that Cuban ships would hereafter be permitted to visit South Korean ports. The ban was lifted as of March 11 after the Seoul government decided to regard Cuba as a non-hostile Communist state.

Aid pact with Sweden. Cuba and Sweden reached a mutual assistance accord May 29, 1972 under which Cuba would receive medical and hospital equipment valued at more than $9 million. Sweden had previously provided Cuba with $5 million to finance two technical institutes, according to reports.

Sugar & the Economy

Sugar harvests lag. Fidel Castro conceded Jan. 12, 1970 that his plan to harvest 10 million tons of sugar during 1970 had run into difficulties. Explaining that heavy rains had set back progress in a number of provinces, Castro also spoke of other difficulties such as "industrial troubles deriving from indispensable adjustments to new investments, unavoidable failures in industrial equipment being subjected to intensive work, operational failures caused by inefficient machine operators, or the inexperience of those who organize or manage the process." Castro warned that the "political, agricultural, and industrial administrations of the provinces must learn where their weakest links are and must ceaselessly attack problems in the political, organizational, and technical fields, assigning their best qualified workers and cadres to solve these problems. We must never lower our guard for a moment."

Castro May 18 expressed disappointment at the crop failure. He had staked the "honor" of the Cuban Revolution on the harvest, saying that the drive would

1970-73: A TIME OF RESTRAINT

be a test of Socialist organization and revolutionary determination.

Underlining the failure, Havana Radio announced July 6 that the education and sugar ministers had been replaced. In what was apparently a significant cabinet shuffle, Sugar Minister Francisco Padron was replaced by Marcos Lage Coello, vice rector of the University of Havana, and Education Minister Jose Llanusa was succeeded by Maj. Belarmino Castilla Mas, a deputy defense minister.

Castro told Cubans July 26 that the effort to meet the 10-million-ton sugar goal had caused bad strains in the economy. Speaking on the 17th anniversary of his unsuccessful attack on the Moncada Barracks in Santiago Province which marked the start of his revolution, Castro conceded that Cubans had "shown very little efficiency. The problem is the responsibility of all of us and mine in particular."

"We were unable to fight a simultaneous battle," he explained. "Our heroic efforts resulted in imbalances in the economy and an increase in our difficulties." Castro added that the nation could "change its leaders right now if it wishes," but pointed out that this would not solve the problems. A solution, he said, could "only be found in a dialogue with the mass of the workers."

Castro called for party functionaries to consult workers before making important decisions and he recommended the establishment of "collective organizations" in factories and state concerns where workers would be represented along with party officials. In addition, he announced the creation of a high level cabinet position to coordinate administrative and economic planning. He did not name anyone to fill the post.

Cuba's 12-month sugar harvest rose to a record high of 8,535,281 tons, the highest ever achieved in Cuba. (The four-month 1952 harvest had reached 7.2 million tons.) In addition, the 1970 production of meat, milk, bread, vegetables, tobacco and clothing had declined due to the massive effort put into the sugar harvest.

(In a speech May 31, Castro had denounced the "irresponsibility" of many Cuban workers, stressing that human rather than technological factors were the "weak point" in Cuba's development.)

In a speech published in the official party newspaper Granma Aug. 3, Labor Minister Jorge Risquet attributed many of the nation's economic difficulties to "extremely low" worker productivity. He criticized the workers for lack of discipline and absenteeism and charged that the 1970 sugar harvest had in reality cost the economy up to three times its value on the world market.

(The U.S. Agriculture Department estimated Nov. 23 in its weekly magazine Foreign Agriculture that Cuba had sold a record 3 million tons of sugar to the Soviet Union in 1970, more than twice the amount sold in 1969.)

Castro Dec. 7 decreed a 1971 sugar harvest goal at 7 million tons and announced that the harvest would officially begin in December. In addition, the 1971 harvest would include the postponement of Christmas and New Year celebrations until July 1971, as was done during the 1970 harvest period.

In a New Year's Eve speech in Havana Dec. 31, 1970, Castro proclaimed 1971 as "the year of productivity" in which the government would launch a "crusade" to increase production and the quality of work and to "eradicate vagrancy, parasitism, and other strange vices of the revolution." Castro described these "vices" as "expressions of ideological weaknesses that a workers' society must root out." His remarks were summarized by Havana radio Jan. 1.

Stressing the importance of reaching Cuba's goal of a 7 million-ton sugar harvest, he said that the harvest schedule was already behind. He added that almost the entire harvest would be cut by hand, with little of the mechanization originally planned. The nation's dependence on sugar exports, which represent about 85% of the nation's overall exports, would be greater in 1971 than ever before, he said.

Castro said Jan. 26, 1971 that the sugar harvest was considerably behind schedule. Noting that only about 15% of the harvest had been cut to date, Castro said: "At such a rate, we will be left with a large quantity of unground cane and the country will suffer terribly." Castro added that he was introducing "revolutionary techniques" to speed up the harvest through mechanization.

Castro confirmed that he was planning to institute burning as a method to speed up the harvest, it was reported in the New York Times Feb. 7. "There is no machine in existence today capable of cutting cane that had not been burned," the premier said. "This is the reality. We cannot mechanize without burning the cane."

But in a May Day speech, Castro then announced that the 1971 sugar harvest target would be cut from 7 million to 6.65 million metric tons of refined sugar.

Castro also announced that Cuba's tobacco harvest would fall 40% below expectations in 1971 due to severe drought in western Cuba.

Castro called on Cubans to work harder and to understand that needed increases in labor efficiency would be "long and difficult" to achieve. He asserted that low labor productivity was Cuba's most serious problem.

Cuba's 1971 sugar harvest was completed July 20 with a total production of over 5.92 million metric tons.

Citing setbacks in sugar output, officials said Feb. 28 that per capita sugar rations would be cut two pounds a month beginning March 1. The normal ration was six pounds a month.

A Havana radio broadcast quoted the government as saying that the cut was necessary to fulfill "export commitments which cannot be decreased beyond certain limits" and to avert "further strain on the economy." Sugar made up 70%-80% of Cuba's foreign exchange earnings.

Production had been reduced by severe drought during the 1971 planting and growing periods and heavy rains in the current harvesting season. Castro, quoted in the Times of the Americas March 1, also cited the smaller amount of weed killer available in 1972.

Sugar official Julio Israel Rodriguez, quoted in the Miami Herald Feb. 21, said the rains had seriously affected the harvest in all provinces. Rodriguez added that it had been necessary to hold up cutting operations "to avoid the difficulties encountered by piling up sugar cane and having it rot on the ground."

The Herald also noted the problem of the soaring rate of fuel oil usage in Cuba's 138 operating sugar mills. Some mills were reported to be using as much as 10-12 gallons of fuel oil to grind a ton of cane, far above the sugar ministry's goal of one gallon per ton. The Times of the Americas said March 1 that as the halfway point in the harvest approached, 16 mills still had not started to grind cane.

The 1972 sugar harvest ended July 18. President Osvaldo Dorticos was quoted July 19 as saying the harvest had been "bad," but "the workers of this nation have made an effort that saves our honor and prestige and meets the vital needs of our economy."

East European diplomatic sources were quoted July 28 as estimating the harvest at 4.1 million tons, lower than recent harvests but higher than the most pessimistic forecasts. Cuba reportedly would still earn as much as $560 million from sugar exports in 1972, since a scarcity of sugar had pushed the world market price up to nearly 10¢ per pound.

In a related development, the Soviet Union would provide Cuba with a factory to build a new type of sugar cane harvester designed jointly by Soviet and Cuban specialists, the newsletter Latin America reported June 16.

Labor developments. Among developments involving workers:

The Labor Ministry Oct. 16, 1970 issued a decree establishing a system of merits and demerits. The decree, which set up "labor merit assemblies" to review each worker's work every six months, was designed to reduce absenteeism and increase productivity.

In line with Premier Fidel Castro's policy of increasing workers' participation in the labor movement, the Cuban Labor Confederation (CTC) ordered secret ballot election of union officers at all work centers, its was reported Oct. 31, 1970.

A conference of industrial workers, held Dec. 5-7, 1970, established a basic industry workers national trade union. Radio Havana reported Dec. 8 that veteran labor leader Agapito Figueroa had been elected secretary-general of the union.

The London newsletter Latin America reported July 28, 1972 that the CTC had started a drive to improve internal administration and bring rural workers into the mainstream of Cuban life. The CTC said that during the past 18 months there had been a 10% increase in its membership, to 1.1 million persons.

Among urban workers, the CTC claimed, union participation was virtually 100%, but in the countryside 150,000 laborers remained to be recruited. Organizers in rural areas reportedly faced local reluctance to shift from small farms to wage-earning agricultural labor, as well as opposition from groups of Jehovah's Witnesses.

(At Pinar del Rio, southwest of Havana, a people's court had sentenced a Jehovah's Witness to 150 days confined agricultural labor for barter activities and spreading "the obscurantist ideas he professes," Havana Radio announced July 17. The man, Pedro Campo Perez, had manufactured furniture illegally and repaired motors for peasants in exchange for agricultural products.)

CTC officials reported progress in elevating the status of Cuban women, estimating that women accounted for 30% of the work force and asserting that male resistance to women holding jobs was waning.

1971 power shortage. The New York Times reported Oct. 3, 1971 that Cuba had been experiencing in the past months the worst power shortage since the 1959 revolution.

The Times cited a speech in which Castro reportedly said the situation was particularly serious in four of Cuba's six provinces, including Havana. Castro also said that the power shortage would not ease before the end of 1972.

Tobacco crop up. The government announced May 19, 1972 that despite harm caused by a tropical storm in 1971, the tobacco crop had shown a 57% increase during the current season.

Oil production falls. Cuba's annual petroleum production had fallen from a peak of 200,000 metric tons in 1970 to 125,000 tons, increasing the island's already heavy dependence on the Soviet Union for oil supply, the Miami Herald reported Sept. 11, 1972. Soviet oil shipments to Cuba had reportedly reached 3.9 million metric tons annually, up by about 75,000 metric tons from 1970.

The decrease in domestic oil production was widely attributed to the failure of the Guanabacoa oil fields east of Havana, discovered in 1968.

Construction industry gains. Improvements in the construction industry were reported in 1972.

The director of the national budgeting department said the construction industry had completed more work during the first nine months of 1972 than in all of 1970–71, it was reported Nov. 3. Improved labor productivity was reported to have been a major factor.

Economy shows gains. Recently published statistics for 1972 showed most sectors of the economy had reached, and some had exceeded, their annual production targets for the second year in a row, the New York Times reported Feb. 4, 1973. Despite continuing problems of mismanagement, the economy was recovering from the disatrous drops in production in 1970, which stemmed from the effort to produce a 10 million ton sugar crop, the Times reported.

The gains, however, had not yet affected the average Cuban, for whom most consumer goods remained strictly rationed, the Times reported. The government Feb. 1 had further reduced meat quotas in view of a shortage attributed to higher prices of imported feed grass, a shortage of fishmeal, droughts during the past three years and the 1971 epidemic of African porcine fever, which necessitated the killing of 600,000 pigs and hogs.

According to the Times, the gains followed a reorganization of the economy, with a greater emphasis on production costs. The government decided to expand or modernize existing plants whenever possible before building new ones, and waged an all-out effort against worker absenteeism. Cubans were encouraged to work harder through a scheme that partially restored material incentives and gave better workers a priority for receiving consumer goods. In several sectors factories and production centers were encouraged to compete with one another in reaching production targets, the Times reported.

Government & Communism

Cabinet changes. The government announced a major cabinet change Aug. 19, 1970, the third in less than two months. Domestic Trade Minister Manuel Luzardo Garcia, a member of the Communist Party Central Committee who had served in the post since the early part of Fidel Castro's regime, was replaced by Capt. Serafin Fernandez Rodriguez, a little-known army officer. Fernandez, until his new appointment, had been in charge of food supplies for the armed forces for seven years.

The government announced Aug. 21 the formation of the Ministry of Merchant Marine and Ports to be headed by Lt. Cmdr. Angel Cheveco Hernandez, a senior naval officer.

Nora Frometa Ilva, general secretary of the Cuban Women's Federation in Camaguey Province, was named minister of light industry, it was reported Oct. 15. She succeeded Enrique Escalona.

It was announced Dec. 4 that Faure Chomon had been replaced as transportation minister by Maj. Antonio Enrique Lusson, a member of the Communist party Central Committee.

Maj. Eddy Sunol Ricardo, an interior vice-minister and member of the Communist Party executive committee, committed suicide July 1, 1971. The newspaper Granma reported that serious injuries Sunol suffered during the Cuban revolution had resulted in a chronic brain disease which reduced his capabilities.

Government reorganized. Cuba's government structure was reorganized Nov. 24, 1972 as seven Cabinet ministers were promoted to vice premier and entrusted individually with specific and broad responsibilities. The move, approved by the Council of Ministers following a "reorientation" of the Communist party, was made "to facilitate the direction, coordination and control of workable central state administrative organs, and to create better conditions for [Premier Fidel Castro] to devote his full attention . . . to achieving the greatest unity and organization of our state."

Each of the seven new deputies would supervise several ministries and previously independent state agencies, and be responsible directly to Castro. With the premier, President Osvaldo Dorticos and First Vice Premier Raul Castro, they would form a new executive committee of the Council of Ministers, whose decisions would have to be followed to the letter by local officials.

Six of the seven new deputies were army officers, continuing a recent trend toward military influence in the government. The lone civilian promoted was Carlos Rafael Rodriguez, an old-line Communist party leader who as minister without portfolio had been Castro's chief foreign policy operative. Rodriguez would be in charge of the Foreign Ministry and the economic, scientific and technical collaboration commission.

The other vice premiers:

Maj. Ramiro Valdes—construction and related agencies; Maj. Guillermo Garcia Frias—communications, transport, merchant marine and ports; Maj. Pedro Miret Prieto—basic industries, mines and metallurgy; Maj. Flavio Bravo Pardo—light industry, food and internal commerce; Maj. Belarmino Castilla Mas—education, culture and science; Maj. Diocles Torralba Gonzalez—sugar.

President Dorticos, long one of Cuba's most powerful men, was assigned control of the Central Bank, the Foreign Trade, Labor and Justice Ministries, the Central Planning Commission and the National Fishing Institute. Raul Castro, the only vice premier before the reorganization, was given no new duties but remained head of the armed forces. However, Premier Castro was said to exercise direct supervision over the armed forces, as well as the Interior and Health Ministries, agrarian reform, the Council of Ministers and the presidential secretariat.

U.S. State Department sources cited by the Associated Press Nov. 26 said they had expected a government reorganization in view of Soviet dissatisfaction with the management of the Cuban economy, particularly the lack of adequate planning.

Havana party. Jose R. Machado Ventura became first secretary of the Communist Party of Havana province, the New York Times reported June 12, 1971.

Party unit enlarged. The Political Bureau had decided to add four members to the Secretariat of the Central Committee of Cuba's Communist Party, El Nacional of Caracas reported Feb. 8, 1973. The new members, added to "strengthen the activities" of the party unit, were: Maj. Antonio Perez Herrero, head of the army's political section; Isidoro Malmierca, subdirector of the National Fishing Institute; Raul Garcia Pelaez, ambassador-designate to the Soviet Union; and Labor Minister Jorge Risquet. The Secretariat had previously had only seven members, including Premier Fidel Castro, First Vice Premier Raul Castro and President Osvaldo Dorticos.

Casas heads forces. It was reported Sept. 22, 1971 that Maj. Zenen Casas had been appointed chief of the armed forces general staff.

Laws offered for public discussion. Five draft laws had been submitted for public discussion at work places, in rural communities, committees to defend the revolution, military units and elsewhere, it was reported Feb. 2, 1973. The laws concerned crimes against the economy, against the family and children and against "the normal development of sexual relations," and covered the improper use of military uniforms and criminal responsibility at age 16.

Other Developments

Prisoners & arrests. Among developments involving political prisoners in Cuba and political arrests:

Sixteen Cuban exiles chained themselves to the conference table in the U.N. Security Council at U.N. Headquarters in New York March 13, 1971. They demanded rights for political prisoners in Cuba. U.N. guards later removed the demonstrators from the empty chamber.

Heberto Padilla, winner of Cuba's 1968 national poetry prize, was arrested in Havana March 20, 1971. He had been criticized for "counter-revolutionary writings." Padilla was then freed April 27 without explanation.

Sixty European and American intellectuals, including Jean-Paul Sartre, Simone de Beauvoir, and Susan Sontag, had signed a letter to Premier Fidel Castro in April expressing their disillusionment with Castro at the treatment of Padilla. The letter, made public in Paris May 20, said the signatories had favored the Cuban revolution but were ashamed at the Padilla case.

The letter was in response to a confession which Padilla was said to have made while in prison. In the confession, circulated outside Cuba by the Cuban press agency, Padilla described himself as a coward, a liar and a "vicious character" who had taken part in counter-revolutionary activities, especially in conversations with foreign intellectuals.

Radio Havana said May 26 that Padilla had denounced the protest letter as "a pretext to attack the Cuban revolution and fuel the reactionary hate against all Socialist countries."

Castro June 6, in a broadcast answering the 60 intellectuals, denied that physical torture had been used to exact the confession from Padilla.

Castro declared that the intellectuals were guilty of the "most infamous calumny" against the Cuban regime and were "cynical enemies of socialism." Castro affirmed that "the noble tradition of never resorting to physical violence and torture" had not yet been violated by the "armed forces of the revolution."

The Miami Herald reported July 22,

1971 that armed forces firing squads had executed three Cubans charged with killing two members of the armed forces and an Interior Ministry agent, stealing their uniforms, weapons and identity documents. Four other Cubans were reportedly sentenced to long prison terms for hiding the condemned men.

Two men who had flown from Florida were reported Nov. 24, 1971 to have been sentenced to four years' imprisonment in Cuba after landing their light plane at a Cuban airfield without permission June 26.

The two men, identified by the U.S. State Department as Steve Ruth and Russell Lease, were convicted of illegal entry and violation of Cuba's airspace.

A revolutionary tribunal sentenced the French photographer Pierre Golendorf, arrested March 19, 1971, to 10 years in prison "for espionage against Cuba for the CIA," the French newspaper Le Monde reported Sept. 3. The report said Golendorf had "worked" for the CIA "under the cover of his professions as a journalist, photographer and translator." Golendorf had repeatedly denied the accusations.

The Inter-American Press Association (IAPA) had announced formation of a special commission to collaborate with other groups on behalf of political prisoners in Cuba, according to the Miami Herald May 21, 1972.

Members of the commission, appointed by IAPA President John C.A. Watkins, included: Horacio Aguirre, director of the Miami Spanish-language newspaper Diario de las Americas; George Beebe, senior managing editor of the Miami Herald; and Guillermo Martinez Marquez, former director of the Havana newspaper El Pais and currently a correspondent for La Prensa of Buenos Aires.

Pedro Luis Boitel, an opponent of the Castro regime, had died earlier in 1972 in a Havana prison, apparently from effects of a hunger strike and mistreatment by prison guards, the Times of the Americas reported July 12.

Boitel, former student president of the engineering faculty at Havana University, had been jailed in 1960 for anti-Castro activities, the Times said. Before his death, he and other inmates reportedly had smuggled out a letter to the United Nations Human Rights Commission describing conditions at the La Cabana prison fortress where they were held.

According to the letter, the prisoners were subjected to "a cruel and inhumane system ... without medical aid, in dark cells....We are living skeletons."

Five legislators from Puerto Rico's Popular Democratic Party Jan. 16, 1973 urged Castro to free the estimated 60,000 political prisoners allegedly held in Cuba. They said the prisoners included 58 newsmen.

Population. The 1970 census indicated a sustained drop in Cuba's birth rate. First results were published in the newspaper Granma Dec. 31, 1970. The census indicated a population of 8,553,395 persons, up from a 1959 estimate of 6,669,000. The population growth rate had declined since the mid-1960s from a 2.5% annual increase to slightly more than 2% a year.

More Cubans in the U.S.—The U.S. Bureau of the Census reported June 11, 1972 that the population of first- and second-generation Cubans in the U.S. had increased by 351% in 1960–70.

A preliminary count by the bureau showed the number of Cubans in the U.S. had risen from 124,416 in 1960 to 560,628 in 1970. Of the 1970 total, 252,520 Cubans lived in Florida.

Rail safety stressed. A rail safety drive got under way in Cuba early in 1971. Transportation Minister Antonio Lusson announced strict disciplinary measures in an attempt to decrease the number of railroad accidents in Cuba, it was reported Jan. 8. A Havana Radio broadcast reported that 195 railroad accidents had taken place in the first 11 months of 1970, causing 43 deaths and 600 injuries. Stressing that Cuba was "determined to eradicate negligence and indiscipline in the railroad sector," Lusson said "we are going to apply drastic disciplinary measures in every violation of the safety regulations and procedures, even when no accident has been caused."

Vagrancy law announced. Radio Havana announced the terms of the new vagrancy law under which vagrants could be sentenced to as much as two years forced labor, it was reported Jan. 13, 1971. The law said all physically and mentally capable male persons between the ages of 17 and 60 had a "social duty to work." Full-time students were exempted.

Those found guilty of chronic absenteeism or vagrancy were subject to penalties of from six months to two years in labor camps. According to the broadcast, the law was to be discussed by Cuban workers in special assemblies to be held between Jan. 10 and Feb. 28 and would go into effect sometime after Feb. 28.

Premier Fidel Castro, in his year's end speech Dec. 31, 1970, had announced that the government planned a major campaign to decrease absenteeism and vagrancy and increase productivity.

Among provisions of the law, which went into effect March 17, 1971:

Whereas: in the new society, work is a social duty for all able-bodied men and women;

Whereas: our people are engaged in a great productive effort to overcome the underdevelopment to which they were subjected during imperialist domination availing themselves of their precious right to create with their own hands the cultural and material goods needed, without foreign appropriation of the product of their work;

Whereas: in contrast to the upright attitude of the vast majority of our workers, there is a numerically small social stratum that, intent on living as parasites, without working, exhibits antisocial behavior and provides a bad example for the new generations;

Whereas: loafing may take different forms, running from those persons who have no work connections whatsoever and are dedicated to a life of idleness and crime, to those who try to disguise their lazy ways with occasional work, quitting one job after another, or even to those who, while having an official work center, are repeatedly absent from their jobs and on whom all disciplinary measures adopted by the labor councils have no effect;

Whereas: the working class condemns all forms of loafing as crimes similar to robbery, unanimously repudiates the negative behavior of the loafers and demands that severe and effective measures be taken against those who, every day, round the clock, steal the social and material goods created through the efforts of the working people;

Whereas: it is necessary to provide our workers and bodies of labor justice with the means to determine and combat the antisocial conduct covered by this law; and

Whereas: in response to the people, it is the duty of the Revolutionary Government to denounce and fight against such manifestations inherited from the old society—and, consequently, adopt measures leading to the eradication of loafing and parasitism.

ON THE SOCIAL DUTY TO WORK

Article 1: All citizens who are physically and mentally fit have the social duty to work.

Article 2: All men from 17 through 60 and all women from 17 through 55 are presumably physically and mentally fit to work.

CHAPTER I. ON THE CRIME OF LOAFING

Article 3: All male citizens of working age who are fit to work and are not attending any of the schools in our national system of education but who are completely divorced from any work center are guilty of the crime of loafing.

CHAPTER II. ON THE PRECRIMINAL STATE OF LOAFING

Article 4: All male citizens of working age who are fit to work and who,

(a) connected with a work center, have abandoned the said work center for more than 15 days without any justification

(b) connected with a work center, have been punished by a labor council two or more times for unjustified absence from work, without any improvement in their behavior

are considered to be in the precriminal stage of loafing.

CHAPTER III. ON PUNISHMENT AND SECURITY MEASURES

Article 5: In such cases as those included in Article 3 of this law, the following punishment may be applied.

(1) The guilty party will be sent to a rehabilitation center for a period of from 6 months to two years, during which time he will do productive work.

(2) The guilty party will be sent to a rehabilitation center for a period of from 6 months to two years, during which time, while working outside the center, it will be his duty to spend the night at the said center.

Article 6: In such cases as those included in Article 4 of this law, the following security measures will be applied:

(1) The guilty party will be sent to a rehabilitation center for a period of no more than one year, during which time he will do productive work.

(2) The guilty party will be sent to a rehabilitation center for a period of no more than one year, during which time, while doing productive work outside the center during working hours, he will spend the night in the said center.

(3) The guilty party, while living at home, will be charged with the duty to work, subject to surveillance by the workers in his work center and the mass organizations in his neighborhood for a period of no more than one year. . . .

CHAPTER V. ON THE ACCUSATION

Article 10: The crime of loafing or the pre-criminal state outlined in this law may be reported by any person or mass organization to a unit of the Department of Public Order or other competent authorities.

In cases of abandonment of work center, the administration is obliged to make the corresponding accusation to a labor justice Regional Appellate Council.

Article 11: If the accused person claims physical or mental disability, he will be examined by a medical commission designated for this purpose, and the commission will decide on his labor capacity. . . .

U.S. professor cites progress. A Temple University (Philadelphia) professor who visited Cuba in August said the island had made so much progress in the last 13 years that he now considered it one of the leading countries in Latin America, the Miami Herald reported Sept. 24, 1972.

Dr. Albert Schatz, a professor of science and education, said he and his wife, who visited Cuba as guests of the Public Health Ministry, had "never met a people as relaxed and confident as the Cubans. That feeling of confidence, and the sense of progress in the country, are what impressed us most." He said the differences between the island and other Latin American countries with which he was familiar were striking.

Public health plan. A program of heightened public health activity in Cuba was revealed late in 1972.

The government planned to sharply increase expenditure and effort on public health measures, which would include investment in cleaning up the environment and insuring proper supplies of drinking water for the entire population, according to a report Nov. 3. It was reportedly the only program of its kind in Latin America.

1973-75: A Period of Accommodation

Barriers Against Cuba Crumble

During the 2-1/2 years that followed the U.S.-Cuban anti-hijacking accord, the Western Hemisphere countries made rapid strides in adjusting to the coexistence in the area of a nominally Marxist Cuba and the hemisphere's anti-Communist nations. By July 1975 the Organization of American States had voted to cancel its diplomatic and economic sanctions against Cuba. It took this action a mere 8-1/2 months after a similar proposal had been rejected by the same body. Prior to the OAS' July 1975 action. however, several nations of the Americas had made their own accommodations to the Cuban problem: they merely ignored sanctions and negotiated arrangements with Cuba as they found suitable.

Mexican trade. Mexico had been the sole Western Hemisphere nation to refuse to break relations with Cuba under the OAS' sanctions policy. But it was not the only country of the hemisphere to trade with Cuba.

A Mexican trade delegation had been visiting Cuba to sell more agricultural and industrial goods in exchange for Cuban nickel and rum (reported March 16, 1973). Under a signed agreement, Cuba would buy $6.4 million worth of Mexican exports.

Cuban Foreign Trade Minister Marcelo Fernandez, during a 1974 trip to Mexico, negotiated an agreement for a Cuba-Mexico shipping link-up "which will eventually reach other Caribbean ports," according to a Havana radio broadcast. Mexico purchased $310 million worth of Cuban goods in 1973, and currently exported corn, beans and steel to the island.

Francisco Javier Alejo, economic adviser to Mexican President Luis Echeverria, had said April 10, at the end of a visit to Havana, that Mexico would systematically expand its trade relations with Cuba. Mexican Foreign Minister Emilio Rabasa had visited Havana March 29–April 1, becoming the first holder of his office to do so since 1959.

The discovery of major new oil deposits in southeastern Mexico was confirmed by the Mexican government Oct. 12, 1974. Horacio Flores de la Pena, Mexico's national patrimony minister, said Oct. 15 that Cuba was the first country to have been offered oil from the new deposits. But the offer, made Sept. 12, was rejected by Cuban Premier Fidel Castro because Mexico asked payment at world prices in cash, the Miami Herald reported Oct. 19.

An 85-member Mexican trade delegation arrived in Havana Dec. 2. A report Dec. 9, following the mission's departure said Cuba agreed to buy $30 million worth of Mexican goods during the visit, and the Mexicans agreed to establish a permanent

73

trade office in Havana and hold a trade fair there in 1975.

Argentine relations. Relations were re-established between Argentina and Cuba following Hector Jose Campora's assumption of office May 25, 1973 as president of Argentina.

Following his inaugural address, Campora flew by helicopter to the presidential palace, where he received the baton of office. Two presidents, Chile's Salvador Allende and Cuba's Osvaldo Dorticos, stood behind Campora throughout.

Campora met with Dorticos May 28 and announced afterwards that Argentina and Cuba had established diplomatic relations. Dorticos hailed the resumption of ties between the two nations as "a gesture of sovereignty and independence."

Emilio Aragones Navarro, a member of the Communist party's Central Committee and director of the National Fisheries Institute, was appointed Cuba's ambassador to Argentina, it was reported June 15.

About 10 days earlier Cuba June 5 had purchased from Argentina 27,000 tons of corn, worth about $3 million, in the first commercial transaction between the two countries in 13 years. Cuba agreed two days later to import another 31,000 tons of Argentine corn, according to the official newspaper Granma June 9.

Argentina Aug. 24 gave Cuba $200 million in credits to buy trucks, tractors, agricultural machinery and other items manufactured in Argentina.

The credits had been announced Aug. 6 by Finance Minister Jose Gelbard, who had said Argentina would follow an independent international economic policy, trading with all countries of the world.

<small>The Italian-owned Fiat-Concord Co. of Argentina signed a pact to export $100 million worth of vehicles to Cuba, it was reported Dec. 30. The U.S.-owned General Motors Corp. had agreed earlier in December to sell 1,500 tractors to Cuba as part of an Argentine credit package to Cuba.</small>

More than 200 Argentine businessmen and government officials went to Havana Feb. 25, 1974 to consolidate buying accords under $1.2 billion in credits that Argentina had given Cuba in 1973.

The Argentine mission, headed by Economy Minister Jose Gelbard, included executives of the Argentine subsidiaries of three U.S. automobile firms—General Motors Corp., Ford Motor Co. and Chrysler Corp.—which were negotiating contracts to sell Cuba 44,000 vehicles worth $130 million–$150 million.

These contracts required the approval of the U.S. government, which had a regulation forbidding U.S. companies to sell goods to Cuba. The U.S. Treasury Department had confirmed Jan. 25 that the three firms had applied for licenses to sell vehicles to Cuba.

Argentine plants of the French firm Citroen and the West German concern Mercedes-Benz had already signed sales contracts with Cuba, it was reported Feb. 26. The Argentine subisidary of Italy's Fiat Motor Co. signed a contract Jan. 16 to ship to Cuba $81 million worth of railroad cars and equipment.

The U.S. agreed April 18 to issue special export licenses to the Argentine subsidiaries of General Motors, Ford and Chrysler to cover the vehicles involved, and the companies then concluded their contracts.

Under a $24.2 million agreement signed in Buenos Aires April 23, Chrysler would ship 9,000 sedans to Havana over the next three years, and establish a sales and maintenance service in Cuba. Under Ford's $30 million contract with Cuba, signed in the Argentine capital April 30, 1,000 cars and 500 heavy trucks would be shipped to Havana in 1974 and an equal number would be exported in 1975–76.

The Argentine subsidiary of General Motors Corp. agreed to sell 6,000 taxis to Cuba for about $30 million, it was reported June 26.

The U.S. had insisted that despite granting the export licenses, its policy toward Cuba had not changed. A State Department spokesman had said April 19 that the auto export decision was an "exception," and that the U.S. continued to support the OAS sanctions against Havana.

In Buenos Aires, the decision had been hailed as a major victory for Argentine foreign policy and evidence that Cuba's enforced isolation was doomed. The newspaper Cronica asserted the U.S. had been forced to admit that the export of cars to Cuba was "a sovereign Argentine decision." The English-language Buenos Aires Herald said the decision "undoubtedly signals the eventual end of the economic blockade of Cuba."

Cuba signed two shipping agreements with Argentina April 26, one for purchase of $33 million worth of ships to be built in Argentine shipyards, and another for use of Argentine technicians and materials in the enlargement and modernization of Casablanca Port in Havana Bay.

Cuba had become Argentina's principal trade partner in Latin America, having purchased more than $500 million worth of Argentine products in less than a year, it was reported July 11.

Dorticos in Chile, Peru. President Osvaldo Dorticos visited Chile and Peru May 31–June 4, 1973 after attending Argentina's presidential inauguration and sealing the resumption of Cuba-Argentine relations. He was received warmly in all three countries.

Dorticos arrived in Chile May 31 and met June 2 with President Salvador Allende. At a press conference June 3, he attacked the U.S. for not recognizing major changes in Latin America and merely continuing to play its role of hemispheric "policeman." He said there would be no contacts to improve U.S.-Cuban relations until the U.S. "unilaterally halts the blockade of Cuba."

Dorticos continued to Peru June 4, where he conferred with President Juan Velasco Alvarado on "continental and Latin American problems." The two presidents praised their countries' processes of change, with Dorticos asserting: "Our revolutions travel different roads, but both point toward the beautiful horizon of continental liberation."

Velasco thanked Premier Fidel Castro for his friendship toward Peru and his concern over Velasco's health. Castro had sent specialists and orthopedic equipment to help Velasco recover from his recent leg amputation, according to a report April 14.

Cuba & Chile. Following the overthrow and death of Chile's Marxist President Salvador Allende Sept. 11, 1973, Castro's Cuba became involved in a propaganda war with the junta that had defeated and replaced Allende.

The junta said Sept. 12 it had expelled 150 Cuban extremists. It broke diplomatic relations with Cuba Sept. 13.

Cuba charged in a complaint to the United Nations Security Council Sept. 12 that the Chilean armed forces had attacked its embassy in Santiago and a Cuban merchant ship off the Chilean coast during the coup Sept. 11. The complaint also said two Cubans in Chile on World Health Organization scholarships had been arrested.

The charge that Allende was murdered was aired in the United Nations Security Council Sept. 17 by the Cuban representative, Ricardo Alarcon. Alarcon denounced the Chilean junta and the U.S., asserting: "It is not difficult to know where the main responsibility lies. The trail of blood spilled in Chile leads directly to the dark dens of the Central Intelligence Agency and the Pentagon."

Alarcon's remarks, interrupted at one point by shouts from angry Cuban exiles in the gallery who opposed the island's Communist government, were subsequently denounced by Chile's new representative to the U.N. and by the U.S. delegate, John Scali. The Chilean delegate, Raul Bazan, charged that Cuba's embassy staff in Chile had been training leftist guerrillas in sabotage. Scali charged Alarcon had "descended" in his remarks to "a new low, even for those who wallow in such words as normal talk."

(Princeton Professor of Politics Paul E. Sigmund asserted in the May–June 1974 issue of Problems of Communism that "Allende ... put two bullets into his head. The automatic rifle that he used was a gift from Fidel Castro.")

Chilean Foreign Minister Ismael Huerta defended the Chilean junta before the U.N. General Assembly Oct. 10.

The delegations of Cuba, the Soviet Union, Algeria, Tanzania and at least 16 other nations walked out of the Assembly as Huerta rose to speak, but there was some applause from Latin diplomats.

Huerta said the armed forces had overthrown Allende to avert a totalitarian takeover largely instigated and supported by Cuba. To support this contention, Huerta read and later distributed to newsmen a handwritten letter which, he said, had been sent to Allende by Cuban Premier Fidel Castro July 29.

In the alleged letter, Castro offered his cooperation "in the face of the difficulties and dangers obstructing and threatening the [Chilean] process." He wrote of the need for Allende to "gain time to organize forces in case the fight breaks out," and urged the president not to "forget for a second . . . the vigorous support offered by the working class."

Huerta charged foreign agents sent principally by Cuba had smuggled into Chile enough Soviet- and Czech-made weapons to equip 20,000 men. He added that more than 13,000 foreign extremists had been admitted to the country under Allende to establish "a parallel army to oppose the regular armed forces." These foreigners, Heurta charged, had become directors of public offices, taken illegal control of factories, and in a few cases, joined Chilean delegations in international negotiations.

Huerta later held a press conference in which he outlined "Plan Z," which, he claimed, had been devised by Cuba and Allende's Popular Unity (UP) coalition to seize "absolute political power" in Chile. The plan, to have been carried out Sept. 17–19, while troops were occupied in national independence anniversary celebrations, allegedly involved assassination of the armed forces commanders, political leaders, and business and management organization executives.

Cuban Ambassador Raul Roa returned to the Assembly after Huerta's address and delivered a bitter denunciation of the junta and of the U.S., which he accused of directing the overthrow of Allende.

He called Huerta "a sergeant of Goebbels," and asserted the Chilean had been telling Nazi-style "big lies" while the junta committed Nazi-style atrocities.

Chilean Ambassador Raul Bazan rose after Roa concluded and repeated Huerta's charges against Cuba. He then attacked Premier Castro personally, asserting Castro had made it his "daily pastime" to watch the execution of political opponents and to invite foreign diplomats to the spectacle.

The attack on Castro caused Roa to shout at Bazan and rush to the podium with a few other Cuban representatives to silence the Chilean. The Cubans were stopped by U.N. guards and other delegates. Eyewitnesses said later that some of the Cubans had carried pistols under their jackets and one had warned, "Be careful, I am armed!"

Sweden's ambassador to Chile, Harold Edelstam, said he and four embassy secretaries had been beaten Nov. 25 by soldiers and police who arrested a Uruguayan woman under their protection.

Edelstam asserted he and his aides were assaulted at a clinic in Santiago as they tried to prevent authorities from seizing Consuelo Alonso Freiria, who had sought asylum three weeks earlier in the Cuban embassy, under Swedish protection since Chile and Cuba broke relations Sept. 13.

The Chilean Foreign Ministry denied Nov. 26 that there had been violence at the clinic, but criticized Edelstam for trying to prevent Alonso's arrest. It alleged Edelstam had acted "improperly" because Alonso had given up diplomatic asylum in leaving the Cuban embassy.

Edelstam had vigorously defended the rights of political refugees in Chile since the military coup Sept. 11. He was credited with single-handedly preventing troops from storming the Cuban embassy and with protecting the estimated 20–32 Chilean and foreign refugees who had sought asylum there.

Troops had surrounded the Cuban embassy Nov. 6 and had arrested a Swedish newswoman and two Chilean chauffeurs of the Swedish embassy attempting to enter the building. Edelstam protested the action the next day and secured the release of the journalist—Margarethe Sourander, wife of Swedish newsman Bo Sourander, arrested and deported earlier—and the drivers. He complained that Swedish embassy automobiles were searched illegally and that he was forced to sleep at the Cuban embassy every night "to protect the refugees."

The Chilean government asserted the Cuban embassy had been surrounded because persons inside it had fired on security forces outside. Edelstam denied this.

Two freighters owned by the Cuban

and Soviet governments were detained by U.S. authorities in the Panama Canal Zone in October and November at the request of Chilean companies demanding delivery of cargo they claimed to have paid for previously.

A Cuban freighter, the Imias, was detained by U.S. federal court order Oct. 2 at the request of Chile's National Sugar Industry and its Vina del Mar Refining Co., which claimed two other Cuban vessels, the Playa Larga and the Marble Island, had failed to deliver more than 18,000 metric tons of sugar purchased for more than $8 million.

The Playa Larga had been unloading its sugar in the Chilean port of Valparaiso Sept. 11, the day of the Chilean military coup, and had escaped with much of its cargo after being bombed and strafed by Chilean air force rebels. It had met the Marble Island a day later in the Pacific and warned it not to proceed to Chile. The Chilean firms had attempted to have the Marble Island detained Oct. 1 in the Panamanian port of Balboa, at the entrance to the Canal, but the vessel had escaped.

Panama officially protested the detention of the Imias Oct. 4, asserting that under international law the U.S. had no legal jurisdiction over a vessel owned by a foreign government.

A Soviet freighter, the William Foster, was detained in the Canal Oct. 13 by order of U.S. federal Judge Guthrie Crowe, at the request of two Chilean firms claiming to have paid $309,000 for some of its cargo, including electrolytic zinc.

An out-of-court settlement was reached on the William Foster at the behest of the U.S. State Department, it was reported Nov. 7. The vessel was freed after it agreed to transfer its Chilean-bought cargo to another Soviet vessel for shipment to Chile via Peru.

The Imias was freed by court order Nov. 13, also at the request of the State Department.

Chilean ex-Sen. Carlos Altamirano, the leftist most sought by Chile's military junta, appeared Jan. 2, 1974 in Havana, where he attended celebrations marking the 15th anniversary of the Cuban revolution.

Altamirano said at a press conference the next day that he had not taken political asylum in Cuba. He asserted he had left Chile with the approval of leaders of his outlawed Socialist Party, and would return when the anti-junta resistance needed him.

Castro backs rebels. In his 1973 May Day speech, Premier Castro said Cuba had not abandoned Latin American revolutionaries trying to overthrow "reactionary oligarchic governments." He was particularly critical of Brazil, which he called "the no. 1 ally of the United States in Latin America." Castro also promised Cuban support for Venezuela if its oil dispute with Washington became more acute.

Guyana deals in 1973. Cuba and Guyana signed a commercial air agreement July 28 that would permit Guyanese citizens to fly to Africa by way of Cuba instead of England.

The state-owned Guyana Timber Ltd. had contracted to sell Cuba $350,000 worth of timber, it was reported July 5. It was the first trade agreement between the two countries.

Canadian dealings. Paul Gerine-Lajoie, president of the Canadian International Development Agency, announced Feb. 26, 1974 that Canada had signed a three-year $9 million technical assistance agreement with Cuba. The aid would be primarily for agricultural and foodstuffs industries, but would also include research/feasibility grants in mining, paper industry innovations, and animal health.

MLW-Worthington Ltd., Canadian subsidiary of the U.S.-based firm Studebaker-Worthington Inc., confirmed March 18 that its representative in Havana had signed a $15 million contract with Cuba for the sale of 30 locomotives. The signing of the contract was in defiance of the U.S. Trading with the Enemy Act of 1962. However, U.S. officials suggested, according to a New York Times report of March 19, the U.S. government was expected to simply permit the sale without official sanction or intervention. The sources also said that a formal diplomatic note sent by Ottawa to Washington Feb. 13 would be ignored. The note argued that the U.S. should not attempt to inhibit Canadian exports "through the parent-subsidiary relationship or in any other way."

The inconclusive but apparent end to this trade deal came five weeks after the parent company had submitted an application for exemption from the U.S. act and left unresolved several problems in the extra-territorial application of U.S. law and the manner in which such application could be circumvented.

MLW-Worthington's U.S. chairman had resigned and was replaced by a Canadian at a board meeting March 8 during which a vote was taken to proceed with the negotiation of the sale. Company President R. L. Grassby said that day the resignation was not related to the proposed sale and expressed the opinion that by voicing their opposition to the sale, the two remaining U.S. directors had protected themselves from prosecution under U.S. law.

Earlier, the Canadian government had strongly favored carrying out the Cuban deal. Prime Minister Pierre Trudeau told the House of Commons March 5 that "the important thing is that the Canadian government has the means to make sure this kind of deal goes through. We have the means to do it and we will exercise them."

Cuba joins Latin Group talks at U.N. Cuba was invited to participate in a caucus of the Latin American delegations to the United Nations Feb. 26, the Washington Post reported March 2, 1973.

Latin American diplomats insisted the decision to allow Cuba to participate in a discussion of regional strategy for an upcoming meeting on a law-of-the sea conference was "unique." They emphasized that Cuba remained outside the official Latin American group at the U.N.

The Cuban delegation had been excluded from similar meetings since 1961.

■ Latin American nations included Cuba in their deliberations at the United Nations' Law of the Sea Conference in Venezuela, it was reported July 13, 1974.

Cuba formally joins U.N. caucus—Cuba participated in a formal caucus of the 26 Latin American delegations to the United Nations Jan. 29, 1975. Thus ended 11 years of Cuban isolation from the Latin group, and marked another step toward full acceptance of the island's Communist government in the hemisphere.

The caucus had met informally since 1963 to prevent Cuban participation. The decision to meet formally this time was made by the caucus chairman for January, Jamaican Ambassador Don Mills, who "decided that enough of this travesty was enough," a Latin American diplomat told the New York Times. The caucus reportedly discussed Latin attitudes toward the U.N.'s work program for 1975.

Ambassador Ricardo Alarcon Quesada, who represented Cuba in the caucus, said of his inclusion: "The Latin American group now reflects the times and the spirit of the U.N. For some in it, it was a transition from the stone age to modern times in one afternoon."

OAS studies Cuba's readmission. The question of readmitting Cuba to the Organization of American States (OAS) was taken up at the OAS General Assembly held in Washington April 4–15, 1973.

■ A working group was established to find a compromise solution on the readmission of Cuba to the OAS. The group included Chile and Brazil, which represented extreme opposite viewpoints on the matter. A majority of delegates reportedly favored an end to Cuba's isolation, but backed away from an outright confrontation with the U.S., which objected to Havana's military links to Moscow and maintained that Cuba was still interfering in other countries' internal affairs.

■ The General Assembly declared that "under the [OAS] Charter, plurality of ideologies is a presupposition of regional solidarity," implying the "duty of each state to respect the principles of nonintervention and self-determination of peoples." In an apparent rebuff to Cuba, however, the assembly reaffirmed its support for a 1972 OAS resolution condemning support by one nation for "subversive, terrorist or armed activities" against another.

The OAS June 4. however, rejected a Venezuelan proposal to invite non-OAS members—presumably Cuba—to the organization's forthcoming deliberations on reform of the inter-American system.

Castro assails U.S., OAS. Premier Fidel Castro denounced the U.S., the Organization of American States and several right-wing Latin American governments in an address, made July 26, 1973, commemorating the 20th anniversary of the revolutionary assault on the Moncada barracks.

Speaking before 20,000 persons outside the old barracks in Santiago, Castro accused the U.S. of using "the most corrupt, unpopular and discredited governments in this continent"—Brazil, Bolivia, Paraguay and Uruguay—to isolate the "progressive and revolutionary states"—Cuba, Chile, Peru, Argentina and Panama.

Castro reiterated Cuba's proposal for a new inter-American organization excluding the U.S., but admitted it was not yet viable "because the U.S. still controls many [Latin] governments." He dismissed current attempts to restructure the OAS, saying "it makes no sense to revive it. Let us allow it to die a natural death."

Castro criticized "certain leaders who consider themselves part of the Third World" who drew parallels between Soviet foreign policy and U.S. imperialism. He called such comparisons "reactionary," stressing that the U.S.S.R. had provided arms to revolutionaries in Cuba, Southeast Asia, Africa and the Middle East.

Chiles on situation. U.S. Sen. Lawton Chiles (D, Fla.), speaking Aug. 31, 1973 on his return from a tour of four Latin American nations, said that many Latin governments appeared ready to disregard OAS sanctions against Cuba and unilaterally resume ties with the island's Communist government. He said such action had "some merit," and should be accepted by the U.S. as an expression of Latin American individuality.

Chiles dismissed the possibility of an early rapprochement between the U.S. and Cuba, asserting: "Right now Cuba doesn't want to resume ties with us. Cuba has an aggressive policy toward the United States. [Premier Fidel] Castro doesn't show any interest [in changing this policy] and I don't think we should take any initiative there."

Cuba asks Puerto Rico independence. Cuba asked that a U.N. committee studying the status of Puerto Rico demand immediate independence for the island, dismantling of U.S. military bases there, and abandonment of plans to build an oil superport on its western coast, it was reported Aug. 18, 1973.

Ricardo Alarcon, Cuba's ambassador to the U.N., charged at a session of the Special Committee on Decolonization that under Puerto Rico's U.S. commonwealth status, "Yankee exploiters" invaded the island and forced natives to emigrate to "the ghettoes of New York and semi-forced labor camps of New Jersey and Florida." He described the planned superport as part of a "genocidal process" in which "greedy minorities" settled in Puerto Rico, "threatening to engulf the people and threatening them with extinction."

The U.N. committee was studying whether to list Puerto Rico as a colony entitled to independence. The U.S. refused to participate, claiming Puerto Rico was not a proper subject for U.N. deliberations. The U.S. maintained the island already enjoyed self-determination, and was free to change its status to either statehood or full independence.

Cuba in new energy group. Ministers of energy and hydrocarbons from 24 hemispheric nations, including Cuba, held their Third Advisory Meeting in Lima, Peru Oct. 29–Nov. 2, 1973 and voted approval to creation of the Latin American Energy Organization (OLADE).

The organization, to be based in Quito,

Ecuador, would work for integration, preservation, coordinated marketing, rational use and defense of all regional energy resources, including oil, coal, and hydroelectric and nuclear power.

Film director denied U.S. visa. The U.S. State Department said Jan. 16, 1974 that it had denied a request by Cuban film director Tomas Gutierrez Alea for an entry visa to accept an award from the National Society of Film Critics in New York.

A visa was also denied to Saul Yelin, director of Cuba's National Film Institute, who had sought to accompany Gutierrez as an interpreter.

The award of $2,000 was for Gutierrez' 1968 film "Memories of Underdevelopment." A spokesman for the critics' society said a U.S. Treasury Department official had warned that it would be a violation of the Trading With the Enemy Act for anyone to receive the award in Gutierrez' behalf.

Denial of the visas "represents a continuation of the U.S. policy toward Cuba," said a U.S. official quoted by the New York Times Jan. 17.

Both Sides Soften, But Sanctions Remain

Interest in U.S. talks. The Cuban ambassador to Mexico, Fernando Lopez Muino, said Jan. 7, 1974 that Cuba would be willing to hold political talks with the U.S. "with the single and irrevocable condition" that Washington end its 12-year economic blockade of the island.

Continued use of the U.S. naval base on the Cuban mainland at Guantanamo was "not important" to Havana, and would not be an obstacle to the talks, the diplomat asserted.

Lopez Muino said the U.S. blockade had become a "farce" because many non-Communist nations, including Japan and most Western European countries, were now trading with Cuba. In addition, several Latin American nations had established diplomatic relations with Havana, he noted.

U.S. Secretary of State Henry A. Kissinger had said Dec. 27, 1973 that "the major obstacle to a rapprochement [between Havana and Washington] has been the hostility of the government of Cuba and its commitment to a revolutionary policy throughout the Western Hemisphere."

U.S. reaction cautious—The U.S. State Department expressed cautious interest in Lopez Muino's declarations Jan. 8.

"We are not dismissing them, we will weigh everything," said department spokesman George S. Vest. He added he did not want to "jump to the conclusion" that Lopez Muino's statements reflected a significant change in Cuban policy. (Cuban embassy sources in Mexico reportedly stressed the ambassador had merely reiterated Cuba's oft-stated policy toward the U.S.)

Eaton, Castro meet—U.S. millionaire industrialist Cyrus Eaton visited Cuba Feb. 5-10 and met with Premier Castro, President Osvaldo Dorticos and other leaders. The Cuban newspaper Granma reported Feb. 9 that Eaton had been invited by Castro and that the two had discussed Cuba's "economic problems."

Eaton, 90, told the New York Times Feb. 12 that U.S.-Cuban relations could be resumed quickly if U.S. Secretary of State Henry Kissinger took up the matter with Castro.

"It would be a fine and swift deal," Eaton said. "I carry no messages from Havana, just the clear understanding that the Cuban government and people are most favorably inclined toward a resumption of relations with Washington."

Eaton said Cuba had meant its signing of an anti-hijacking accord with the U.S. in 1973 to be a friendly gesture. "But every time Castro makes a friendly gesture, some lughead in the State Department thinks we have him over a barrel. That is why I believe that any negotiations must be conducted by an official of Mr. Kissinger's caliber, not any State Department functionary," he asserted.

U.S. efforts to improve relations with Cuba. The question of improving U.S.-Cuban relations was discussed by U.S. Secretary of State Henry A. Kissinger during talks in Mexico City Feb. 21-23, 1974 with the foreign ministers of 24 Latin American and Caribbean nations. Cuba was the only Latin American nation not represented at the conference.

The economic and political blockade of Cuba was brought up in Kissinger's private working session with his colleagues Feb. 22. Guyana's Foreign Minister Shridath Ramphal reportedly asked the U.S. secretary what kind of "Western Hemisphere community" he had in mind if Cuba were excluded.

Kissinger said at a press conference Feb. 22 that Tlatelolco was "not the appropriate forum to discuss Cuba." However, he was reported to have privately indicated he would support the recent application by Argentine subsidiaries of U.S. motor companies for licenses to sell cars to Cuba, a move that would reverse the U.S. policy of total economic blockade of the island.

The issue was brought up again at the General Assembly of the OAS, held April 19-May 1 in Atlanta, Ga.

To prepare for the assembly, Kissinger had met privately in Washington April 17-18 with the foreign ministers of 24 hemispheric nations. Their talks stressed economic issues, particularly trade, but also touched on sensitive political issues such as the continued isolation of Cuba from the inter-American system.

In moves to defuse the Cuba issue, the U.S. agreed April 18 to issue export licenses to Argentine subsidiaries of three U.S. automobile firms—General Motors, Ford and Chrysler—to sell cars and trucks to Cuba. The U.S., furthermore, did not object to the taking of a poll of OAS members to determine whether to invite Cuba to a projected hemispheric foreign ministers' meeting in Buenos Aires in March 1975.

The U.S. insisted that its approval of the export licenses did not presage a change in its Cuba policy, and officials said the decision responded to threats by Argentina to nationalize the U.S. subsidiaries if they were not allowed to sell to Cuba.

Argentine Foreign Minister Alberto Vignes April 20 called for ending the blockade of Cuba, describing it as "unrealistic and anachronistic." Peruvian Foreign Minister Miguel Angel de la Flor agreed, calling the blockade "an obstacle to the renewal of inter-American relations which weakens the institutions."

Continuation of the boycott was supported by the Chilean foreign minister, Rear Adm. Ismael Huerta, who charged: "Castroism continues to be an aggressive policy of intervention and constitutes a danger for peace and security in the continent."

Kissinger said April 21, as he left Atlanta to return to Washington, that the U.S. "will not be establishing diplomatic relations with Cuba." U.S. officials had said April 20 that Kissinger had omitted mention of Cuba in his addresses to the OAS assembly to avoid weakening President Nixon's support in the U.S. against efforts to impeach him, the Miami Herald reported April 22.

A step toward ending the isolation of Cuba was taken April 24 when Colombian Foreign Minister Alberto Vasquez Carrizosa called for consultations within the OAS to consider lifting its sanctions. "Each day, the sanctions become more fragile and less efficient," Vasquez said, after referring to the recent U.S. approval of auto sales to Cuba by U.S. affiliates in Argentina, and recent improvements in U.S. relations with other Communist governments.

Cuthbert Joseph, foreign minister of Trinidad & Tobago, called April 25 for an immediate decision to lift the Cuba embargo "by simple majority" vote. Joseph opposed Vasquez Carrizosa and other foreign ministers who favored ending the sanctions only by a two-thirds vote of the Assembly.

In the U.S., meanwhile, the Senate Foreign Relations Committee April 23 unanimously approved a resolution calling for an end to the U.S. trade embargo of Cuba and a resumption of U.S.-Cuban relations. The measure, introduced by Senator Jacob Javits (R, N.Y.), was a rider on a State Department budget bill, and was not binding on President Nixon.

Donald Kendall, chairman of PepsiCo Inc. and a close friend of Nixon, said April

23 that Congress should continue to ease the way for foreign subsidiaries of U.S. firms to trade with Cuba.

Latin nations oppose embargo. Latin American nations continued to apply pressure on the OAS and the U.S. during 1974 to end the diplomatic and economic embargo of Cuba. Among the moves:

- Mexican Foreign Minister Emilio Rabasa, a major opponent of the sanctions, met with U.S. Secretary of State Henry Kissinger June 8 and with Kissinger and President Ford Aug. 29. Cuba was discussed at each meeting. Rabasa said Aug. 29 that Kissinger did not indicate the U.S. would block moves among Latin nations to lift the sanctions. Kissinger said the U.S. would study the matter, Rabasa reported.

- Outgoing Colombian President Misael Pastrana Borrero urged the OAS July 23 to reconsider the isolation of Cuba. President-elect Alfonso Lopez Michelsen and Venezuelan President Carlos Andres Perez said Aug. 3 that they intended to resume relations with Cuba. Perez, however, noted his country's "commitments" to the OAS and said he would first support an initiative to lift the OAS sanctions.

(Premier Fidel Castro had made friendly references to Venezuela July 26, and Perez cited these in his statement. Castro added Cuba was prepared to cooperate with the majority of governments in the Americas which were unwilling to obey "the dictates of imperialism" and were capable of pursuing an independent foreign policy.)

- Costa Rican Foreign Minister Gonzalo Facio said Aug. 27 that the sanctions would be lifted before November. He asserted 17 OAS member states—one more than the required two-thirds majority—were prepared to vote against the measures.

(Diplomatic sources quoted by the Washington Post Sept. 7 said Cuban Foreign Minister Raul Roa had met secretly with U.S. representatives in Switzerland while on an official visit there Aug. 27–Sept. 3. Roa denied this Sept. 7 and reaffirmed Cuba's long-standing refusal to begin talks with the U.S. unless Washington lifted its economic embargo of the island.)

The OAS sanctions were imposed in 1964 because of Cuba's alleged interference in the internal affairs of Venezuela. Venezuela's OAS representative, Jose Maria Machin, said Sept. 19 that his country now had "no grievance to air" with Cuba.

Panama ties renewed. Cuba and Panama officially resumed diplomatic, economic and cultural relations Aug. 22, 1974.

U.S. aide visits. Pat M. Holt, chief of the staff of the U.S. Senate Foreign Relations Committee, visited Cuba June 29–July 8, 1974. He conferred with Premier Castro and other officials. After returning to the U.S., he issued a report calling the trade embargo of Cuba a "failure" and urging a change in U.S. policy toward the island.

Holt's trip was arranged by correspondence between Castro and Sen. J. William Fulbright (D, Ark.), the committee's chairman, and was planned as a "fact-finding" mission to inform the committee on Cuban "reality." The U.S. State Department said July 5 it had approved the trip "reluctantly" and stressed it signified no change in U.S. policy toward Havana.

The department Sept. 5 also approved reluctantly the request of two committee members, Sens. Jacob Javits (R, N.Y.) and Claiborne Pell (D, R.I.) to visit Cuba in the next few weeks.

Holt, who met with Castro July 6, said in his report that "Cubans would welcome better relations with the United States." However, Cubans emphasized the lifting of the U.S. trade embargo as "the sine qua non of a change in Cuban policy toward the United States," he declared.

Holt asserted the ostensible reason for the isolation of Cuba—Castro's support for revolutionary movements in the hemisphere—had been "at a minimal—one might even say trivial—level for years in other than an ideological sense. Cuban policy now recognizes that there is more than one road ... to economic development. The Cubans have been particularly impressed by the military government of Peru."

Holt said there were still shortages of goods in Cuba, "but they are more of an inconvenience than a hardship." With the help of "massive assistance from the Soviet Union and high world commodity prices," he stated, "the Cubans are on the verge of making their system work—that is to say, of constructing a Socialist showcase in the Western Hemisphere."

Holt said the Cuban per capita gross national product was among the highest in Latin America, and "while some slums are visible, the extremes of poverty that can be seen throughout the rest of Latin America simply are not visible there."

Kalman Silvert, a New York University professor and a Ford Foundation program adviser for Latin America, also visited Cuba in July, the Washington Post reported Aug. 24. Frank Mankiewicz, director of Sen. George McGovern's (D, S. Dak.) 1972 presidential campaign and currently head of the National Executive Council, visited Cuba July 17–20 and filmed about 12 hours of talks with Premier Castro.

Mankiewicz said Aug. 2 that Castro envisioned a resumption of normal relations with the U.S., but added there was "more to the problem" than the lifting of the U.S. trade embargo. "That is one of the tangibles," Mankiewicz stated, "but there are some intangibles too." He asserted Castro was willing to offer some concessions to the U.S.

Castro had said July 2 he would be willing to meet with Kissinger if the embargo were lifted. He said there was "no moral or logical justification for the blockade," and called Kissinger "a realistic man."

Ford on policy toward Cuba. At a televised news conference Aug. 28, 1974, U.S. President Gerald R. Ford was asked whether he contemplated any change in U.S. policy toward Cuba.

Ford said that policy was determined by the sanctions voted by the Organization of American States (OAS) "and we abide by those actions." If Cuba changed its policy toward the U.S. and its Latin neighbors, he said, "we, of course, would exercise the option, depending on what the changes were, to change our policy. But before we made any change, we would certainly act in concert" with the other OAS members.

Javits, Pell see Castro. U.S. Senators Jacob Javits (R, N.Y.) and Claiborne Pell (D, R.I.) visited Cuba on a personal factfinding mission Sept. 27–30, 1974. They conferred with Premier Castro and other government officials on the possible renewal of relations between Washington and Havana.

Javits said on their return to Washington that he and Pell felt "the Cuban government, Premier Castro particularly, were interested in working for better relations with the United States."

The two senators met with Castro for three hours Sept. 29, one day after the Cuban leader delivered a blistering attack on the U.S. in a speech commemorating the 14th anniversary of the founding of the grass-roots Committees for the Defense of the Revolution (CDRs). Senators Javits and Pell, who watched the speech on television, said they took strong exception to it in their meeting with Castro, but it did not otherwise affect their visit to Cuba.

At a midnight news conference after their talk with Castro, the senators said the premier had been "very cordial" and had discussed with them all outstanding problems between the U.S. and Cuba.

Javits said he had forcefully outlined U.S. objections to Cuban policies, including the separation of Cuban families, expropriation of U.S. property, and alleged torture and summary executions. "I have no euphoria about settling these profound problems," Javits added. Pell noted that the senators had "even asked to see some political prisoners." (Javits and Pell had talked to political prisoners on a housing construction project in Havana before their meeting with Castro, the New York Times reported Sept. 30.)

The two senators had met Sept. 28 with President Osvaldo Dorticos and Foreign Minister Raul Roa, and had listened to a speech on Cuba's health administration. Javits said Cuba had made "fantastic medical progress" in recent years.

The senators visited Cuba without the sanction of the State Department, which granted them visas for the trip but twice asked them to postpone it "in the national interest," according to press reports. Both were members of the Senate Foreign Relations Committee, which they briefed immediately after returning to Washington.

Sen. Gale McGee (D, Wyo.), a member of the committee, said Sept. 30 that Javits and Pell had brought home "no surprises," but that their visit to Cuba had made further talks between Havana and Washington possible and had generally "loosened the situation."

Javits said at a press conference Oct. 1 that a thaw in U.S. relations with Cuba would lead to a reduction of Soviet presence on the island, which would be "good for us and good for the Russians" because it would ease friction between Moscow and Washington.

It would be wrong "to believe that the Soviets can be replaced in Cuba," Javits said, but "their presence can be greatly reduced by an improvement in relations." He noted that Havana's harbor was "full of Russian ships, and Russian money is pouring into the country ... This is not good for America."

Sen. James Buckley (R-Conservative, N.Y.) urged Sept. 30 that the U.S. require Cuba to "renounce its alliance with the Soviet Union" in exchange for any improvement in relations. He said Cuba, with Soviet help, had built a deepwater port at Cienfuegos which could easily become a forward base for Soviet nuclear submarines in the Caribbean. He added that Cuba's intelligence services were financed by Moscow to such an extent that they were virtually a "Western office of the KGB."

Buckley called Oct. 1 for a national debate "before we plunge ahead" and renew relations with Cuba. "We seem to be caught on a drift moving us uncritically toward a relaxation of sanctions against the Castro regime," he said.

Another Republican senator, Barry Goldwater (Ariz.), had expressed strong reservations about the trip by Javits and Pell and the momentum toward improved U.S.-Cuban relations. "As long as [Cuba] is under Communist control, we should ignore her," Goldwater said Sept. 28.

Castro blasts U.S.—Castro severely criticized the U.S. in his speech Sept. 28 on the anniversary of the creation of the CDRs.

He denounced President Ford's recent appeals to oil producers to cut their prices, asserting world inflation was due not to high petroleum prices but to the U.S. "war budget" of "hundreds of billions of dollars." The implicit threats in Ford's appeals constituted an attempt to divide Third World countries, he added.

Castro denounced Ford's defense of covert U.S. activities to undermine the government of the late Chilean President Salvador Allende, asserting that Washington now "openly proclaims the right to intervene by any means, no matter how illicit, dirty or criminal, in the internal processes of the nations of the hemisphere." The "clean and revolutionary blood of Allende, who was assassinated Sept. 11, 1973, is an indelible stain on the North American government," he declared.

Castro praised Venezuela for raising its oil prices, and urged all Latin American nations to support Caracas in this move. He warned that U.S. policy toward Venezuela would harden as soon as it nationalized the oil and iron industries, both currently controlled by U.S.-based corporations.

Castro also urged Venezuela to come to the aid of other Latin nations, investing part of its growing oil wealth in the development of hemispheric neighbors.

Castro scorned the Organization of American States, which was considering lifting its political and economic sanctions against Cuba. The premier described the agency as a "prostitute, shameless and ridiculous," and called for creation of a parallel organization which excluded the U.S.

Castro's words were cheered by hundreds of thousands of Cubans who attended the speech. Twenty-nine U.S. journalists accompanying Sens. Javits and Pell to Cuba also attended the address.

The Commission on U.S.-Latin American

Relations, an independently financed organization of U.S. businessmen, scholars and former government officials, sent a report to President Ford Oct. 29 urging him to end the U.S. trade embargo of Cuba and make other major changes in U.S. policy toward Latin America.

"The United States should change its basic approach to Latin America and the Caribbean," the report declared in its opening sentence. "We strongly believe that the policies which the United States has inherited from the past—including many of their most basic assumptions and goals—are inappropriate and irrelevant to the changed realities of the present and the trends of the future."

The report warned that if the U.S. did not end its policy of isolating Cuba, it might become the isolated nation "as one Latin American country after another renews relations" with Havana. "Economically, the U.S. embargo is ineffective," the report added. "It may serve as much to deny American manufacturers a chance to compete for exports as it does to deprive the Cuban regime of supplies."

OAS retains Cuba sanctions. The Organization of American States (OAS) upheld its diplomatic and commercial embargo of Cuba at a meeting of hemispheric foreign ministers in Quito, Ecuador Nov. 12, 1974.

A resolution to lift the embargo failed to gain the required two-thirds majority of the 21 nations that had signed the Inter-American Treaty of Reciprocal Assistance, or Rio Treaty, under which the sanctions were imposed. Twelve countries voted for the resolution, three voted against, and six—including the U.S.— abstained.

The favorable votes were cast by Venezuela, Colombia and Costa Rica, which jointly introduced the resolution Nov. 10, and Argentina, Ecuador, El Salvador, Honduras, Mexico, Panama, Peru, the Dominican Republic and Trinidad & Tobago. Chile, Paraguay and Uruguay voted against the resolution, and Brazil, Bolivia, Haiti, Guatemala and Nicaragua joined the U.S. in abstaining.

Opponents of the embargo had predicted Nov. 8, when the Quito meeting began, that they had the 14 votes needed to pass the resolution. However, Bolivia and Guatemala, which had publicly opposed the embargo, decided during the meeting to abstain.

Diplomats quoted by the Washington Post Nov. 13 explained that the Bolivian government had shifted after an abortive coup attempt against President Hugo Banzer Suarez and that the Guatemalan foreign minister had been told that his country's military officers would not stand for a vote to lift the embargo.

The U.S. refused to take part in the debate on the embargo, and was criticized for it by supporters of the resolution, particularly Venezuelan Foreign Minister Efrain Schacht Aristeguieta and Colombian Foreign Minister Indalecio Lievano. Lievano asserted Nov. 12 that the U.S. "does not have any policy" toward Latin America.

Foreign Minister Gonzalo Facio of Costa Rica blamed the U.S. for the resolution's failure, calling Washington's professed neutrality "negative." "We have helped the United States when they needed us, and now that we need their help they do nothing," Facio asserted Nov. 11.

The chief U.S. delegate, Undersecretary of State Robert S. Ingersoll, explained Nov. 12 that the U.S. had remained silent "because we wished to avoid even the appearance of influencing by our remarks or our actions the outcome of this meeting. We have not voted no and we have not worked against the resolution."

Ingersoll said the U.S. had opposed the Quito meeting, but had been "persuaded by other nations that [the embargo] should be discussed."

The 12 supporters of the resolution issued a statement Nov. 12 assailing the embargo as "anachronistic, ineffective and inconvenient" and warning that the resolution's failure "seriously compromises the authority of the OAS." They called the requirement of a two-thirds majority "absurd" and "contrary to the democratic sense that should govern international bodies."

The statement implied that more OAS nations would join the seven that already ignored the sanctions. However, Ecuador, an opponent of the embargo, said Nov. 16

that it would not renew relations with Cuba in the near future.

Jamaican Mines Minister Allan Isaacs called Nov. 16 for a new hemispheric organization which included Cuba and excluded the U.S. Jamaica was an OAS member but was ineligible to vote at Quito.

Juana Castro, sister of Cuban Premier Fidel Castro, and Carlos Prio Socarras, a former Cuban president, traveled to Quito on behalf of Cuban exiles, reportedly at the invitation of Chile. However, they were placed under police custody Nov. 7 when they attempted to hold a press conference. Ecuadorean officials said they had been admitted on the condition that they make no declarations.

(Anticommunist Cuban exiles exploded a bomb at OAS headquarters in Washington, D.C. Nov. 9, causing an estimated $100,000 damage. Cuban exiles were presumed responsible for explosions at the Bolivian embassy and a Brazilian cultural center in Quito Nov. 7.)

Bars Keep Falling, Sanctions Finally End

Latin sugar cartel. Cuba and 19 other nations of Latin America and the Caribbean formed sugar producer's union to protect world sugar prices, currently at record levels.

Formation of the cartel, called the Group of Latin American and Caribbean Sugar Exporting Countries, was announced Nov. 28 by Francisco Cano Escalante, president of the Mexican National Sugar Commission, following a meeting of representatives of the member nations Nov. 25–27 on the island of Cozumel, off Mexico's Caribbean coast.

Castro hint on U.S. relations. Premier Castro said in an interview in the Dec. 1, 1974 issue of Oui, a U.S. sex magazine, that relations between Cuba and the U.S. "should exist, and we hope peacefully, because we are not interested in wars or aggressions." Sol Linowitz, a former U.S. ambassador to the OAS, said Dec. 17 that U.S. Secretary of State Kissinger had implied to him that Washington might support lifting the two-thirds vote rule which enabled the OAS to retain the sanctions.

A Harris Poll published Dec. 16 reported that U.S. citizens approved a renewal of relations with Cuba by a 50%–34% margin, virtually unchanged from 1973.

The U.S. had approved a record 814 requests in 1974 by citizens seeking to travel to Cuba, it was reported Feb. 2, 1975.

Ties with Bahamas established. Cuba established diplomatic relations with the Bahamas Nov. 30, 1974.

Venezuelan & Colombian ties resumed. Cuba resumed full relations with Venezuela Dec. 30, 1974.

Of the 12 members of the Organization of American States (OAS) which voted in November to lift sanctions against Havana, Venezuela was first to renew relations. Colombia, which also had voted to lift sanctions, announced Dec. 23 that it would allow local affiliates of multinational corporations to resume exports to Cuba. Foreign Minister Indalecio Lievano said his government would consider renewing ties with Havana in 1975.

Premier Fidel Castro had said Nov. 30 that Cuba welcomed renewed relations with all OAS member states that had voted to lift the sanctions. However, he again rejected the possibility of Cuba rejoining the OAS, asserting Cubans were "patiently waiting for that imperialist instrument to disintegrate."

Cuba and Colombia agreed March 6, 1975 to resume full diplomatic relations. Lievano called this another step toward "dismantling the Cold War in Latin America."

The next day Cuba released six Colombian sailors who had been imprisoned in Cuba 10 months earlier when the British ship on which they worked was captured "violating Cuban territorial waters."

Kissinger hints U.S. policy change. Secretary of State Kissinger said March

1973–75: A PERIOD OF ACCOMMODATION

1, 1975 that the U.S. was prepared to move in a new direction" in its policy toward Cuba, and that he would consult with Latin American leaders on ways to end Cuba's hemispheric isolation during a scheduled visit to the region in April.

Kissinger's remarks, made at a Civic Club luncheon in Houston, were interpreted in the U.S. press as an overture to the government of Premier Fidel Castro.

Kissinger said the U.S. would "consider changes in its bilateral relations with Cuba" if the Organization of American States lifted its diplomatic and commercial embargo of the island, presumably at its General Assembly in May. However, he asserted the U.S. decision would be "heavily influenced by the external policies of the Cuban government," particularly its "military relationships with countries outside the hemisphere."

"Fundamental change cannot come," Kissinger said, "unless Cuba demonstrates a readiness to assume the mutuality of obligation and regard upon which a new relationship must be founded."

"We see no virtue in perpetual antagonism between the United States and Cuba," he declared. "We have taken some symbolic steps to indicate that we are prepared to move in a new direction if Cuba will."

These steps presumably included government approval Feb. 14 of a sale of office furniture to Cuba by the Canadian subsidiary of Litton Industries, Inc. and the easing Feb. 17 of travel curbs on Cuban diplomats at the U.N. (The Cubans were newly permitted to travel within a 250-mile radius of New York City. They had been restricted to a 25-mile radius.)

Lifting of the travel restrictions had been suggested to the Ford Administration earlier by Sens. Jacob Javits (R, N.Y.) and Claiborne Pell (D, R.I.), who visited Cuba in 1974, and by Sen. Edward Kennedy (D, Mass.) who declared Feb. 9 that the U.S. policy of isolating Cuba in the Western Hemisphere had been a failure.

Kennedy introduced a bill in the Senate March 4 to end the U.S. embargo on trade with Cuba as well as punitive measures against third countries and shipping companies that dealt with the island. Javits and Pell introduced a resolution asking President Ford to consider taking steps to improve relations with Cuba and to report to the Senate by June on what he had accomplished.

Two other senators had urged a change in the Administration's policy before Kissinger's Houston address. Sen. John J. Sparkman (D, Ala.), chairman of the Senate Foreign Relations Committee, said in a statement in the Congressional Record that "our policy of isolating Cuba has been a failure, and it is time to reexamine that policy with a view toward ending the futile economic boycott and restoring normal relations," it was reported Feb. 3. Sen. Gale McGee, (D, Wyo.), chairman of the Senate Subcommittee on Western Hemisphere Affairs, said "this isolationist policy is a luxury we cannot afford, especially at a time when our relations with the rest of the hemisphere are subjected to serious problems over economic matters," it was reported Feb. 8.

The U.S. Defense Department warned in its annual report that Cuba, aided by the Soviet Union, was successfully exploiting anti-U.S. sentiment in several Latin American nations, the Miami Herald reported Feb. 22. The report added that Latin America was a crucial area in U.S. foreign policy, where "hostile foreign influence" could "endanger the security of the United States."

U.S. gestures—There were continued indications of U.S. desire to normalize relations with Cuba. Among them:

U.S. State Department official Kempton B. Jenkins told the Mexican newspaper Excelsior April 21 that Cuba had stopped exporting subversion, had freed the majority of its political prisoners and had abolished forced labor camps, and that its relations with the Soviet Union were more technical than military. Consequently, Jenkins said, "Cuba is not a threat to the United States."

A law professor and three law students from Havana University were allowed to enter the U.S. April 21 to attend an international moot court competition in Washington. They were the first Cubans in many years to be admitted to the U.S. for a private professional meeting, according to the Washington Post.

It was reported April 22 that a few days earlier Cuba had released four U.S. citizens serving prison terms for marijuana smuggling. The terms were not yet completed.

U.S. Representative Jonathan Bingham (D, N.Y.) introduced a bill in the House of Representatives April 24 to end the trade embargo of Cuba. The bill matched one introduced in the Senate earlier by Senator Edward M. Kennedy (D, Mass.).

The Washington-based Association of American Chambers of Commerce in Latin America May 4 asked the Ford Administration to end the prohibition on trade with Cuba by U.S.-based firms in Latin America.

McGovern visits; Castro asks improved ties. U.S. Senator George McGovern (D, S.D.) visited Cuba May 5–8, 1975 at the invitation of Premier Fidel Castro. During the visit Castro publicly called for improved relations between Havana and Washington.

At a press conference late May 7, between extended talks with McGovern, Castro asked the U.S. to end its commercial embargo of Cuba. He vigorously denied reports that Cuba had participated in the assassination of President John F. Kennedy in 1963, and he accused the U.S. Central Intelligence Agency of making several attempts on his own life.

Then, facing the American television cameras, Castro said in English: "We wish friendship. We belong to two different worlds but we are neighbors. One way or another we owe it to ourselves to live in peace."

Castro asked the U.S. to lift restrictions on sales of medicine and food to Cuba to show its willingness to resolve its longstanding disputes with Havana. These included U.S. demands that Cuba return $2 million brought in from the U.S. on a hijacked airplane in 1972, and that Cuba release nine American political prisoners.

McGovern, who called for an end to the embargo, said May 8 that Castro had agreed to consider granting both U.S. demands and, as a symbolic gesture, to allow the parents of Luis Tiant, a Cuban-born pitcher for the Boston Red Sox baseball team, to travel to the U.S. to see their son play before he ended his major league career. McGovern added that Castro was "very much interested" in his suggestion that U.S. and Cuban baseball and basketball teams play each other as a gesture to ease relations between the two countries.

In the U.S., officials said May 8 that the Ford Administration welcomed Castro's apparent overture, but that it would not make any major unilateral moves until the Organization of American States lifted its sanctions against Cuba. Ron Nessen, President Ford's press secretary, noted that Castro "seems to have accepted what the U.S. refers to as the mutuality of obligation. Any change in status would involve the mutuality of obligations."

A U.S. State Department official, Robert Funseth, said the Ford Administration had "made it clear to Cuba that we are prepared to improve our relations." Another State official said the U.S. would like to see further gestures by Castro such as the reuniting of Cuban families currently split between the two countries.

At the May 7 press conference Castro indicated that the resignation of President Richard M. Nixon and the end of U.S. involvement in Vietnam might help restore good relations between Havana and Washington. He said Nixon had "a personal hostility to Cuba and many counter-revolutionary friends," but Ford did not. As for Vietnam, Castro said Cuba's strong opposition to U.S. policy there made it "very difficult" to improve bilateral relations.

Regarding the Kennedy assassination, Castro said Cuban involvement would have been "absurd, irresponsible, crazy and a very dangerous measure." He asserted that although Kennedy had approved the abortive Bay of Pigs invasion against Cuba, the late president was "an intelligent man who had begun to understand the errors of his policies, and perhaps Kennedy would have made some steps toward improving relations with Cuba."

Turning to the CIA, Castro said it was "not news to us" that the agency reportedly had tried to kill him and other Cuban officials after they took power in 1959. He said his security men "for many years" had uncovered plots against his government by persons allegedly trained by the CIA, and in some cases supplied with weapons from the U.S. naval base at Guantanamo in eastern Cuba.

Castro met with McGovern for an hour late May 6, after McGovern dined with Cuba's top foreign policy officials, Raul Roa and Carlos Rafael Rodriguez, and he spent nearly eight hours with the U.S. senator the next day, personally chauffeuring him on a tour of a state dairy farm, a "new town" and a rum factory outside Havana.

McGovern said May 7 that he and Castro agreed the end of the U.S. embargo against Cuba was "inevitable." He noted that the embargo had been "very difficult" for Cuba, but had failed to fully isolate the island from its hemispheric neighbors.

McGovern praised Cuba's educational system May 6, and he said May 8, summarizing his impressions of the island, that "the people are healthy, the morale is high, and Mr. Castro obviously has achieved a warm relationship of confidence with his people."

Upon his return to Washington May 9, McGovern said the next move in easing U.S.-Cuban relations was up to the Ford Administration. He asked the administration May 13 to begin sending food and medicine to Cuba as a first step toward lifting the trade embargo against the island.

(Another U.S. Senator, Charles Percy, [R, Ill.] called May 6 for an end to the embargo. He said the U.S. should act independently of the Organization of American States.)

Four-nation oil deal planned. Mexico, the Soviet Union, Cuba and Venezuela planned to cooperate in selling crude oil and petroleum to countries that lacked an oil-producing capacity, it was announced in Havana May 20, 1975.

The proposed agreement, revealed by Mexican Information Minister Jose Campillo Sainz, was in the form of a triangular trading company through which the oil commitments of one nation could be filled by another if the buyer were situated closer to the latter producer. Campillo said Mexico had granted Cuba a revolving credit line of $20 million to be used for Cuban purchase of Mexican machinery, equipment and industrial raw materials.

Dominican infiltration charged. Dominican Republic authorities arrested hundreds of members of unions and of opposition parties in June 1975 in raids ostensibly connected with a search for three leftist guerrillas who had allegedly infiltrated the country from Cuba.

The arrests began June 5, with more than 250 persons reported jailed by June 7. The army and police issued a joint communique June 7 charging that three Dominican guerrillas had entered the country "from Cuba" June 2 to prepare a terrorist campaign against the government. The three were identified as Claudio Caamano, Toribio Pena Jaquez and Manfredo Casado, all well-known leftists.

The alleged guerrilla landing was immediately ridiculed by major opposition leaders, including ex-President Juan Bosch of the Dominican Liberation Party, who charged the government had fabricated the guerrilla story to justify increased "repression" against Dominicans. However, troop reinforcements were sent June 8 into the area of the alleged infiltration, near San Jose de Ocoa, west of Santo Domingo.

The army reported June 20 it had seized three Puerto Rican Socialists June 2 after they allegedly delivered the leftist guerrillas to the Dominican coast in a boat. The three held a press conference June 23 and admitted they had acted on orders from Puerto Rican Socialist leader Juan Mari Bras, but added they had not known their passengers' identities or plans. Mari Bras immediately denied their allegation.

The Puerto Ricans later denied having transported the guerrillas, telling a judge June 27 that the Dominican armed forces had "pressured" them into making false confessions. They told their lawyers June 27 they had been tortured.

The newsletter Latin America commented June 13 that although the alleged guerrillas might have landed in the Dominican Republic, any support for them from Cuba was unlikely, as Cuba was cultivating good relations in the Caribbean. Even U.S. officials discounted the possibility of Cuban support, the newsletter reported.

OAS lifts Cuba sanctions. The U.S. joined 15 Latin American countries July 29, 1975 in voting to end diplomatic and commercial sanctions imposed against Cuba by the Organization of American States.

A resolution passed at a meeting of OAS foreign ministers in San Jose, Costa Rica, allowed signatories of the Inter-American Treaty of Reciprocal Assistance (Rio Treaty), under which the sanctions were invoked, to "normalize or conduct" relations with Cuba "at the level and in the form that each state deems advisable." The sanctions, imposed in 1964, were already being ignored by seven of the treaty's 21 signatories.

Costa Rican Foreign Minister Gonzalo Facio, a major opponent of the sanctions for the past three years, said after the vote that "more countries will establish relations with Cuba." But it was considered doubtful that the U.S. would renew ties with the island in the near future, according to press reports. William Mailliard, chief U.S. delegate to the San Jose meeting, would say only that there might soon be "conversations that might lead to some kind of normalization" between Havana and Washington.

There was also no indication that Cuba might seek readmission to the OAS. Premier Fidel Castro had denounced both the OAS and the Rio Treaty at a press conference in Havana June 20, calling the latter a "shameful alliance between the shark and the sardines" under which the U.S. hoped to keep Latin America disarmed to allow multinational corporations to continue to "exploit" the continent.

Voting to lift the sanctions, in addition to the U.S., were Argentina, Bolivia, Colombia, Costa Rica, Ecuador, El Salvador, Guatemala, Haiti, Honduras, Mexico, Panama, Peru, the Dominican Republic, Trinidad & Tobago, and Venezuela. Three nations—Chile, Paraguay and Uruguay—voted against the resolution, and two—Brazil and Nicaragua—abstained. Guatemala switched from abstention to a favorable vote in a gesture of "solidarity" with the majority.

Although the resolution against the sanctions received a two-thirds majority vote, it had needed only a simple majority following approval of an amendment to the Rio Treaty at a meeting of OAS delegates in San Jose July 16–26. Other reforms of the treaty approved by the delegates included an endorsement of "ideological pluralism" in the Americas and a controversial clause on "collective economic security" in the hemisphere.

The U.S. voted against the economic security amendment, asserting July 23 that "this is not the time, nor the Rio Treaty the opportunity, to try to resolve the complex economic problem."

Delegates and newspaper reporters characterized the U.S. as a prime mover in the effort to lift the Cuba sanctions at San Jose. Mailliard had committed the U.S. vote against the sanctions July 15, saying that Washington wanted Cuba to become an issue for bilateral negotiation.

Only one incident of violence was reported in connection with the San Jose meeting. The Costa Rican ambassador to the U.S., Rodolfo Silva, escaped injury July 18 when a bomb exploded near him on a street in Washington, D.C. A man calling himself "the Cuban scorpion" claimed responsibility for the explosion in a telephone call later to the Miami offices of United Press International. He claimed membership in a group whose "goal is to punish anyone who recognizes Cuba."

The Costa Rican government carefully screened applicants for visas to visit the country beginning June 1, in an effort to avert demonstrations related to the OAS meeting. Foreign Minister Facio said two anticommunist Cuban exile leaders—Carlos Prio Socarras, former president of Cuba, and Juanita Castro, sister of Fidel Castro—would not be allowed into Costa Rica for the meeting, according to press reports June 1. Other Cuban exiles were screened out as well, according to reports.

The decision to hold the special OAS meeting in Costa Rica had been made at the Fifth OAS General Assembly, held in Washington, D.C. May 8–19 with the foreign ministers of most members attending. The Assembly approved a Mexican proposal May 17 to review the OAS' diplomatic and commercial sanctions against Cuba.

The proposal, approved 14-4 with five abstentions, scheduled a meeting for July in Costa Rica to reform the article in the Inter-American Treaty of Reciprocal Assistance which required a two-thirds majority vote to lift the Cuba sanctions.

Although the U.S. abstained on the vote for the Costa Rica meeting, Mexican Foreign Minister Emilio Rabasa said he was certain Washington would eventually vote to lift the sanctions.

Voting for the Mexican proposal were Colombia, Costa Rica, Peru, Argentina, Ecuador, Haiti, Honduras, Jamaica, Panama, the Dominican Republic, Trinidad & Tobago, Venezuela and Grenada (Grenada became the 24th active member of the OAS May 8). Voting against it were Chile, Nicaragua, Paraguay and Uruguay, and abstaining with the U.S. were Brazil, Bolivia, El Salvador and Guatemala. The delegation from Barbados, which already enjoyed relations with Cuba, was absent during the vote.

The isolation of Cuba was discussed in private meetings among the delegates, but it was not on the General Assembly's agenda, which concentrated on other issues.

CIA Plots Vs. Castro

Book details CIA activities. A book describing day-to-day operations by the U.S. Central Intelligence Agency (CIA) in three Latin American countries was published in London by Penguin Books, it was reported Jan. 14, 1975. The book indicated that CIA activity in Latin America was focused on combating Castro's Cuba.

The book, "Inside the Company: CIA Diary," was written by Philip Agee, who had worked for the agency in Ecuador, Uruguay and Mexico in 1960-68.

Agee described the CIA as an instrument to frustrate revolution and protect capitalism.

The book listed nearly 250 persons whom Agee called officers, local agents, informers or collaborators of the CIA. They included businessmen, labor and student leaders, and politicians in the countries where Agee served; in Mexico, Agee named as collaborators two former presidents, Gustavo Diaz Ordaz and Adolfo Lopez Mateos, and the current president, Luis Echeverria Alvarez.

Agee said that during his years in Latin America, the CIA's main objective was to counteract Cuban influence in the hemisphere. He described CIA infiltration of local political parties, cooperation with local police forces to eliminate leftist subversives, tampering with local mail services, and wiretapping embassies of Communist countries.

The truth of Agee's account was not questioned, according to press reports. Miles Copeland, a former high-ranking CIA official, said in a review of the book in the British magazine the Spectator: "The book is... an authentic account of how an ordinary American or British 'case officer' operates... All of it... is presented with deadly accuracy."

CIA linked to assassinations. Daniel Schorr, Washington correspondent for CBS News, said Feb. 28, 1975 that a CIA inquiry had developed evidence of agency involvement in assassination plots against at least three foreign leaders. Schorr said that President Ford was concerned that public disclosure of the plots would embarrass the U.S. and damage relations with one foreign nation.

Schorr reported that the assassination plots had been uncovered by James R. Schlesinger, CIA director for part of 1973, when he asked agency employes to report to him any questionable activities with which they were familiar. In August 1973, Schorr said, Schlesinger prohibited such activities.

Ford was reportedly orally informed of the involvement in December 1974 by William E. Colby, current CIA director, who at that time also gave Ford a written report on covert domestic activities of the agency.

The Washington Post reported March 6 that the CIA was concerned about the effect of investigations into the agency's alleged involvement in assassination plots against Fidel Castro of Cuba, the late Rafael Trujillo of the Dominican Republic and the late Patrice Lumumba of the Congo (now Zaire).

The CIA refused comment on the report, the Post said.

According to an unidentified government source, the Post said, the CIA had acknowledged in private that two episodes in Cuba and the Dominican Republic might have been carried forward by persons with close agency connections. The source insisted that the killing of Lumumba in 1961 had been done by individuals not in contact with U.S. intelligence.

The Post also identified a former Army captain and CIA operative named Bradley Ayers, who related that he had accidentally discovered in 1963 a team of marksmen trained in Miami for "an assassination effort against Castro." Ayers said John Roselli, reputedly a top Mafia figure, was the case officer for the team. Ayers added that the team's captain "made jokes" about the assassination, "quite frankly."

The Post also noted that an account of CIA involvement in the 1961 killing of Trujillo was contained in "Inside the Company," the recently-published diary of ex-CIA operative Philip B. Agee. Agee wrote that the late Ned P. Holman, a CIA station chief in Latin America, had admitted being "deeply involved in planning the assassination, which was done by Cuban exiles from Miami using weapons we [the CIA] sent through a diplomatic pouch."

CIA death plot against Castro claimed. Two aides of the late Robert F. Kennedy said that he had told them in 1967 that the CIA had collaborated with the Mafia in a plot to assassinate Castro, the New York Times reported March 10, 1975. According to Adam Walinsky and Peter B. Edelman, assistants to Kennedy when he was attorney general and a senator, Kennedy told them he had played an active role in aborting the plot.

Kennedy "told us that he had discovered that the CIA had made a contract with the Mafia to hit Castro," Walinsky said. Kennedy had also disclosed to them, Walinsky said, that he had received "assurances in writing" from the CIA that the attempted assassination had been called off. Neither man knew how Kennedy had learned of the alleged plot, although Walinsky noted that Kennedy had learned of CIA-Mafia connections while serving as a member of a Presidential panel reviewing the CIA's planning for the Bay of Pigs invasion of Cuba in 1961.

Meanwhile, Time magazine reported March 9 that "credible sources" within the CIA contended "that the CIA enlisted the hired-gun help of U.S. Mafia figures in several unsuccessful attempts to kill Cuban Premier Castro both before and shortly after the CIA-planned Bay of Pigs invasion." Time said the CIA received the help of John Rosselli and San Giancana, reputed members of the Mafia.

L. Fletcher Prouty, retired Air Force colonel who once served in the Defense Department's Office of Special Operations, said April 27 that in "late 1959 or 1960" he had handled a Central Intelligence Agency request for a small, specially equipped Air Force plane to fly a two-man assassination team into Cuba to kill Premier Castro.

The men, both Cuban exiles, were "equipped with a high-powered rifle and telescopic sights" and "knew how to get to a building in Havana which overlooked a building where Castro passed daily," Prouty said.

The plane, an L-28 "Heliocourier," returned safely to Eglin Air Force Base in Florida, he said, but the "Cuban exiles as far as I know were picked up between where they were left off and town."

Prouty explained that he had come forward now only because of criticism Richard Helms, director of the CIA in 1966–73, had directed at Daniel Schorr, who had reported that President Ford was worried that investigations of the agency would uncover assassination plots against foreign leaders. Helms, who had just emerged from over three hours of testimony before the Rockefeller Commission April 26, angrily said, "I don't know of any foreign leader that was ever assassinated by the CIA." Before his statement, Helms had directed profanities at the CBS-TV newsman and had referred to him as "killer Schorr" for reporting that the "CIA goes around killing people."

Prouty said he was upset because he was "positive" that Helms knew about the mission to kill Castro. At the time of the mission, Prouty said, Helms was in almost total control of clandestine CIA operations against Cuba.

CIA, government links cited. The interior ministers of nearly all Latin American governments "collaborated" with the U.S. Central Intelligence Agency, according to David A. Phillips, former chief of CIA operations in Latin America.

Phillips told a press conference in New York May 10, 1975 that although the officials worked with the agency, they did not know "everything that the agency does" in their countries. The CIA's major preoccupation in Latin America was uncovering "the activities being prepared" by the Soviet and Cuban intelligence services, he added.

Phillips denied that the agency had organized the overthrow of any Latin American head of state—notably, the late Chilean President Salvador Allende—but he conceded that "this type of operation might have been discussed as a possibility."

Former President Jose Figueres of Costa Rica had said in an interview March 9 that most Latin American presidents collaborated with the CIA, and that he personally had worked "in 20,000 ways" for the agency. Figueres praised the CIA for its "excellent work in espionage and counterespionage," but he expressed regret that the agency had frustrated several plots against Latin American military dictators on which he had worked during the past three decades.

Rockefeller Panel ends CIA probe. The blue-ribbon Presidential commission investigating charges of illegal domestic activities by the Central Intelligence Agency (CIA) completed its probe May 12, 1975. The panel was known as the Rockefeller Commission since its chairman was Vice President Nelson A. Rockefeller.

C. Douglas Dillon, vice chairman of the panel, said that "with one or two major exceptions" the CIA's domestic activities were peripheral and connected in one way or another to the legitimate work of the agency. The commission's report was submitted to President Ford June 6 and made public June 10, but Ford withheld the section of the report concerning assassination plots against foreign leaders.

Henry A. Kissinger, secretary of state, and James R. Schlesinger, secretary of defense, gave closed-door testimony before the commission May 5. Speaking to reporters afterward, Kissinger said that neither he nor the National Security Council (NSC), which he directed, had been involved in domestic spying. Moreover, Kissinger pointed out that while the NSC was supposed to direct the CIA, the NSC was not alone in having a direct channel to the CIA.

Schlesinger, who headed the CIA for six months in 1973, supported Kissinger's contention that the CIA had received directions from "senior officials" in the Nixon White House who were not members of the NSC.

In his remarks May 12, Dillon confirmed for the first time that the commission had looked into allegations that the CIA had been involved in plots to assassinate foreign leaders. Acknowledging that these allegations concerned Cuban Premier Fidel Castro and Rafael Trujillo, the Dominican Republic dictator assassinated in 1961, Dillon declined to discuss any conclusions the commission might have reached. He confirmed that the commission had delved into the allegations at the request of President Ford.

On the matter of the assassination of President Kennedy in 1963, another subject of investigation, Dillon said that he had "no knowledge" that Kennedy had been killed in retaliation for CIA assassination plots against Castro. (Schlesinger May 5 had labeled such theories as "simply preposterous.")

This re-examination of the Kennedy assassination had been prompted by charges by Dick Gregory, the comedian and activist, that a film of the assassination clearly showed Kennedy being shot from the front and not from behind as the Warren Commission had found. The evidence indicated that the assassination was a CIA plot, Gregory said. A news photograph, taken shortly after the killing, purportedly showed Dallas police holding men resembling convicted Watergate burglars E. Howard Hunt Jr. and Frank Sturgis, both of whom were CIA employes at the time.

Other conspiracy theorists suggested that Oswald acted as an agent for the Soviet Union. However, CBS News reported May 9 that Lt. Col. Yuri I. Nosenko of the Soviet secret police, the KGB, who defected to the U.S. 10 weeks after the assassination, told the CIA that the KGB had considered Lee Harvey Oswald mentally unstable and possibly a U.S. agent.

Another theory was based on Oswald's visit to Havana only a few months before the assassination. According to proponents of the theory, Oswald acted on orders from Cuban Premier Castro, who was retaliating against attempts by the CIA to assassinate him.

Former President Lyndon B. Johnson was said to have believed Castro was connected with the assassination. In her syndicated newspaper column April 24, Marianne Means related a conversation she had with Johnson about a year before his death in 1973. Johnson told her in confidence, Means wrote, that he thought Oswald had acted alone but was under either "the influence or the orders" of Castro. Lee Janos, a former aide to Johnson, also wrote that Johnson had speculated shortly before his death "that Dallas had been in retaliation for the thwarted attempt" to kill Castro, it was reported April 28.

However, Castro May 7 called the theory untrue, and said it would have been "irresponsible" for Cuba to have involved itself in the Kennedy slaying.

Meanwhile, it was reported by the New York Times May 20 that the Rockefeller Commission and a select Senate committee investigating U.S. intelligence operations had obtained secret FBI memos supporting publicized charges that the CIA had contracted with Mafia in 1961 to kill Castro.

According to the Times' sources, J. Edgar Hoover, then director of the FBI, wrote a detailed memorandum to Robert Kennedy in May 1961 informing the attorney general that apparent connections between racketeers Sam Giancana and John Rosselli had been uncovered by the FBI. The memo, a source said, indicated that the FBI had requested and received a CIA briefing about the agency's dealings with the pair. Hoover did not use the term "assassination" or equivalent euphemisms, but described the CIA's relationship to Giancana and Rosselli as "dirty business."

Kennedy, who ordered a vigorous follow-up on the matter, was eventually briefed by top CIA officials in May 1962. According to one unnamed source, Kennedy's only response was to tell the CIA that if it wanted to deal with organized crime again, it should come to him first.

Subsequently, the Times said, Kennedy informed Hoover of what he had learned. In turn, Hoover wrote another memorandum in which he expressed concern that Giancana might "blackmail" the U.S. government. This memorandum was then filed and its existence kept secret from everyone except a select group at the bureau, the Times reported.

In the 1960s, Giancana and Roselli had been the subjects of federal probes of organized crime. Giancana had spent most of 1964 in jail for refusing to answer questions before a federal grand jury in Chicago. The Justice Department considered bringing Giancana before a second grand jury, but later decided otherwise and prosecution was halted. Giancana subsequently moved to Mexico.

The middle-level Justice Department decision to stop prosecuting Giancana was based on reasoning that another attempt to bring him before a grand jury would be harassment. William Hundley, a Washington attorney formerly in charge of the organized crime section of the department, said he had been unaware of Giancana's connection to the CIA and had not been pressured by his superiors.

Rosselli, also under Justice Department scrutiny during the mid-1960s, was convicted of failing to register as an alien and of conspiracy to rig card games at a Los Angeles club. At one point, the Times said, Rosselli's lawyers sought clemency for their client on the grounds of his cooperation with the CIA. Justice Department files, a Times source said, gave no

1973-75: A PERIOD OF ACCOMMODATION

indication that favorable action was taken.

Another version under investigation in Washington involved a story—parts reported as early as 1967 by Jack Anderson, the syndicated columnist—that Giancana and Rosselli had been recruited for CIA work by Robert Maheu, the former manager of the Las Vegas, Nevada interests of Howard R. Hughes, the billionaire recluse. According this scenario, reported by the Times May 20, the involvement of the Mafia in the affair was one facet of an "elaborate" cover story for a government assassination plot.

"'If Castro had been killed, it would then be possible to make it appear that the mob did the job because Castro had cut off their gambling interests in Havana,'" said a Times source familiar with the scenario. For their part, the source said, gangland leaders would say the assassination had been their work.

According to an Associated Press report May 24, the Rockefeller unit had obtained the minutes of a 1962 White House meeting during which the assassination of Castro had been discussed. Although the idea was dismissed, the AP's unnamed sources said, an assistant to Robert S. McNamara, then secretary of defense, two days later ordered the Central Intelligence Agency to prepare contingency plans for the assassination of Castro. That memo was quickly withdrawn, one AP source indicated, adding, however, that other U.S.-sponsored plots against Castro were subsequently planned.

The sources said the April 10, 1962 meeting had been attended by McNamara, Secretary of State Dean Rusk, CIA Director John A. McCone and McGeorge Bundy, national security adviser to President Kennedy. The McNamara assistant who wrote the memorandum was then-Col. Edward G. Lansdale. The minutes described a meeting of a special group known as Operation Mongoose, which was responsible for all covert activities against Castro.

Time and Newsweek magazines reported May 25 that discussions on deposing or eliminating Castro from power were held at the highest levels of the Kennedy Administration. Time cited "credible" sources who said that President Kennedy and his brother, then-Attorney General Robert F. Kennedy, angry over the 1961 defeat of CIA-backed Cuban exiles at the Bay of Pigs, ordered U.S. government agencies to find some means to "depose" Castro. Whether the Kennedys authorized assassination attempts against the Cuban leader was still unclear, Time said.

Newsweek, which attributed its report to a "highly placed intelligence source," said a major effort had been made by the Kennedy Administration to "get rid" of Castro. "Like several other informants," Newsweek said, "this source was careful to say that the intention had been to 'eliminate' Castro; there were at least perfunctory hopes that he could be removed from power without shedding his blood. But this source implied strongly that the decision, made at the highest levels of government, did not preclude outright assassination."

Kennedys said to seek Castro removal. Maj. Gen. Edward G. Lansdale (ret.) told the New York Times in a phone interview May 30, 1975 that in late 1961 Attorney General Robert F. Kennedy, acting on behalf of President Kennedy, instructed him to prepare contingency plans to depose Castro.

Although he said he had never been ordered by either Kennedy brother to plan the assassination of Castro, Lansdale, a retired Air Force general and expert in counter-insurgency warfare, conceded that in later operational planning, assassination as a possible means of removing Castro from power might have been contemplated.

In November or December 1961, Lansdale said, Robert Kennedy asked him to come up with contingency plans to remove Castro. The planning focused on picking a cadre of Cubans from exile groups in the U.S. This politically cohesive group was to be then sent to Cuba, where it would hopefully foment a popular uprising against Castro, Lansdale said. He added that this idea was "never feasible" because he was unable to find the "20 or 30" Cubans necessary.

Lansdale, who indicated the plan had been formulated because of intelligence reports that Castro was negotiating with the Soviet Union, said he could not remember writing a memorandum, mentioned in press reports May 24, concerning the possible assassination of Castro. Nonetheless, he explained, he knew as he prepared the plan that "operationally down the pike, something like this could emerge—not only assassination but other things like defamation of character," which would be in the form of propaganda attacks discrediting Castro in the eyes of his supporters.

John A. McCone, director of the CIA 1961-1965, also shed light on CIA plots against Castro. Speaking to newsmen after giving secret testimony to the Senate select committee June 6, McCone confirmed that the CIA had planned and undertaken steps to assassinate Castro. McCone, who claimed not to have been told of the attempts on Castro's life even after he became head of the agency, said all of the schemes were "aborted" and that the principal effort was stopped soon after the failed Bay of Pigs invasion in April 1961. He had become aware of the CIA's efforts after reviewing agency files in the previous few months, McCone said.

McCone said the chain of command for the assassination plots against Castro was murky "because the people involved are dead," including Presidents Eisenhower and Kennedy, former Attorney General Robert F. Kennedy, former CIA Director Allen Dulles and former Secretaries of State John Foster Dulles and Christian Herter.

Kennedy scores Rockefeller 'innuendos'. Sen. Edward M. Kennedy (D, Mass.) June 16, 1975 criticized Vice President Nelson Rockefeller for implying that John F. Kennedy and Robert F. Kennedy might have been involved in CIA assassination plots against Cuban Premier Castro.

Rockefeller June 15 had suggested that the late president and his brother might have been aware of CIA plots to kill foreign leaders. Stating that the evidence with regard to assassinations was inconclusive, the vice president added, "I think it's fair to say that no major undertakings by the CIA were done without either the knowledge and/or the approval of the White House."

President Ford, who made the Rockefeller commission's findings public June 10, said he would not release a section of the commission's report on assassinations because it was "incomplete and extremely sensitive."

Given Rockefeller's "failure to fulfill his duty on the issue," Kennedy said, "I hope he'll have the decency to maintain his silence ... Such comments come with especially bad grace from the Vice President whose own CIA commission avoided the question of assassination and passed the buck to Congress."

Giancana slain, Rosselli talks. Sam Giancana, Chicago crime boss linked to CIA murder plots against Castro, was shot to death June 20 in his suburban Oak Park, Ill. home. Police said they had no leads on the killers of Giancana, 65, who was described by a spokesman for the Chicago Crime Commission as the city's most powerful mobster since Al Capone.

Meanwhile, John Rosselli, reputedly Giancana's West Coast lieutenant, testified June 24 before the Senate Select Committee on Intelligence in closed session for more than two hours. (The committee had also planned to question Giancana.)

According to Sen. Frank Church (D, Ida.), the committee's chairman, who spoke to reporters afterwards, Rosselli's testimony had "filled in, in much greater detail [the plot] and did not depart from what has been published in the press."

The published reports Church referred to said that Robert Maheu, a former Federal Bureau of Investigation agent and later a key aide to billionaire industrialist Howard R. Hughes, recruited Giancana and Rosselli on behalf of the CIA to direct an assassination plot against Castro. The racketeers, who established a base of operations in Miami Beach, were asked by the CIA in late 1960 to arrange the poisoning of the Cuban premier, his younger brother, Raul Castro, and Ernesto Che Guevara, the late Argentine revolutionary leader. The plot was subsequently aborted, the reports said, because the assassin inside Cuba entrusted with the mission was never able to get close enough to the Cuban leaders to poison their food as planned. The purpose of the killings was to create a leadership vacuum that would make Cuba ripe for counter-revolution, the reports indicated.

(Rosselli was murdered the following year; his body was found in an oil drum in the bay near Miami in August 1976.)

Castro offers data on CIA death plots. Cuban Premier Fidel Castro, in a report turned over to the Senate Select Committee on Intelligence July 30, 1975, said he and other Cuban leaders had been targets of at least 24 Central Intelligence Agency assassination attempts between 1960 and 1971.

The allegations were set down in an 86-page report delivered to Sen. George S. McGovern (D, S.D.) by the Cuban government. McGovern, who had visited Cuba in May, made public a summary of the charges and submitted the full report, along with accompanying photographs, to the Senate committee.

Listing 24 separate plots against Castro, the report repeatedly linked the CIA to the aborted assassination attempts. Some of the plots were attributed without elaboration to groups "with CIA connections," while other efforts were said to involve "CIA agents." On several occasions, the report said, anti-Castro groups used the U.S. Naval base at Guantanamo in eastern Cuba as a haven and supply point for weapons to be used.

Sen Frank Church (D, Ida.), chairman of the Senate committee, said Oct. 5 that the CIA, over a span of "many years," made actual attempts to assassinate Castro.

Church, who said his committee had obtained evidence of actual attempts on Castro's life during the Eisenhower, Kennedy and Johnson Administrations, indicated that no conclusive evidence had been found showing that any of the presidents ordered or even knew of CIA involvement in assassination plots against foreign leaders. "We have no hard evidence that directly relates this activity to any order that was given by any president," Church said under questioning on the ABC television program "Issues and Answers."

Church confirmed a disclosure by committee member Walter Mondale (D, Minn.) Oct. 4 that the CIA during the early 1960s established an official "executive action" group to develop plans for removing foreign leaders by means that included assassination. Mondale said that Richard Helms, director of the CIA from 1966 to 1973, and Richard Bissell, former head of the agency's covert operations, had claimed that "they had 'higher-level' authorization . . . for setting up and running an institutionalized assassination capability within the CIA called 'executive action.'" However, "when we pressed them, neither Helms nor Bissell would say that any president, or anyone representing a president ever gave specific orders to undertake an assassination or develop assassination plans and capabilities," Mondale said.

Senate assassination report. The Senate Select Committee on Intelligence Nov. 20, 1975 made public a report that U.S. government officials had ordered the assassination of two foreign leaders and had been involved in assassination plots against three other foreign officials. Although four of the five leaders were assassinated, none of them died as the direct result of the assassination plans initiated by U.S. officials, the report concluded.

According to the committee's 347-page report, which was released over the opposition of the Ford Administration, Fidel Castro of Cuba and Patrice Lumumba of the Congo (now Zaire) were the targets of death plots originated in Washington. The others—Rafael Leonidas Trujillo of the Dominican Republic, Ngo Dinh Diem of South Vietnam and Gen. Rene Schneider of Chile—died as the result of coup plots, which U.S. officials had encouraged or were at least privy to.

The committee said it was unable to determine if any president had explicitly ordered the death of a foreign leader.

Among details of the report:

Plots vs. Castro—The Senate report said that as early as March 1960, CIA officials had begun plotting against Castro. Among the various schemes that were suggested:

Between 1960 and 1965, the CIA instigated at least eight separate plots against Castro, but none was successful. A box of the Cuban leader's favorite cigars contaminated with botulism toxin was delivered by the CIA to an unidentified person in Cuba in February 1961, but there was apparently no attempt to pass them on to Castro.

Robert Maheu, a former Federal Bureau of Investigation agent and later an aide to millionaire industrialist Howard R. Hughes, was contacted in August 1960 by Col. Sheffield Edwards, director of the CIA office of security, who had proposed that a member of the crime syndicate that formerly ran gambling operations in Cuba be used to kill Castro. Maheu in turn contacted racketeer John Roselli, who was told by Maheu that "high government officials" wanted to eliminate Castro.

Accepting the proposal, Roselli travelled to Miami, where he recruited exiled Cubans for the job and also met with CIA agents, who supplied poisoned pills, money and electronic gear for the assassination. A Cuban working in Castro's favorite restaurant was to administer the poison when he received the word. However, the signal did not come and the waiter returned the pills and money.

The poisoning plan was reactivated in April 1962 by CIA agent William Harvey, who turned the poisoned pills and $5,000 worth of arms and radio equipment over to a Cuban contact. (No evidence that an attempt on Castro's life occurred was uncovered, however.)

In early 1963, "Task Force W," a covert CIA group assigned to covert operations in Cuba, studied and rejected a plan to place an exploding seashell in an area in which Castro was known to skin dive.

In January 1963, a skin diving suit contaminated with a poisonous fungus was prepared as a gift to Castro from James Donovan, U.S. negotiator for the release of Cuban prisoners. This plan failed because Donovan decided to give Castro an uncontaminated suit.

An unidentified highly placed Cuban leader met with Desmond Fitzgerald, chief of the CIA special affairs staff, in August 1963 and offered to kill Castro with a high powered rifle. Fitzgerald later told in-house CIA investigators that he had rejected the offer.

In a meeting in Paris November 22, 1963, the day President Kennedy was assassinated, Fitzgerald offered a Cuban agent a poison ball point pen with a hypodermic needle too small to be felt. The agent rejected the device as amateurish.

From 1963 until early 1965, the CIA arranged for the delivery of arms and explosives for use against Castro. (The committee's report did not contain specifics on these attempts.)

Authorization—The committee acknowledged in its report that it had encountered difficulties in determining if any U.S. president had authorized a plot to assassinate a foreign leader. President Nixon had explicitly authorized the CIA to foment a military coup against Allende, an assignment the CIA undertook and failed at. There was no evidence to implicate Nixon in the bungled kidnapping attempt that resulted in Schneider's death, the report said.

Available evidence permitted the "reasonable inference that the plot to assassinate Lumumba was authorized by President Eisenhower," but this was not certain.

With regard to Castro, Diem and Trujillo, the committee report said it was impossible on the basis of the evidence uncovered to conclude that any incumbent president was involved in their deaths.

However, the report did conclude that Allen Dulles, director of the CIA during the Eisenhower Administration, had taken part in the plots against Castro and Lumumba.

McCone, who succeeded Dulles as the CIA's director, might not have known of the plots against Castro and Lumumba, the report said. But Richard Helms, director of plans under McCone and later CIA director, took part in the plots, the report said.

The committee found that in some cases officials withheld information about the assassination plots from their CIA superiors and other government officials. The report specifically criticized Bissell and Helms. Helms withheld information from President Johnson and Attorney General Robert F. Kennedy on the plots against Castro. In addition, Helms did not tell McCone of the CIA's use of underworld figures to try to kill Castro when McCone became CIA director.

Bissell on several occasions "had the opportunity to inform his superiors about the assassination effort against Castro." Yet "he either failed to inform them, failed to do so clearly or misled them."

The report said that attempts to pinpoint responsibility for various assassination plots often foundered because of bureaucratic techniques that diffused or disguised individual responsibility. "Plausible denial" insulated high officials from the covert activities of subordinates in order that these senior officials would be able to deny culpability in case the activities were discovered. To establish "plausible deniability," officials frequently resorted to "circumlocution and euphemism."

These latter techniques, the report said, were used by senior officials to deliver instructions indirectly, or by subordinates to report indirectly on their activities. The committee also found that senior officials issued "generalized instructions" that were vague enough that they could be interpreted in several ways. An example, the report said, was the order to "get rid of the Castro regime."

"The system of executive command and control was so ambiguous that it is difficult to be certain at what level assassination activity was known and authorized. This situation creates the disturbing prospect that government officials might have undertaken the assassination plots without it having been incontrovertibly clear that there was explicit authorization from Presidents."

Excerpts from report—Among excerpts from the Senate report:

To put the inquiry into assassination allegations in context, two points must be made clear. First, there is no doubt that the United States government opposed the various leaders in question. Officials at the highest levels objected to the Castro and Trujillo regimes, believed the accession of Allende to power in Chile would be harmful to American interests and thought of Lumumba as a dangerous force in the heart of Africa. Second, the evidence on assassinations has to be viewed in the context of other, more massive activities against the regimes in question. For example, the plots against Fidel Castro personally cannot be understood without considering the fully authorized comprehensive assaults upon his regime, such as the Bay of Pigs invasion in 1961 and Operation Mongoose in 1962.

Once methods of coercion and violence are chosen, the probability of loss of life is always present. There is, however, a significant difference between a cold-blooded, targeted, intentional killing of an individual foreign leader and other forms of intervening in the affairs of foreign nations. Therefore, the committee has endeavored to explore as fully as possible the questions of how and why the plots happened, whether they were authorized, and if so, at what level.

The picture that emerges from the evidence is not a clear one. This may be due to the system of deniability and the consequent state of the evidence which, even after our long investigation, remains conflicting and inconclusive. Or it may be that there were in fact serious shortcomings in the system of authorization so that an activity such as assassination could have been undertaken by an agency of the United States government without express authority.

The committee finds that the system of executive command and control was so ambiguous that it is difficult to be certain at what levels assassination activity was known and authorized. This situation creates the disturbing prospect that government officials might have undertaken the assassination plots without its having been incontrovertibly clear that there was explicit authorization from the Presidents. It is also possible that there might have been a successful "plausible denial" in which Presidential authorization was issued but is now obscured. Whether or not the respective Presidents knew of or authorized the plots, as chief executive officer of the United States, each must bear the ultimate responsibility for the activities of his subordinates. . . .

Two of the five principal cases investigated by the committee involved plots to kill foreign leaders (Lumumba and Castro) that were instigated by American officials. . . .

The Cold War setting in which the assassination plots took place does not change our view that assassination is unacceptable in our society. In addition to the moral and practical problems discussed elsewhere, we find three principal defects in any contention that the tenor of the period justified the assassination plots:

First, the assassination plots were not necessitated by imminent danger to the United States. Among the cases studied, Castro alone posed a physical threat to the United States, but then only during the period of the Cuban missile crisis, and assassination was not advanced by policymakers as a possible course of action during the crisis.

Second, we reject absolutely any notion that the United States should justify its actions by the standards of totalitarians. Our standards must be higher, and this difference is what the struggle is all about. Of course, we must defend our democracy. But in defending it, we must resist undermining the very virtues we are defending.

Third, such activities almost inevitably become known. The damage to American foreign policy, to the good name and reputation of the United States abroad, to the American people's faith and support of our government and its foreign policy is incalculable. This last point—the undermining of the American public's confidence in its government—is the most damaging consequence of all. . . .

There was insufficient evidence from which the committee could conclude that Presidents Eisenhower, Kennedy, or Johnson, their close advisors, or the Special Group authorized the assassination of Castro.

The only suggestion of express Presidential authorization for the plots against Castro was Richard Bissell's opinion that Dulles would have informed Presidents Eisenhower and Kennedy by circumlocution only after the assassination had been planned and was underway. The assumptions underlying this opinion are too attenuated for the committee to adopt it as a finding. First, this assumes that Dulles himself knew of the plot, a matter which is not entirely certain. Second, it assumes that Dulles went privately to the two Presidents—a course of action which Helms, who had far more covert action experience than Bissell, testified was precisely what the doctrine of plausible denial forbade CIA officials from doing. Third, it necessarily assumes that the Presidents would understand from a "circumlocutious" description that assassination was being discussed.

In view of the strained chain of assumptions and the contrary testimony of all the Presidential advisors, the men closest to both Eisenhower and Kennedy, the committee makes no finding implicating Presidents who are not able to speak for themselves.

Helms and McCone testified that the Presidents under which they served never asked them to consider assassination.

There was no evidence whatsoever that President Johnson knew about or authorized any assassination activity during his presidency.

The CIA officials involved in the targeted assassination attempts testified that they had believed that their activities had been fully authorized. . . .

The evidence points to a disturbing situation. Agency officials testified that they believed the effort to assassinate Castro to have been within the parameters of permissible action. But Administration officials responsible for formulating policy, including McCone, testified that they were not aware of the effort and did not authorize it. The explanation may lie in the fact that orders concerning overthrowing the Castro regime were stated in broad terms that were subject to differing interpretations by those responsible for carrying out those orders.

The various Presidents and their senior advisors strongly opposed the regimes of Castro and Trujillo, the accession to power of Allende, and the potential influence of Patrice Lumumba. Orders concerning action against those foreign leaders were given in vigorous language. For example, President Nixon's orders to prevent Allende from assuming power left Helms feeling that "if I ever carried a marshal's baton in my knapsack out of the Oval Office, it was that day." Similarly, General Lansdale described the Mongoose effort against Cuba as "a combat situation," and Attorney General Kennedy emphasized that "a solution to the Cuba problem today carries top priority." Helms testified that the pressure to "get rid of Castro and the Castro regime" was intense, and Bissell testified that he had been ordered to "get off your ass about Cuba."

The 1967 Inspector General's Report on assassinations appropriately observed:

The point is that of frequent resort to synecdoche—the mention of a part when the whole is to be understood, or vice versa. Thus, we encounter repeated references to phrases such as "disposing of Castro," which may be read in the narrow, literal sense of assassinating him, when it is intended that it be read in the broader figural sense of dislodging the Castro regime. Reversing the coin, we find people speaking vaguely of "doing someting about Castro" when it is clear that what they have specifically in mind is killing him. In a situation wherein those speaking may not have actually meant what they seemed to say or may not have said what they actually meant, they should not be surprised if their oral shorthand is interpreted differently than was intended.

The perception of certain Agency officials that assassination was within the range of permissible activity was reinforced by the continuing approval of violent covert actions against Cuba that were sanctioned at the Presidential level, and by the failure of the successive administrations to make clear that assassination was not permissible. . . .

The failure of agency officials to inform their superiors of the assassination efforts against Castro is particularly troubling.

On the basis of the testimony and documentary evidence before the committee, it is not entirely certain that Dulles was ever made aware of the true nature of the underworld operation. The plot continued into McCone's term, apparently without McCone's or the Administration's knowledge or approval.

On some occasions when Richard Bissell had the opportunity to inform his superiors about the assassination effort against Castro, he either failed to inform them, failed to do so clearly, or misled them.

Bissell further testified that he never raised the issue of assassination with non-CIA officials of either the Eisenhower or Kennedy Administration. His reason was that since he was under Dulles in the chain of command, he would normally have had no duty to discuss the matter with these Presidents or other Administration officials, and that he assumed that Dulles would have "circumlocutiously" spoken with Presidents Eisenhower and Kennedy about the operation. These reasons are insufficient. It was inexcusable to withhold such information from those responsible for formulating policy on the unverified assumption that they might have been "circumlocutiously" informed by Dulles.

The committee finds the reasons advanced for not having informed those responsible for formulating policy about the assassination operation inadequate, misleading and inconsistent. Some officials viewed assassination as too important and sensitive to discuss with superiors, while others considered it not sufficiently important. Harvey testified that it was premature to tell McCone about the underworld operation in April 1962, because it was not sufficiently advanced; but too late to tell him about it in August 1962, since by that time Harvey had decided to terminate it. On other occasions, officials thought disclosure was someone else's responsibility; Bissell said he thought it was up to Dulles, and Harvey believed it was up to Helms.

The committee concludes that the failure to clearly inform policymakers of the assassination effort against Castro was grossly improper. . . .

While we do not find that high Administration officials expressly approved of the assassination attempts, we have noted that certain agency officials nevertheless perceived assassination to have been authorized. Although those officials were remiss in not seeking express authorization for their activities, their superiors were also at fault for giving vague instructions and for not explicitly ruling out assassination. No written order prohibiting assassination was issued until 1972, and that order was an internal CIA directive issued by Director Helms. . . .

Relations With Communist & Third World Nations

London expels Cuban. It was reported March 24, 1973 that Cuban diplomat Aristides Diaz Rovirosa had been declared persona non grata by Britain earlier in the year for allegedly spying for the Soviets. He was said to have been part of a largely Latin network formed by the Russians to replace the 105 Soviet officials expelled from Britain in September 1971.

The reports said that Gerardo Peraza, a second secretary at the Cuban embassy, had defected in November 1971, apparently to the U.S.

Soviet thermoelectric contract. The Cuban regime signed a $30 million contract with the Soviet Union to expand the Mariel thermoelectric installations west of Havana, aiming at an increase in capacity from 200 megawatts to 500, it was reported Aug. 24, 1973.

Brezhnev visits. Soviet Communist Party General Secretary Leonid Brezhnev and a team of Soviet economic and political specialists visited Cuba Jan. 28–Feb. 3, 1974. They conferred with Fidel Castro and other officials on a wide range of topics, including world affairs and Soviet aid to Cuba.

The visit, Brezhnev's first to the island, had originally been scheduled for the end of 1973. Its postponement was attributed to Brezhnev's reluctance to jeopardize East-West detente by appearing publicly at celebrations of the 15th anniversary of the Cuban revolution.

A joint Cuban-Soviet communique published Feb. 4, after Brezhnev's departure, expressed hopes that detente would be strengthened and warned that "opponents of detente and advocates of a return to the Cold War are becoming more active in the United States."

The message stressed that the Soviet Union and Cuba shared a "complete identity" of views on international affairs. It demanded an end to the U.S. economic and political blockade of Cuba and to U.S. naval presence on Cuban soil at Guantanamo. It also condemned the Chilean military junta, expressed "solidarity with the people of Latin America who are waging just struggles for national liberation and ... social progress," and denounced "the imperialist policy of interference in the affairs of Latin America."

The communique made veiled attacks on China, suggesting that Cuba now fully supported the Soviet Union's campaign against Peking. It decried "hegemonistic and chauvinistic tendencies which contradict the internationalist course of communism," and backed the Soviet proposal for a collective security system in Asia, opposed by China.

(The Chinese official news agency Hsinhua denounced alleged Soviet military and economic "infiltration and expansion" in Latin America Feb. 4.)

The communique stressed plans for "wider cooperation" between Cuba and the Soviet Union in economic planning and administration, and noted Soviet pledges of "continued assistance" to the island.

Brezhnev and his party had arrived in Havana Jan. 28 to what the news agency EFE called "the warmest, most enthusiastic and massive" welcome given by Cubans to a foreign dignitary. Premier Castro, First Vice Premier Raul Castro, President Osvaldo Dorticos, members of the Politburo, members of the Central Committee and Secretariat of the Communist Party, and high-ranking armed forces officers were on hand with thousands of cheering citizens.

Castro and Brezhnev addressed a rally of an estimated one million Cubans Jan. 29. Castro said the Soviet Union had granted Cuba trade terms and long-range credits which were a model for relations between an industrial nation and a small country. "The Soviet Union ... does not own in our homeland a single mine, business or public service. It has not invested a single cent in Cuba expecting profit," Castro declared.

In a presumed reference to China, Castro condemned "pseudo-leftists and renegades of the revolutionary movement who, from allegedly Marxist stances, revile the Soviet Union, wretchedly betraying proletarian internationalism and serving the interests of imperialism."

Castro asserted "the idea of peaceful coexistence between states with different social systems is gradually making headway in international relations," and pledged Cuban support for Brezhnev's "efforts to overcome world tension and to achieve an end to the arms race."

Brezhnev said Cuba was not "an object of exploitation or of capitalist investments" to the Soviet Union, nor "a strategic base out of which influence is expected." He asserted "Soviet weapons in the hands of Cubans are not for attacking anyone."

Brezhnev stressed that Communists were not "supporters of the export of revolution." Revolution "ripens within the territory of one country or another," he said. "How and when it sprouts, and what form and methods are employed are the business of that country." The statements recalled Soviet opposition to Cuba's earlier but now abandoned policy of directly supporting Latin American guerrilla movements.

Havana radio broadcasts announced Jan. 31 that Brezhnev had pledged technical aid to Cuba to search for new sources of petroleum as part of an intensified "scientific exchange" between the Soviet Union and its allies.

Brezhnev received Cuba's highest award, the Jose Marti medal, Feb. 1. Cuba and the Soviet Union signed an aviation convention the next day. Havana radio broadcasts said only that it was a scientific and technical pact between Cuba's Civil Aeronautics Institute and the Soviet Civil Aviation Ministry.

Brezhnev departed for Moscow Feb. 3, and Soviet Foreign Minister Andrei Gromyko, who had accompanied him throughout the Cuban visit, flew to the U.S. for conferences with President Nixon and U.S. Secretary of State Henry Kissinger. His trip spurred speculation that the Soviet Union would press for a thaw in U.S.-Cuban relations.

Raul Castro in U.S.S.R. & Yugoslavia. First Vice Premier Raul Castro visited the U.S.S.R. Feb. 6–20, 1974 on the invitation of the Soviet Communist Party Central Committee. He arrived only three days after Soviet Party General Secretary Leonid Brezhnev ended a visit to Havana.

Castro proceeded Feb. 20 to Yugoslavia, where he conferred with state and Communist Party leaders and toured the country until Feb. 28.

While Castro was in Yugoslavia, the East German Communist Party chief and premier, Erich Honecker and Horst Sindermann, were in Cuba for talks with Premier Fidel Castro and other officials. The East Germans arrived in Havana Feb. 20 and departed Feb. 27.

Polish pact. Cuba and Poland April 2, 1973 signed a credit agreement covering the sugar industry and Havana shipyards, among other sectors. Polish President Henryk Jablonski made an official visit to Cuba at the end of April, reported in Granma's weekly edition May 6.

Husak visits. Czechoslovak Communist party Secretary General Gustav Husak visited Cuba April 3–7, 1973. He met with Premier Castro in what he called an atmosphere of "profound mutual understanding and agreement." He became only the second person, after Chilean President Allende, to be awarded the National Order of Jose Marti, given to heads of state and political leaders who had done "outstanding work in the struggle for solidarity and against imperialism."

Ceausescu visits. Romanian President Nicolae Ceausescu visited Cuba Aug. 29–Sept. 1, 1973 during a tour of Latin America.

He was met at the Havana airport Aug. 29 by Premier Castro, First Vice Premier Raul Castro, and President Osvaldo Dorticos. Ceausescu and his delegation subsequently discussed with Cuban officials economic and commercial cooperation, and Latin American politics, according to El Nacional of Caracas Aug. 31.

1973–75: A PERIOD OF ACCOMMODATION

Ties with Arab nations. Cuba and Algeria June 7, 1973 reached a new trade agreement in which, among other points, Cuban sugar exports to Algeria were fixed for 1974–76.

Algerian President Houari Boumedienne visited Cuba April 12–16, 1974 for talks with Premier Castro and other officials. He was decorated with the Jose Marti medal, Cuba's highest award, soon after his arrival.

The Washington Post reported that Cubans were training South Yemeni pilots to fly MiG-21 jet fighters, according to the newsletter Latin America June 29, 1973.

Kuwait and Cuba established diplomatic relations at the ambassadorial level, it was reported May 14, 1974.

Israeli Defense Minister Moshe Dayan said in a U.S. TV interview March 31, 1974 that about 3,000 Cuban troops had been deployed in Syria as part of a Soviet-aided military buildup in Syria. The London Times confirmed the Cuban presence April 2 and reported the unit was believed to have about 110 tanks.

The U.S. Defense Department April 2 confirmed the presence of Cubans in Syria, but said they only numbered 100–500 men believed serving as replacements in a Syrian armored brigade. A department spokesman said he did not know what functions they were performing in the unit. He said the Cubans had been in Syria "for some months" but was not certain they were there during the October war.

Israel's radio military commentator, Gen. Haim Herzog, had said in a broadcast April 1 that the Cuban force was probably in Syria at the Soviet Union's instigation. The presence of the Cubans was believed to have been known by Israel for some time, but newsmen were not permitted to mention them.

Chairman Yasir Arafat of the Palestine Liberation Organization (PLO) arrived in Havana Nov. 14 following his departure from New York, where he had addressed the U.N. General Assembly the previous day. Arafat conferred with Castro and other Cuban officials through Nov. 17 and then flew to Algeria.

The U.N. Assembly Nov. 22 approved a resolution, co-sponsored by Cuba, all Arab nations and several Third World countries, declaring that the Palestinian people had the right to independence and sovereignty.

Visitor from Hanoi. Havana played host to a top Hanoi official in 1974.

North Vietnamese Premier Pham Van Dong visited Cuba March 22–28. At a rally in Havana March 26, he accused the U.S. and South Vietnam of violating their accords with Hanoi. Premier Castro pledged continued Cuban economic aid for the reconstruction of North Vietnam—Havana was believed to have sent annual sugar shipments—and vowed to send more Cuban work brigades to build roads, schools and hospitals in the war-torn country.

Communists meet. Communist Party leaders from 24 Latin American and Caribbean nations held a four-day meeting in Cuba in June 1975 and issued denunciations of both the U.S. and China.

In a document released in Havana June 16, after the conference ended, the Communists denounced U.S. imperialism as their "principal and common enemy" and criticized the Chinese government for recognizing Chile's military junta and for supporting unnamed "groups of pseudorevolutionaries who ... divide the left, attack the Communist parties, block the progressive process and often behave as agents of the enemy at the core of the revolutionary movement."

The document offered other leftist parties in Latin America "mutual respect" and "a frank and total analysis" which would lead to leftist unity and achievement of a "second independence" for the continent.

Nonaligned conference. Cuba was among 76 Asian, African and Latin American member nations and nine observer nations at the fourth conference of nonaligned nations, held in Algiers Sept. 5–9, 1973.

The relationship of the Soviet Union to the underdeveloped countries became a dramatic issue at the meeting, with Cuban Premier Fidel Castro struggling against a tendency to include the U.S.S.R. among the imperialist nations, or at least among the industrial powers whose interests clashed with those of the Third World.

Libyan leader Muammar el-Qaddafi criticized "imperialist colonialism" on the part of both the U.S. and the Soviet Union in his address to the conference Sept. 6, although he said he remained a friend of the U.S.S.R. Qaddafi criticized Cuba's presence at the conference on the grounds it was aligned with the Soviet Union. Libya had submitted a proposal that both the Soviet and U.S. navies be barred from the Mediterranean, while Mali and Mauritania, both Islamic West African nations, demanded that the Soviet Union be specifically named in a resolution denouncing imperialism in the Third World, it was reported Sept. 8. Tunisian President Habib Bourguiba, referred Sept. 7 to the "peaceful coexistence of Coca Cola and vodka" at the possible expense of the Third World.

Castro strongly defended the Soviet Union in a speech Sept. 7, leading Prince Norodom Sihanouk, former Cambodian leader living in exile in Peking, to obtain rebuttal time to criticize Soviet recognition of the Lon Nol government in Cambodia. (Sihanouk obtained full recognition for his exile government from Oman, Zaire and a few other African countries at the conference.) Castro reportedly angered the Algerian hosts when he tried to prevent the representatives of Brazil and Bolivia from addressing the conference Sept. 9, because of their alleged allegiance to U.S. imperialism.

Among other resolutions passed by the conference at its closing session was one stating that the nonaligned countries would take "individual and collective measures" to help Arab countries oust Israeli forces from territory occupied in the 1967 war. The Arab nations had hoped for a declaration calling for the severance of diplomatic relations with Israel, but opposition or indifference among Asian and Latin American delegations forced a more moderate resolution. But in a surprise move, Castro announced that his country would sever relations with Israel, in what was seen as an attempt at reconciliation with Qaddafi and the Algerian leaders.

Cuba aids SELA formation. Cuba played a major role in the formation in 1975 of SELA (the Latin American Economic System), a regional unit including Cuba and excluding the U.S. The scheme had been proposed in 1974 by Mexican President Luis Echeverria Alvarez and Venezuelan President Carlos Andres Perez after the Organization of American States had refused (temporarily, as it turned out) to lift its sanctions against Cuba.

Castro Jan. 3, 1975 expressed his support for the proposed new organization. Castro had discussed the proposal earlier with Horacio Flores de la Pena, Mexico's minister of national patrimony. Castro said Jan. 3 that he had no objection to multinational corporations—envisioned in the system—"if they are Latin American and serve to develop" the region.

Perez and Echeverria issued a joint communique March 22 which denounced the U.S. Trade Reform Act as "a coercive instrument which contradicts the principles of equity which should prevail in international relations ... [and] represents a flagrant violation of the basic principles of the inter-American system [the OAS], which is frankly in crisis."

The communique proposed that the OAS be changed so it "takes into account ... the right of each nation to adopt the political and economic system which most suits it," in apparent reference to Cuba, which was still under an OAS diplomatic and commercial embargo. It suggested that Article 17 of the Inter-American Treaty of Reciprocal Assistance, under which the Cuba sanctions were imposed, be amended so a two-thirds majority was no longer required to lift such "coercive measures."

Cuba was among 25 Latin American and Caribbean nations whose representatives signed the SELA charter Oct. 17 at the end of a three-day meeting in Panama City.

Echeverria in Cuba. Mexican President Luis Echeverria Alvarez visited Cuba Aug. 17-22, 1975 at the end of a world tour. He was welcomed Aug. 17 by an estimated 500,000 citizens who cheered him in the streets of Havana. Echeverria exchanged praise with Premier Fidel Castro and asserted the Cuban revolution provided "unquestionable evidence that our time is one of social change, that our era is one of reaffirmation of the Third World, and that our task is to build a more just and humane society." Mexico had maintained relations with the Castro government since its inception and had led the successful effort in July to lift the sanctions imposed against the island by the Organization of American States (OAS).

Other Foreign Affairs

Venezuelan plane hijacked to Cuba. Four professed members of the People's Revolutionary Army (Zero Point), a guerrilla group, hijacked a Venezuelan airliner with 42 people aboard May 18, 1973 and flew it to Cuba, where the guerrillas requested political asylum.

The hijackers, led by Zero Point leader Federico Bottini, seized the plane on a domestic flight from Valera to Barquisimeto. They claimed to have a bomb, and threatened to blow up the aircraft unless the government released 79 "political prisoners," including the leading leftist guerrillas in captivity. They also accused security officials of torturing detainees.

The plane was ordered first to Curacao, where it refueled, then to Panama City, where five passengers were allowed to deplane, and then to Merida, on the Yucatan peninsula in Mexico. It continued early May 19 to Mexico City, where an official told the hijackers the Venezuelan government refused to discuss their demands.

The Mexican official, Miguel Nazar, persuaded the guerrillas not to destroy the plane and offered them either political asylum in Mexico or whatever assistance they needed to reach Cuba. They chose the latter, and the plane, with Nazar aboard, proceeded to Havana, where the hijackers were taken into custody by Cuban police. The plane and passengers were returned to Venezuela May 20.

Nicaraguan prisoners freed, flown to Cuba. Eight guerrillas of Nicaragua's Sandinista Liberation Front invaded a party at a Managua businessman's home Dec. 27, 1974 and seized several prominent officials. Through the mediation of the Roman Catholic archbishop of Managua, the guerrillas subsequently negotiated the release of more than a dozen imprisoned comrades, payment of a large ransom and safe-conduct to Cuba.

The hostages were freed Dec. 30 and the guerrillas and released prisoners were flown to Havana accompanied by the archbishop, Msgr. Miguel Ovando y Bravo, the papal nuncio in Managua and the Mexican and Spanish ambassadors to Nicaragua.

Because of strict press censorship, there was some confusion as to how many prisoners were released and how much ransom was paid. Most foreign reports put the freed prisoners at 14 and the ransom at $1 million.

The party invaded by the Sandinistas was at the home of Jose Maria Castillo, a former agriculture minister, who was killed when he apparently tried to resist the guerrillas. Two or three guards at the home (reports varied) were also killed. The Sandinistas took more than 30 hostages—including Foreign Minister Alejandro Montiel Arguello and Ambassador to the U.S. Guillermo Sevilla Sacasa—but they missed Turner Shelton, the U.S. ambassador and guest of honor, who had already left.

The guerrillas demanded the mediation of Archbishop Ovando, release of 18 imprisoned comrades, a $5 million ransom, and wage raises for all maids, workers, employes and National Guardsmen. After Ovando agreed to mediate Dec. 28, they began releasing hostages, retaining only 13 by Dec. 30.

Anti-hijack pact with Colombia. Colombia and Cuba July 22, 1974 signed an agreement to prevent the hijacking of planes and ships between their borders.

U.S. hijack money returned. U.S. Sen. John J. Sparkman (D, Ala.) announced Aug. 11, 1975 that Cuba had returned to the U.S. airline Southern Airways nearly $2 million extorted from the airline by three U.S. hijackers who landed in Havana in 1972.

U.S. continues dispute over relations—Sparkman, chairman of the Senate Foreign Relations Committee, called Cuba's action "very solid evidence that the Cuban government is genuinely interested in pursuing a policy of improved relations with the United States." He asked the Ford Administration to respond by immediately lifting restrictions on the sale of food and medicine to Cuba, and by eventually ending the U.S. trade embargo against the island.

Cuba had attempted to return the money to Southern Airways in 1972 in a check drawn on the Cuban government's account with Chase Manhattan Bank in New York, but the account had been frozen by the U.S. government in 1961 in retaliation for the expropriation of U.S. property in Cuba. The new payment was drawn on a Cuban account with the Royal Bank of Canada.

The payment was apparently made in response to a personal plea to Cuban Premier Fidel Castro by Sparkman, who described himself as an old friend of Southern Airways president Frank Hulse. Castro first announced his intention to make the payment in a letter to Sparkman May 30 and a subsequent letter to Senator George McGovern (D, S.D.) which McGovern released June 16.

McGovern said in a speech reported July 4 that Castro had "made a number of important gestures" toward improving relations with the U.S. and that there was no longer any "excuse to postpone the Cuban detente." He dismissed claims by some Ford Administration officials that the Cuban government was an "exporter of revolution," asserting: "After Vietnam, Chile and other [U.S. Central Intelligence Agency] outrages, our righteousness about exported violence must sound hollow and hypocritical—especially to a country which was invaded at the Bay of Pigs and whose leader has been the target of American assassination attempts."

Another critic of U.S. policy toward Cuba, Rep. Jonathan Bingham (D, N.Y.), charged July 23 that the State Department apparently sought to prolong U.S.-Cuban problems indefinitely by opposing a bill Bingham had introduced in the House to end the trade embargo against the island.

William D. Rogers, assistant secretary of state for inter-American affairs, had testified against the bill June 11 at a hearing by two subcommittees of the House International Relations Committee. Rogers warned that Congressional action regarding the embargo would "take away an important element of executive discretion" in the matter and "further complicate the task of putting relations with Cuba on a solid and mutually satisfactory basis."

Rogers said that "the legacy of over a decade of antagonism and diversion of trade relations elsewhere, together with the complex question of Cuba's attitude toward and respect for private enterprise and private property, as reflected in the vexed issue of compensation for claims, will restrain any great expansion of business" between the U.S. and Cuba.

However, Rogers admitted that Cuba's economy was steadily expanding and that the State Department had received requests from more than 100 firms for information about prospects for trade with Cuba.

President Ford had said in an interview with the French magazine L'Express June 14 that there were no prospects for a change in U.S.-Cuban relations in 1975 "because there has been no apparent change in the attitude of Premier Fidel Castro." Ford apparently referred to allegedly continued Cuban support for Latin American leftist guerrilla movements.

(Cuban Deputy Premier Carlos Rafael Rodriguez had asserted in London recently that Cuba supported only Latin American governments that were progressive or had progressive elements, and not leftist insurgent movements, the Washington Post reported May 31. He denied that his government backed insurgents in Chile, Uruguay or Paraguay, asserting: "The objective conditions for armed struggle exist in many places in Latin America, but the subjective conditions are not there yet." Rodriguez said Cuba would seek normal relations with the U.S. once the U.S. trade embargo were lifted, the Post reported.)

Embassy bomb blast in Lima. A spokesman for the Cuban embassy in Lima, Peru said Feb. 5, 1974 that a package bomb had exploded in the embassy the day before, wounding a woman attache and damaging the building. Stamps and postmarks on the package indicated the bomb was sent from Mexico.

Refugee leader slain in Miami. Jose de la Torriente, former Cuban minister of agriculture, was killed by a sniper's bullet in his home in Miami April 13, 1974. A political leader of Cuban exiles living in Miami, Torriente had been accused by Cuban Premier Fidel Castro of working for the U.S. Central Intelligence Agency (CIA). A Cuban group calling itself "Zero" took responsibility for Torriente's killing April 17.

U.S. airlift ends. The Cuba-Miami airlift, which had taken nearly 261,000 Cuban refugees to the U.S. since 1965, ended with two flights April 6, 1973.

France ousts Cubans. France July 10, 1975 expelled three Cuban diplomats believed to have links with a fugitive terrorist. The terrorist, known as "Carlos," was sought for the killing of two French counterespionage agents and a Lebanese informer in a Paris apartment June 27. Carlos, 25, was Ilich Ramirez Sanchez, the son of a wealthy Venezuelan Communist lawyer. Said to be connected with terrorist organizations around the world, he was the target of an intensive police dragnet in France, Great Britain and a number of other countries, but had eluded authorities.

The French interior ministry spokesman, Andre Mousset, in announcing the Cuban expulsions, expressed the belief that the intelligence services of "certain nations" had significantly aided the terrorist network. The spokesman said the expelled officials—Raul Sainz Rodriguez, first secretary for cultural affairs, Ernesto Herrera Reyes, chief of protocol, and Pedro Zamora Lara, deputy cultural attache—had been "constant visitors" to Carlos' Paris apartment.

Mousset told reporters that "the Carlos affair is one of the most important cases of international terrorism to come to the attention of any Western police force in recent years. It provides categoric proof of the unity of action of the terrorist groups operating in Europe and elsewhere, as well as of the close links between the terrorist networks and certain foreign intelligence services." He added that two Venezuelan women, who had been in touch with Carlos and the three Cubans, were also being expelled. The women were identified as Lema Palomares Duque and Albaida Salazar.

The Cuban embassy in Paris issued a statement July 10 denying any involvement in terrorist activities.

Record '73 trade reported. Foreign Trade Minister Marcelo Fernandez said Cuba's 1973 foreign trade reached a record $2.6 billion, double the 1968 volume, it was reported May 19, 1974.

Australian Prime Minister Gough Whitlam had announced May 8, 1973 that Australia was easing its trade curbs against Cuba and other Communist nations.

British deals promoted—The Cuban regime received a $16.8 million credit from the National Westminister Bank of London Sept. 17, 1974 to buy capital plant and equipment from British manufacturers. A 23-member British trade mission, the first to visit Cuba in 22 years, arrived in Havana Nov. 8, and Premier Castro conferred with its leader on agricultural problems Nov. 14.

Spanish credit & ties. Spain granted Cuba a $900 million credit as part of a trade agreement under which Cuba would buy Spanish ships and transportation equipment and Spain would buy Cuban sugar and other goods, according to a Havana radio broadcast reported by the Associated Press Dec. 18, 1974.

The agreement was reached in Havana by Cuban officials and Spanish Trade Minister Nemesio Fernandez Cuesta, who returned to Madrid Dec. 17.

Cuba and Spain exchanged ambassadors April 11, 1975. Since the early 1960s, the two nations had conducted affairs on the charge d'affaires level although the ties were officially on the ambassadorial level.

Vatican relations set. Archbishop Agostino Casaroli, secretary of the Roman Catholic Church's Council for Public Affairs, visited Cuba March 28–April 5, 1974 as a guest of the Cuban Episcopal Conference. He was the first high Vatican official to visit Cuba since the Communists took power.

Casaroli met with church officials, President Osvaldo Dorticos, Vice Premier Carlos Rafael Rodriguez and Premier Fidel Castro. Casaroli said after returning to Rome that Castro had visited him at the apostolic nunciature in Havana April 4 and they had had "a profound talk, really at quite responsible levels."

Cuba officially normalized relations with the Vatican Dec. 20.

Ties with Bonn & Iran. Cuba resumed diplomatic relations with West Germany Jan. 16, 1975 and established ties with Iran Feb. 10. The West German ties had been broken by Bonn in 1963 to protest Cuban recognition of East Germany.

Government & Politics

Judicial reform set. A sweeping reform of the judiciary, to go into effect later in 1973, was reported by the London newsletter Latin America Aug. 17.

There would be a new People's Supreme Court, with four chambers dealing with criminal, civil and administrative and military offenses, and crimes against state security. Below these would be the People's Provincial Courts, with civil and criminal chambers to deal with cases warranting sentences of up to six years' imprisonment. At the local level, People's Basic Courts would deal with offenses warranting up to six months' imprisonment.

Those convicted of crimes against the state would be sentenced according to their participation in or responsibility for the crimes if they were civilians, and would receive the death penalty if they belonged to the armed forces, according to Raul Amaro Salup, a prospective judge of the chamber on crimes against state security. All those convicted would have the right of appeal, and would be able to engage a lawyer or conduct their own defense.

The private practice of law would be banned, and lawyers would be compelled to join collective offices, of which there were currently 50, Latin America reported.

Matanzas elections. Residents of Matanzas Province elected representatives empowered to choose candidates for new municipal assemblies which eventually would cover the island, it was reported May 10, 1974.

The elections began the government's first effort to give Cuba a formal democratic structure since the revolution 15 years ago. Matanzas was chosen first because of its small size and population.

Further Matanzas elections took place June 30, runoffs July 7. All citizens over 16 years of age were eligible, and more than 90% reportedly turned out. They elected 1,114 delegates to municipal assemblies from among 4,712 candidates. The municipal delegates in turn chose 150 from their number to be regional delegates (Matanzas was divided into five regions) and the regional delegates elected 68 provincial representatives. Provincial representatives retained their regional and municipal status, according to the Journal.

Some 50% of the delegates elected were members of the Communist Party, which had a national membership of only 200,000, the Journal reported.

Following the elections, executive committees of delegates at each level began a massive inventory of everything from trucks to manpower in the province to determine the real needs of each area, the Journal reported. The national bureaucracy had often been faulted for not knowing these needs, and sending insufficient or excessive supplies to different localities. Delegates also began setting up local agencies to solve local problems more swiftly.

Although the assemblies were charged with directing economic and cultural affairs and services within the province, they would not control transportation and industry, and would conform to national priorities and standards of health and education set by the Politburo, the Journal noted.

The Wall Street Journal reported Dec. 4 that Matanzas' newly elected municipal, regional and provincial assemblies had begun to operate in this experiment to decentralize and improve public administration.

The experiment, known as "Popular Power," was expected to be extended to Cuba's other provinces if it succeeded in Matanzas. Premier Castro said July 26 that the process of democratization would culminate with elections in 1976 for a national governing council.

New constitution planned. Premier Castro said Oct. 25, 1974 that a panel headed by Blas Roca, a member of the Communist Party's Central Committee, had begun to draft a new constitution to replace the one of 1940. He said the draft should be ready for submission to the Politburo and the Council of Ministers in February 1975. It would later be reviewed by the First Congress of the Communist Party, scheduled for November 1975, and submitted to a referendum.

The draft was published by the official newspaper Granma April 10.

Cubans April 28, 1975 began public discussions of the draft of the new constitution.

The draft declared that Cuba was a socialist state of laborers, peasants and other manual and intellectual workers, with maximum power exercised by the people through popular assemblies and with the Communist Party designated as "the superior force in the society," according to the Cuban news agency Prensa Latina.

The "supreme organ of the state" would be the National Assembly of the People's Power, elected every five years by all citizens over the age of 16. The assembly's powers would include election of a Council of State composed of a president, a first vice president, five vice presidents and 24 other members. The council president would be the chief of state and head of the Cuban government.

The assembly sessions would be public, unless this was agreed to harm the national interest, and assembly members would be unsalaried. Legislation could be proposed by the state labor union and other mass organizations, and by citizens who obtained 10,000 signatures for their proposals.

The draft guaranteed "the freedom and inviolability of the individual," and freedom of speech and the press "as they conform to the goals of socialist society." It also endorsed religious freedom so long as "faith or beliefs do not oppose the revolution, education or the defense of the fatherland." Free education and health care were also guaranteed.

The draft reaffirmed Cuba's repudiation as "illegal and void" of all treaties, agreements or concessions undertaken "under conditions or inequality" or violating or diminishing the state's "sovereignty over any part of the nation's territory."

It offered asylum in Cuba to persons who were persecuted for fighting for "the democratic rights of the majorities, for national liberation, against imperialism, fascism, colonialism and neocolonialism." It also offered asylum to persons who fought for an end to racial discrimination or for the rights of "workers, peasants and students."

Cubans had also held public discussions on a new Family Code, enacted March 8, which guaranteed full equality between men and women and established the right of women to participate fully in the nation's political, cultural and economic life. The code eliminated legal distinctions between legitimate and illegitimate children, and declared that a marriage could be dissolved if a court found it to have "lost its meaning for the couple, their children and society."

(The divorce rate in the metropolitan district of Havana had risen to 48% in 1972, the newsletter Latin America reported July 18. Officials expected the rate to decline once the equality of women and the importance of their work role became socially accepted, the newsletter reported.)

Blas Roca asserted May 12, 1975 that Cuban exiles who had not participated in activities against the Castro government would still be considered Cuban citizens.

Castro had said earlier that all Cuban exiles were "no longer Cuban," according to press reports.

Other Developments

Troops aid in economic development. Cuba was increasing armed forces reserve training to free regular troops for sectors of the economy that were short of manpower, according to the head of the armed forces, First Vice Premier Raul Castro, April 16, 1973.

Other economic events. Cuban Foreign Trade Minister Marcelo Fernandez told an international sugar conference in Geneva that Cuban sugar production for 1973 had already passed 5 million tons, 1.2 million tons ahead of the 1972 pace, it was reported May 18, 1973.

Sugar production had been reported behind schedule early in April because of industrial breakdowns, irregular cane supplies and bad weather.

Cuban raw sugar production rose from 4.4 million tons in 1972 to 5.2 million in 1973 and 5.8 million in 1974, then declined to 5.5 million in 1975. Cuban sugar exports totaled 4.14 million metric tons in 1972, 4.797 metric tons in 1973 and 5.37 million metric tons in 1974. Of these totals, the U.S.S.R. imported 1.097 million metric tons (26.5% of the total) in 1972, 1.661 million (34.6%) in 1973 and 1.9 million (35.4%) in 1974. Other Communist countries imported 1.197 million (28.9%) in 1972, 1.351 million (28.2%) in 1973 and 1.37 million (25.5%) in 1974.

Cuba had become the world's second leading exporter of lobster, after Australia, and the rapidly expanding fishing industry had become a major source of foreign income (reported July 7, 1973). Living and working conditions in Cuba's fishing ports had also improved dramatically.

The government announced production in the basic industry sector had reached 101% of its target for the first half of 1973, an increase of 16% over the same period of 1972, it was reported Aug. 3.

Ordoqui freed. Authorities had released Joaquin Ordoqui Mesa, a former armed forces deputy minister placed under house arrest in 1965 for maintaining "questionable cultural contacts with an enemy agent" in Mexico, the London newsletter Latin America reported May 4, 1973.

Ordoqui's suspension from the Communist party was confirmed despite official admission that there was no conclusive proof of his "collaboration with the enemy." Ordoqui had consistently denied such collaboration.

Pena dies. Lazaro Pena, 73, secretary general of the Cuban Workers Federation (CTC) and a member of the Communist

CUBA: ESTIMATED PRODUCTION OF SELECTED FARM PRODUCTS

[In 1,000 metric tons]

Item	1972	1973	1974
Rice, rough	350	375	400
Beans, dry	23	23	23
Tobacco	40	45	50
Cassava	30	30	25
Sugar, raw	4,388	5,250	5,800
Bananas	50	50	45
Coffee	29	29	29
Beef and veal [1]	186	162	162
Pork [1]	37	44	44
Milk	540	579	585

[1] Dressed carcass weight.

Source: Based on FAO Production Yearbook, 1972, Granma, Jan. 9, 1974, FAO rice trade intelligence, and FAS.

Party's Central Committee, died March 11, 1974 after an illness. The government declared 36 hours of mourning and displayed Pena's body in the Plaza of the Revolution in Havana before burial March 13.

Roberto Veiga Gonzalez, head of the CTC's governing commission in Oriente Province, succeeded Pena as the nation's top labor leader, it was reported March 20.

Illiteracy low. Education Minister Jose Ramon Fernandez asserted the illiteracy rate in Cuba was only 4%, concentrated among adult citizens, it was reported Nov. 11, 1974. He said that Cuba had spent $700 million on educational programs in 1974.

Cuba 2nd militarily in region. Cuba was second only to Brazil in leadership in Latin America in number of active military servicemen and combat aircraft, according to U.S. Air Force magazine statistics reported by the news agency Efe Jan. 4, 1975.

Brazil had 358,000 active soldiers, followed by Cuba with 329,000 and Argentina with 162,000. Brazil had 230 combat aircraft, while Cuba had 205 and Argentina 132.

1975-77: Conflicting Objectives

Relations With U.S. Develop

Cuba and the U.S. continued to provide evidence, during the latter half of 1975 and on through 1976 and 1977, that leaders of both countries wanted to establish normal relations with each other if possible. The pursuit of conflicting objectives—exemplified by Cuba's military adventure in Angola —made this common goal difficult to achieve. Yet there were distinct improvements in U.S.-Cuban relations during this period.

U.S. eases trade embargo. The U.S. relaxed its economic embargo against Cuba Aug. 21, 1975, announcing that it would allow foreign subsidiaries of U.S. firms to sell goods to the island and that it would stop penalizing other nations that traded with Cuba.

The State Department and White House emphasized that the action was only a response to the recent decision of the Organization of American States to lift its sanctions against Cuba, and not a conciliatory gesture aimed at improving relations with the government of Premier Fidel Castro.

Castro called the action "a positive gesture," but he said Cuba would not negotiate a resumption of full relations with Washington until the trade embargo were lifted entirely. He described the embargo as a "dagger" aimed at Cuba's heart.

The changes in U.S. policy, as announced by the State Department, were the following:

■ Licenses would immediately be granted to permit "transactions between U.S. subsidiaries and Cuba for trade in foreign-made goods when those subsidiaries are operating in countries where local law or policy favors trade with Cuba." (Trading licenses would still be required, subject to U.S. regulations on exporting strategic goods, technology and U.S.-made components.)

■ Nations whose ships and aircraft carried goods to or from Cuba would no longer be "penalized by loss of U.S. bilateral assistance."

■ The Ford Administration would modify regulations that prevented refueling in the U.S. by foreign merchant vessels engaged in trade with Cuba.

■ The Administration would ask Congress to change legislation prohibiting nations that traded with Cuba from receiving U.S. food aid under Public Law 480.

White House spokesman Ron Nessen minimized the importance of the policy changes, asserting they did not "really relate to bilateral relations with Cuba."

Nessen said any further moves toward improving relations with Havana would "really depend on Cuba's attitude," including its policy toward claims by Washington on U.S. property and assets nationalized by the Cuban government.

State Department spokesman Robert Funseth noted several other issues separating the U.S. from Cuba, including "family visits in both directions; American citizens who are prisoners in Cuban jails;... Cuban's attitude on Puerto Rico [Cuba favored Puerto Rican independence], and whether Cuba is prepared to follow a clear practice of nonintervention everywhere in the hemisphere." Funseth admitted that "there certainly has been a reduction in Cuban intervention" in Latin America since 1961, when the U.S. imposed the embargo.

In Havana, Castro asserted the embargo had cost Cuba more than the compensation demanded by the U.S. for its nationalized property. Lifting of the embargo, he said, would be "a minimum condition of equality and dignity which will make it possible" for Havana and Washington to discuss their conflicts fairly.

Regarding claims in some U.S. sectors that Cuba still "exported revolution" to Latin America, Castro said: "The revolution cannot be exported... What we should talk about is the attempt by the U.S. to export counterrevolution" to Cuba, Chile, the Dominican Republic and other Latin American nations.

In the U.S., relaxation of the embargo was praised by Senators George McGovern (D, S.D.) and Jacob Javits (R, N.Y.), and criticized by Senator Jake Garn (R, Utah) and Rep. Jonathan Bingham (D, N.Y.). Garn accused the Ford Administration of acting with "no apparent regard for Senate opinion." Bingham, who favored lifting the embargo entirely, charged that the relaxation "leaves the U.S. in an even more ridiculous posture than before. Goods manufactured abroad under American auspices can now be sold to Cuba, but goods produced by American workers still cannot."

Castro admits error on 1962 missile crisis. Sen. McGovern disclosed Aug. 15, 1975 that when he had met Castro in Cuba in May, the Cuban premier had conceded that he made a mistake in seeking a showdown with President John F. Kennedy in 1962 during the Cuban missile crisis. Castro reportedly said: "I was furious when [Soviet Premier Nikita Khrushchev] compromised [with Kennedy]. But Khrushchev was older and wiser. I realize in retrospect that he reached the proper settlement... If my position had prevailed, there might have been a terrible war. I was wrong."

Castro also disclosed that Kennedy later had intended to work out a reconciliation with Cuba, the New York Times reported Aug. 23. Castro said he received a message from Kennedy to that effect from a French newsman on the day Kennedy was assassinated in 1963.

Cuba hosts parley for P.R. independence. Representatives of 79 countries and 18 international organizations attended a conference in Havana Sept. 6–8, 1975 to support the small Puerto Rican independence movement.

The delegates issued a declaration condemning Puerto Rico's commonwealth status with the U.S. as "the most flagrant act of colonialism" in Latin America. Cuban President Osvaldo Dorticos asserted at the end of the meeting that Puerto Rican independence was "not negotiable with the U.S."

Secretary of State Henry Kissinger charged Sept. 9 that Cuba was interfering in internal U.S. affairs and damaging its chances for normalizing relations with Washington. Castro replied Sept. 29 that there would "never" be a normalization if it meant Cuba must abandon support for an independent Puerto Rico. Cuban representative Ricardo Alarcon Quesada reaffirmed this position before the United Nations General Assembly Oct. 8, calling the independence movement an "admirable example of national resistance."

The U.N.'s Decolonization Committee had held hearings on Puerto Rico Aug. 14–15 but had postponed until 1976 consideration of a resolution that would give the independence movement permanent observer status in the U.N. The committee heard Aug. 14 from three leaders of the splintered movement—Juan

Mari Bras, secretary general of the Puerto Rican Socialist Party; Sen. Ruben Berrios of the Puerto Rican Peace Council, and Noel Colon Martinez of the Independence Party. Mari Bras alleged that repression against advocates of independence had been increased recently by the Puerto Rican police in close association with the U.S. Central Intelligence Agency, Federal Bureau of Investigation and Secret Service.

Officials in Washington did not attach great importance to the independence movement, noting that it had not won more than 5% of the vote in any Puerto Rican election.

U.S.-Cuban baseball barred. A series between teams of United States and Cuban all-stars was vetoed by the State Department after Cuba became involved in the Angolan conflict, the New York Times reported Jan. 7, 1976.

The games, scheduled for March 21 and 22 in Havana, had been planned by two producers, Barry Jagoda and Richard Cohen. They reached agreements with the Cuban government and with Bowie Kuhn, the commissioner of baseball. ABC Sports had agreed to buy the broadcast rights to the games for $165,000.

Cuban Troops in Angola & Other African Countries

Cubans aid Soviet-backed force. Cuba admitted in the fall of 1975 that Cuban soldiers were fighting in Angola against the Portuguese and on the side of the Soviet-supported Popular Movement for the Liberation of Angola.

Unidentified sources in Lusaka, Zambia had claimed Oct. 23 that Cuban mercenaries were fighting alongside MPLA forces in Angola, the London Times reported. About 1,500 Cuban troops were alleged to be in Angola or en route from the Congo Republic where Cuban ships had reportedly docked in late September and early October.

Independence brings rival Angolan regimes—Angola's liberation movements proclaimed two distinct governments in the war-aggrieved nation Nov. 11 as Portugal granted independence to its final African colony.

In ceremonies in Luanda Nov. 10, Vice Adm. Leonel Cardoso, the last Portuguese high commissioner in Angola, announced the transfer of sovereignty to "the Angolan people," indicating that Portugal was not yet recognizing the authority of any of the nationalist movements, still waging battle throughout Angola.

Shortly after midnight Nov. 11 the Popular Movement for the Liberation of Angola (MPLA) proclaimed its leader, Agostinho Neto, president of the People's Republic of Angola. The proclamation and subsequent celebrations were conducted in Luanda, the Angolan capital and stronghold of the MPLA which also controlled the band of territory across the middle of the nation.

Hours later in Nova Lisboa, the joint formation of the People's Democratic Republic of Angola was announced by the National Front for the Liberation of Angola (FNLA) and the National Union for the Total Independence of Angola (Unita). The two movements had agreed in Kinshasa, Zaire Nov. 10 to form a joint government headed by a 24-member National Revolutionary Council.

The Luanda government of the Soviet-backed MPLA was promptly recognized Nov. 11 by the former Portuguese colonies of Mozambique, Guinea-Bissau, Cape Verde and Sao Tome e Principe. Other nations recognizing the MPLA regime that day included Cuba, the U.S.S.R. and other Communist countries.

The U.S. and other Western nations withheld recognition of either regime. In denying U.S. recognition, U.S. Secretary of State Henry A. Kissinger charged Nov. 11 that the MPLA was using Cuban as well as Soviet arms; he further stated that Havana's involvement in Angola was one of the reasons for Washington's delaying improvement in relations with Cuba.

The MPLA was soon embroiled in war, supported by Cuban troops, against the FNLA and Unita forces.

Unita leader Jonas Savimbi charged Dec. 11 that it was the Soviets and not the MPLA that had asked Cuba to send personnel to Angola to fight against the Unita and FNLA forces. Savimbi asserted that the Cubans, who were operating the sophisticated Soviet weapons for the MPLA, were being used "as cannon fodder."

Cuba's intervention in Angola on the MPLA's side further strained Havana's relations with the U.S., which was supporting the MPLA's opponents, the National Front for the Liberation of Angola and the National Union for the Total Independence of Angola. President Ford said that because of Cuba's support for the MPLA and for the Puerto Rican independence movement, "there is no chance for a quick resumption of relations" between Havana and Washington, it was reported Dec. 11.

President Ford Dec. 16 expressed through a spokesman his "serious concern" over the involvement of the Soviet Union and Cuba in Angola and appealed for "discussion in the Congress of the geopolitical significance of that part of Africa to the United States and the West."

Premier Fidel Castro paid tribute Dec. 18 to Cuban soldiers fighting in Angola and other nations, asserting "the history of the world revolutionary movement will recall this example of selflessness and heroism." The Cuban army had "shed its blood more than once in other countries threatened by imperialist aggression," Castro declared.

Castro asserted Dec. 22 that Cuba would continue to aid the MPLA and the Puerto Rican independence movement, even at the cost of continued hostility from the U.S. He accused the U.S. of plotting with "racist South Africa" to take over Angola in order to exploit its "riches in minerals and oil."

A representative of the MPLA thanked Cuba and the Soviet Union Dec. 21 for their "concrete acts" of assistance, which had enabled the movement to "face French and American tanks and cannon used by South African expansionists to invade Angola." The delegate, Lucio Lara, addressed the First Congress of the Cuban Communist Party in Havana.

In a related development, the government of Barbados asked Cuba Dec. 18 to stop using the West Indies island's airport at Bridgetown as a refueling stop for aircraft carrying Cuban soldiers to Angola. Barbados acted after receiving complaints from the U.S. Barbados, the easternmost island in the Caribbean, lay some 2,000 miles from Cuba and about 4,000 miles from the African coast.

Cuban troops in other countries—The news magazine U.S. News and World Report asserted Nov. 30, 1975 that Cuba had sent more than 5,000 regular troops to 10 countries for use "as a revolutionary force against the interests of the United States and China, and for the Soviet intelligence network."

The countries were Angola, Syria, South Yemen, Congo Republic, Tanzania, Equatorial Guinea, Guinea, Somalia, Guinea-Bissau and Sierra Leone, according to U.S. intelligence sources cited by the magazine.

U.S. officials quoted by the Miami Herald Nov. 26 had said there were about 400 Cuban military advisers in the Congo Republic and 200–300 advisers each in Malawi, Mozambique, Guinea, Cameroon and Gabon. The Cubans' duties included training African soldiers in guerrilla warfare tactics and the use of mortars and recoilless rifles, the sources reported.

U.S.S.R., Cuba criticized on Angola. President Ford spoke out strongly at his news conference Dec. 20, 1975 against Soviet and Cuban involvement in Angola.

It was "harmful" for any foreign power "to try to dominate that country," Ford said. Soviet activity in Angola, he asserted, "certainly does not help the continuation of detente."

"I want to get it on record as forcefully as I can," Ford continued, "to say the action of the Cuban government in an effort to get Puerto Rico free and clear of the United States" as well as Cuba's involvement in Angola "erodes any chance for improvement of relations" with the U.S.

The President also was critical of the Senate's vote to cut off funds for U.S. covert military support of Unita and FNLA.

In a statement released Dec. 19, Ford had called the Senate action "a deep tragedy for all countries whose security depends" on the U.S. "Ultimately," he said, "it will profoundly affect the security of our country as well."

"The issue in Angola is not, never has been and never will be a question of the use of U.S. forces," the President stressed. "The sole issue is the provision of modest amounts of assistance to oppose military intervention by two extra-continental powers, namely the Soviet Union and Cuba."

How could the U.S. take the position, Ford asked, that these countries could "operate with impunity" with troops and "massive amounts of military equipment while we refuse any assistance to the majority of the local people who ask only for military equipment to defend themselves?"

State Secretary Henry Kissinger held a news conference Dec. 23 to emphasize that the U.S. would continue to oppose imposition of a Soviet-backed regime in Angola.

While pledging that no American forces would be sent to Angola, Kissinger said the U.S. would continue to supply its available military aid to the Angolan factions fighting the Soviet-backed faction and to press for diplomatic solution, primarily through the Organization of African Unity. He spoke of $9 million still in the pipeline for covert military aid and said the U.S. would make "every effort" militarily with that aid.

The issue at hand "is not whether the country of Angola represents a vital interest to the United States," he continued. "The issue is whether the Soviet Union, backed by a Cuban expeditionary force, can impose on two-thirds of the population its own brand of government." If the U.S. support in Angola ended, he said, "we are practically inviting outside forces to participate in every situation in which there is a possibility for foreign intervention, and we are, therefore, undermining any hope of political and international order."

Cubans fight in central Angola. It was reported in late December 1975 that Cuban troops were reinforcing MPLA forces in the fighting in central Angola.

The Cuban newspaper Granma reported Dec. 26 that MPLA forces had taken the town of Cariango in central Angola. Foreign intelligence sources in Johannesburg said Dec. 31 that the Cuban forces in Angola had doubled to 7,500 men as the MPLA launched an all-out offensive to secure territorial gains before an Organization of African Unity emergency meeting on Angola in January.

Cuba vows continued MPLA support— Cuban Deputy Premier Carlos Rafael Rodriguez said Jan. 11, 1976 that Cuba would continue sending troops to the MPLA despite any resolution the Organization of African Unity might adopt regarding foreign intervention in Angola.

In an informal talk with U.S. correspondents in Havana, Rodriguez said Cuba would withdraw its support only if MPLA leader Agostinho Neto so requested. This was reiterated by Cuban Premier Fidel Castro in a Jan. 15 statement to foreign journalists.

The deputy premier, in his remarks, declined to comment on a U.S. government estimate that there were approximately 7,500 Cuban troops fighting alongside the MPLA.

He said Cuban aid had first become substantial in the spring of 1975 when the three Angolan movements' coalition government collapsed and the MPLA asked Havana to send advisors. Cuba responded by sending 230 military advisors to train the MPLA forces and only stepped up its aid after "Oct. 23 [when] the South Africans suddenly came into Angola," Rodriguez stated.

A spokesman for the tenuous Unita-FNLA coalition based in Huambo (formerly Nova Lisboa) said Jan. 11 that MPLA troops were being supported by more than 13,000 non-Angolans: 10,000 Cubans, 700 Russians and 2,500 "other foreigners."

Zaire Jan. 15 charged that Cubans had supported MPLA forces in firing rockets into the Zaire town of Dilolo, 14 miles from Angola.

Along the southern front, in central Angola, the Financial Times of London reported Feb. 2 that MPLA and Cuban forces had taken the key port city of Lobito.

Cuba defies Azores refueling ban. Despite objections from the Portuguese government, Cuba was using the Azores Islands to refuel aircraft carrying soldiers and arms to Angola, it was reported Jan. 18, 1976.

Cuban planes had refueled on Santa Maria Island in the Azores Dec. 20–30, 1975, but Portugal had subsequently barred Cuban stopovers there. The stopovers resumed Jan. 10 and continued Jan. 15 despite formal objections made by Portugal to the Cuban ambassador in Lisbon Jan. 13, according to reports.

The U.S. State Department said Jan. 19 that it had made strong protests against Cuban refueling in the Azores.

OAU deadlocks on Angola. An extraordinary session of the Organization of African Unity (OAU) concluded its meetings of African heads of state and other high national officials in Addis Ababa, Ethiopia Jan. 13 without agreeing to a single resolution on the Angolan crisis it had convened to discuss.

A one-sentence communique was issued at the end of the meetings, which had begun Jan. 10. It stated that, after "seriously considering the Angolan problem, the assembled heads of state decided to adjourn and request the bureau of the 12th summit to continue to follow the Angolan problem closely." (The "12th summit" was the annual OAU summit meeting, scheduled for Mauritius in June.)

The 46-member organization had a 22–22 split in the voting on the Angolan issue, with two nations abstaining. They were Ethiopia, the host state, and Uganda, whose president was the OAU's chairman for the year.

Representing the group of states that opposed recognition of the Soviet-backed Popular Movement for the Liberation of Angola, Senegal had sponsored a resolution calling for the formation of a government of national unity by the three Angolan parties—the MPLA, the National Front for the Liberation of Angola (FNLA) and the National Union for the Total Independence of Angola (Unita). The resolution also condemned all foreign intervention, citing explicitly Soviet, Cuban and U.S. roles, as well as that of South Africa.

Led by Nigeria, the pro-MPLA nations, all of whom had recognized the Luanda-based movement's government, opposed the Senegal resolution and advocated OAU recognition of the MPLA regime and condemnation of South Africa alone for its role in the civil war. A last-minute compromise was offered by Nigeria in a resolution that would have expressed commitment to, rather than recognition of, the MPLA; the resolution also would have deplored "other foreign intervention" in addition to South African participation—though without naming the "other" nations intended. However, the Nigerian proposal was rejected by the anti-MPLA states.

Role of foreign forces seen mounting—The Johannesburg Star reported Jan. 20 that in fighting along the central Angolan battle front, Angolans were serving in an essentially supporting capacity to white foreign forces. In major battles at Cela—which, the Star said, pitted 3,000 Cuban-led MPLA soldiers against "thousands of white" troops supporting Unita fighters—and Luso, as well as at other sites, this situation was regarded as prevalent, according to the Star.

Estimates of the number of South African and Cuban troops continued to change in statements from different quarters. The U.S. State Department said Jan. 16 that, though Cuba had committed 6,000–7,000 troops to the MPLA, Havana actually had a total of 9,500 troops in the area, a number of them stationed in the Congo, a major shipment point for Soviet arms deliveries.

Zaire announces mercenary ban—President Mobutu Sese Seko, a major supporter of the Western-backed forces fighting in Angola, Feb. 3 barred any foreign mercenaries from passing through Zaire en route to fight in the war-ravaged nation. Jonas Savimbi, leader of the pro-Western Unita movement, told reporters in Kinshasa that day that Mobutu had only made the statement to balance an earlier condemnation of Cuban and Soviet involvement in Angola.

Kissinger says Cuba 'exports revolution.' U.S. Secretary of State Kissinger had concluded that Cuba had resumed "exporting revolution" on its own initiative, now to Angola, the Sahara and possibly other places outside the Western Hemisphere, the New York Times reported Feb. 5, 1976.

However, Kissinger had decided not to express himself publicly on the issue, preferring instead to press the Soviet Union to end its intervention in Angola on behalf of the Popular Movement for the Liberation of Angola (MPLA), the Times reported. Kissinger reasoned that he had no diplomatic leverage with Cuba, while he did have leverage with the U.S.S.R. because of the U.S.-Soviet detente, the newspaper said.

Kissinger reportedly had rejected the widely held theory that Havana had been forced by Moscow to send the 11,000 Cuban troops now reported to be fighting for the MPLA. "I believe the Cubans went in there with flags flying," he was quoted as saying.

Kissinger was echoed by two unidentified Soviet officials quoted by the Times. "We did not twist their arms," said one official about the Cubans in Angola. "We didn't even have to twist their arms. The Cubans wanted to go in."

Both Soviet officials said Cuban military advisers had gone to Angola to train MPLA recruits in the spring of 1975, before Soviet advisers had appeared in the Angolan capital of Luanda, the Times reported. Cuba's deputy premier for foreign affairs, Carlos Rafael Rodriguez, had said Jan. 10 that Havana had sent 250 advisers to Angola in June 1975.

Cuba had also sent military advisers to other countries in Africa and the Middle East, and there were unconfirmed press and intelligence reports that 300 Cubans were in Algeria to train and assist troops fighting against Morocco in the disputed Sahara, the Times noted.

Cuba's intervention in Angola was disturbing Venezuela and nations in the Caribbean, the Miami Herald reported Jan. 24. "Angola shows that [Cuban Premier Fidel] Castro has the capacity, the strength and the will to mount a large-scale military intervention," said a Venezuelan cabinet official quoted by the Herald. "If he can do it in Africa, so far from home, he also can do it anywhere in the Caribbean."

Some Venezuelan officials were convinced that Cuban airplanes taking troops to Angola were refueling in Guyana, Venezuela's neighbor on the eastern Caribbean coast of South America which recognized the MPLA government, the Herald reported. The presence of Cuban troops in Guyana would be a serious matter to Venezuela, which claimed more than half of Guyana in a territorial dispute, and to neighboring Brazil, the newspaper noted.

It was at Venezuela's initiative that the Organization of American States (OAS) had imposed its embargo in Cuba in 1964, after it was discovered that Cuba was aiding leftist revolutionaries against the Caracas government. The OAS had lifted the embargo in 1975, with many nations arguing that Cuba had stopped "exporting revolution" in the Western Hemisphere after the failure of Cuban guerrillas led by Ernesto "Che" Guevara who fought the Bolivian government in 1967.

Inside Cuba, the Angolan intervention had caused more complaining than any issue in recent years, according to diplomats quoted by United Press International Feb. 4. Complaints were voiced at Communist Party meetings, and some militia reserves had resisted recruitment for service in the African country, UPI noted.

The Cuban people had been told officially of the Angolan intervention only within the last two weeks, UPI reported, and no public mention had been made of Cuban casualties in the Angolan war.

Ford scores Castro. President Ford denounced Castro Feb. 28, 1976 as he campaigned in Florida for the support of Cuban-Americans in the state's March 9 presidential primary election.

Speaking at a naturalization ceremony in Miami for 1,121 persons, most of them Cuban refugees, Ford cited the Cuban military intervention in the Angolan civil war in declaring that the Castro regime was "acting as an international outlaw."

"My Administration will have nothing to do with the Cuba of Fidel Castro," he said. "It is a regime of aggression. And I solemnly warn Fidel Castro against any temptation to armed intervention in the Western Hemisphere. Let his regime, or any like-minded government, be assured the United States would take the appropriate measures."

The President pledged to "speed up" the process of naturalizing Cuban immigrants.

Castro tours Eastern Europe & Africa. Castro won additional Communist and African support for Cuba's involvement in Angola as he visited Yugoslavia, Bulgaria, Algeria and Guinea March 6–16, 1976, conferring with their presidents and with leaders of other African nations.

Castro made the stops on his return to Havana after attending the 25th Congress of the Soviet Communist Party in Moscow. The Cuban premier was accompanied by a large delegation including Deputy Premier Carlos Rafael Rodriguez and other members of the Politburo and the Central Committee of the Cuban Communist Party.

Castro arrived in Yugoslavia March 6, traveling immediately to the Adriatic resort island of Brioni for two days of talks with President Josip Broz Tito. Tito commended Cuba March 6 for its "broad contribution" to the victory of the Popular Movement for the Liberation of Angola in the Angolan civil war. However, press accounts noted that Tito, who reportedly disliked the Cuban and Soviet military buildup in Africa, referred to Cuba's aid to Angola as a nonaligned nation rather than to Cuban achievements on the battlefield.

Castro continued March 8 to Bulgaria, where he met with Communist Party First Secretary Todor Zhivkov. He moved on March 12 to Algeria, where he conferred for three days with President Houari Boumedienne and expressed Cuba's support for the republic recently declared in the Western Sahara by the Algerian-backed Polisario front. Castro met March 14 with Polisario leader Mohamed Lamine Ould Ahmed and with Oscar Montero, minister of state of Mozambique.

In Algiers March 14 Castro rejected recent warnings by President Ford and Secretary of State Kissinger of the U.S. against further Cuban military adventures abroad. "In the first place," he said, "Ford is not my father ... We Cubans don't lose sleep over anything."

Castro arrived in Conakry, Guinea March 14 and met there March 15–16 with President Ahmed Sekou Toure and Presidents Agostinho Neto of Angola and Luis Cabral of Guinea-Bissau. A communique said the leaders "reviewed the struggle of the Angolan people against South Africa" and reaffirmed "the unity of progressive forces" against white minority regimes on the continent.

Kissinger stresses warning. Kissinger stressed anew March 22 his warning to Cuba that the U.S. "will not accept further Cuban military interventions abroad."

The warning was specifically related to the Cuban intervention in Angola and the possibility of any intervention in Rhodesia, where the white minority government was confronting demands by the black majority for rule.

In a speech in Dallas, Kissinger gave assurance that the U.S. would neither support the white minority government in Rhodesia nor condone foreign military intervention. He affirmed "two equal principles of our policy—our support for majority rule in Africa and our firm opposition to military intervention."

World peace was more likely to be threatened "by shifts in the local regional balances," Kissinger said, than by strategic nuclear attack. "We are not the world's policeman," he continued, "but we cannot permit the Soviet Union or its surrogates to become the world's policeman either."

"It does no good to preach strategic superiority while practicing regional retreat," he asserted.

Kissinger repeated his message at a news conference in Dallas March 23. "We stand strongly for majority rule and a rapid political change in southern Africa," he said, "not to be brought about by outside military forces." He refused under questioning by reporters to rule out any move by the U.S., including military invasion of Cuba, in the event Cuba ignored the warnings about new armed intervention in southern Africa. It would be "impossible for any senior official to put out ahead of time all the things the United States will or won't do and all the circumstances that may arise," he said. "We have pointed out the dangers to Cuba. We are serious about what I have said."

U.N. censures South Africa on Angola. The United Nations Security Council adopted a resolution March 31 condemning what it termed South Africa's aggression against Angola but made no mention of Cuban or Soviet activities there.

The council vote was 9–0, with five abstentions by the U.S., Great Britain, France, Italy and Japan. China did not participate in the vote.

The U.S. and other nations abstaining had objected to the resolution because it did not condemn as well the involvement of other states, particularly the Soviet Union and Cuba, in the Angolan war. Huang Hua, the Chinese representative, March 26 vigorously denounced the "vicious and ferocious new czars" in Moscow and called for the immediate withdrawal of Soviet military personnel and "their foreign mercenaries" from Angola.

The Angolan representative, Pascal Luvalu, who said his government hoped to be admitted soon to the U.N., insisted March 26 that it was "ridiculous to speak of Soviet or Cuban interference" in Angola because the assistance they provided was neither part of any expansionist policy nor a violation of sovereignty.

Mikhail Kharlamov, the acting Soviet delegate, deplored China's statement and told the Security Council March 30 that the U.S.S.R. was continuing to give "moral, political, diplomatic and other types of support" to Angola. He lauded the contribution of the Cuban forces who had fought in Angola, labeled "mercenaries" by the Chinese delegate, and further accused China itself of having "sent armed mercenaries" to Angola.

The Cuban representative, Ricardo Alarcon Quesada, showed the Council photographs March 29 which he said depicted Chinese advisers in Angola, "close to the bandits of the "CIA," and charged that China was acting as "the public relations agent of Africa's worst enemies." He said the victory of the "Angolan revolutionaries" had raised new hopes among the "millions of men and women who are oppressed in southern Africa," an allusion to the black majorities in white-minority ruled South Africa and Rhodesia.

William Scranton, the U.S. delegate, charged March 31 that Cuba and the Soviet Union were serving their own "global objectives" in intervening in Angolan affairs and said that more than 13,000 Cuban soldiers remained in Angola.

Scranton asked: "What are they doing there? Against what threat are they staying there? Who are the imperialists?" The Cuban representative contended, in response, that "imperialist" threats against Angola persisted.

Cuba sets troop withdrawal. In a letter to the premier of Sweden, Cuban Premier Fidel Castro said Cuban troops would be withdrawn from Angola at a rate of 200 a week. By the end of 1976, Castro told Premier Olof Palme, Cuban forces in the southwest African nation would be reduced "drastically."

Castro authorized Palme, who received the letter May 21, to divulge its contents to U.S. Secretary of State Henry A. Kissinger. Kissinger, who was in Stockholm on an official visit, was notified of Castro's letter May 24.

The letter was the first indication that Cuba would conduct a pullout of the troops it had sent to Angola.

Cuban President Osvaldo Dorticos May 26 indicated that the withdrawals would be carried out with the consent of Angolan President Agostinho Neto. Dorticos warned the U.S. not to demand evidence of the pullout.

Angolan Premier Lopo de Nascimento May 25 confirmed that some Cuban units were leaving the country. Information Director Luis de Almeida said that day that the MPLA had "appealed to Cuba for help . . . last fall and has now decided that the situation is sufficiently under control that the Cuban troops can begin to withdraw." Almeida said there were a total of 12,000 Cuban armed personnel in Angola, a figure regarded as low by Western analysts who estimated that as many as 15,000 18,000 Cuban troops were in Angola.

In Luxembourg May 25, Kissinger said the letter was "a positive development." He added, however, that the withdrawal rate of 200 soldiers a week "should be speeded up." U.S. officials said Kissinger had asked Palme to tell Cuba that the U.S. still insisted upon a total withdrawal of Cuban troops from Angola. The U.S. had said it would not consider recognizing the Luanda regime until such action were taken.

(According to U.S. estimates reported May 25 by the New York Times, if withdrawals of Cuban troops were to have begun at the end of May at a rate of 200 a week, at least 7,400 would remain in Angola at the year's end.)

In his letter, Castro also said Cuba had no intention of sending troops to other countries in southern Africa or in Latin America to aid "liberation movements." "I do not wish to become the crusader of the 20th century," Castro said.

In the letter, Castro said he was writing in response to an article by the Swedish premier in a Swedish newspaper, criticizing Havana for its military intervention in Angola.

Cubans reported in Red Sea area. Cuban troops and military advisers were joining Soviet elements in the Red Sea-Persian Gulf region as part of a general buildup in the area, according to qualified intelligence sources cited by the New York Times April 5, 1976.

British sources said some 650 Cuban troops had arrived recently in Somalia, where there were already some 2,500 Soviet military advisers and a large stock of naval and air force supplies including air-to-surface and surface-to-surface missiles, the Times reported.

There were also 60-70 Cuban pilots and missile technicians in Somalia, according to the Times. Elsewhere in the region, Cuban pilots reportedly were training airmen in Southern Yemen and Cuban advisers reportedly were aiding antigovernment guerrillas in the Dhofar district of Oman.

U.S., Western European and Israeli intelligence sources generally agreed that the U.S.S.R. and Cuba sought to establish military supremacy in the area and win control of the exit from the Persian Gulf through the Strait of Hormuz and the southern entry to the Red Sea and the Suez Canal, the Times reported. This, the sources noted, would enable Moscow to cut off oil supplies in the event of a confrontation with the European powers of the North Atlantic Treaty Organization, which obtained 60% of their petroleum from the Middle East, the Times said.

A secondary target in the Communist buildup was likely to be the French Territory of Afars and Issas, whose port city of Djibouti was at the southern entrance to the Red Sea, the Times reported. France would abandon the territory at the end of 1976, leaving behind only one infantry brigade for security.

Soviets & Cubans in Africa. A June 13, 1976 report in the New York Times described a Pentagon map that depicted the Soviet and Cuban military presence in Africa. Soviet personnel, arms and money were shown in Somalia, Uganda, Mozambique and the Sudan in eastern Africa; in Egypt, Libya and Algeria in northern Africa, and in Mali, Guinea, Nigeria and Angola in western Africa.

Fifty Cubans were placed in Somalia in military capacities and 310 in Guinea. The map showed 11,400 Cubans in Angola. However, an official of the North Atlantic Treaty Organization said the figure was higher, estimating it at about 15,000-16,000 Cubans. The official also noted that there had been no evidence of a Cuban withdrawal from Angola as had been signaled by Premier Fidel Castro.

U.S. arms pledge to Kenya & Zaire—The U.S. agreed in principle to provide Kenya and Zaire with military equipment to bolster their armed forces in the face of Soviet and Cuban military buildups in neighboring African countries. The agreements, which required approval by the U.S. Congress, were reached during a visit to the two nations June 15-19 by U.S. Secretary of Defense Donald Rumsfeld.

Neither Kenya nor Zaire received U.S. grant military aid, although both countries received credits to buy arms through the foreign military sales program. Zaire would receive $28 million and Kenya $5 million in 1977.

In Nairobi June 15-17, Rumsfeld reached agreement to provide Kenya with

12 F-5 jet fighters valued at more than $70 million. Pentagon officials described the Kenyan agreement as one of the single largest U.S. arms sales ever made to an African nation. With a small, ill-equipped army of 7,500 men, Kenya had sought the aircraft to counter the threat posed by Soviet arms in Somalia and Uganda.

The Zaire agreement was for $50 million worth of armored vehicles and anti-tank weapons. In Kinshasa June 17–19, Rumsfeld conferred with officials on Zaire's concern over the buildup of Soviet arms and Cuban personnel in neighboring Angola.

The planned sales to Kenya and Zaire were separate from the credit program.

Neto visits Cuba. Angolan president Agostinho Neto visited Cuba July 23–29, 1976.

At a July 26 rally marking Cuba's national day, Premier Fidel Castro pledged to increase the number of Cuban technicians and economic advisers in Angola. He said that a pull-out of Cuban forces from Angola was under way, but he assured Neto of continued Cuban military aid. (A U.S. State Department official quoted in the Sept. 22 Washington Post, reported that 3,000 Cuban soldiers had left Angola, leaving 10,000 still in the country.)

Cuban aid vs. guerrillas. Cuban forces were reported in the fall of 1976 to be assisting the Angolan government against guerrillas of the National Union for the Total Independence of Angola (UNITA), whose attacks had increased over the past months.

South African observers near the Angolan border in Namibia (South-West Africa) said that heavy fighting was apparent in early November as the government attempted to destroy UNITA resistance before Nov. 11, the first anniversary of Angolan independence. By Nov. 10, the South Africans reported, UNITA forces were in retreat to the bush near the Zambian border. The government, with the aid of both Cuban troops and guerrillas of the South-West Africa People's Organization (SWAPO), had succeeded in closing off much of the Angolan-Namibian border, cutting off UNITA communication and supply lines, the reports said.

More than 8,000 Angolan refugees were reported to have fled into Namibia since the major anti-UNITA campaign began Oct. 29, according to the Nov. 12 London Times. The South African government had set up a temporary camp in Omungwelume for the refugees, who belonged to the same tribe as Africans in northern Namibia. The South African police Nov. 12 reported that a group of Angolan and Cuban soldiers Nov. 3 had crossed into Namibia and had forced a group of refugees to return at gunpoint to Angola.

Cuba's Version of Angola Affair

Angola war role detailed. Excerpts of the first official version of Cuba's involvement in the Angolan civil war were released Jan. 9, 1977 by Cuba's news agency, Prensa Latina, and reprinted by the Washington Post in three installments Jan. 10–12.

The account was written by Gabriel Garcia Marquez, the celebrated Colombian novelist. Garcia Marquez, a communist, had visited Cuba several times in the past two years and had been in regular touch with President Fidel Castro.

Cuba's intervention in Angola, Garcia Marquez wrote, was "the end result of a continuous policy toward Africa." Since 1963 Cuba had given military aid to various black African liberation movements, notably the National Revolutionary Council of the Congo, which fought against forces of former Congolese Premier Moise Tshombe. Cuban revolutionary leader Ernesto (Che) Guevara fought alongside 200 Cuban troops in the Congo in April–December 1965, according to Garcia Marquez.

Cuban contacts with the Popular Movement for the Liberation of Angola (MPLA) reportedly began in 1965, when Angola was a Portuguese colony. MPLA leader Agostinho Neto, now president of Angola, visited Havana in 1966, Garcia Marquez wrote.

In May 1975, when the Portuguese were preparing to leave Angola and the

MPLA was embroiled in a civil war with the National Front for the Liberation of Angola (FNLA) and the National Union for the Total Independence of Angola (UNITA), Neto reportedly asked for a shipment of Cuban arms. In July he asked Cuba to send instructors to open and run four military training camps, Garcia Marquez wrote. The Cuban government appealed to Otelo de Carvalho, then Portugal's chief of security, for permission to send the men to Angola, but Carvalho did not immediately reply, according to Garcia Marquez.

The decision to send troops to fight in Angola was made at a meeting of the Cuban Communist Party's top leaders Nov. 5, Garcia Marquez wrote. Cuba reportedly went ahead without Portuguese permission because it felt the MPLA was on the point of being defeated by the FNLA and South African mercenaries.

A Cuban battalion of 650 men was flown to Angola over 13 days beginning Nov. 7. The first flight carried 82 "well-trained warriors, with a high level of political and ideological formation," Garcia Marquez wrote. Cuban troopships followed, bearing thousands of soldiers plus armored vehicles, guns and explosives. They docked in Angola Nov. 27 and Dec. 4, 7 and 11.

Cuban instructors immediately set up the four training camps requested by Neto, and Cuban soldiers helped the MPLA drive FNLA troops from the outskirts of Luanda. Over the next few months more than 15,000 Cuban soldiers helped the MPLA drive its foes out of Angola and consolidate rule over the country. "Cuban aid reached such a level," Garcia Marquez wrote, "that at one point there were 15 Cuban ships on the high seas bound for Luanda."

The air and sea crossings were long and arduous because Cuba's planes and ships were old and overcrowded and because the U.S. intervened to hinder the Cuban aid effort, according to Garcia Marquez. U.S. threats reportedly forced Barbados and Guyana to deny refueling facilities to Cuban planes. And Cuban troopships "were the target of all sorts of provocations by North American destroyers, which followed them for days on end, and by war planes that buzzed them and photographed them," Garcia Marquez wrote.

President Castro followed the Angolan conflict closely. "At the start of the war, when the situation was especially pressing," Garcia Marquez wrote, "[Castro] stayed in the general staff command room as long as 14 hours at a stretch, without eating or sleeping, as if he were on the campaign. He followed the progress of battles, using colored indicators on wall-sized tactical maps, and was in constant contact with the battlefield high command [of the MPLA]."

Cuba's intervention in Angola was kept secret within the island until Castro acknowledged it at the December 1975 congress of the Cuban Communist Party. Families of soldiers fighting in Angola were ordered to reveal nothing, and some families did not even know that their relatives, who were officially on maneuvers, had been sent to Africa.

After the MPLA's success, Castro and Neto agreed in March 1976 on a Cuban troop-withdrawal program, Garcia Marquez wrote. "They decided that the withdrawal would be gradual but that as many Cubans as needed would remain in Angola as long as needed to build a modern and strong army, able to guarantee the future internal security and independence of the country without outside help," according to the Colombian author.

Garcia Marquez gave no figures on Cuban troop withdrawals.

Garcia account questioned. A report questioning the Garcia Marquez account of Cuba's involvement in Angola was written by Robert Moss, a former editor with The Economist of London. Moss's report appeared as a series in the Toronto Globe and Mail beginning Jan. 31. Moss said Cuban soldiers had been operating in Angola several months before Nov. 5, 1975, the date on which the Cubans officially said they had decided to intervene.

According to Moss, Cuban Deputy Foreign Minister Carlos Rafael Rodriguez had revealed in a December 1975 speech

1975-77: CONFLICTING OBJECTIVES

that there were 230 Cuban military instructors with the MPLA as of the spring of 1975. In August 1975, MPLA Defense Minister Iko Carreira visited Moscow to ask for Soviet troops. Moscow had turned down the request, fearing a confrontation with the U.S., but had suggested Carreira request help from Cuba. The Soviets had given Cuba assurances of direct Soviet intervention if the U.S. blockaded Cuba or sent troops to Angola, Moss reported.

More Cuban military instructors arrived in Luanda Aug. 16, 1975, and shipments of military equipment and troops were reported in September and October. By Nov. 11, 1975, Angola's independence day, there were 4,000 Cuban troops in the country, 2,500 of them in Luanda, Moss said.

Further African Developments

Castro again tours Africa. Castro visited eight Arab and black African nations March 1–April 2, 1977. Castro conferred with the national leaders and with Cuban soldiers and civilians who were stationed in some of the countries.

Castro's itinerary, often improvised on short notice, was: Algeria March 1; Libya March 1–10; South Yemen March 10–12; Somalia March 12–14; Ethiopia March 14–16; Tanzania March 17–21; Mozambique March 21–23; Angola March 23–31, and Algeria again March 31–April 2. After leaving Algeria, Castro paid an unscheduled visit to East Germany April 2–4 and then flew on to Moscow to meet with Soviet leaders.

Castro conferred with Algerian President Houari Boumedienne during a brief stopover in Algiers March 1, after which he flew to Tripoli. During his 10-day stay in Libya, Castro toured the country and conferred extensively with the head of government, Col. Muammer el-Qaddafi. The two leaders signed an agreement March 10 to increase economic, commercial, scientific and cultural exchanges between Cuba and Libya.

The two governments were secretive about Castro's talks with Qaddafi, but newspapers reported that the two leaders had discussed the civil war in Ethiopia, among other topics. In their final communique March 10, Castro and Qaddafi denounced "imperialist maneuvers against the Ethiopian revolution," presumably referring to Sudanese support for opponents of Ethiopia's military government.

Castro began an unscheduled visit in Ethiopia March 14, after two-day stops in South Yemen and Somalia. Despite official secrecy about Castro's talks with these countries' leaders—South Yemen's President Salem Ali Rubaye, Somalia's President Mohamed Siad Barre and Ethiopia's Lt. Col. Mengistu Haile Mariam—Western diplomats and newspapers reported that the principal topic of discussion was Ethiopia's conflict with Somalia over the future of the French Territory of the Afars and Issas (Djibouti), which was scheduled to become independent in June.

Castro reportedly urged Ethiopia, Somalia and South Yemen—all of which had leftist governments—to form an alliance that would keep Djibouti independent and serve as a "common anti-imperialist front." This plan, endorsed by the Soviet Union, was opposed by the U.S., Egypt, Sudan and Saudi Arabia, which were using offers of economic aid to try to entice Somalia out of the Soviet sphere of influence. Castro's chief obstacle in promoting the alliance was Somalia's claim to sovereignty over Djibouti and a part of eastern Ethiopia. The Ethiopian government, which used Djibouti as its major port, wanted the territory to be independent.

Lt. Col. Mengistu supported the proposed alliance, according to the Cuban newspaper Granma March 15. (Mengistu also asked Castro to give his government military support against Eritrean and other rebels, but Castro made no commitment, according to diplomatic sources quoted by the Washington Post March 17.)

Castro left Ethiopia March 16, but he did not arrive at his next scheduled destination—Dar es Salaam, Tanzania—until the next day. Newspapers speculated that he had returned to Somalia or South Yemen to continue pressing his alliance plan.

In Tanzania, Castro addressed other African issues. He said March 20 that Cuba could not afford to give more aid to Tanzania because of its economic and military commitments to the Angolan government. At a press conference in Dar es Salaam March 21, Castro denied that Cuban soldiers had been involved in a recent invasion of Zaire, and he said Cuban troops would not be sent to aid black nationalist guerrillas in Rhodesia or Namibia (South-West Africa). "We believe the struggle for independence is primarily a task which belongs to the people concerned themselves," Castro said. "Independence is not bought from abroad."

The Cuban leader made an unscheduled visit to Mozambique March 21, where he conferred with President Samora Machel. Castro continued to Angola March 23 for a nine-day visit that was considered the highlight of his African tour.

Castro declared March 24 that Cuba would "not place any limit on its cooperation" with Angola and would give the Luanda government "all the aid it needs." At a rally March 28, Castro pledged continued military support for Angola despite U.S. opposition. "The day will come when Angola has sufficient military units, tanks, cannon, airplanes and soldiers to confront all imperialist aggression," he said. "How many years, how many [Cuban] soldiers will stay in Angola? We don't have to discuss that with Yankee imperialists."

Following Castro's departure from Angola, the Luanda government April 2 issued a joint communique in which Castro and Angolan President Agostinho Neto pledged to "support with all the means at hand, the just struggle for the liberation of the peoples of South Africa, Zimbabwe [Rhodesia] and Namibia."

Castro ended his African tour in Algeria. On arriving in Algiers March 31, he said: "Just like Christopher Columbus, I have discovered a continent in struggle. I have been able to evaluate the possibilities of a long and protracted liberation struggle, which can only be victorious."

Castro flew April 2 to East Germany, which was believed to be one of the Communist nations most deeply involved in African politics, providing military and economic support for black liberation movements and left-leaning black governments, according to Reuters. Castro conferred with East German leaders, presumably about his tour.

The Cuban leader arrived in Moscow April 4, where he was hugged at the airport by Soviet Communist Party leader Leonid Brezhnev, Premier Alexei Kosygin, and President Podgorny, who had returned from Africa only the day before. The presence of the top Soviet leaders at the airport and the warmth of their greeting signaled the great importance they gave Castro's visit, according to press reports. Castro conferred with the Soviet leaders in Moscow April 5-6.

Young on Cubans in Africa. Andrew Young, U.S. representative to the United Nations, visited Africa as an ambassador from the new Carter Administration Feb. 3-10, 1977. The visit and events both preceding and following it were marked by a series of policy observations in which Young appeared to be differing from Administration positions.

The first of Young's controversial policy observations concerned Angola. It was made in a television interview days before his trip, on Jan. 25. Young had remarked that the presence of Cuban troops there brought "a certain stability and order" to Angola.

Secretary of State Cyrus Vance, at a news conference Jan. 31, said the presence of any outside forces in Angola was "not helpful to a peaceful solution." The matter was one "that should be settled by the Africans themselves," Vance said.

The official State Department position, released Feb. 2 by spokesman Frederick Brown, was that "neither Ambassador Young nor the secretary condones the presence of Cuban troops in Angola."

Young said April 11 that the U.S. had found itself getting into hard positions in Africa because it had made "cold war" assessments of developments there, based on a paranoia about Communism.

At a State Department news conference called by Young to explain his sometimes controversial outspokenness on foreign policy, Young said, "The only thing I'm thinking is, don't get paranoid about a few Communists." He cited several instances in Africa, specifically mentioning Egypt, Nigeria, Zambia and Tanzania, in which he said the U.S. had concluded that Soviet or Chinese military or economic aid meant Communist domination. This was not the case, he said.

Young argued that the developmental needs of African countries, even those with avowedly Marxist governments, would sooner or later persuade them to turn to the U.S. and the West for assistance and trade. "We don't have to fear Communism in the area of economic competition," Young said. "We do almost everything so much better than they do that the sooner the fighting stops and the trading starts, the quicker we win."

Again and again at the news session, Young said the U.S. had to get away from "knee-jerk reactions" and examine what was really going on in Africa before making policy.

In calling for this reassessment of policy, Young defended the remark that had embroiled him in controversy soon after he assumed his U.N. post: that the presence of Cuban troops had contributed to "stability" in Angola. He noted that Cuban forces were helping to defend the Gulf Oil Co. installations in the Angolan province of Cabinda against two antigovernment guerrilla groups. In this instance, he said, the Cubans were helping to keep the oil flowing to the West, which was vital to Angola's economy.

Of the 10,000 or so Cubans reported to be in Angola, Young said: "We don't known how many are troops and how many are" agriculturalists, physicians and technicians helping to fill the vacuum left by the flight of several hundred thousand Portuguese from Angola just before it became independent.

"I'm not defending what the Russians and the Cubans did in Angola," he said. "But once they are there, it seems to me that there needs to be a realistic assessment of what their role is."

Young toured Africa again May 10–24, making his first stop in Abidjan, capital of the Ivory Coast, where he attended a four-day meeting of more than 30 U.S. ambassadors to various African countries. The meeting, which had begun May 9, was the first comprehensive conference on U.S. Africa policy in recent years to include diplomats. It reflected the Carter Administration's desire for both a cohesive U.S. policy and for closer consultations with U.S. diplomats.

Although the meeting was confidential, the discussions were believed to reflect the division of opinion among the ambassadors over the influence of the U.S.S.R. in Africa. The diplomats were split between those who saw a Cold War threat in the growing Soviet and Cuban influence and those who favored fostering closer relations with radical African states. (Young appeared to ally himself with the latter.)

Young then irked U.S. officials May 26, when he suggested in London that the presence of Cuban military advisers in Ethiopia "might not be a bad thing" if they could halt the killings there. Only the day before, the State Department had expressed official concern about the Cubans' reported presence in Ethiopia. Moreover, Vice President Walter Mondale, speaking shortly after Young made his remarks, reiterated that the U.S. would view the sending of Cuban troops to Ethiopia as "very serious" and a "destabilizing factor."

One important official whose support for Young appeared unshaken by the latest controversy was President Carter. At a news conference May 26, Carter said he knew of "no instance when Andy Young has violated" Administration policy. In an interview published in the June 6 U.S. News and World Report, Carter said there had been no disagreement between himself and Young "on the thrust of our policy or statements on Africa."

Cubans involved in Zaire invasion? Cuba as well as the Soviet Union was accused of aiding the National Front for the Liberation of the Congo (FNLC) in an invasion of the Zaire province of Shaba (Katanga) March 8, 1977. Captured FNLC weapons and rebels were shown to newsmen April 20 in Kinshasa, capital of Zaire, as evidence.

Two prisoners of war displayed in the capital April 20 told reporters they had been trained in Angola by Cubans, who had escorted them to the Zaire border. However, according to a report April 26 in the Washington Post, when the prisoners had been captured they had said no Cuban troops had crossed into Shaba. They had said they had been given assistance by "whites" in Angola who were presumed by observers to be Portuguese.

From the start of the conflict, Mobutu had charged the Soviet Union, Cuba and Angola with masterminding the invasion by the Katangan rebels. All three countries repeatedly had denied the charges, calling the conflict a purely internal uprising.

King Hassan II of Morocco April 18 said he had direct proof of Cuban involvement in the conflict. At an interview with French reporters, he said a Moroccan commander in Shaba had interrogated a prisoner who had revealed the presence of "white Angolans and Cubans" among the Katangan secessionists.

Zairian sources said in Paris that seven Cubans had been captured in the fighting in Mutshatsha in Shaba.

African nations that rallied to support Mobutu, either orally or with troops and supplies, were influenced not only by the desire to halt the spread of separatist movements in African states but by opposition to foreign intervention in the continent. Senegalese President Leopold Senghor May 3 strongly condemned Soviet and Cuban military intervention in Africa and warned the U.S. and the U.S.S.R. against interfering in African affairs. He made his remarks during a meeting with West German Chancellor Helmut Schmidt in Bonn.

Cubans in Ethiopia. The U.S. State Department said May 25, 1977 that it had reports of the arrival of 50 Cuban military advisers in Addis Ababa and warned Cuba that intervention in Ethiopia "could impede the improvement of [Cuban] relations" with the U.S.

A State Department spokesman said the U.S. had no confirmation of reports that 400–500 Cuban troops would be dispatched to Ethiopia in the future, but added that the U.S. "will be watching closely" any Cuban activity in Africa.

In an ABC-TV interview broadcast in the U.S. May 24, Cuban President Fidel Castro had denied there were Cuban military advisers in Ethiopia, saying all Cuban nationals in the country were "accredited as diplomatic personnel." He did not rule out sending military instructors if requested to do so by the Ethiopian government.

The Egyptian Middle East News Agency had reported April 17 that about 200 Cuban commandos had arrived in Ethiopia to help train government troops in the war against Eritrean separatists.

U.S. Rep. Ronald Dellums (D, Calif.) said June 1 that Cuba planned to increase its personnel in Ethiopia by 311—but that they consisted only of doctors and medical technicians. Dellums, who met with President Castro in Havana May 28, said the Cuban leader had assured him that the Cubans now in Ethiopia were not military instructors but "diplomatic personnel." Dellums said he was convinced that "Cuba will send no troops to Ethiopia." He briefed President Carter June 3 on his meeting with Castro.

In a TV interview broadcast to the U.S. June 9, Castro again discussed his African policies. He denied having sent Cuban troops or military advisers to Ethiopia. But he revealed that Cuba had halted its military withdrawal from Angola in April after France and Morocco sent troops to Zaire to help the Zairian government fight separatist rebels in Shaba.

(Although France had airlifted Moroccan troops to Zaire, it denied having sent French troops or airmen to the African country.)

Ethiopian radio said Sept. 16 that 71 Cuban medical personnel had arrived the day before. The report said the Cuban aid was the result of a recent agreement between the two countries.

The State Department estimated Nov. 14 that there were 400 Cuban officers and soldiers assisting Ethiopian forces in the Ogaden region. A spokesman said the increase in Cuban aid meant that there were at least 550 Cubans providing military and civilian assistance to Ethiopia, up from 50 in May.

A State Department estimate Nov. 4 had put the total of Soviet and Cuban military advisers at 250, of which 150 were estimated to be Cubans. Cuba the next day had denied stationing troops, in reply to previous charges by Somali President Mohamed Siad Barre that there were 15,000 Cuban troops in Ogaden.

Aid vs. Angola revolt. Angolan government troops backed by Cubans May 27, 1977 suppressed a rebellion by supporters of two purged government officials. Rebels demanding the reinstatement of Nito Alves, former interior minister, and Jose Van Dunem, a former army political commissar, had briefly captured the national radio station that morning and the international airport in Luanda, the Angolan capital. The two men had been expelled from the ruling Popular Movement for the Liberation of Angola (MPLA) May 21, reportedly because of their hard-line pro-Soviet stance and their opposition to establishing diplomatic relations with Western countries.

The New York Times reported June 20 that in the fighting, Cuban troops had played an important part in putting down the coup despite Neto's denials of Cuban participation.

In addition to facing internal dissent, the ruling party was engaged in a struggle against several anti-MPLA guerrilla groups. The National Front for the Liberation of Angola (FNLA) had issued a communique claiming "resounding victories" over Cuban and Angolan forces, according to a report May 31 in the Financial Times (London). The communique said that FNLA forces controlled the northern third of the country, and that Cuban-backed MPLA forces held only the large cities. A spokesman for the Front for the Liberation of the Enclave of Cabinda (FLEC) May 4 said the rebels have driven back a Cuban-led offensive in the oil-rich province. The spokesman said FLEC held two-thirds of Cabinda.

In an earlier development, a South African official April 13 reported that about 700 Angolans had fled into Namibia (South-West Africa) since March to escape fighting. A South African broadcast March 30 had reported that more than 1,000 Angolan civilians had been killed since March 28 by Angolan troops, Cubans and guerrillas of the South-West Africa People's Organization.

Cuba sent 4,000 additional soldiers to Angola to help contain opposition guerrilla activity, the South African Press Association reported Sept. 11. Quoting Angolan refugee sources, the agency said economic problems and the conflict in the southern half of the country with the Union for the Total Independence of Angola required the presence of extra troops. Total Cuban troop strenth in Angola was estimated at almost 20,000 as a result of the new arrivals.

Zambia to accept aid. Zambian President Kenneth Kaunda disclosed July 8, 1977 that he had accepted in principle the offers of military aid from Cuba and Somalia to defend Zambia against Rhodesian attacks. He said such aid would be requested only if Zambia were in serious need of help.

Somalia breaks relations. In a surprise move Nov. 13, 1977, Somalia ordered all Soviet advisers to leave and broke diplomatic relations with Cuba. The Somali action was the abrupt climax of a steadily worsening diplomatic crisis resulting from the U.S.S.R.'s pro-Ethiopia stance in the Horn of Africa conflict.

The announcement came after an emergency session of the central committee of Somalia's ruling Socialist Revolutionary Party. Soviet advisers, said to number at least 1,500, were given a week to leave, while Cuban personnel were given 48 hours. The announcement indirectly accused the U.S.S.R. and Cuba of having "brazenly interfered in the struggle of the peoples fighting for their liberation from the Ethiopian government," a reference to the Somali-backed guerrillas in the Ogaden region of Ethiopia.

The termination of the Soviet-Somali cooperation agreement meant the loss of a number of important Soviet military bases in the country and possibly a weakened Soviet military position in the Indian Ocean. The Soviets had established naval and air facilities at Berbera in the north and Kismayu in the south, as well as bases elsewhere in the country.

The U.S. Nov. 14 expressed satisfaction over the Somali move. The State Department said Somalia was in "a far better position to pursue a truly nonaligned foreign policy" as a result, and it ruled out any U.S. moves to fill the Soviet vacancy. A U.S. spokesman blamed the troubles in the Horn of Africa on the increased Soviet and Cuban military involvement, adding that "African problems should be solved by Africans themselves."

U.S. warns Cuba on Africa buildup. The U.S. government warned Cuba Nov. 17 that its growing military involvement in Africa "will have an impact on the pace and even the possibility of normalizing relations" between Washington and Havana.

"We believe that the presence of large numbers of Cubans in Africa is bound to have an unsettling effect and is a threat to peace in Africa," said a spokesman for the U.S. State Department.

The Carter Administration previously had played down the Cuban role in Africa in its effort to move toward full relations with the government of President Fidel Castro. But a new study by the National Security Council (NSC) had convinced top Administration officials that Cuba was building up its forces in Africa as part of a broad policy to establish and protect pro-Cuban and pro-Soviet governments throughout the continent, according to the New York Times Nov. 17.

The study estimated that Havana had sent 4,000 to 6,000 new troops to Angola since July, raising the Cuban presence there to about 19,000 military personnel and 4,000 civilian advisers. In addition, there were more than 3,000 Cuban soldiers, civilian advisers, technicians and medical aides in 15 other African nations, the NSC study said.

The study gave the following breakdown of Cuban strength in Africa:
Algeria: 35 medical aides.
Angola: 19,000 military, 4,000 civilian advisers.
Benin: 10-20 security advisers.
Cape Verde: 10-15 medical aides.
Congo: 300 military, 100-150 technicians.
Equatorial Guinea: 300-400 advisers, about half military.
Ethiopia: 400 military advisers, 300 medical aides.
Guinea: 300-500 advisers, most of them military.
Guinea-Bissau: 100-200 advisers, two-thirds of them military.
Libya: 100-125 military advisers.
Malagasy Republic (Madagascar): 30 military advisers.
Mozambique: 600-750 advisers, including 150 technicians.
Sao Tome e Principe: 75-80 medical aides.
Sierra Leone: 100-125 military advisers.
Tanzania: 350-500 advisers, mostly technicians.
Uganda: Possibly 25 military advisers (unconfirmed report).

A U.S. official noted that the Cuban commitment in Africa was "fairly sizable" considering Cuba's small population (estimated at 9.3 million in 1975). "We have to be seriously disturbed by the implications of the growing military presence in Africa and raise a warning flag about it," the official told the New York Times.

The Carter Administration was said to be worried that Cuba's involvement in Africa might have been encouraged by the Soviet Union, although there was no specific evidence of this.

The State Department left the clear impression that the Cuban buildup in Africa had stymied progress toward renewing U.S.-Cuban relations. "In the light of the military activity," the spokesman said, "it appears we have gone as far as we can go at this time."

Castro bars pressure on Africa. Fidel Castro asserted Dec. 5, 1977 that Cuba's military presence in Africa was not negotiable and had nothing to do with Cuba's relations with the U.S.

Speaking with reporters after meeting with two U.S. congressmen in Havana, Castro rejected the Carter Administration's persistent calls for a gradual Cuban pullout from Africa. "It has nothing to do with Carter, it has nothing to do with the U.S.," he said. "If it becomes an issue, it's going to be an impediment."

The American congressmen—Reps. Frederick W. Richmond (D, N.Y.) and Richard Nolan (D, Minn.)—had given Castro a message from President Carter urging Cuba to "get out of Angola." The message came a few days after Andrew Young, the U.S. ambassador to the United Nations, implied in a speech that Cuba was aiding African governments that kept power by "killing off the opposition."

Young continued his criticism of Havana Dec. 6, charging that the Soviet Union and Cuba were "contributing to the

1975-77: CONFLICTING OBJECTIVES

escalation of death and destruction in Africa." Young said the two communist nations should "assist Africans in the task of nation-building" instead.

Castro reaffirmed his position Dec. 24 after receiving a letter from 40 U.S. senators urging him to cut back Cuba's military involvement in Africa. Speaking to the closing session of the National Assembly in Havana, Castro accused the Carter Administration of conducting a "policy of blackmail" against Cuba.

Castro said Cuba would "never trade our ties with the Third World for a smile from the U.S., for the smallest concession on their part." He acknowledged that trade relations with the U.S. would benefit Cuba, but he said they would not be "decisive." "Our relations with the Soviet Union and the socialist camp are decisive, and the U.S. will never be able to replace those relations," he declared.

U.S.-Cuban Relations Under Jimmy Carter

Jimmy Carter succeeded Gerald R. Ford as U.S. President in January 1977, and major progress was soon visible in the effort to normalize U.S.-Cuban relations. By the end of May, the two countries had agreed on a formula for an exchange of diplomats—but not for the resumption of full diplomatic relations.

CIA linked to '71 swine fever. With at least tacit approval from the U.S. Central Intelligence Agency, operatives linked to anti-Castro terrorists had introduced the African swine fever virus into Cuba in 1971, the New York newspaper Newsday reported Jan. 1, 1977.

Six weeks after the virus was introduced, a Cuban outbreak of the fever forced the slaughter of 500,000 pigs to prevent a nationwide animal epidemic. The previously unexplained outbreak—the only one ever to occur in the Western Hemisphere—was called the "most alarming event" of 1971 by the United Nations' Food and Agriculture Organization.

African swine fever was a highly contagious and usually lethal disease that infected only pigs and, unlike swine flu, could not be transmitted to humans.

A U.S. intelligence source told Newsday that early in 1971 he was given a sealed, unmarked container at Ft. Gulick in the Panama Canal Zone, a U.S. Army base where the CIA operated a paramilitary training center for career personnel and mercenaries. The source said he was instructed to turn over the container to an anti-Castro group. He gave it to someone in the Canal Zone who took it by boat to a fishing trawler off the Panamanian coast. The source said he was not told until after the Cuban outbreak that the container held swine fever virus.

A CIA-trained Cuban exile who was involved in the operation told Newsday that he was on the trawler when the virus was put aboard. He said the container was carried to Navassa Island, a tiny, deserted U.S. property between Jamaica and Haiti. From there it was taken to Cuba in late March 1971, where it was given to other operatives on the southern coast near the U.S. Navy base at Guantanamo Bay.

Cuban officials said the first sick pigs in Cuba were found in Havana about May 6. A non-Soviet bloc agricultural technician then in Cuba said the disease easily could have gone undetected for months, Newsday reported. Newsday's sources said they had no direct knowledge of whether the virus from Ft. Gulick was responsible for the outbreak in Havana, 500 miles northwest of Guantanamo.

Neither the intelligence source nor the source on the trawler could confirm that the operation was approved by the CIA. Another intelligence source in Miami said: "In a case like this, [the CIA always would have] plausible deniability." A CIA spokesman, asked by Newsday to comment, said: "We don't comment on information from unnamed and, at best, obscure sources."

Cuban officials said the island's entire pork production was halted until the disease was confined to Havana Province and eradicated by slaughtering the infected pigs and burning their remains.

U.S. makes overtures. The U.S. made a number of qualified public overtures to Cuba in early 1977, culminating in President Jimmy Carter's announcement March 9 that he would end restrictions on travel to the island.

In reply, President Fidel Castro told American visitors to Cuba that he was very interested in improving relations with the U.S., particularly in resuming trade. However, Castro reacted angrily to the Carter Administration's attempts to link improved relations and greater observance of human rights in Cuba.

U.S. Secretary of State Cyrus Vance said in mid-January that Washington would consider the release of Cuban political prisoners as "one indication that Cuba is seriously interested in starting a dialogue with the U.S." Vance made the statement during his confirmation hearings before the Senate Foreign Relations Committee. The committee released the testimony Jan. 27.

Vance said Feb. 3 that the U.S. hoped to hold direct talks with Cuba on a possible renewal of the 1973 U.S.-Cuban antihijacking pact, which was scheduled to expire April 15 and which Castro had vowed not to renew. At those talks, Vance said, it would be "constructive" if the two nations discussed their other major differences.

In an interview broadcast on the CBS Evening News program Feb. 9, Castro said he thought it was possible for Cuba and the U.S. to establish normal relations. He said that if Carter wished, "I will with pleasure talk with him." Castro called Carter a "man of morals," adding, "I think that a man like Carter may abide by a policy of international principles, not the Marxist principles nor the capitalist principles, but rather the principles accepted universally among the people."

A spokesman for Carter said Feb. 19 that the President considered Castro's remarks "interesting and positive."

Rep. Jonathan Bingham (D, N.Y.), a proponent of normalized U.S.-Cuban relations, conferred twice with Castro during a visit to Havana Feb. 10–15. Bingham said in Washington Feb. 16 that Cuba would not begin full negotiations with the U.S. until Washington lifted its ban on exports of food and medicine to the island. Cubans considered the ban "a knife at their throat," Bingham said.

Even after normal relations were established, Bingham warned, the U.S. could not expect Cuba to pull all its troops out of Angola or to stop advocating independence for Puerto Rico. It might take years to arrange payment of compensation to U.S. companies that were seized by Castro's government, the congressman added.

Carter said Feb. 16 that he would "very much like to see the Cubans remove their soldiers from Angola and let the Angolan natives make their own decisions about their government . . . [That] would be a step toward full normalization of [U.S.] relations with Angola. The same thing applies ultimately to the restoration of normal relationships with Cuba.

"If I can be convinced that Cuba wants to remove their aggravating influence in this hemisphere, will not participate in violence in nations across the oceans, will recommit the former relationships which existed in Cuba toward human rights, then I would be willing to move toward normalizing relationships with Cuba," Carter declared.

Vance met Feb. 25 with seven Cuban exile leaders who claimed to represent the views of many of the more than 600,000 Cubans who emigrated to the U.S. after Castro took power in 1959. The seven, including former Cuban President Carlos Prio and several leaders of the abortive 1961 Bay of Pigs invasion, said they were unalterably opposed to U.S. negotiations with the Castro government.

Castro met Feb. 26 and 27 with Benjamin C. Bradlee, executive editor of the Washington Post. In an account of the talks, published by the Post March 6, Bradlee said Castro admired Carter but was "appalled" by his remarks linking improved U.S. relations to greater respect for human rights in Cuba.

"If one message came ringing loud and clear through conversations with Castro," Bradlee reported, "it was this: Don't talk to Fidel Castro about human rights; he truly believes he has nothing to learn from the U.S. on this particular subject."

"What does Cuba have to learn about human rights, [Castro] asks, from the country that mounted an invasion of Cuba and has relentlessly tried to assassinate Cuba's leader for 20 years?" Bradlee wrote. "These attempts are no longer speculative, but fully documented by the Senate's Church Committee, [Castro] notes."

As other reasons for discounting U.S. concern over human rights, Castro cited U.S. military involvement in Vietnam, U.S. racial discrimination, American "businessmen [who] regularly bribe public officials of other countries," the Watergate scandal, and U.S. support for "every totalitarian regime in Latin America," Bradlee reported.

Castro also expressed dismay at Vance's willingness to meet Cuban exile leaders, who, Castro said, were "known by Cubans to personify everything that was corrupt in pre-Castro Cuba or involved in the Bay of Pigs invasion," Bradlee wrote. (However, Bradlee noted, news of Vance's meeting with the exiles was censored in Cuba.)

Asked what single thing the U.S. could do to open a new era in Cuban-American relations, Castro recommended that Washington end its trade embargo of the island. Such a move would create goodwill toward the U.S. in Europe and the Third World and would allow Cuba to purchase badly needed products ranging from tomato seeds to spare auto parts, Castro said.

Cuban Foreign Trade Minister Marcelo Fernandez said March 4 that Cuba was eager to buy a wide variety of American goods from foodstuffs and fertilizers to heavy industrial equipment. In return Cuba could sell the U.S. sugar, rum, cigars and raw materials including chrome, copper and nickel.

Vance proposed March 4 that Havana and Washington discuss a broad range of issues without preconditions. Meanwhile, persons close to President Carter made apparently contradictory statements on the U.S. trade embargo. Vice President Walter Mondale said March 4 he thought the U.S. was "far short" of a decision to lift the embargo. Charles Kirbo, a close friend and adviser to the President, predicted that Cuba and the U.S. would develop normal trade relations by the end of 1977, according to a published report March 5.

Finally, the State Department approved Castro's suggestion that U.S. athletic teams go to Cuba for friendly competition. A team of college basketball players from South Dakota was authorized to go to Cuba at the end of March or beginning of April, the Washington Post reported March 5. And authorization was given March 8 for professional baseball to send a team to Cuba.

Castro specifically had invited the New York Yankees, defending champions of the American League, but baseball commissioner Bowie Kuhn said March 8 that he would send only an all-star team composed of players from both the American and National Leagues. Kuhn said there might not be enough time to assemble such a team before the U.S. baseball season officially opened in early April.

In a related development, an Arlington Va. travel agent who recently took 20 colleagues on a tour of Cuba, said the island was ready to accept U.S. tourists, the Washington Post reported Feb. 8. Alex Lopez said 50 new hotels were under construction in Cuba. The island had a goal of 300,000 tourists by 1980, he said. The U.S. travel agents visited vacation sites, hospitals, factories and government ministries on their tour.

Carter reports 'indirect dialogue' on Cuba. President Carter Feb. 16 linked improved diplomatic relations with Cuba to the ending of Cuban interference in other countries, particularly Angola, and a restoration of human rights in Cuba itself.

Speaking informally at the Agriculture Department during a question-and-answer session with its employees, Carter said:

"I would like very much to see the Cubans remove their soldiers from Angola and let the Angolan natives make their own decisions about their government.

We've received information from indirect sources that [President Fidel] Castro and Cuba have promised to remove those troops. And that would be a step toward full normalization of relationships with Angola.

"The same thing applies ultimately to the restoration of normal relationships with Cuba.

"If I can be convinced that Cuba wants to remove their aggravating influence from other countries in this hemisphere, will not participate in violence in nations across the oceans, will recommit the former relationship that existed in Cuba towards human rights, then I would be willing to move toward normalizing relationships with Cuba as well."

In another informal setting Feb. 12—a

news conference of sorts while the President strolled around his home town of Plains, Ga.—Carter had pinpointed human rights as the key to improved relations between Cuba and the U.S. He expressed hope that recent conciliatory talk by Castro "can be followed up by mutual efforts to alleviate tensions and reduce animosities."

Carter did not identify his "indirect sources" of information, but President Jose Lopez Portillo of Mexico mentioned the subject of Cuban-U.S. relations at the conclusion of a two-day visit with Carter Feb. 15. Meeting with newsmen in Washington, Lopez Portillo said with regard to normalizing diplomacy between the U.S. and Cuba, "If the United States or Cuba require our good offices, we would be only too happy to make any effort in that regard, but I don't think it will be necessary because there seems to be goodwill on both sides."

Rep. Jonathan B. Bingham (D, N.Y.) also reported on the subject Feb. 15 after returning from a visit to Cuba and more than eight hours of talks with Castro. While Castro insisted that the U.S. embargo on trade with Cuba was barring negotiations on normalizing relations, Bingham reported, "There are several subjects that can and should be discussed without any preconditions immediately."

He said Castro had indicated his willingness to hold discussions with the Carter Administration on such subjects as a 200-mile fishing limit, cultural and sports exchanges and joint efforts to curb spread of a sugar cane blight.

Bingham had gone to Cuba Feb. 10 in his role as chairman of the subcommittee on economic policy and trade of the House International Relations Committee.

Bingham also reported that Cuban officials had told him the number of Cuban troops in Angola had been reduced by one-half since the preceding spring. He said that Castro and others had informed him, however, that Cuba would keep troops in Angola for some time and leave only when requested by the Neto government or possibly the Organization of African Unity.

At a news conference Feb. 23, Carter again brought up the subject of the denial of human rights in Cuba.

Any "substantial move in our relationship with Cuba," he said, "would have to await further discussions with them indirectly, and also some tangible evidence . . . that they are willing to restore basic human rights in Cuba, involving the number of prisoners. . . ,their attitude toward overseas adventures such as the one in Angola and other matters."

Cuba was one of the topics discussed when Carter answered questions from 42 citizens in 26 states during a two-hour, telephone call-in radio broadcast from the White House March 5.

The program, the first conducted by a U.S. president, was carried on the CBS radio network with CBS anchorman Walter Cronkite serving as moderator.

The President said that he "would like to do what I can to ease tensions with Cuba" but that "I don't know yet what we will do." Carter continued:

"Before any full normalization of relations can take place, though, Cuba would have to make some fairly substantial changes in their attitude.

"I would like to insist, for instance, that they not interfere in the internal affairs of countries in this hemisphere and that they decrease their military involvement in Africa and that they reinforce a commitment to human rights by releasing political prisoners that have been in jail now in Cuba for 17 or 18 years, things of that kind.

"But I think before we can reach that point we'll have to have discussions with them, and I do intend to see discussions initiated with Cuba quite early on reestablishing the antihijacking agreement, arriving at a fishing agreement between us and Cuba since our 200-mile limits do overlap between Florida and Cuba. And I would not be averse in the future to seeing visitation rights permitted as well."

As for the possibility of the New York Yankees playing an exhibition baseball game in Cuba this season, Carter said, "It's a possibility, yes."

■ American and Cuban delegations met in New York March 24–29 for the first round of negotiations on an agreement to regulate fishing in waters between the two countries. The talks, described by the State Department as "the first formal, face-to-face negotiations" between the U.S. and Cuba in 16 years, were occasioned by the recent establishment by both countries of 200-mile fishing zones. Since Cuba was only 90 miles from the Florida coast, an accord was needed to define each country's area of jurisdiction. The State Department said March 29 that "substantial progress" had been made in the fishing talks, which would resume "in the near future."

1975-77: CONFLICTING OBJECTIVES

■ U.S. officials disclosed March 28 that State Department and Cuban representatives had held several secret meetings in the U.S. between November 1974 and November 1975 to discuss bilateral issues and the normalization of relations. The talks, begun at the initiative of then-Secretary of State Henry Kissinger, apparently broke down because of Cuba's military intervention in the Angolan civil war.

U.S. to lift travel bans. President Carter announced March 9 that restrictions on travel by U.S. citizens to Cuba, Vietnam, Cambodia and North Korea would be lifted March 18.

Speaking at a news conference in Washington, Carter said he had "long been concerned" over the restrictions and feared they might constitute a violation of human rights, as defined by the 1975 Helsinki Agreement.

"I want to be sure that we don't violate those rights," Carter said, noting that a conference would be held in Yugoslavia in June to assess compliance with the agreement's provisions. The President admitted that the U.S. had been "culpable in some ways" by restricting travel within the country by some foreigners and by refusing visas to "those who disagree with us politically."

"I think it is entirely appropriate," Carter said, "for our country to take the leadership role and let the world say that the focal point for the preservation and protection of human rights is in the U.S."

Carter stressed that the U.S. did not have formal relations with the countries affected by the travel ban and added that such relations were "a doubtful prospect at this time."

The executive order that imposed the travel restrictions had to be renewed every six months. The current order expired March 18. The lifting of the ban meant U.S. citizens could now travel to any nation that would admit them.

It had always been possible for members of Congress, journalists, scholars, public-health officials, some athletes and some persons traveling for humanitarian reasons to get the restrictions removed from their U.S. passports, the Washington Post noted March 9.

However, the banned countries had taken differing attitudes to visits by Americans.

Thousands of Americans had visited Cuba since restrictions on travel to the island were imposed in 1960.

■ The Carter Administration March 25 eased currency restrictions on American visitors to Cuba. Under a new Treasury Department regulation, U.S. citizens who obtained visas to visit Cuba could spend U.S. dollars there and could buy up to $100 worth of Cuban pesos for personal use every six months. A visitor buying goods in Cuba was required to bring them back to the U.S. in his personal luggage.

U.S. team, senators & others visit—A team of basketball players from two South Dakota universities visited Cuba April 4–8, 1977 with a 90-member American delegation that included three members of the U.S. Congress—Sens. George McGovern and James Abourezk, both Democrats of South Dakota, and Rep. Les Aspin (D, Wis.).

The basketball team, representing the University of South Dakota and South Dakota State University, toured the island and lost two games to a taller and stronger Cuban national team. A third game was canceled to give the weary American players a rest.

The U.S. legislators, meanwhile, met with Cuban officials to discuss ways of improving relations between Havana and Washington. McGovern, Abourezk and Aspin met April 7–8 with Gen. Raul Castro, Cuba's defense minister, who was overseeing the Cuban government while his brother, President Fidel Castro, was on a month-long tour in Africa and the Soviet Union. McGovern and Aspin remained in Cuba after the South Dakota basketball team left. They met April 9 with Fidel Castro, who had returned from Moscow earlier that day.

Raul Castro April 8 said the basketball team's visit was an important step in restoring normal relations between Havana and Washington. Addressing American reporters during a break in his talks with McGovern, Abourezk and Aspin, Castro compared U.S.-Cuban relations to a bridge in wartime. "I think it was you who blew it up, but I won't say it," Castro said. "The war has ended and now we are reconstructing the bridge brick by brick—90 miles from Key West to Varadero. It takes a long time. At the end of the bridge we can shake hands, without winners or losers."

McGovern said after the talks that Raul Castro had demanded cancellation of the U.S. trade embargo against Cuba as a precondition for negotiations on other bilateral issues, such as reparations for the $1.8 billion worth of U.S. assets nationalized by Cuba after the 1959 revolution. McGovern said he agreed with Castro. "The embargo has never made any sense from the standpoint of U.S.-Cuban relations," he asserted. "[The U.S.] can trade with Peking, we can trade with Moscow. I don't see why not with Havana."

McGovern said Castro also had complained about overflights by the American SR-71 reconnaissance plane. According to Castro, the overflights began in September 1974 and were repeated on 16 later occasions, the last flight occurring Jan. 11. Castro said Cuba had protested privately to the U.S. three or four times but had received no response. Castro noted, however, that no overflights had occurred since the inauguration of President Carter.

Aspin said Castro had repeated his brother's earlier denial that Cuban troops had participated in the recent invasion of Zaire from Angola. Castro also told the U.S. legislators that Cuba was reducing its military force in Angola but was sending more "civilian technicians" there.

McGovern and Aspin met with Fidel Castro April 9 at Santa Maria del Mar, on the Caribbean coast outside Havana. Castro told reporters that day that the U.S. was torn between "the idealism of President Carter and the realism of the country." He said he would like to follow U.S.-Cuban developments a little longer before meeting with Carter.

Castro expressed satisfaction with the basketball team's visit and the recent lifting of U.S. restrictions on travel to Cuba, but he said full normalization of U.S.-Cuban relations would "take time."

U.S. tourists would be received in Cuba "with respect and friendship," Castro said, although "we don't have many hotels." "In these years of revolution," he explained, "no one has tried to create feelings of hostility toward the North American people. We have criticized the government. We have criticized the system. Instilling hatred is easy. What is hard is developing political conscience and culture."

McGovern said April 11, after returning to Washington, that Fidel Castro had insisted on the repeal of the U.S. trade embargo as a condition for the renewal of the 1973 anti-hijacking agreement between the U.S. and Cuba, which would expire April 15 on Cuba's initiative. Castro said, however, that he would enforce the agreement even after the lapse of the formal pact. He also indicated that even a partial lifting of the embargo could open the way for negotiations on other bilateral issues, McGovern said.

McGovern said he had given Castro a message from President Carter assuring Castro that the U.S. wanted to work for a normalization of U.S.-Cuban relations and expressing appreciation of Cuba's cooperation in recent fishing negotiations with the U.S. In response, McGovern said, Castro had called Carter "an idealist, a religious man and a good man."

McGovern said he would press Carter to repeal the trade embargo. (McGovern already had proposed a partial lifting of the embargo, to permit trade in food and medicines, as an amendment to the State Department authorization bill that was being considered by the Senate Foreign Relations Committee.)

The South Dakota senator said he would also work to expand U.S. athletic and cultural exchanges with Cuba, and to set up an exchange program for Cuban and American college students. Cuba had agreed to send its basketball team to play college teams in the U.S., and to host exhibition baseball games between a Cuban team and an all-star team from the U.S. major leagues, McGovern said. U.S. baseball commissioner Bowie Kuhn said the exhibition could be arranged for the fall of 1977 or spring of 1978.

■ American citizens from Puerto Rico and the U.S. mainland were among 87 volunteers of the 10th "Venceremos Brigade" who arrived in Cuba April 8 to help with sugar harvesting and construction work until mid-May. Some 200

American volunteers were reported in Cuba by April 11. They planned to build a monument to Cuban soldiers killed in Angola, according to the London Times.

■ Fifty-two businessmen from Minnesota visited Cuba April 18–22 for talks with Cuban officials in anticipation of a relaxation of the U.S. economic blockade. Cuban officials spoke frankly about the island's serious economic problems, and held out the prospect of substantial but not massive U.S.-Cuban trade once the embargo was lifted. President Castro met with all 52 Minnesotans April 20, and then conferred with 16 of them the next day. The 16 represented food and financial concerns.

Castro said Cuba was interested in exporting nickel, iron ore and other items to the U.S., and in buying industrial machinery and other American products. He went out of his way to praise President Carter, according to press reports, citing the "political courage" of Carter's recent energy message.

The businessmen's trip was sponsored by the Greater Minneapolis Chamber of Commerce and arranged with the help of Minnesota's Democratic senior senator, Hubert Humphrey. Castro sent boxes of cigars to Humphrey, Vice President Walter Mondale and Sen. McGovern. The Minnesota businessmen delivered them during a stopover in Washington on their return trip to Minneapolis.

■ The U.S. Treasury Department May 13 announced it would allow travel agents to arrange group tours to Cuba. Heretofore, only individuals had been allowed to travel to the island, with exceptions made for certain government-sponsored groups.

The MTS Daphne, the first U.S. cruise ship to sail to Cuba in 16 years, left New Orleans May 15 for Havana. The eight-deck liner was filled to capacity with more than 300 tourists and jazz musicians Dizzy Gillespie and Earl (Fatha) Hines. The departure was protested by several hundred Cuban exiles including President Castro's sister, Juanita. The passengers were received enthusiastically in Havana, where the U.S. musicians performed a well-received concert May 18. The visit ended May 19.

Mackey International Airlines, a small Miami-based company, canceled its plans to operate regular flights to Cuba after a bomb exploded in its Fort Lauderdale offices early May 25. Anti-Castro Cuban exiles claimed credit for the blast, which caused property damage but no casualties.

U.S.-Cuban fishing agreements. The U.S. and Cuba signed two fishing agreements April 27, 1977 following three days of talks in Havana. The first pact set provisional boundaries for fishing zones between the two countries, and the second covered terms under which Cuban fishermen would be allowed to fish for certain species in surplus supply within the U.S. zone.

A seven-man State Department delegation had arrived in Havana April 24 for the fishing talks. The group was headed by Terence Todman, assistant secretary of state for inter-American affairs, who was the first high-ranking U.S. diplomat to visit Cuba since 1961. Todman and four other members of the delegation returned to the U.S. April 28. The two other delegates remained in Cuba until May 2 to interview some of the 27 U.S. citizens held in Cuban jails.

(A State Department letter made public by Sen. Jesse Helms [R, N.C.] May 13 said eight of the U.S. prisoners were serving terms ranging from 20 to 30 years on sentences for political crimes handed down in the 1960s. The other 19 Americans were serving terms for common crimes, according to the letter written by Douglas J. Bennett Jr., assistant secretary of state for congressional relations.)

The fishing accord was published in Havana May 25. It would allow Cuban vessels to fish off the U.S. coast for a total catch to be determined by U.S. authorities. Cuban ships also would be able to call at U.S. ports to obtain supplies and equipment and to undergo repairs.

U.S. panel votes to ease trade curbs. The U.S. Senate Foreign Relations Committee May 10, 1977 approved an amendment to allow Cuba to buy medicine, food and agricultural supplies from the U.S. The legislation was later modified to appease opponents of trade with Cuba.

The amendment, to a pending State Department authorization bill, was a diluted version of a measure proposed by Sen. George McGovern (D, S.D.) with the apparent blessing of President Carter. McGovern had suggested a complete lifting of the embargo on U.S.-Cuban trade in agricultural products and medicine.

A majority of the committee had opposed McGovern's original proposal, arguing that it would give away vital U.S. bargaining power in future negotiations with Cuba. The State Department had shared this objection, although it did not say so until after the compromise amendment was passed by a 10–6 vote.

The following day, on the initiative of committee member Jacob K. Javits (R, N.Y.), the panel voted to give President Carter authority to halt shipments to Cuba at any time.

Passage of the May 10 amendment was greeted with little enthusiasm in Cuba, whose leaders had demanded a complete lifting of the U.S. trade embargo as a prerequisite for further negotiations on outstanding U.S.-Cuban disputes. President Fidel Castro said May 11, "The partial abolition of the economic blockade against Cuba is inadequate and does not resolve [our] problem with the U.S. government."

Nevertheless, observers saw the amendment as one more step toward normal relations between Havana and Washington. Cuba was eager to buy U.S. medicine and food, although it was desperately short of foreign exchange with which to make the purchases.

The Senate June 16 approved the State Department authorization after Sen. Robert Dole (R, Kan.) had provoked debate with an amendment saying Cuba should not be recognized and that the U.S. trade embargo against the country should not be even partially lifted unless Cuba withdrew its troops from Africa, paid $1.8 billion in compensation to U.S. companies for confiscated property and met several other conditions.

An attempt to table, and so kill, the Dole amendment failed, 39–53. However, the Senate then adopted, 54–37, a compromise amendment offered by Byrd.

Byrd's amendment simply said that U.S. negotiators with Cuba should not disregard Cuban activities in Africa and that the negotiations should proceed on a reciprocal basis.

U.S. & Cuba to exchange diplomats. The U.S. and Cuba agreed May 30, 1977 to exchange diplomats by establishing "interest" offices in each other's capital.

The agreement, announced in Havana June 2 and in Washington the following day, was considered an important step toward a resumption of full diplomatic relations between the two governments. But U.S. officials stressed that full ties would have to wait until American and Cuban negotiators resolved a number of outstanding disputes.

Within the next two or three months, according to the agreement, each country would place in the other's capital an "interest section" consisting of eight to 10 diplomats and consular officials. Each section would occupy its country's former embassy in the foreign capital, but under another nation's flag—the U.S. section under the Swiss flag, and the Cuban section under the Czechoslovakian banner.

The interest sections would discuss a wide range of bilateral issues, performing much of the work of embassies but without the traditional protocol. The senior diplomat of each section would hold the rank of counselor, the third rank behind ambassador and minister, according to a U.S. State Department spokesman.

The Carter Administration warned that while the agreement represented "an improvement" in U.S.-Cuban affairs, it was not "tantamount to diplomatic relations." Jody Powell, President Carter's press secretary, said the establishment of interest sections could be seen "as a step—primarily a procedural step—that will make it less difficult to have discussions that hopefully can resolve the substantial differences that still exist" between Havana and Washington.

Among the "differences" to which Powell alluded were Cuban demands that the U.S. lift its trade embargo of the island,

and U.S. demands that Cuba pull its troops out of Africa, release its American prisoners, show more respect for human rights, grant visiting rights in Cuba and the U.S. to members of divided families, and compensate American companies whose assets were seized by the Communist government.

The arrangement establishing interest sections had been proposed by the U.S. and accepted by Cuba virtually without amendment, according to the New York Times June 4. The agreement was signed in New York after only one day of negotiations by Pelegrin Torras, Cuba's deputy foreign minister, and William H. Luers, U.S. acting secretary of state for inter-American affairs.

Republicans oppose renewed ties—Leaders of the U.S. Republican Party criticized the Carter Administration's moves toward renewed relations with Cuba, asserting the Cuban government had not yet made sufficient concessions to the U.S.

Sen. Robert Dole (Kan.) said June 3 that he would introduce legislation barring any future improvement in U.S.-Cuban relations until Havana removed its troops from Africa; released Americans jailed in Cuba on political charges; restored guarantees of human rights for its citizens; paid the $1.8 billion in compensation claimed by U.S. companies nationalized in Cuba; renewed the lapsed anti-hijacking agreement with the U.S., and guaranteed the future security of the U.S. naval base at Guantanamo Bay in eastern Cuba.

Senate Minority Leader Howard Baker (Tenn.) had said earlier that Cuban military involvement in Africa made this "the worst time in history" for Washington to seek diplomatic relations with Havana, it was reported June 5. "I can't believe for one minute that Cuban troops are in Ethiopia, or other parts of Africa, as an extension of Cuban foreign policy," Baker said. "They're there as surrogates for Russia, and this is exactly the wrong time for the United States to get cozy with Cuba."

Former President Gerald Ford expressed a similar view in a talk with newsmen in Houston, it was reported June 5. "I think it would be a mistake to resume diplomatic relations with Cuba as long as Cuba has 15,000 to 20,000 troops in Angola," Ford declared. Washington and Havana could renew ties "under certain conditions," he said, but not while Cuba was "expanding its military operations... doing the things they're doing to promote communism."

Rep. Clair W. Burgener (R, Calif.), in a statement printed in the Congressional Record June 10, warned against lifting the trade embargo against Cuba and establishing full relations until Castro "shows some good faith." As "evidence of lack of good faith," Burgener declared:

"First. He expropriated $1.8 billion of American private property, the largest seizure in the history of the American countries. Eighty-nine percent of that was owned by corporate interests and their shareholders but $233 million was owned by private citizens and $13 million by churches and educational institutions.

"Second. I will not belabor this one but certainly he has flouted the principle of self-determination by interfering in the Angolan civil war, with some 10,000 to 12,000 Cuban troops still there.

"Third. He holds thousands of political prisoners and I have evidence and testimony that this is undisputed. In terms of human rights this does not match our President's efforts at all at the present time.

"Fourth. He unilaterally in April canceled the hijacking agreement. We feel this is a very important agreement to both countries. It was entered into and it worked but he unilaterally canceled it. Is this evidence of good faith? I submit that it is not.

"Fifth. Finally, there are at least 18 Americans held, 18 of our own citizens held in Cuban prisons. Eleven are held for the crimes of hijacking or drugs, and so on, and we have no quarrel with that, but at least seven are political prisoners in the country of Cuba and are held for political reasons.

"Mr. Chairman, it seems to me, why should we be the first to turn the other cheek? Why not have Mr. Castro demonstrate some good faith and then we can begin to ease tensions.

"Mr. Chairman, I will make one final point here. Anna Balbis, who is the exiled Second Secretary who formerly served in the Communist Cuban Embassy in Peking, recently at Dartmouth College stated there are 50,000 Cubans being held as political prisoners, in 56 prisons, in 26 concentration camps and 108 prison farms in Cuba."

Rep. Donald M. Fraser (D, Minn.), during the same discussion, told the House:

"I do not think there is any question but what the Castro government is guilty of human rights violations, but we have never applied that standard to the recognition of any country around the world. If we did, we ought to break relations with the Soviet Union, most of Eastern Europe, southern Africa, and most of the countries of Latin America. We would stop having diplomatic personnel in most of the countries around the world.

"The fact is, we have interests that we have to work out with Cuba. The 200-mile fishing zone has required contact, and we have had negotiations on that. There will be Americans in Cuba, and their interests have to be loked after.

"I think we do need to look at some of these issues. I am very much opposed to Cuban involvement in Angola, but we are going to be better off if we can talk to them than if we cannot. This does not involve diplomatic recognition in any event, but having some American personnel on the ground which are able to look after American interests and look after the interests we have, such as the commercial situation, seems to me to make sense."

Rep. Ronald V. Dellums (D, Calif.), also supporting a relaxation of tensions with Cuba, told the House the same day:

"I would like to place my argument in a much larger context. The nations of the world have a profound obligation to address critical and complex questions. The issues the world faces include disarmament, economic questions, ecological issues, issues with respect to the shortage of food in the world, and so forth.

"Mr. Chairman, these are enormous questions, important issues, issues that transcend nations themselves.

"It would seem to me that we cannot get on with the business of dealing with those problems until we have some ability to communicate.

"What are we afraid of from a tiny nation 90 miles off our coast, a nation of 9.5 million people?

"They certainly do not pose a military threat to this country.

"It seems to me, Mr. Chairman, that we have an obligation to begin to speak with each other because at some point we have to move past our nationalism in order to deal with the issue of the survival of human life on the face of the Earth and we ought to start this by beginning to communicate.

"If we are able to communicate with the Soviet Union and if we are able to communicate with China—these are the two powerful Communist nations—then why should we be fearful of these tiny Communist nations? Maybe it is because they cannot bomb us back, and because they cannot bomb us back we refuse to deal with them, and we kick them around on the floor of Congress. It seems fundamentally absurd that with respect to these small countries we refuse to deal with them.

"We talk about Cuba spreading communism around the world yet we have no problem in dealing with China and with the Soviet Union.

"But here, Mr. Chairman, is a tiny little country of 9.5 million people and we refuse to deal with them.

"Finally, Mr. Chairman, many people object also to Cuba being involved in Angola, but I stand here as one appreciative of their involvement in Angola, because if they had not been involved in Angola, then one of the most racist, repressive nations in the world would have marched through and taken over Angola, and I would have been totally opposed to that development."

Rep. Dante B. Fascell (D, Fla.) told the House July 11 that if the U.S. "fails to secure the resolution of certain important outstanding issues before the normalization of relations with Cuba continues any further, then any satisfactory resolution of these issues will be endangered, or perhaps foreclosed." Fascell continued:

"... Certainly the United States should not take actions which would significantly benefit Cuba prior to agreement to resolve such issues.

"I must emphasize at the outset that I have no quarrel at all with establishing better communications between the two countries. It is of paramount importance to realize, however, that before there can be a restoration of relations between the United States and Cuba, our Government must secure the satisfactory settlement of a number of difficult and vital issues of contention.

"There are at least four such issues which must be resolved prior to further significant normalization of relations. First, there is the continued holding of American citizens as political prisoners in Cuban jails. Second, there are serious questions concerning Cuba's record on human rights. Third, we are continually hearing reports of Cuba's active and increasing involvement in the internal affairs of certain African countries, Angola being an example. And, finally, there is Cuba's failure to provide any settlement for the extensive expropriations of the property of U.S. citizens, expropriations which were clearly in violation both of international law and of basic human rights.

"It is my strong conviction that all of these issues must be resolved before there can be full resumption of normal diplomatic and economic relations between the United States and Cuba. Our failure to resolve these issues prior to the full resumption of relations with Cuba would represent nothing less than the sacrifice of interests which are of key importance to U.S. citizens and which represent American policy goals of the highest order. If we ignore these issues, Cuba will secure the objectives which it seeks to attain, economic and political, while the United States overlooks those principles of human rights and international law which we have in the past so strongly defended. Any movement to resume relations which is blind to these concerns must be opposed.

"I would like to review the problem that began in 1959 with the expropriation by Cuba of property owned by literally thousands of U.S. nationals, in both their individual and their corporate capacities. In reviewing this problem, I will also trace the efforts which I and many others have made to secure just and fair compensation for these tremendous losses.

"Before reviewing this problem I would like to make it clear that my conviction in this matter is based on more than what might be called 'traditional' international law. Under traditional international legal principles the citizens of every state are entitled to just compensation for deprivation of their private property by a foreign state. This principle is so time-honored and based on such elementary notions of fairness that it alone justifies our condemnation of Cuba's action of depriving U.S. nationals of their private property. Indeed, our State Department has described this Cuban action as being 'manifestly in violation of those principles of international law which have long been accepted by the free countries of the West. It is in essence, discriminatory, arbitrary and confiscatory.'

"What must be realized, however, is that such deprivations represent nothing less than an abridgment of one of the fundamental human rights. I am referring to the right of a person to his property.

"The Universal Declaration of Human Righs, adopted by a vote of 48 to 0 by the General Assembly of the United Nations in 1948 and generally recognized as being declaratory of customary international law, provides explicitly for the protection of private property. And similar protection is afforded in the protocols to the European Convention on Human Rights and in the American Convention on Human Rights. The latter has been signed by 12 Latin American countries, all of them neighbors to ourselves and Cuba, and it provides in article 21 that—

No one shall be deprived of his property except upon payment of just compensation . . .

"It is on just such a guarantee that I base my present concern.

"I am sure that all of us support and are proud of the United States' commitment to the protection of human rights throughout the world. But this commitment should not blind us to our duty to champion the human rights of our own nationals no less than those of foreign nationals abused by their own countries. Indeed, I should think that our primary duty is to our own citizens. And it is in the spirit of protecting these American citizens whom all of us represent that I approach the problem of Cuban expropriations.

"Shortly after the Castro regime seized power in Cuba in January of 1959 it expropriated thousands of property holdings of U.S. citizens in express retaliation against the U.S. suspension of the import quota and the special pricing arrangements for Cuban sugar. These expropriations took various forms, including outright confiscation, interventions, nationalizations, and purportedly legal squeeze-outs.

"For example, pursuant to its Agrarian Reform Law of May 1959, Cuba expropriated American-owned farms and rural properties. Under Cuban Law No. 653 of November 1959, all pending applications for further exploration of American-owned ore concessions were canceled arbitrarily, and new applications were ignored or disapproved. By the Urban Reform Law of October 1960, Cuba effected a cancellation of all mortgages on properties in the country. And by certain resolutions issued pursuant to Law No. 851 of July 1960, Cuba authorized the nationalization of American banks and of any Cuban concerns in which Americans owned majority interests.

"I could continue citing Cuba's confiscatory "laws" and actions at length, but irrespective of the details, the principle is crystal clear: Cuba's action in expropriating the private property of U.S. nationals was an outright violation of international law and a deprivation of the basic human right to property.

"Our course, many of the persons deprived of their property by these illegal actions undertook to secure redress for their losses. To begin with, a number of U.S. claimants brought actions in the Cuban courts, under Cuban laws which purported to provide safeguards against arbitrary deprivations by the Cuban Government. These efforts proved to be unavailing. If nothing else, however, they did demonstrate that compensation was never a realistic possibility under Cuban law as applied by Castro. Indeed, an American court has held as much.

"In October of 1964, the Congress adopted a bill which I sponsored, the Cuban Claims Act of 1964, which amended the International Claims Settlement Act of 1949 so as to add to it title V; authorizing the determination of the validity and amount of each claim by a U.S. national against Cuba. This amendment provides for the adjudication of these Cuban claims by the Foreign Claims Settlement Commission of the United States.

"It should be emphasized that title V does not provide for payment of the losses that result from the Cuban expropriations. The statute provides only for the "preadjudication" by the Commission of the validity and amounts of such claims and the certification of the findings to the Secretary of State. This certification is meant to provide the Secretary of State with information for use in the future negotiation of a claims settlement agreement with Cuba. Since no such negotiation has occurred, the U.S. nationals who have had their claims adjudicated in this manner have received nothing as yet by way of compensation. The Cuban Claims program is, therefore, a presettlement adjudication of claims, meant to determine the validity and amount of each American claim and to provide a benchmark for our Government in its future settlement negotiations with Cuba.

"The Foreign Claims Settlement Commission began to administer the Cuban Claims program, as I have just described it, on November 1, 1965, and finished its job in July of 1972. In that time the Commission adjudicated almost 9,000 claims for compensation, claims for properties ranging from small agricultural and shopkeeping interests to large industrial enterprises.

"Of these almost 9,000 claims, the Commission certified awards in 5,911, which in the aggregate represent losses again certified by the Commission, of $1,851,-057,358. To break these figures down further, 898 corporate claims were awarded, representing in amount a total of $1,578,498,839.55. Individual claims awarded totaled 5,013 and represent in amount $221,049,729.14. I refer anyone interested in pursuing more details regarding these thousands of claims to the 1972 annual report of the Foreign Claims Settlement Commission.

"Let me add that this total of over $1.8 billion does not include any element of interest from the date of the takings, nor does it attempt to take into account the rapid inflation of the past two decades, nor does it include an extremely large claim by the U.S. Government itself for the loss of certain Cuban nickel interests. If interest were added, the total claims of the United States on behalf of its nationals through December 31, 1977, would be on the order of over $3 billion.

"Thus, Cuba's expropriation of the property of U.S. nationals since January of 1959 represents the largest single expropriation by one country recorded by history up to the present time.

"What I now insist upon is that these interests of American nationals be vigorously defended by our Government

1975-77: CONFLICTING OBJECTIVES

as it proceeds to establish a new relationship with the Government of Cuba. Failure by the United States to secure a just and fair settlement of these claims would constitute a severe default in our Government's protection of the rights of her citizens. Equally, it would establish a precedent which would place the property rights and, therefore, the fundamental human rights of American citizens in worldwide jeopardy.

"I have heard reports that the State Department intends to make a monetary settlement of the Cuban expropriations an element in the plan for improving our relations with Cuba. I applaud this sentiment, if, indeed, it has been expressed with conviction. But intentions are not actions, and we must make certain that a settlement is a prerequisite to the full normalization of relations with Cuba. We are defending here fundamental human rights of American citizens, rights which we must advocate for all peoples, but on which we must insist for our own citizens.

"It is with this understanding that I advocate the protection of the rights of our citizens under the international laws of the world community."

A study by a Washington-based research group showed that most Americans wanted renewed relations with Cuba but under terms that heavily favored the U.S., it was reported Aug. 8. The study, made by Potomac Associates and based partly on a Gallup poll conducted in mid-April, said 59% of those polled favored establishing normal relations with the Castro government, although 51% saw Cuba as a threat to U.S. security. The poll found 52% opposed to a partial lifting of the trade embargo before normal relations were established, and 59% opposed to paying Cuba reparations for damages caused by the embargo or the Bay of Pigs invasion. In addition, those polled wanted Cuba to pull its troops out of Africa (46% to 35%) and to release American political prisoners from its jails (62% to 23%).

Castro doubts early resumption of full ties—In a TV chat broadcast in the U.S. June 9, Castro said he was "honestly and seriously interested in improving relations" with the U.S., but he doubted that full diplomatic ties could be established soon. "Maybe in Carter's second term, between 1980 and 1984," he said. He described the President as "an idealistic man with certain ethical principles that have their roots in his religious convictions. He is a well-prepared man, . . . an intelligent man, and also . . . a man who trusts himself."

Castro again dismissed as insufficient a measure adopted by the Senate Foreign Relations Committee that would allow Cuba to buy American medicine, food and agricultural supplies but would bar Cuba from selling its own products to the U.S. Under these terms, he said, Cuba "would not buy anything at all in the U.S., not even an aspirin for a headache, and we have lots of headaches."

U.S. & Cuban 'interest' offices open—The U.S. and Cuban governments Sept. 1 established "interest sections" in each other's capitals.

The 10-man offices would occupy their governments' former embassy buildings and function as virtual embassies despite the absence of normal diplomatic relations between the two countries. The Cuban office in Washington officially would be part of the Czechoslovakian Embassy to the U.S., and the American office in Havana would be part of the Swiss Embassy there.

Establishment of the offices brought the U.S. and Cuba one step closer to full diplomatic ties, which were broken by Washington in January 1961. But officials of both countries said normal relations could not be expected soon. Both sides wanted to negotiate a number of bilateral issues first, and the Carter Administration wanted to downplay Cuban relations while it sought Senate ratification of the new Panama Canal treaties.

U.S. and Cuban officials hailed their steady rapprochement at a ceremony opening the Cuban office in Washington Sept. 1. Philip C. Habib, U.S. undersecretary of state for political affairs, said creation of the interest offices was "a beginning, not an end. It is not a big step, but it is a significant one just the same." The new offices would allow the U.S. and Cuba to "speak to each other directly," although "the dialogue won't always be an easy one," Habib said. The "ultimate goal" of President Carter's policy toward

Cuba was "full friendship," he declared.

The head of the Cuban interest office, Ramon Sanchez Parodi, said his government was prepared "to analyze deeply and with a constructive spirit . . . those matters that the U.S. government considers as issues of the existing conflicts between our two countries." These issues presumably included the human rights situation in Cuba, the fate of American prisoners held by the Communist government, Cuba's military role in Africa and the $1.8 billion in claims against the Cuban government by American companies and individuals.

Sanchez Parodi said his government could not renew relations with Washington until the U.S. lifted its trade embargo against Cuba. He also said the U.S. must clamp down on "the aggressive actions" carried out by Cuban exiles "against Cuba from U.S. territory." He noted that the initiative for opening the interest offices had come from the U.S., but he added, "Cuba has always been open to establishing normal relations between our two countries."

The U.S. office in Havana was headed by Lyle Franklin Lane, 51, a career foreign service officer who would hold the rank of counselor in Cuba. Lane had served previously in Costa Rica, Ecuador, Guatemala and Peru, most recently as deputy chief of the U.S. Embassy in Lima. The chief U.S. consular official in Havana would be Thomas L. Holladay, 31, who had been working in the State Department's Office of the Coordinator of Cuban Affairs.

Neither interest section immediately occupied its embassy building because each site was being repaired after 16 years of neglect. The Cuban government was charging the U.S. about $250,000 to renovate the American Embassy in Havana, while the U.S. was charging Cuba four times that amount to fix up its properties in Washington, the Washington Post reported Aug. 16. President Fidel Castro said this showed that the Cuban people were very honest and American wages were too high, but the Post noted that the U.S. was importing much of the equipment and supplies for its Havana embassy, thereby reducing the cost of Cuban work on the renovation.

Cuba frees Americans. The Cuban government announced June 3, 1977 that it would free 10 American prisoners immediately and review the cases of the other 20 U.S. citizens jailed on the island.

The 10 favored prisoners, all aged 20–30 and held by Cuba on drug charges, were flown to Mexico June 12 on to the U.S. the next day. U.S. consular officials in Mexico City said the former prisoners appeared to be in good health.

A State Department spokesman June 3 asked Cuba to show "compassionate consideration" for the 20 American prisoners that stayed behind, some of whom were elderly persons held for years on political grounds. Cuba held seven Americans for "crimes against the state," according to the Miami Herald June 8.

President Castro said Aug. 11 that he would allow more than 80 U.S. citizens to leave Cuba with their families. The Americans always had been free to go but had refused to leave without their Cuban-born wives and children.

Castro made the announcement at the end of a four-day visit to Cuba by U.S. Sen. Frank Church (D, Ida.). Church said the Cuban leader's action was "a very important, humane gesture of goodwill" that was certain to please President Carter.

Castro also agreed to free the crews of two U.S.-registered boats that had been seized recently in Cuban waters. Church had told him that the wife of one of the crew members was dying of cancer. Another crew member was reported to be a nephew of Charles G. (Bebe) Rebozo, a close friend of former President Richard Nixon. His boat reportedly was carrying a large cargo of marijuana when it was seized.

Castro & Church discuss disputes—Sen. Church had arrived in Cuba Aug. 8 on a U.S. Air Force plane, the first to land in Cuba in 16 years. He said he hoped his visit would help "heal the wounds" between the U.S. and Cuba, a phrase he used often during his visit. Castro replied at one point that there were "wounds" but no "cancer" in U.S.-Cuban relations.

U.S. officials said Aug. 8 Church's visit to Cuba was of "enormous importance" to Carter. The senator met with the President before departing for Havana, and he also conferred with Carter's national security adviser, Zbigniew Brzezinski.

Church spent most of Aug. 9 and 10 with Castro, but they did not get down to substantive talks until late in the second day. Then they discussed a wide range o problems, including Cuba's economic straits, its military presence in Africa, U.S. detente with the Soviet Union, the Panama Canal, the U.S. trade embargo against Cuba and the fate of seven American citizens jailed in Cuba for allegedly carrying out subversive activities sponsored by the Central Intelligence Agency.

Castro and Church reportedly made progress on the last issue, which Carter considered a key obstacle to good relations between the U.S. and Cuba. A member of Church's party said Castro had agreed to "review the seven [prisoners] on a case-by-case basis," the New York Times reported Aug. 12. Castro, Church and their aides declined to give more details of the two leaders' talks.

At a press conference before his return to the U.S. Aug. 11, Church thanked Castro for giving him "three days of his time" and said he believed they had become personal friends. Castro in turn praised Church as an "important, courageous politician" who was "capable, serious and intellectual . . . a man you can talk to."

Church later told reporters: "I found [Castro's] views to be reasonable, objective and surprisingly moderate. Most surprising of all, he did not display bitterness toward the U.S. . . . If any man had a reason to be embittered it might have been him."

Church said that during their talks Castro had never requested a specific concession from the U.S. The Cuban leader "clearly hopes that relations will continue to improve and [he] looks forward to the end of the embargo," Church said. "But he said he understands the complexities of American politics, and he sees it more difficult for President Carter to make a decision than for him to do so."

Church said Castro had conceded that the new U.S.-Panamanian agreement on the Panama Canal, which some American conservatives considered a "giveaway" to Panama, would increase pressure on Carter not to make any deal with Cuba that appeared to grant Cuban demands.

Americans & relatives leave—Fifty-five U.S. and Cuban citizens flew from Havana to Florida Sept. 22 as the Cuban government began allowing American residents of Cuba to emigrate with their Cuban relatives.

The emigrants were flown in a U.S. Air Force plane to the Homestead air base near Miami. It was unclear how many of them were U.S. citizens and how many were Cubans. The New York Times counted 29 Americans and 26 Cuban relatives; Reuters said it was 31 Americans and 24 Cubans, and the Miami Herald gave two conflicting counts—31 Americans and 24 Cubans in its lead news article, and 16 Americans and 39 Cubans in a news analysis essay.

The emigrants were greeted by Joseph Aragon, a special assistant to President Carter on issues concerning Hispanic Americans. Aragon read a message from Carter calling the release of the emigrants "the first in what we hope will be a series of similar humanitarian actions on the part of the government of Cuba."

Carter's message also expressed hope that "in the near future we shall begin to see the bringing together of other families, both Cuban and Americans, who have been separated over long periods of time, which can only be measured in terms of anguish."

The U.S. State Department estimated that there were 55 more American citizens in Cuba with about 200 close Cuban relatives. About half of the Americans wished to be repatriated, a department spokesman said. They would be departing for the U.S. as soon as their papers were processed.

U.S. prisoner to be freed—The U.S. State Department said Dec. 13 that Cuba would release a 63-year-old American prisoner it had held for 14 years.

The prisoner, Frank Emmick, was a former businessman who had been jailed in 1963 on charges of heading operations of the U.S. Central Intelligence Agency (CIA) in Cuba. Emmick denied the charges, but admitted to having smuggled a letter out of Cuba in 1972 or 1973 to Richard Helms, then director of the CIA, the Washington Post reported Dec. 7. U.S. Reps. Frederick W. Richmond (D, N.Y.) and Richard Nolan (D, Minn.) had urged President Castro to release Emmick during their visit to Cuba earlier in December. They reminded Castro that Emmick had suffered two heart attacks in prison and recommended his release as a "humanitarian" gesture.

Anti- & pro-Cuban underground. The U.S. State Department Aug. 3 said the U.S. was giving Cuba information on terrorist acts being planned against the island by Cuban exiles in Miami and elsewhere. An assistant U.S. attorney in Miami said Aug. 15 that a planned raid on Cuba by exiles based in Miami had been foiled earlier in the summer when federal and Florida State agents informed the Cuban government of the plot, seized three armed boats to have been used in the raid and arrested one boat's owner. He was Pedro Gil, a member of Brigade 2506, the Miami-based organization of veterans of the 1961 Bay of Pigs invasion.

Cuban spies in the United States and Canada had provided limited aid to a violent American radical group in the late 1960s and early 1970s, according to a secret report by the Federal Bureau of Investigation, revealed by the New York Times Oct. 9. Several members of the radical group, which called itself the Weather Underground, were helped by Cuban agents to leave and re-enter the U.S. at times when they feared arrest by American authorities, the FBI reported.

Progress expected to be slow. Fidel Castro acknowledged Sept. 29, 1977 that there was a "certain improvement" in U.S.-Cuban relations, but he said the process of normalizing ties would be "long and slow." Addressing a crowd of one million persons in Havana's Revolution Square, Castro reasserted that U.S.-Cuban relations could not improve substantially until the U.S. lifted its trade embargo against the island. He also demanded that the U.S. remove its naval base from Guantanamo Bay in eastern Cuba, a base Castro often had called "a dagger in Cuba's heart."

Castro said he was willing to discuss the $1.8-billion worth of claims by U.S. businesses that Cuba had nationalized since 1959. But he said the U.S. first must compensate Cuba for damages caused by the 16-year trade embargo and by the Bay of Pigs invasion and other U.S. "aggressions."

Castro sent Foreign Trade Minister Marcelo Fernandez Font to Washington Oct. 3 to discuss U.S.-Cuban trade once relations were normalized. Fernandez told a conference of U.S. businessmen that the compensation demanded by Castro was higher than the $1.8 billion claimed from Cuba by the U.S.

Fernandez said that once the trade embargo was lifted, U.S. exports to Cuba might reach $350 million in the first year of "normal trade" and pass the billion-dollar mark within three or four years. But he said this volume could be reached only if the U.S. fully opened its markets to Cuba by restoring Cuba's most-favored-nation trading status and by giving the island special tariff preferences.

U.S. officials were less sanguine about the early possibilities for U.S. exports to Cuba. They noted that certain restrictions were imposed by the 1974 Trade Act and that Cuba was quite short of hard currency reserves.

Fernandez said Cuba was interested in buying American foodstuffs, animal feeds, drugs, fertilizers, ferrous and non-ferrous metals and machinery, and other industrial equipment including entire plants. In exchange, Cuba wanted to sell the U.S. sugar, tobacco, shellfish and nickel.

In another U.S.-Cuban development, the U.S. quietly ended its 14-year-old practice of "blacklisting" foreign ships that called at Cuban ports. Under the policy, such vessels were forbidden to haul U.S. government-generated cargo (such as foreign aid or agricultural commodities) or to refuel in U.S. ports. The policy change was decided by the National Security Council June 10 but not announced by the Maritime Administration until Sept. 7.

Petroleum products refined in Cuba were entering the U.S. through oil brokers in Venezuela, the Netherlands and

France, according to a report in the Caracas Daily Journal Oct. 20. The Cuban products were purchased from the brokers by "foreign-based firms operating in the eastern United States," the Journal's source said.

U.S. businessmen visit Cuba—A delegation of several dozen business executives from Massachusetts visited Cuba Oct. 24-28 to discuss trade opportunities in the event that the U.S. dropped its economic embargo of the island.

President Castro told the executives Oct. 26 that they should not expect normal U.S.-Cuban relations soon. "After 17 years of confrontation and bad relations," he said, "the situation cannot be changed in a few months." The Carter Administration needed time, he noted, to resolve the controversy over the Panama Canal treaties and to tackle other problems.

Castro said the Carter Administration was friendlier toward Cuba than previous U.S. governments had been, but he charged that the U.S. was still trying to foment rebellion in Cuba. Terrorists trained by the U.S. Central Intelligence Agency were still attacking Cuba from bases in the U.S., he asserted.

Castro said his government had freed "almost all" the American prisoners in Cuban jails, holding on to only "a few ... who were part of hijackings, and three or four important CIA agents." Cuba did not plan to free these prisoners, he said, although the lifting of the U.S. trade embargo might "facilitate new releases."

Massachusetts Lt. Gov. Thomas P. O'Neill Jr. accompanied the delegation and spoke with two of the American prisoners. They told him that prison conditions in Cuba were improving steadily. O'Neill was allowed to take home a tape of his conversations with the prisoners as a gift to their families.

(The last American prisoner freed by Cuba was Maria del Carmen Ruiz, who was jailed in 1969 for alleged "crimes against the [Cuban] state." Her release, confirmed by the U.S. State Department Oct. 13, apparently was related to the release in the U.S. of Angel Figueroa Cordero, a Puerto Rican nationalist who was jailed in 1954 for wounding five U.S. congressmen.)

Twenty university professors from the U.S. and Cuba met secretly for five days in October at a Yale University facility in New York State, it was reported Nov. 9. The thirteen Americans and seven Cubans discussed a wide range of topics of "scholarly interest," according to the meeting's organizer, Prof. Alfred Stepan of Yale.

Link to JFK death doubted. Data released by the U.S. Federal Bureau of Investigation Dec. 7, 1977, in response to a Freedom of Information Act request, indicated that FBI investigators doubted that Fidel Castro had been involved in the assassination of John F. Kennedy.

The massive files apparently contained little that was dramatic or new. The documents showed that former FBI Director J. Edgar Hoover was confident that Lee Harvey Oswald had killed Kennedy. They also showed, however, that Hoover, at least for a time, entertained some doubt as to whether Oswald had acted alone.

One document, a memorandum dated Dec. 12, 1963 in which Hoover described for his aides a telephone conversation he had had with J. Lee Rankin, counsel for the Warren Commission, gave a succinct account of Hoover's views:

"I said I personally believe Oswald was the assassin; that the second aspect as to whether he was the only man gives me great concern.... [Hoover noted that the FBI had] several letters, not in the report because we were not able to prove it, written to him [Oswald] from Cuba referring to the job he was going to do, his good marksmanship, and stating when it was all over he would be brought back to Cuba and be presented to the chief; but we do not know if the chief was [Cuban leader Fidel] Castro.... I urged strongly that we not reach the conclusion Oswald was the only man."

However, other documents released Dec. 7 showed that the FBI had doubts, which were shared by Hoover, as to the authenticity of the letters that suggested Oswald was part of a Cuban conspiracy to assassinate Kennedy.

According to the files, two letters appeared to be involved. The first—described in the Hoover memo—referred to a job Oswald was going to do that required accurate shooting. The letter, signed "Pedro Charles" and addressed to Oswald, was intercepted in Dallas Dec. 5, 1963. It was suspect because of its dates: although dated Nov. 10, 1963 (before the Nov. 22 assassination of Kennedy), it had a Havana postmark of Nov. 28. (Presumably, Charles was a Cuban agent.)

The second letter, which was dated Nov. 27 and postmarked from Havana Nov. 28, was addressed to the then-Attorney General, Robert Kennedy. The letter, signed "Mario del Rosario Molina," claimed that Oswald had killed Kennedy at the orders of Charles. The letter said Charles had met Oswald in Miami two months earlier and paid him $7,000.

An FBI examination of the two letters, described in the files, determined that both letters had been typed on the same machine. Also, the examination showed that the same type of pen and ink had been used to sign both letters.

A report from the bureau's intelligence division, dated Dec. 11, 1963, concluded that it seemed "clear that this matter represents an attempted hoax, possibly perpetrated by some anti-Castro group seeking to attach blame to the Castro government."

Another document showed that Hoover was inclined to share the view that the letters were an attempted hoax.

Terrorism Hampers Detente, Castro Cancels Hijack Pact

One of the barriers to the efforts to normalize U.S.-Cuban relations was the continuation of terrorist actions—by both sides in the strife between Castro's regime and anti-Castro exiles. The bombing of a Cuban airliner, in which Castro claimed that the U.S. CIA was implicated, resulted in Castro's abrogation of the U.S.-Cuban anti-hijacking agreement.

Cuban jetliner crashes after bombing. A Cuban passenger jet plunged into the Caribbean Sea Oct. 6, 1976 after one or two bombs exploded on board following takeoff from the island of Barbados. All 73 passengers and crew members were reported killed.

The bombing, attributed to Cuban exiles and Venezuelans who opposed Premier Fidel Castro, had wide repercussions. Castro blamed the sabotage on the U.S. Central Intelligence Agency and renounced an anti-hijacking treaty with the U.S.; Venezuela discovered plans by Cuban exiles for terrorist actions in the U.S. and six other countries, and Cuban exiles were linked to the recent murder of Orlando Letelier, the Chilean ex-Cabinet minister.

At least 16 persons were arrested in Trinidad & Tobago and Venezuela in connection with the bombing. Trinidadian police Oct. 7 seized Hernan Ricardo and Freddy Lugo, two Venezuelan citizens who had boarded the Cuban jet in Trinidad Oct. 6 and left it in Barbados, returning to Trinidad the same day. The Cuban-born Ricardo admitted placing two bombs on the airliner, Trinidadian authorities said Oct. 18.

Ricardo and Lugo told Trinidadian police that they were employed by a private-detective agency in Caracas that was staffed by Cuban exiles. The Venezuelan government confirmed Oct. 14 that it had arrested 10 persons in connection with the bombing. Among them were Luis Posada, head of the detective agency, and Orlando Bosch, chief of the Command of United Revolutionary Organizations (CORU), an anti-Castro umbrella group. At least four more employes of the detective agency were reported to have been arrested in Caracas Oct. 15.

(CORU had been formed recently by Cuban Action, the Cuban National Liberation Front, the Bay of Pigs Veterans' Association, the April 17th Movement and the National Cuban Movement, according to U.S. intelligence sources quoted by the New York Times Oct. 11. The exile groups were based in Venezuela, Nicaragua, the Dominican Republic and Miami, it was reported Oct. 19.)

Bosch had been convicted of a bazooka attack on a Polish ship in Miami in 1968 and had been paroled by U.S. authorities after serving four years of a 10-year prison sentence. He had entered Venezuela in September by using a forged Costa Rican

1975-77: CONFLICTING OBJECTIVES

passport, Venezuelan authorities said Oct. 14.

Castro voids hijack pact, accuses U.S. Castro said Oct. 15, 1976 that he was canceling the 1973 anti-hijacking agreement between Cuba and the U.S. because the CIA had "participated directly" in the bombing of the Cuban airliner.

Speaking to several hundred thousand persons in Havana's Revolution Square, Castro said the bombing was carried out by "mercenaries" in the pay of the CIA. The U.S. agency was responsible for eight other 1976 attacks on Cuban officials or property abroad, Castro charged.

U.S. Secretary of State Henry Kissinger denied the charges Oct. 15. He said that "no official of the U.S. government, no one paid by the American government, no one in contact with the American government has anything to do" with the airplane sabotage. "We will hold the government of Cuba strictly accountable for any encouragement of hijacking and any encouragement of terrorism that may flow from its renunciation of the treaty," Kissinger said.

Castro said that Cuba would respect the treaty's terms until April 15, 1977, in compliance with a clause that required the parties to give six months' notice before cancellation. He added that he would be willing to discuss the agreement with the next U.S. administration "on the basis of a definite end of all acts of aggression and hostility against our homeland." Castro said that Cuba would never encourage air piracy and that it would continue to respect its anti-hijacking pacts with Canada, Mexico, Venezuela and Colombia.

Castro said the sabotage of the Cuban jet had been tied to the CIA by "absolutely reliable" Venezuelan journalists. He charged that Hernan Ricardo, who reportedly took credit for the bombing, was a CIA agent.

(Ricardo's connection to the CIA was not confirmed by other sources, but Cuban exiles and U.S. officials told the New York Times Oct. 20 that Posada and Bosch, under arrest in Venezuela in connection with the bombing, had been trained by the CIA and used in actions against the Castro government after 1960.)

Castro made it clear that he thought the CIA still sought to assassinate him. He said that the CIA had asked one of its agents in Havana to provide information about Castro's itinerary during a projected visit to Angola in November for that country's independence celebrations. The CIA operative was a double agent who had been passing information to the Cuban government for 10 years, Castro said.

Castro listed the eight other anti-Cuban terrorist attacks that he blamed on the CIA as:

■ An attack on two Cuban fishing boats April 6 by private launches from Florida. One Cuban fisherman was killed.

■ The bombing of the Cuban Embassy in Lisbon, Portugal April 22, in which two persons died.

■ The bombing of the Cuban mission to the United Nations in New York July 5.

■ The explosion of a bomb in a suitcase that was about to be loaded onto a Cuban airliner in Kingston, Jamaica July 9.

■ A bomb explosion July 10 in the offices of British West Indian Airways of Barbados, which represented the Cuban airline in Barbados.

■ The slaying of a technician of the Cuban National Fisheries Institute in Merida, Mexico July 23 during an abortive attempt to kidnap the Cuban consul there.

■ The abduction of two employes of the Cuban Embassy in Buenos Aires, Argentina Aug. 9.

■ A bomb explosion in the office of the Cuban airline in Panama Aug. 18.

Castro noted that all the attacks had followed Cuba's military intervention in the Angolan civil war, which had been sharply criticized by the U.S.

Venezuela expels U.S. journalists— Three U.S. journalists who flew to Venezuela to report on the plane-sabotage case were detained by police after their arrival Oct. 21 and deported to the U.S. the next day.

Venezuela gave no explanation for the action against Taylor Branch, a columnist for Esquire magazine; John Rothchild, a free-lance writer accompanying Branch, and Hilda Inclan, Latin American affairs reporter for the Miami News. The Washington Post reported Nov. 1 that the journalists had been expelled because they recognized Ricardo Morales Navarrete, the Disip officer in charge of security at Maiquetia International Airport, as a Cuban exile who had been a paid informant of the U.S. Federal Bureau of Investigation in Miami in the late 1960s.

Morales had been a key witness against Orlando Bosch in 1968 when Bosch was convicted of firing a bazooka at a Polish ship in Miami. A few years later a bomb had exploded in Morales' car in Miami, and Morales had blamed Bosch for the attack. Morales had moved to Venezuela in 1975. Since then, there were conflicting reports that Morales had patched up his differences with Bosch and that he had lured Bosch to Venezuela for arrest, according to the Oct. 24 Miami Herald. Morales refused to confirm or deny either report, the Herald said.

Joseph Leo, an FBI agent attached to the U.S. Embassy in Caracas, had been in contact with Bosch's alleged fellow saboteurs, Luis Posada and Hernan Ricardo, the Washington Post reported Oct. 25.

The report, confirmed by the U.S. Embassy, appeared to contradict U.S. Secretary of State Henry Kissinger's recent assertion that "no one in contact with the American government has had anything to do" with the crash of the Cuban jetliner Oct. 6.

Leo had maintained "a casual acquaintance with Luis Posada when Posada was a Disip official," an embassy spokesman told the Post. Leo had helped Ricardo obtain a one-year U.S. business visa earlier in 1976 for a trip to Puerto Rico on a photographic assignment for Vision magazine, the spokesman said. Vision denied any association with Ricardo, the Post noted.

Leo's name and telephone number also appeared in the appointment book of a third alleged saboteur, Freddy Lugo, the Post said. The U.S. Embassy spokesman denied that Leo had had any personal contact with Lugo.

Leo's contacts with the alleged saboteurs first had been raised by Guyanese Premier Forbes Burnham, who charged Oct. 17 that the U.S. was ultimately "responsible" for the Cuban plane crash. Burnham accused the U.S. of attempting to "destabilize" his socialist government.

Burnham's charges caused a sharp deterioration of ties between the U.S. and Guyana, U.S. State Department officials said Oct. 21. Frederick Z. Brown, a State Department spokesman, charged Oct. 20 that "the Burnham speech contained baldfaced lies." A Guyanese spokesman replied Oct. 21 that the U.S. had "overreacted" with "crudity and rudeness."

Venezuela indicts 4 in Cuban jet crash. A district judge in Caracas, Venezuela Nov. 2, 1976 charged four Cuban exiles with the murder of the 73 persons who had died in the bomb-caused crash of the Cuban airliner Oct. 6.

Judge Delia Estaba Moreno issued indictments for "qualified homicide and manufacture and use of war weapons" against Orlando Bosch, Luis Posada, Hernan Ricardo and Freddy Lugo. All pleaded not guilty.

At first, there was some doubt as to whether the defendants would be tried in civil or military court. An impartial civil trial was considered unlikely because the civil courts were openly political and some of the defendants had ties to the Venezuelan police and government, the Washington Post reported Oct. 31. Venezuelan judges were appointed by the ruling Democratic Action Party, were allowed to make their investigations in secret and were not required to explain their decisions. Defendant Luis Posada was a former operations chief of Disip, the Venezuelan political security police, which was in charge of the local investigation of the Cuban jet crash.

(The Venezuelan police and government also had ties to other Cuban exiles who supported actions against the Cuban government, making a fair civil trial of the alleged saboteurs even less likely, the Miami Herald noted Oct. 24. Hildo Folgar, a Cuban-born gynecologist, was a personal friend and family physician of

Venezuelan President Carlos Andres Perez. Orlando Garcia, another Cuban exile, was deputy director of Disip and security adviser to Perez. Bernardo Viera Trejo, a public relations man who reportedly had been seen with Orlando Bosch, had worked for Perez' presidential campaign in 1973.)

Lawyers for the four defendants said that it would be very difficult to prove the prosecutor's case. They held that there was no evidence that the explosion that caused the Cuban jet to crash was caused by a bomb. They also said that if a bomb were the cause, there was no proof that the bomb was manufactured by the defendants. Sebastian Alvarez, attorney for one of six other Cuban exiles who were arrested in the case and later released without charge, said Nov. 2 that the only evidence in the case was the "divination" of the judge.

Nevertheless, an investigator in the case told the Caracas newspaper El Nacional Oct. 30 that the government had "more than 50 proofs" of conspiracy by the defendants. The Cuban Embassy in Caracas said Nov. 4 that it had given Venezuela additional evidence including bomb fragments recovered from the plane's wreckage by Cuban divers.

Among the evidence against the defendants, according to press reports:

■ A taxi driver taking Hernan Ricardo and Freddy Lugo to their hotel in Trinidad Oct. 6 heard them discussing the plane's bombing and laughing over it, the Washington Post reported Nov. 3.

■ Trinidadian police said they had proof that Ricardo had contacted Luis Posada from the hotel. Police also said that both Posada's girlfriend and his secretary in Caracas had confirmed that they had passed on this message from Ricardo to Posada: "The truck has left with a full load," the Post reported. (The truck and load presumably referred to the Cuban plane and the bombs.)

■ Ricardo had cabled Cuban exiles in Caracas during his brief stay in Barbados Oct. 6, asking for a "considerable" sum of money, El Nacional reported Oct. 30. Some of the money was sent to him, the newspaper said.

■ Trinidadian police confiscated baggage belonging to Ricardo. The baggage contained floor plans of the Cuban embassies in Venezuela, Mexico and Jamaica and plans of various airports in the Caribbean with their schedules of foreign flights, El Nacional reported Oct. 31. The plans presumably would be used to facilitate terrorist attacks against Cuban officials and/or property.

Ricardo and Lugo, both of whom were professional photographers, told the Caracas newspaper El Mundo Oct. 26 that they had gone to Barbados only to check camera prices. Trinidadian police said Oct. 22 that Ricardo the previous day had tried to commit suicide in jail by slashing a wrist. He was taken to a hospital that day and released soon afterward.

Suspects get military trial—The four Cuban suspects accused of bombing the Cuban airliner were being tried secretly by a Venezuelan military court, the Miami Herald reported Oct. 10, 1977.

Although the airplane crashed off the coast of Barbados, the trial was being held in Venezuela because two of the defendants were arrested in Caracas and the other two were seized in countries (Barbados and Trinidad and Tobago) that did not want the trial for fear it would hurt their tourist industries.

The trial had begun in a civilian court, but it was moved to a military court after Cuban exiles bombed a Venezuelan air force jet in Miami Aug. 14. Venezuelan President Carlos Andres Perez requested the transfer to a military court on the grounds that the Miami bombing made the trial a matter of "national security."

The defendants' attorneys resigned to protest the transfer and the Venezuelan attorney general asked the Supreme Court to rule on its constitutionality.

Perez had filed a civil suit against one of the defendants, Orlando Bosch, for telling a Venezuelan newspaper July 4 that Perez had once authorized him to use Venezuela as a base for anti-Cuban operations. Bosch said Perez recently had betrayed the cause of Cuban exiles because he desired good relations with the government of Cuban President Fidel Castro. (Under Venezuela's penal code, disrespectful statements about the president were punishable with prison sentences.)

Cubans blamed for U.S.-based terrorism. Militant pro-Castro and anti-Castro Cuban groups in the Miami area were engaged in terrorist activities in the U.S. and Latin America, according to testimony given before a U.S. Senate subcommittee in May 1976 and released Aug. 22.

The testimony was given before the Judiciary Committee's subcommittee on internal security by Lt. Thomas Lyons, a member of the Dade County Public Safety Dept., and Raul J. Diaz of the department's organized crime, terrorist and security unit. They said that as many as 50 Cuban groups of various political shadings had been operating in Miami at any one time, many of them involved in local actions in Cuba, Mexico and Central and South America.

Some Cuban exiles "use Dade County as a base for international terrorism against allied governments of Cuba, Cuban shipping, Communists, purported Communists and individuals who take a stand against their terroristic-type tactics," Lyons said. During the last two years there had been four homicides in Dade County "with strong indicators on each that the motivations were political in nature and terroristic in design," he declared.

Diaz said that some pro-Castro groups had infiltrated exile organizations in Miami and made plans to assassinate Latin American diplomats and foreign ministers. He did not mention CIA efforts to use Cuban exiles in Florida to kill Premier Fidel Castro.

Antonio Gonzalez, an anti-Castro Cuban exile, had said Aug. 18 that there were as many as 500 pro-Castro agents operating in the Miami area. Gonzalez made the statement in Jacksonville in testimony at the trial of Rolando Otero, a fellow exile, on charges of exploding several bombs in Miami in 1975.

Gonzalez, testifying under a grant of immunity, said he and Otero had plotted to assassinate Castro during a planned visit to Venezuela, but Castro had called off the visit after the plot was discovered by agents of the Cuban government and the U.S.' Federal Bureau of Investigation. FBI agent Robert Ross, in testimony Aug. 17, had told the jury of the plot.

Terrorist plans discovered—Venezuelan police had discovered plans by right-wing Cuban exiles to carry out terrorist attacks in the U.S., Venezuela, Trinidad & Tobago, Barbados, Guyana, Panama and Colombia, the Caracas newspaper El Nacional reported Oct. 19.

Existence of the plans was confirmed by Venezuelan and U.S. officials who were quoted by the New York Times Oct. 20. Some of the attacks already had taken place, including the recent bombing of Guyana's consulate in Trinidad, El Nacional said. Guyana had an avowedly socialist government that enjoyed good relations with Cuba.

The plans were discovered in a police raid on the Caracas home of Luis Posada, the Cuban exile arrested in connection with the Oct. 6 Cuban airliner bombing. Police reportedly confiscated terrorist "equipment" in the raid.

Some of the terrorists had held high positions in the Venezuelan government, according to Venezuelan officials quoted by the Oct. 21 New York Times. Posada had held an important post in Venezuela's police intelligence agency until 1975. Venezuelan President Carlos Andres Perez, the officials added, had used the Cuban exiles to maintain contact with the Chilean military government, with which Venezuela had strained diplomatic relations.

In another development, Aldo Vera Serafin, a Cuban exile who had once served in Castro's government, was shot to death in a San Juan suburb Oct. 25. Vera had broken with Castro in the early 1960s and moved to Puerto Rico, where he had joined the Fourth Republic, an anti-Castro group said to have connections with Orlando Bosch. Police would not speculate on political motives for Vera's murder.

Cuban exiles tied to Letelier slaying—Venezuelan police had linked Cuban exiles to the murder in Washington Sept. 21 of Orlando Letelier, the Chilean ex-Cabinet minister, El Nacional reported Oct. 19, 1976.

After arresting Orlando Bosch, leader of the anti-Castro group CORU, police learned that Bosch had told associates that the bomb that killed Letelier had been placed under his car by two Cuban exiles, Ignacio and Guillermo Novo, the Caracas newspaper reported.

The Novo brothers had been indicted in the U.S. in 1965 on charges of firing a bazooka at the United Nations, according to the Oct. 20 Washington Post. The indictments were later quashed on grounds that confessions had been taken from the Novos in violation of their constitutional rights. Guillermo Novo was convicted in 1974 in connection with a 1969 bombing incident and sentenced to six months' imprisonment and five years' probation, the Post reported.

A Venezuelan government source told the Post that the Chilean government had helped finance terrorism by Cuban exiles against the Castro government. "We've known it for years, but there's no way to do anything about it," the source said. That source and others told the Post that Orlando Bosch was one of several Cuban exiles who regularly made trips to Santiago, Chile.

U.S. intelligence sources also had received tips linking Bosch and CORU to Letelier's assassination, the New York Times reported Oct. 12. The sources said that the U.S. Federal Bureau of Investigation had learned that Cuban exile groups had carried a long-time grudge against Letelier for his role in improving relations between Cuba and Chile under the government of the late Chilean President Salvador Allende.

The U.S. State Department disclosed Oct. 15 that it had asked Venezuela to return Bosch to the U.S. for allegedly violating the terms of his parole. The U.S. did not make a formal request for Bosch's extradition, but asked Venezuela to put Bosch on a U.S.-bound airplane so he could be arrested on arrival.

The U.S intelligence sources quoted by the Times Oct. 12 said that the FBI and the CIA apparently had ruled out the possibility that Letelier was killed by agents of DINA, Chile's secret police. The officials said they understood that killing Letelier could not have served the purposes of Chilean President Augusto Pinochet Ugarte, who had complete control over DINA, the Times reported.

Venezuelan police denied the report that Bosch had told them that the Novo brothers had planted the bomb that killed Letelier, the Washington Post reported Oct. 21.

Guillermo Novo, who lived in Union City, N.J., denied Oct. 20 that he or his brother had been involved in Letelier's assassination.

A spokesman for the Institute for Policy Studies, which had employed Letelier at the time of his death, said Oct. 18 that the FBI was sending one or two agents to Venezuela to investigate possible links between Cuban exiles there and Letelier's murder. The FBI refused to confirm or deny the report, the Washington Post said Oct. 20.

The institute spokesman said that the Novo brothers, whom the institute suspected of having killed Letelier, had "worked directly with DINA, the Chilean secret police."

Unnamed investigators told the Washington Post Sept. 7, 1977 Letelier probably had been killed by right-wing Cuban exiles hired by DINA (as the Chilean secret police had then been called). By late 1977 the investigation was focusing on the Cuban exile community in the U.S., particularly in Florida and New Jersey.

A federal grand jury in Washington that was still investigating Letelier's death had called at least 21 Cuban exiles to testify, according to the Miami Herald Sept. 10. At least 14 of the exiles were residents of Miami; others lived in New York and New Jersey, and one lived in Mexico. Most of the subpoenaed exiles belonged to the small Cuban Nationalist Movement or to Brigade 2506, the organization of veterans of the Bay of Pigs invasion.

Guillermo Novo had appeared before the grand jury at least twice. He denied to the jury that he had gone to Chile in 1975 to see Orlando Bosch. The denial resulted in a perjury charge, and Novo promptly disappeared.

A close associate of Novo, Dionisio Suarez Esquivel, had been in jail since April for refusing to testify before the grand jury despite a grant of immunity.

Letelier a Soviet/Cuban agent?—Rep. Larry McDonald (D, Ga.) asserted in statements in the Congressional Record June 23-24, 1977 that documents found in Letelier's briefcase indicated that he was employed by the Cuban secret service (DGI). McDonald said in his statements:

"**The documents show that Letelier served as a Soviet agent operating un-**

der the direction of the Cuban DGI. His job was to serve as an agent of influence to utilize Members of Congress and other prominent persons to promote Communist goals in the Western Hemisphere. When the press first began carrying stories on this matter, Letelier's associates in the leftist think-tank, Institute for Policy Studies, launched a disinformation campaign to obscure the truth about Cuban operations in Washington using Letelier....

"Letelier's DGI case officer was Julian Torres Rizo, who serves the Cuban intelligence apparatus as their top man in the United States. His cover is First Secretary of the Cuban Mission to the United Nations. Part of Rizo's DGI responsibility includes liaison with such terrorist-connected groups as the Prairie Fire Organizing Committee—above ground apparatus of the Weather Underground—and the Puerto Rican Socialist Party—the parent organization of the FALN terrorists—as well as support groups for foreign terrorist organizations such as the Palestine Liberation Organization and the Chilean MIR terrorists.

"Rizo has used the Cuban diplomatic pouch to transmit material from his agents to Cuba and to obtain Cuban instructions and documents for his agents. For example, on December 12, 1965, Letelier gave Rizo two envelopes of material to be transmitted via pouch to Havana. A week later, on December 19, Rizo gave Letelier some packages that had been sent to him via pouch from Cuba.

"Another agent of Rizo, who had been closely associated with Letelier is Juan Gabriel Valdes, an active member of the Chilean Marxist-Leninist organization MAPU–OC. Valdes, who has been to Cuba a number of times, has had the honor of being Rizo's guest for lunch. On September 14, 1976, Valdes wrote a letter to Emilo Brito, a high ranking DGI official in the American Department of the Central Committee of the Communist Party of Cuba. After mentioning his contact with Rizo, Valdes wrote—

I hope to visit Cuba again during the first months of the coming year and I am looking forward to having the pleasure of talking with you again

"On March 29, 1976, Letelier had written to Beatriz Allende Fernandez, who lives in Cuba and is the wife of one of the top DGI officials—

Juan Gabriel Valdez (MAPU–OC) who up till now has been in New York (at this moment he is in Cuba. Possibly you have seen him) will also be transferring to work more directly with me in Washington.

"Rizo has been very proud of his acceptance by respectable Americans. Last year he boasted that he had been able to gain access to the library of the Council on Foreign Relations for his wife, who had been assisting him on DGI operations through his contact with Abraham Lowenthtal, an official of the CFR. Lowenthal, now head of the Latin American section of the Woodrow Wilson Center of the Smithsonian Institute advised a member of my staff that he did not remember Rizo specifically but that he did remember making arrangements for someone at the mission to utilize the library, which could be used only by permission, sometime over a year ago.

"Rizo was first identified by American intelligence as a DGI agent, when he served as member of the crew of a Cuban ship taking the Venceremos Brigade to Cuba. Rizo, since surfacing 3 years ago as a 'Cuban diplomat,' has been very close to former members of the Venceremos Brigade, some of whom received terrorist training in Cuba. One of Rizo's responsibilities is checking out Americans who apply for visas to visit Cuba. The visitors, including members of the Venceremos Brigade and the National Lawyers Guild, fill out lengthy biographical questionnaires which Rizo then uses to check on their backgrounds.

"Beatriz Allende Fernadez, who is the daughter of the late Salvador Allende former Marxist ruler of Chile, was Letelier's main contact in Cuba. A series of letters between her and Letelier were found in the briefcast—see Documents 2, 3, and 4. In her letter of May 8, 1975, Allende advised Letelier that she would send him a thousand dollars a month from Cuba for his expenses. She stated:

Now I am sending you five thousand in order not to have to send it monthly.

"As part of the disinformation campaign to defend Letelier, his associate at the Institute for Policy Studies wrote in the Washington Post of February 18, 1977—

The Unidad Popular sent Letelier money to pay expenses incurred for this kind of work. The treasurer of the Unidad Popular is Beatriz 'Tati' Allende, the slain Presi-

1975-77: CONFLICTING OBJECTIVES

dent's daughter; she lives in Cuba, with her Cuban husband and children. But the party's treasury is not in Cuba. Its funds were raised in Western Europe and in the United States from labor unions and social democratic parties, and from religious groupings. None of the money sent to Letelier came from the Cuban government.

"The associate, Saul Landau, had told a similar story to Washington Post reporter, Lee Lescaze, which appeared in the Washington Post on February 17, 1977. Landau did not bother to explain why money raised in Western Europe could not be sent to the United States through normal banking channels. By sending it from Cuba it had to be smuggled in. Beatriz Allende's own account appeared in the Washington Post on April 30, 1977. She claimed that—

> The money has been collected by Chile support committees throughout the world— donated by labor unions, political parties and humanitarian organizations.

"She went on to say:

> Since I am in charge of one of these accounts, I had the task of sending Letelier $1,000 a month; a minimal amount of money to help him to defray the expenses incurred by Chile solidarity work; to live, he worked at the Institute for Policy Studies, without abandoning the central objective of his life, which was the struggle against fascism. As you can see, there is nothing mysterious about the remittance of $1,000 which we Chileans sent Letelier through our own channels.

"Allende did not identify "our own channels" but the nature of those channels may be indicated by her statement—

> We will not hide our gratitude for those who give us their generous solidarity in such difficult moments, and especially that given by revolutionary Cuba.

"Landau, who orchestrated the disinformation campaign, has a long record of Castroite activities. On April 25, 1961, Herbert Romerstein testified before the Senate Subcommittee on Internal Security about a meeting that he had covered of a Communist youth organization called Advance on January 28, 1961, where Saul Landau, 'made a speech on behalf of the Fair Play for Cuba Committee.' (Communist Appeal to Youth Aided by New Organizations, pg. 13.) . . .

"I have asked the Justice Department to investigate whether Isabel Letelier, the widow of Orlando Letelier, has been operating in the United States in violation of the Foreign Agents Registration Act. . . .

"Orlando Letelier wrote to Beatriz Allende on March 29, 1976, about the "Human Rights Committee" which his wife Isabel was directing. Letelier wrote warning Allende not to reveal the Cuban connection of his wife's committee. He said:

> I think that given the nature of its 'sponsors' and of the front that this Committee is taking care of in the United States, it is preferable that information about it not be spread from Havana, because you know how these 'liberals' are. It is possible that congressmen serving as patrons could be afraid that they would be linked with Cuba, etc., and eventually drop their support of the Committee, which is quite important at this time."

Airline office in Spain bombed—A bomb exploded Nov. 7, 1976 in the Madrid office of Cubana de Aviacion, the Cuban national airline, causing heavy damage but no casualties.

Responsibility for the blast was claimed by the Command of United Revolutionary Organizations (CORU), a Cuban exile group. Orlando Bosch, reputed leader of CORU, was under arrest in Venezuela in connection with the bombing of a Cubana jetliner off Barbados Oct. 6.

A man claiming to represent CORU telephoned offices of the Associated Press in San Juan, Puerto Rico Nov. 9 and said the Madrid bombing was "a continuation of the war against [Cuban Premier] Fidel Castro." The caller said that Cuba "will be liberated only with the sweat and blood of its sons in exile."

Cuban exile leader slain. Juan Jose Peruyero, 46, a leader of Miami's anti-Castro Cuban exiles, was shot to death Jan. 7, 1977 by unidentified gunmen. Police described the killing as a "political assassination." Peruyero was a former president of the Bay of Pigs Invasion Brigade Veteran Association.

Peruyero was the seventh Cuban exile leader to die in the last three years. During the same period, about 100 bombs were exploded in the Miami area and a number of reporters, both Cuban and American, had received death threats.

Exiles vow more attacks. Militant Cuban exiles in Miami Aug. 31, 1977 said they would continue "all kinds of actions to fight against the Communist tyranny" in Cuba. The threat was made by Brigade 2506, an organization of veterans of the 1961 Bay of Pigs invasion. The group was under surveillance by the Federal Bureau of Investigation, and its activities were being reported to the Cuban government as part of a joint U.S.-Cuban effort to curb terrorism.

Prisoners & Human Rights

Kennedy scores regime on prisoners. U.S. Sen. Edward M. Kennedy (D, Mass.) criticized the Cuban government for refusing to allow representatives of international organizations to observe the condition of political prisoners on the island, the Miami Herald reported Aug. 28, 1976.

Kennedy said that several members of his staff had visited Cuba recently and asked the government to allow the International Red Cross, Amnesty International and the International Commission of Jurists to visit the island and make the inspection. The requests had been ignored, Kennedy said.

The staff members had been permitted to visit some prisons in which conditions appeared to be adequate, Kennedy said, but had been denied access to jails the government considered to be "maximum security" installations.

Kennedy, an advocate of normalized relations between the U.S. and Cuba, warned Havana that "the process of normalization . . . must inevitably include the conditions of human rights and of the political prisoners."

Latin group scores Cuba. At the 1976 General Assembly of the Organization of American States, held in Santiago, Chile June 4–18, the Inter-American Commission on Human Rights appealed to Cuba to take immediate steps to end what the commission called "cruel, inhuman and degrading" treatment of Cuban political prisoners, it was reported June 11. A report by the commission, which did not visit Cuba, said individuals and organizations had given it information that provided a "solid basis" for the belief that Cuba treated its political prisoners with "complete disdain."

At the 1977 OAS General Assembly, held on the Caribbean island of Grenada June 14–22, the commission June 17 submitted a report on rights abuses in Cuba. But the assembly rejected the report on the ground that Cuba was not an OAS member.

Castro on political prisoners. Fidel Castro discussed political prisoners and other issues in a TV interview broadcast in the U.S. June 9, 1977.

Under questioning from ABC-TV correspondent Barbara Walters, Castro admitted that Cuba held between 2,000 and 3,000 political prisoners, having once held "more than 15,000 prisoners" when "the activity of the United States was more intensive against Cuba." It appeared to be the first time Castro had estimated the number of political prisoners in Cuba since a 1967 interview in which he put the figure at 20,000.

(The U.S. State Department estimated there were currently between 10,000 and 15,000 political prisoners in Cuba, it was reported June 9.)

Exile commandos freed. The government freed two Cuban-born anti-Communists who had been jailed in the 1960s for infiltrating the island from exile to carry out subversive activities, it was reported Aug. 2, 1977.

Manuel Humberto Reyes, who reentered Cuba before the 1961 Bay of Pigs invasion, had been held for 15 years. Carlos Ibarra Vasquez had been arrested in 1969 when he tried to organize a resistance group in eastern Cuba.

Upon their release both men went to Venezuela, where Ibarra held citizenship through his Venezuelan father. They told reporters in Caracas that they had been held in tiny, one-man cells and had been forbidden to speak for more than three years, but that they had never been tortured.

The two prisoners were freed following

appeals to President Castro from officials of the U.S., Venezuela and Panama, according to Cuban exile sources in Miami.

Amnesty group on abuse. Amnesty International reported Sept. 17, 1977 that there were about 5,000 political prisoners in Cuba and that some of them were subjected to beatings and others forms of mistreatment.

Amnesty International said Cuban political prisoners were treated well if they agreed to be "rehabilitated," that is, if they accepted political indoctrination and participated in government work projects. But if the prisoners continued to oppose the government, they were beaten, denied adequate nourishment and put in solitary confinement in dark, unsanitary cells. Some prisoners had been killed by guards, and others were held after their prison term had ended, Amnesty International said.

Amnesty said the majority of political prisoners in Cuba had opted for rehabilitation, but some, like former guerrilla commander Huber Matos, had maintained their opposition to the government and suffered the consequences.

Amnesty added that prison conditions in Cuba had improved in the last few years. The government had "closed the worst ... penal institutions and there are indications of great progress in [prison] conditions, with the exception of the Boniato jail in Santiago." Prison guards at Boniato had killed some prisoners, Amnesty reported.

Other Foreign Developments

Torrijos in Cuba. Brig. Gen. Omar Torrijos, Panama's military strongman, visited Cuba Jan. 10-15, 1976 for talks with Premier Fidel Castro on bilateral issues and on Panama's negotiations with the U.S. over the future of the Panama Canal and Zone.

The two leaders signed an assortment of cultural and technical exchange pacts and agreed that Panama should be patient in the canal negotiations. Agreement on the canal issue undermined leftist Panamanian students who sought an immediate takeover of the canal, according to press reports.

Torrijos thanked Castro Jan. 12 for advising him in recent years "not to fight on a hook" cast by the U.S., and he said Panama would continue to negotiate "calmly" for a new canal treaty. "We are—remember this—in a process of [national] liberation, and one of the means by which that can be reached is through negotiations," Torrijos declared Jan. 15.

Castro publicly advised caution on the canal issue Jan. 12, telling Torrijos: "Time is on our side in the struggle against the imperialists. The struggle of the Panamanian people is not very easy because Panama is small. But to the 1.2 million Panamanians we can now add nine million Cubans." As an example to Torrijos, Castro cited Cuba's tolerance of U.S. naval presence at Guantanamo Bay in eastern Cuba.

Torrijos was awarded Cuba's Jose Marti medal in a ceremony shortly after his arrival in Havana Jan. 10. He was accompanied on the trip by more than 200 Panamanians including workers, students, farmers, businessmen, military officers, folk dancers and Roman Catholic priests.

Trudeau visits Cuba. Canadian Prime Minister Pierre Elliott Trudeau Jan. 24-Feb. 2, 1976 visited Mexico, Cuba and Venezuela in an effort to stimulate Canadian trade with the three Latin American nations and promote Canada's economic and political identity as a power in its own right, not just as part of a U.S.-dominated North American presence.

Trudeau came under sharp criticism from opposition politicians in Ottawa for his Cuban sojourn. To charges that he had, by his visit, condoned Cuban participation in the Angolan war, the prime minister responded in the House of Commons Feb. 3 that he had been "brutally frank" with Premier Fidel Castro on Canada's views on the Cuban role there, calling the intervention "a serious mistake." He maintained that cancellation of the scheduled visit would have constituted an "unproductive slight to Cuba."

During the Jan. 26-29 talks in Cuba,

Castro had declared that relations between Ottawa and Havana were "better than ever." Canadian officials deemed the visit highly successful, in marked contrast to Trudeau's Jan. 24–26 talks in Mexico with President Luis Echeverria Alvares where no discernible progress on any issue was reported.

According to figures reported in the Toronto Globe and Mail Jan. 30, Canada ran an annual trade deficit of $1 billion with Venezuela, due to oil imports, while enjoying a $75 million surplus in trade with Cuba during the first six months of 1975.

Soviet trade pact. Cuba and the Soviet Union Feb. 6, 1976 signed a five-year trade agreement that was expected to double the volume of trade between them, according to Cuban sources quoted by the Reuters news agency.

The pact, signed in Moscow, was Cuba's first long-term trade accord with a foreign country. More than half of the island's foreign trade was with the Soviet Union; trade exchanges between the two countries in 1976 would amount to about $3.4 billion, according to a protocol signed along with the five-year pact.

Colombia trade pacts signed. Cuba and Colombia had signed preliminary trade agreements covering steel, fish, paper and textiles following a visit to Cuba by a 70-man Colombian delegation headed by Alberto Galeano Ramirez, director of the Colombian Foreign Trade Institute, it was reported Feb. 20, 1976.

Guyana military involvement denied. The Guyanese government denied foreign reports that Guyanese paramilitary forces were being trained by Cuban and Chinese advisers.

The reports originated in Brazil, Venezuela and the U.S. The most detailed of them, a "confidential report" quoted by the Venezuelan magazine Resumen Feb. 23, 1976, said Guyana had three paramilitary installations, and a fourth under construction, where Cuban and Chinese advisers assisted in the "political indoctrination, military training and agricultural instruction" of thousands of Guyanese youths. Other Guyanese traveled to Cuba for training and indoctrination, Resumen reported.

Resumen's article was immediately denounced by government officials in Georgetown and Guyanese representatives in Venezuela and Brazil. Foreign Minister Frederick Wills called the article "wicked and malicious," it was reported March 3, and other officials charged it was part of a U.S.-inspired "destabilization" campaign against Guyana's socialist government, it was reported March 10.

The Washington Post reported March 10 that there was no evidence of Cuban or Chinese military presence in Guyana, although there were camps where Guyanese teenagers underwent voluntary paramilitary training and instruction in Guyanese history and culture, the government's cooperative socialist doctrine, and agricultural methods.

Resumen's "confidential report," the Post added, had been leaked by the Venezuelan embassy in Georgetown, which received it from Patrick Tenassee, a Guyanese employe of the American Institute for Free Labor Development (AIFLD) and long-time opponent of Premier Forbes Burnham. The AIFLD had received more than $11 million in contracts from the U.S. State Department's Agency for International Development since 1968 to strengthen labor organizations throughout Latin America, the Post reported. It had also provided cover in Uruguay for operatives of the U.S. Central Intelligence Agency, according to the Post.

Burnham admitted March 3 that there were Cuban, Chinese and East German advisers in Guyana, but he said they worked only on agricultural and industrial projects.

Concern grew in Venezuela, Brazil and the U.S. over rumors that Georgetown had allowed Cuban aircraft to refuel in Guyana en route to Angola to deliver Cuban soldiers to fight in the African nation's civil war. Burnham denied the rumors March 6, but he said he would consider allowing Cuban planes to refuel in Guyana if they were carrying soldiers to aid Mozambique in its current conflict with Rhodesia. Burnham called for a

1975-77: CONFLICTING OBJECTIVES

united international front against Rhodesia's white minority government.

Cuba-Oswald link questioned. Associated Press (AP) reports March 20 and 21, 1976 described recently released Central Intelligence Agency (CIA) documents about the assassination of President John F. Kennedy. One memo, from the CIA to the Warren Commission, charged with investigating the assassination of President Kennedy, said that a defector had told the CIA that Lee Harvey Oswald may have been in contact with Cuban intelligence officers seven weeks before killing Kennedy.

This information, together with the defector's assertion that the Cuban intelligence service tightened its security immediately after Kennedy's assassination, was given to the Warren Commission in May 1964. A CIA June 1964 memo remarked that the commission "saw no need to pursue this angle any further."

A CIA memo prepared in May 1975 for the Rockefeller Commission asserted, however, AP said, that it "was the opinion at the working level, particularly in the counter-intelligence component in the CIA, in 1964" that the Warren Commission report "should have left a wider 'window' for this contingency [the involvement of a foreign conspiracy in Kennedy's assassination]."

The 1975 memo specified two leads that it held the Warren Commission had not adequately followed up, AP said. One was testimony to the commission by a friend of Oswald, Nelson Delgado, that Oswald had told him in 1959 that he (Oswald) had contacts with Cuban diplomatic officials. The other lead was a statement allegedly made by Cuban leader Fidel Castro to a news correspondent on Sept. 7, 1963, that "U.S. leaders would be in danger if they helped in any attempt to do away with leaders of Cuba."

An AP report March 1 said that sources on the Senate Intelligence Committee had said that day that the committee had evidence that Earl Warren, head of the Warren Commission, had been informed of CIA attempts on Castro's life, but not until three years after the commission finished its investigation.

Pope on progress effort. Pope Paul VI said March 25, 1976 that he looked "with sympathy on the efforts of the Cuban leaders to promote cultural, economic and social progress" among the Cuban people. The work of the Catholic Church in protecting human rights "finds fertile ground in Cuba due to its long tradition of Christian civilization," the pontiff added.

The pope spoke on receiving the credentials of Cuba's new ambassador to the Holy See, Jose Antonio Portuondo. The Vatican maintained full diplomatic relations with only one other Communist country, Yugoslavia.

U.S. political platforms. Both U.S. parties mentioned Cuba briefly during 1976 in the political platforms they prepared for the U.S. presidential elections. The Democratic platform said:

> Relations with Cuba can only be normalized if Cuba refrains from interference in the internal affairs of the United States, and releases all U.S. citizens currently detained in Cuban prisons and labor camps for political reasons. We can move towards such relations if Cuba abandons its provocative international actions and policies.

The Republican platform said:

> By continuing its policies of exporting subversion and violence, Cuba remains outside the inter-American family of nations. We condemn attempts by the Cuban dictatorship to intervene in the affairs of other nations; and, as long as such conduct continues, it shall remain ineligible for admission to the Organization of American States.
>
> We shall continue to share the aspirations of the Cuban people to regain their liberty. We insist that decent and humane conditions be maintained in the treatment of political prisoners in the Cuban jails, and we will seek arrangements to allow international entities, such as the International Red Cross, to investigate and monitor the conditions in those jails.

U.S. businessmen visiting island. U.S. businessmen were visiting Cuba quietly, anticipating the day when relations between Havana and Washington were sufficiently improved to allow a resumption of normal commercial activities, the Wall Street Journal reported Sept. 27, 1976.

The visits were legal, but U.S. passports were not valid for trips to Cuba and U.S. money could not be used there without authorization. To circumvent these restrictions, Americans entered Cuba from such countries as Jamaica and Mexico using loose-leaf visas that could be discarded later. Cuban officials paid for the businessmen's expenses on the island.

The visitors generally avoided publicity, but it was known that executives of PepsiCo Inc. had recently been in Cuba, the Journal reported. Kirby Jones, a former aide to Sen. George McGovern (D, S.D.), told the Journal that he had escorted executives of five major U.S. corporations to Cuba in recent weeks and that he would chaperon officers of eight other U.S. companies in the next two months. The president of one commodities firm, I.S. Joseph Co. of Minneapolis, openly admitted having visited Cuba in 1975.

(The reported visit of PepsiCo officials to Cuba angered anti-Castro Cuban exiles in the U.S., the Journal reported. "A lot of Pepsi machines were ordered out of Cuban establishments" in Miami, a leader of Miami exiles told the Journal. A reporter for the Florida television station that reported the visit said one PepsiCo franchise had canceled about $300,000 worth of advertising with the station after the report.)

Portuguese accord. A Cuban agreement with Portugal took place during 1976.

Cuba and Portugal signed a declaration of intent on trade to facilitate exports of Cuban sugar and of Portuguese chemicals, ship components and electrical equipment, it was reported Sept. 14.

Cuba spurns OAS. Cuban Foreign Minister Raul Roa Sept. 14 reaffirmed Cuba's determination "never" to rejoin the Organization of American States.

Burmese relations. Cuba established diplomatic relations with Burma Oct. 11, 1976.

U.S. firm linked to Bay of Pigs raid. United Brands Co. of the U.S., then known as United Fruit Co., had actively participated in the 1961 Bay of Pigs invasion of Cuba at the request of the U.S. Central Intelligence Agency, according to a book published Oct. 21, 1976.

The book, titled "An American Company: The Tragedy of United Fruit," was written by Thomas P. McCann, a former vice president of the firm. McCann said United Fruit had dealt directly with the late Robert F. Kennedy, then U.S. attorney general, in planning the Bay of Pigs invasion. The CIA's main contact at the firm was the late J. Arthur Marquette, then vice president in charge of steamships and terminal operations, McCann said.

McCann quoted Marquette as saying that Kennedy "wanted us to supply two of our freighters to convey men, munitions and material during that invasion. The arrangements were made, and it was all very cloak and dagger: our own board of directors didn't know about it, and certainly only a handful of us with the company were party to the secret."

After the abortive invasion, McCann said, the logs of the two ships were sent to Washington, sealed with wax and then returned to the company. "As far as I know, they are still in company vaults—the official record of our participation in that fiasco permanently safe from public view," McCann said.

Burke Wright, United Brands' current public relations director, said he was unable to find anyone in the company who knew about its participation in the invasion, the Miami Herald reported Oct. 23.

Canada seizes fishing boats. Canadian destroyers Nov. 8, 1976 seized three Cuban fishing boats that had violated Canada's 12-mile fishing limit.

Two of the vessels, a trawler and a factory ship which processed the catch, were boarded by Fisheries Department officers who arrested their captains. The third, a trawler, turned for the open sea and was intercepted by a Canadian destroyer outside the 12-mile limit.

The captains, two Soviets and one Cuban, were ordered to proceed to the port of Halifax. They pleaded innocent Nov. 9 to charges of entering Canadian waters without permission, a charge that carried a maximum penalty of a $C2,000 fine and/or one month in jail. After an insurance company representing the vessels had presented a letter of intent Nov. 9 in

1975-77: CONFLICTING OBJECTIVES

which it promised to pay the fines and costs incurred in keeping the vessels in port, Canada granted them permission to remain in Halifax and allowed the crews to take shore leave.

All three vessels were fined Jan. 4, 1977 after their representatives pleaded guilty in a Halifax court.

Two of the vessels, a trawler and a factory ship, were fined the maximum of C$2,000 each. A second trawler was fined C$1,500.

Fishing limit set at 200 miles. Cuba March 1, 1977 extended to 200 miles the limits of its territorial waters within which it would control or ban fishing by foreign vessels. The U.S., which imposed a similar limit the same day, reduced the distance in specific areas to avoid conflict with the fishing claims of Cuba, Mexico and Canada.

Nicaragua accuses Cuba re guerrillas. The Nicaraguan government charged Nov. 16, 1976 that Cuba was training and infiltrating Nicaraguan leftists into Nicaragua for a guerrilla war against President Anastasio Somoza Debayle. The government also denied a recent charge by Cuban Premier Fidel Castro that Nicaragua was a base for Cuban exiles who staged attacks against Cuba and other countries that enjoyed good relations with the Castro government.

As guerrilla warfare in Nicaragua continued to expand, Somoza charged Nov. 7, 1977 that an international communist plot had emerged. This plot, he said, received "the direct and open aid of the current communist government of Cuba, which not only has given asylum and protection to Nicaraguan and other foreign subversive elements, but has given them all manner of help, principally training and propaganda, in open violation of the fundamental principles of international law."

The Sandanista National Liberation Front denied receiving anything but moral support from Cuba. In an interview published by the New York Times Oct. 26, Sandinista leader Plutarco Hernandez insisted that the guerrillas received no money or arms from Cuba, and said none of them had been trained in Cuba since 1970.

"If we had received more effective support from Cuba or from any other country," Hernandez said, "we'd have been in power a long time ago. Our problem is that we've had to fight entirely alone. But it also means that when we achieve victory we will owe nothing to any outsiders."

Comecon to build nuclear plant. Comecon, the Communist bloc's economic association, would build the first atomic power station in Cuba, the Soviet news agency Tass reported Jan. 6, 1977.

Under an agreement signed in Moscow in April 1976, the first stage of the plant would have "an output capacity of 440 megawatts." Cuban President Fidel Castro had said the plant eventually would have twice that capacity.

Canada expels 'spies.' Canada Jan. 10, 1977 ordered the deportation of five Cubans, including three members of the Cuban Consulate in Montreal, on charges of recruiting and training intelligence agents to be sent to Rhodesia.

According to an official in the External Affairs Department, the three consular staff members had been ordered "withdrawn" and the Department of Immigration had issued deportation orders against two more Cubans living in Canada on nonimmigrant status. "On the basis of investigations," the official said, "it was determined that there was an intelligence operation being conducted in Canada involving the Cuban nationals in contravention of their status in Canada."

The Canadian government refused further comment on the case, but a report in the Jan. 10 Gazette, a Montreal newspaper, cited details first reported by the Sunday Mail of Salisbury, Rhodesia. According to the report, the existence of the Montreal operation was revealed by a U.S. citizen, David Bufkin, who said he had been recruited and trained by the Cubans. He was also reported to have spied on the Cubans for the U.S. Central Intelligence Agency.

Cuba Jan. 12 admitted having used its Montreal consulate as a base for recruiting agents but denied "any actions ... that would interfere with normal relations between Canada and Cuba."

The Cuban Foreign Ministry in Havana said it had recruited informants to operate against the National Front for the Liberation of Angola (FNLA), not against the Rhodesian government as had been suspected. Cuba accused the FNLA of attacking Cuban diplomats and said it was a "normal right" to gather intelligence on the group. The Canadian Department of External Affairs refused to comment on the Cuban statement, saying it had been issued to journalists and thus was not an official intergovernmental communication.

Four Cubans who had been ordered expelled from Canada in connection with the case left for Havana Jan. 12. They were: Montreal Consul General Jesus Rodriguez Verdes, Vice Consul Rene Valenzuela Acebal, consular employe Raul Hernandez Cuesta and Hector Arazoza Rodriguez, a lecturer at McGill University in Montreal. Fernando E. Rivero Milan, third secretary at the Cuban Embassy in Ottawa, was in Cuba on leave and was informed he would not be permitted to return to Canada.

Canadian Solicitor General Francis Fox disclosed Jan. 16 that the Cuban Consulate in Montreal had been under Canadian police surveillance for several months.

In a radio interview, Fox said the Royal Canadian Mounted Police (RCMP) had been aware of illegal Cuban activities before the disclosure by Bufkin of the Cuban espionage recruiting and training taking place there. Fox added that the CIA had denied employing Bufkin. Fox said the CIA and the RCMP had an "understanding ... that there would be no CIA operatives operating in Canada without our permission." He added, "We were definitely not advised that he [Bufkin] was a CIA operative."

Spanish accord. Cuba also came to a new agreement with Spain during 1977.

Spain and Cuba signed a trade protocol for 1977 that included a reduction in the price of Cuban sugar to be purchased by Spain, it was reported Feb. 20. The agreement provided for bilateral trade totaling $280 million–$300 million. Spain was Cuba's second-largest trading partner behind the Soviet Union.

Castro visits Jamaica. Fidel Castro visited Jamaica Oct. 16–21, 1977 in an evidently successful effort to strengthen ties between Cuba and Jamaica and to bolster the political position of Prime Minister Michael Manley.

To the apparent approval of many Jamaicans, Castro projected a moderate image, denying that Cuba sought to interfere in the affairs of other countries, offering Jamaica extensive aid, giving advice on economic problems and warmly praising the socialist programs of Manley's government.

Nevertheless, Castro's visit was protested by the opposition Jamaica Labor Party (JLP) and other conservative sources. The JLP charged that Castro was a "Communist dictator" and urged Jamaicans to boycott all public functions at which he appeared.

The party's leader, Frank Phipps, said Oct. 16 that the visit was "ill-conceived and inopportune." He said Castro was "an individual with a history of interference in the internal affairs of Jamaica and other countries, who preaches subversion and revolution in the entire hemisphere."

The Kingston newspaper The Gleaner also criticized the visit, it was reported Oct. 23. Gleaner columnist Wilmot Perkins wrote that the visit was one of many "circuses" to which Jamaicans were being treated to cover up the "reality of worsening poverty, worsening unemployment [and] worsening crime."

Castro arrived in Kingston Oct. 16 to a warm greeting from Governor General Florizel Glasspole, Prime Minister Manley and members of the foreign diplomatic corps, including the U.S. ambassador to Jamaica. Manley praised Castro as a "hero to the peoples of the Third World" and "one of the great leaders of the 20th century." Manley also denounced "agents of imperialism" who had tried to prevent Cuba's friendship with Jamaica, and he called for an end to all international sanctions against Cuba, presumably including the U.S. trade embargo of the island. [See below]

Castro praised Manley's programs during a motorcade across Jamaica Oct. 18. He said that Manley was working to improve housing, employment and the general economic opportunities of Jamaicans, and that the Cuban people supported him.

Wherever he went in Jamaica, Castro stressed Cuba's eagerness to help the beleaguered island economically. He promised buses for a Cuban-built school, tractors for a sugar cooperative, prefabricated housing plants for construction workers and Cuban doctors, teachers and technicians wherever they were needed.

"We are willing to bring to Jamaica all our experience in agriculture, cattle-raising, public health, education, economic development, fishing, sports—in everything we can," Castro said at a rally in Montego Bay. "Our universities are open to you, our research centers, hospitals, technological institutes—we shall never keep a secret from you. Anything that might be useful for us, we are willing to offer to you."

Castro wept as he embraced Manley before his return to Cuba Oct. 21.

Domestic Events

Communist Party congress. The First Congress of the Cuban Communist Party was held in Havana Dec. 17–22, 1975 with more than 3,000 Cuban delegates and representatives of 82 foreign Communist parties attending.

The Congress heard a 10-hour "report to the nation" from Premier Fidel Castro, the party's first secretary, and it approved the final draft of Cuba's new constitution and the guidelines of the island's first five-year economic plan.

Foreign delegates attending the congress included Mikhail Suslov, leading Soviet ideologist; Gen. Vo Nguyen Giap, defense minister of North Vietnam; Janos Kadar, first secretary of the Hungarian Communist Party; Todor Zhivkov, first secretary of the Bulgarian Communist Party; Georges Marchais, leader of the French party, and Alvaro Cunhal of the Portuguese party.

The congress was opened Dec. 17 by Armed Forces Minister Raul Castro, who introduced his brother, Premier Fidel Castro. In a speech which consumed that day's session and stretched into the Dec. 18 session, Premier Castro detailed the history of the Cuban revolution since 1959 and denounced the U.S., notably its Central Intelligence Agency, which had conspired in several attempts to assassinate him.

Castro cited a number of "errors" by the revolution's leaders, including the setting of unrealistically high goals for the sugar harvest in 1970, the complete nationalization of trade in 1967, and the tendency of the Communist Party to dominate public administration in 1965–70. The revolution would not have succeeded, Castro noted, without the aid of the Soviet Union against the U.S.' "aggressive and unscrupulous imperialism."

Castro said the CIA had "organized dozens of attempts against the lives of the leaders of the Cuban revolution," contracting "leading members of the Mafia" in some plots. He praised as a "positive step" the publication of a report on the assassination plots by an investigative panel of the U.S. Senate.

Castro outlined the five-year economic plan, which would concentrate on industrial development rather than agricultural expansion and would introduce profitability as a standard for judging state-owned businesses.

"The profit criteria will tell us which is the most technologically backward factory, the most expensive, the industry in which we must make investments first, the one in which we have to substitute first a new industry," Castro said. But "the fundamental object is not profits as in capitalism but the satisfaction of the spiritual and material needs of the people," he added.

Some of the profits would remain in the hands of the workers' cooperative at each enterprise for use in "resolving social problems and providing prizes for the most distinguished workers," Castro continued. Each business would also have "a determined autonomy in the use and the management of the resources . . . to sell or rent idle material, undertake marginal production by their own decision and so on, without affecting the principal production plan," he declared.

The five-year plan would concentrate on achieving an annual 6% growth rate in goods, not counting services, Castro said. Sugar production was scheduled to grow by 30%-40%, from the present 5.5 million tons to more than 8 million tons by 1980.

Record school attendance reported. More than three million Cubans—a third of the population—attended schools or colleges at the beginning of the 1975-76 school year, setting a record for the island, the regime reported Aug. 28, 1975. The education budget rose in 1975 from $750 million to $875 million.

Constitution enacted. Cuba's new constitution was officially proclaimed Feb. 24, 1976 at a Havana ceremony led by Raul Castro, the armed forces minister and first deputy premier. Castro announced that in the national referendum on the new charter Feb. 15, 5,602,973 citizens had voted, with 5,473,534 voting yes and 54,070 voting no.

The charter declared that Cuba was a socialist state ruled by its people through a pyramid of elected assemblies culminating in the National Assembly of People's Power. It recognized the leading role of the Communist Party and institutionalized the social and economic changes brought about by the regime of Premier Fidel Castro since 1959.

The constitution recognized freedom of expression, the press, religion and association so long as they did not oppose the government or the principles of the revolution. It provided for state control of the information media, among other national sectors.

Elections. About five million Cubans went to the polls Oct. 11, 1976 to elect members of 169 municipal assemblies.

The assemblies, composed of 11,000 members elected from more than 30,000 candidates, later elected 14 provincial assemblies and the National Assembly of People's Power. The national assembly, to be Cuba's highest legislative body, was then inaugurated in December.

Candidates for the municipal assemblies had been selected in August by "assemblies of neighbors" in small villages, districts and groups of city blocks. Citizens over the age of 16 were eligible to vote.

Premier Fidel Castro said after voting Oct. 11 that the municipal assembly elections were "a significant step forward in the consolidation and institutionalization of the revolution."

Assembly meets, names Castro president. The National Assembly of People's Power, Cuba's new legislature, convened in Havana Dec. 2, 1966, completing the reorganization of the Cuban government.

The assembly Dec. 3 elected Gen. Fidel Castro to be president of the new Council of State. The post effectively combined Castro's old office of premier, now abolished, and the presidency of the republic, heretofore held by Osvaldo Dorticos. Castro, who was also first secretary of the Cuban Communist Party, would be the "supreme power of the nation," according to a Cuban radio broadcast.

Dorticos fell in the hierarchy to be a member of the Council of State. Blas Roca, an old-line Communist, was elected president of the assembly Dec. 2.

In his opening speech to the assembly Dec. 2, Castro urged the 481 deputies to carry on a "tireless criticism of our work" and to avoid "all personality cults." Deputies should observe "the constant practice of self-limitation and modesty," in contrast to "the corrupt and haughty coterie [who had] betrayed Marxism-Leninism" in China, Castro said.

Castro sharply criticized members of the Organization of Petroleum Exporting Countries, charging that by raising oil prices they were "crushing underdeveloped countries." Castro denounced Saudi Arabia and Iran but praised what he called "progressive positions" taken by Venezuela, Algeria, Libya, Kuwait and Nigeria.

The assembly convened on the 20th anniversary of Castro's 1956 landing on the Cuban coast with an 82-member guerrilla force. Two years later the insurgents overthrew dictator Fulgencio Batista and established a largely ad hoc administration under Castro's leadership. The assembly meeting climaxed a process of systematizing the administration and sorting out the tasks of the Communist Party, the government and the labor organizations. Cuban administrative procedures now showed increased similarity to those of Eastern Europe, the Financial Times of London said Nov. 30.

The national assembly deputies had been elected Nov. 2 by the 10,725 members of Cuba's 169 municipal assemblies. Among the national assembly deputies were Castro, the 13 members of the Communist Party's Politburo, writers Alejo Carpentier and Nicolas Guillen, and Cuba's heavyweight boxing champion, Teofilo Stevenson.

The municipal delegates also elected members of the island's 14 provincial assemblies. Under the new constitution Cuba had 14 provinces of roughly equal size and population, and one special municipality, the Isle of Pines off the southwestern coast. Cuba previously had only six provinces.

The new administrative structure broke down as follows:

■ Municipal assemblies would be responsible for schools, hospitals, stores, hotels, cinemas, public utilities and municipal transport. They also would select magistrates to preside over the municipal people's courts.

■ Provincial assemblies would regulate intercity transport and provincial trade, and would elect judges to the provincial courts.

■ The national assembly would control all basic industries, establish the national education curriculum and appoint supreme court judges. It would also act as the national legislature, considering all laws proposed by the Council of State.

Municipal and provincial delegates would serve 2½-year terms and national delegates would serve five-year terms. All would continue in their existing jobs, receiving extra leave only when assembly meetings conflicted with normal work hours. The assembly jobs were unpaid but delegates would receive "a daily allowance equivalent to their salary and whatever additional expenses they may incur in the exercise of their duties." The Constitution stressed that assembly service carried no additional privileges or benefits, and that delegates could be recalled by their constituencies at any time.

The new structure was expected to reduce the state bureaucracy by 20%-25% and concentrate the remaining bureaucrats at the local level, according to the Oct. 29 London newsletter Latin America. Under the old system only 16% of Cuba's 250,000 state bureaucrats dealt with problems at a municipal level, while 38% operated at a regional level, Latin America said.

Fidel Castro Sept. 27, 1976 gave a detailed outline of Cuba's economic problems, laying the main blame on the fall in world sugar prices.

In a speech before 500,000 persons in Havana, Castro noted that the price of sugar had dropped from 65.5¢ a pound in November 1974 to 7.5¢ a pound Sept. 23. In addition, Cuba was suffering a severe drought which had put sugar production 25% below target levels and affected Cuban agriculture across the board.

Because sugar brought Cuba more than 80% of its export earnings, the island faced a shortage of foreign exchange. Consequently, Castro said, Cuba would be forced to slow down its economic development, reduce trade with the West and increase its dependence on aid from Communist countries, especially the Soviet Union. Austerity measures would be imposed, including a cut in electricity output to conserve fuel; replacement of artificial-fiber imports with Soviet cotton, and reduction of the coffee ration from 43 grams a week to 30 grams (about one ounce).

Castro expressed gratitude for the Soviet Union's extensive aid to Cuba, saying: "Without the support of the Communist bloc and the Soviet Union, I don't know how a country like ours could solve its problems." He noted that Moscow was paying five times more than the world market price for Cuban sugar, was providing the island with all its oil and fuel and was selling Cuba wheat below world market prices.

The Soviet Union also was giving Cuba aid in the electrical, mechanical-engineering and steel sectors, Castro said.

(Cuba's problems were compounded by a fall in sugar production in Eastern Europe and the Soviet Union, which forced the Communist countries to take more Cuban sugar and left the island with less sugar to use in financing imports from the West. Moscow took 1.8 million tons of Cuban sugar in 1974 and 2.9 million tons in 1975, the Miami Herald reported Sept. 30. In addition, the Soviet Union had raised the price of petroleum it sold to Cuba by more than 40%, the Herald said.)

Castro charged that the U.S. had helped to drive down the price of sugar by tripling its import taxes to protect the U.S. sugar industry, thereby putting more sugar on the world market. This action was "brutal aggression," Castro charged.

Cuba had no more hope of producing oil in significant quantities and would build nuclear plants to satisfy its growing energy needs, according to the U.S. weekly Oil and Gas Journal March 2. Cuba produced only 3,000 barrels of crude oil per day, and was forced to import 150,000 barrels daily from the Soviet Union, the Journal reported.

Documents

1976 Constitution

The 1976 Cuban Constitution was approved by Cuban voters in a national referendum Feb. 15, 1976 and was proclaimed Feb. 24. The text follows:

PREAMBLE

We, the Citizens of Cuba,
 heirs and continuators of the creative work and the traditions of combativity, firmness, heroism and sacrifice fostered by our ancestors;
 by the slaves who rebelled against their masters;
 by those who awoke the national consciousness and the Cuban ardent desire for country and liberty;
 by the patriots who in 1868 launched the wars of independence against Spanish colonialism and those who in the last drive of 1895 brought them to the victory of 1898, which victory was usurped by the military intervention and occupation of Yankee imperialism;
 by the workers, peasants, students and intellectuals who struggled for over fifty years against imperialist domination, political corruption, the absence of people's rights and liberties, unemployment and the exploitation of capitalists and landowners;
 by those who promoted, joined and developed the first organization of workers and peasants, spread socialist ideas and founded the first Marxist and Marxist-Leninist movements;

by the members of the vanguard of the generation of the centenary of the birth of Marti who, imbued with his teachings, led us to the people's revolutionary victory of January;

Basing Ourselves
on proletarian internationalism, on the fraternal friendship, help and cooperation of the Soviet Union and other socialist countries, and on the solidarity of the workers and the peoples of Latin America and of the world;

Guided
by the victorious doctrine of Marxism-Leninism;

Aware
that all the regimes of man's exploitation of man cause the humiliation of the exploited and the degradation of the human nature of the exploiters;
that our Revolution uplifted the dignity of the country and of Cubans; and
that only under socialism and communism, when man has been freed from all forms of exploitation—slavery, servitude and capitalism—can the full dignity of the human being be attained;

And Having Decided
to carry forward the triumphant Revolution of the Moncada and of the Granma of the Sierra and of Girón under the leadership of Fidel Castro, which sustained by the closest unity of all revolutionary forces and of the people won full national independence, established the revolutionary power, carried out democratic changes, started the construction of socialism and, under the direction of the Communist Party, continues said construction with the objective of building the communist society;

We Declare
our will that the law of laws of the Republic be guided by the following strong desire of José Marti, at last achieved:

I wish that the fundamental law of our republic be the tribute of Cubans to the full dignity of man;

And Adopt, by means of our free vote in a referendum,
the following

CONSTITUTION

CHAPTER I. POLITICAL, SOCIAL AND ECONOMIC PRINCIPLES OF THE STATE

ARTICLE 1. The Republic of Cuba is a socialist state of workers and peasants and all other manual and intellectual workers.

ARTICLE 2. The national symbols are those which have presided for over one hundred years in the Cuban struggles for independence, the rights of the people and social programs:
the flag of the lone star;
the hymn of Bayamo;
the coat of arms of the royal palm.

ARTICLE 3. The capital of the Republic is the city of Havana.

ARTICLE 4. In the Republic of Cuba all the power belongs to the working people who exercise it either directly or through the assemblies of People's Power and other organs of the state which derive their authority from these assemblies.

The power of the working people is sustained by the firm alliance of the working class with the peasants and the remaining strata of urban and rural workers under the direction of the working class.

ARTICLE 5. The Communist Party of Cuba, the organized Marxist-Leninist vanguard of the working class, is the highest leading force of the society and of the state, which organizes and guides the common effort toward the goals of the construction of socialism and the progress toward a communist future.

ARTICLE 6. The Young Communist League, the organization of the vanguard youth, under the direction of the Party, works to prepare its members as future members of the Party and contributes to the education of the new generations along the ideals of communism, by means of their participation in a program of studies and in patriotic, labor, military and scientific activities.

ARTICLE 7. The Cuban socialist state recognizes, protects and stimulates the social and mass organizations, such as the Central Organization of Cuban Trade Unions, the Committees for the Defense of the Revolution, the Federation of

Cuban Women, the National Association of Small Farmers, the Federation of University Students of Cuba, the Federation of Intermediate Education Students, the Union of Pioneers of Cuba and others which, having risen from the historic process of struggles of our people, gather in their midst the various sectors of the population, represent specific interests of the same and incorporate them to the tasks of edification, consolidation and defense of the socialist society.

In its activities the state relies on the social and mass organizations, which, in addition, directly fulfill the state functions that are intended to be assumed by the same according to the Constitution and the law.

ARTICLE 8. The socialist state:
(a) carries out the will of the working people and
—channels the efforts of the nation in the construction of socialism;
—maintains and defends the integrity and the sovereignty of the country;
—guarantees the liberty and the full dignity of man, the enjoyment of his rights, the exercise and fulfillment of his duties and the integral development of his personality;
—fastens the ideology and the rules of living together and of conduct proper of a society free from man's exploitation of man;
—protects the constructive work of the people and the property and riches of the socialist nation;
—directs in a planned way the national economy;
—assures the educational, scientific, technical and cultural progress of the country;

(b) as the power of the people and for the people, guarantees
—that no man or woman, apt to work, be without employment with which to contribute to the good of society and to the satisfaction of individual needs;
—that no disabled person be left without adequate means of subsistence;
—that no sick person be left without medical care;
—that no child be left without schooling, food and clothing;
—that no young person be left without the opportunity to study;
—that no one be left without access to studies, culture and sports;

(c) works to achieve that no family be left without a comfortable place to live.

ARTICLE 9. The Constitution and the laws of the socialist state are the judicial expression of the socialist relationships of production and of the interests and the will of the working people.

All organs of state power, its leaders, officials and employees function within the limits of their respective competency and are under the obligation to observe strictly the socialist legality and to look after the respect of the same in all levels of society.

ARTICLE 10. The Cuban socialist state exercises its sovereignty over the entire national territory, which consists of the island of Cuba, the Isle of Pines and all other adjacent islands and keys; over the territorial waters in the extension prescribed by law; and over the air space corresponding to the above.

The Republic of Cuba rejects and considers illegal and null all treaties, pacts and concessions which were signed in conditions of inequality, or which disregard or diminish its sovereignty over any part of the national territory.

ARTICLE 11. The Republic of Cuba is part of the world socialist community, which constitutes a fundamental premise for its independence and development in all orders.

ARTICLE 12. The Republic of Cuba espouses the principles of proletarian internationalism and of the combative solidarity of the peoples, and

(a) condemns imperialism, the promoter and supporter of all fascist, colonialist, neocolonialist and racist manifestations, as the main force of aggression and of war, and the worst enemy of the peoples;

(b) condemns imperialist intervention, whether direct or indirect, in the internal and external affairs of any state; and, therefore, armed aggression and economic blockade, as well as any other form of economic coercion and of interference with or threat to the integrity of the states and to the political, economic and cultural elements of the nations;

(c) considers wars of aggression and of conquest to be international crimes; recognizes the legitimacy of the wars of national liberation, as well as of armed resistance to aggression and conquest; and considers that its help to those under attack and to the peoples that struggle for their liberation constitutes its internationalist right and duty;

(d) recognizes the right of the peoples to repel imperialist and reactionary violence with revolutionary violence and to struggle by all means within their reach for the right to determine freely their own destiny and the economic and social system in which they choose to live;

(e) works for an honorable and lasting peace, based on respect for the independence and sovereignty of the peoples and on their right to self-determination;

(f) establishes its international relations on the principles of equality of rights, sovereignty and national independence of the states and on mutual interest;

(g) bases its relations with the Union of Soviet Socialist Republics and with other socialist countries on socialist internationalism, and on the common objectives of the construction of the new society, fraternal friendship, cooperation and mutual assistance;

(h) aspires to establish along with the countries of Latin America and of the Caribbean—freed from foreign domination and internal oppression—one large community of nations joined by the fraternal ties of historical tradition and the common struggle against colonialism and imperialism, in the same desire to foster national and social progress;

(i) develops fraternal relations and relations of collaboration with the countries that uphold anti-imperialist and progressive positions;

(j) maintains friendly relations with those countries which—although having a different political, social and economic system—respect its sovereignty, observe the rules of coexistence among states and the principles of mutual conveniences, and adopt an attitude of reciprocity with our country;

(k) determines its affiliation with international agencies and its participation in international conferences and meetings, bearing in mind the interests of peace and of socialism; of the liberation of the peoples; of the progress of science, technology and culture; of international exchange; and the respect for our country's own national rights.

ARTICLE 13. The Republic of Cuba grants asylum to those who are persecuted because of their struggle for the democratic rights of the majorities; for national liberation; against imperialism, fascism, colonialism and neocolonialism; for the abolition of racial discrimination; for the rights and the replevin of workers, peasants and students; for their progressive political, scientific and artistic activities; for socialism and peace.

ARTICLE 14. In the Republic of Cuba rules the system of socialist economy based on the socialist property of all the people over the means of production and on the abolition of man's exploitation of man.

ARTICLE 15. The socialist state property, which is the property of the entire people, becomes irreversibly established over the lands that do not belong to small farmers or to cooperatives formed by the same; over the subsoil, mines, woods, waters, means of communication; over the sugar mills, factories, chief means of transportation; and over all those enterprises, banks, installations and properties that have been nationalized and expropriated from the imperialists, the landholders and the bourgeoisie; as well as over the people's farms, factories, enterprises and economic, social, cultural and sports installations built, fostered or purchased by the state and those which will be built, fostered or purchased by the state in the future.

ARTICLE 16. The state organizes and directs the economic life of the nation in accordance with the central plan of socioeconomic development in whose elaboration and execution the workers of all the branches of the economy and of the other spheres of social life have an active and conscious participation.

The development of the economy serves the purpose of strengthening the socialist system; of satisfying increasingly better the material and cultural needs of the society and of the citizens; of promoting the flowering of the human personality and of its dignity; and serves the progress and the security of the country; and the national capacity to fulfill the internationlist duties of our people.

ARTICLE 17. The state organizes enterprises and other economic entities for the administration of the socialist property of the entire people.

The structure, powers and functions of the state enterprises and economic entities of production and of services and the system of their relations are prescribed by law.

ARTICLE 18. Foreign trade is the exclusive function of the state. The law determines which are the state enterprises, institutions and officials authorized to carry out import and export transactions; and which are those invested with legal power to sign commercial agreements.

ARTICLE 19. In the Republic of Cuba rules the socialist principle of "from each according to his ability, to each according to his work."

The law establishes the regulations which guarantee the effective fulfillment of this principle.

ARTICLE 20. The state recognizes the right of small farmers to own their lands and other means of production, according to what the law stipulates.

Small farmers have the right—according to their free and voluntary determination—to group themselves, in such a way and following such requirements as are prescribed by law; or to join the state plans for the purposes of agricultural production and of obtaining state loans and services.

The state supports the individual and cooperative production of small farmers, which contributes to the growth of the national economy.

ARTICLE 21. Small farmers have the right to sell their land with the previous authorization of the state agencies, as prescribed by law. In all cases, the state has preferential right to the purchase of the land while paying a fair price.

Land leases, partner ownership, mortgages and all other forms which entail a lien on the land or partial cession of the rights and title to the land which is property of the small farmers are all prohibited.

The establishment of agricultural cooperatives in the instances and ways prescribed by law is authorized.

Ownership of the cooperatives constitutes a form of collective ownership on the part of the peasants in those cooperatives.

ARTICLE 22. The estate guarantees the right of citizens to ownership of personal property in the way of earnings and savings derived from their own work, to their place of residence provided that they have legal title to it, and to their other possessions and objects which serve to satisfy their material and cultural needs.

Likewise, the state guarantees the right of citizens to ownership over their personal or family work tools, as long as these tools are not employed in exploiting the work of others.

ARTICLE 23. The state recognizes the right of political, social and mass organizations to ownership of the goods intended for the fulfillment of their objectives.

ARTICLE 24. The law regulates the right of citizens to inherit legal title to a place of residence and to other personal goods and chattels.

The land owned by a small farmer may only be inherited by the heirs who are personally involved in its cultivation, save for the exceptions prescribed by law.

With regard to goods which are part of cooperatives, the law prescribes the conditions under which said goods may be inherited.

ARTICLE 25. The expropriation of property for reasons of public benefit or social interest and with due compensation is authorized.

The law establishes the method for the expropriation and the bases on which the need for and usefulness of this action is to be determined as well as the form of compensation, taking into account the interest and the economic and social needs of the person whose property has been expropriated.

ARTICLE 26. Citizens who suffer damages, or injuries unjustly caused by a state official or employee while in the performance of his public functions have the right to claim and obtain the corresponding indemnification as prescribed by law.

ARTICLE 27. To insure the wellbeing of citizens, the state and society are the protectors of nature. It falls within the jurisdiction of the legally qualified agencies and of each and every citizen to watch over the cleanliness of the waters and of the air, and to protect the flora and the fauna.

CHAPTER II. CITIZENSHIP

ARTICLE 28. Cuban citizenship is acquired by birth or through naturalization.

ARTICLE 29. Cuban citizens by birth are:

(a) those born in Cuba, with the exception of the children of foreign persons at the service of their government or international organizations;

(b) those born abroad from a Cuban father or mother, prior to the fulfillment of the formalities stated by law;

(c) those born outside the territory of the Republic from a Cuban father or mother and who have lost their citizenship, provided they apply for Cuban citizenship according to the procedure stated by law;

(d) foreigners who, by virtue of their exceptional merits won in the struggles for Cuba's liberation, were considered as Cuban citizens by birth.

ARTICLE 30. Cuban citizens by naturalization are:

(a) those foreigners who acquire Cuban citizenship in accordance with the regulations established by law; and

(b) those who contributed to the armed struggle against the tyranny overthrown on January 1, 1959, provided they show proof of this in the legal established form.

ARTICLE 31. Neither marriage nor its dissolution affect the citizenship status of either of the spouses or their children.

ARTICLE 32. Cuban citizenship is lost by:

(a) those who become citizens of another country;

(b) those who without the Government's permission serve another nation in military functions or in posts entailing authority or jurisdiction;

(c) those who on foreign territory conspire or act in any way against the people of Cuba and their socialist and revolutionary institutions;

(d) naturalized Cubans residing in the country where they were born, unless they express their desire to maintain Cuban citizenship to the corresponding consular authority every three years;

(e) naturalized citizens who accept double citizenship.

The law may determine crimes and causes of unbecoming behavior that may lead to the loss of citizenship by naturalization through a nonappealable judgment by a court.

The formalization of the loss of citizenship by the reasons stated in clauses (b) and (c) is made effective by a decree issued by the Council of State.

ARTICLE 33. Cuban citizenship may be regained in those cases and ways specified by the law.

Chapter III. The Family

ARTICLE 34. The state protects the family, motherhood and matrimony.

ARTICLE 35. Marriage is the voluntarily established union between a man and a woman in order to live together. It is based on full equality of rights and duties for the partners, who must see to the support of the home and the integral education of their children through a joint effort compatible with the social activities of both.

The law regulates the formalization, recognition and dissolution of marriage and the rights and obligations deriving from such acts.

ARTICLE 36. All children have the same rights, regardless of whether or not they were born out of wedlock. Any qualification on the nature of the relationship is abolished.

No statement shall be made either with regard to the difference in birth or the civil status of the parents in the registration of the children's birth or in other documents that mention parenthood.

The state guarantees, through adequate legal means, the determination of and recognition of paternity.

ARTICLE 37. The parents have the duty to provide nourishment for their children; to help them to defend their legitimate interests and in the realization of their just aspirations; and to contribute actively to their education and integral development as useful well-prepared citizens for life in a socialist society.

It is the children's duty, in turn, to respect and help their parents.

Chapter IV. Education and Culture

ARTICLE 38. The state orients, foments and promotes education, culture and science in all their manifestations.

Its educational and cultural policy is based on the following principles:

(a) the state bases its educational and political policy on the scientific concept of the world established and developed by Marxism-Leninism;

(b) education is a function of the state. Consequently, educational centers belong to the state. The fulfillment of the educational function constitutes a task in which all society participates and is based on the conclusions and contributions made by science and in the closest relationship between study and life, work and production;

(c) the state must promote the communist education of the new generations and the training of children, young people and adults for social life.

In order to make this principle a reality, general education and specialized education of a scientific, technical or artistic character are combined with productive work, research with a view to development, physical education, sports and participation in political and social activities.

(d) education is provided free of charge. The state maintains a broad scholarship system for students and provides the workers with multiple opportunities to study, with a view to the universalization of education.

The law establishes the integration and structure of the national system of education and the extent of the compulsory education and defines the minimum level of general education that every citizen must acquire.

(e) artistic creativity is free as long as its content is not contrary to the Revolution. Forms of expression of art are free;

(f) in order to raise the level of culture of the people, the state foments and develops artistic education, the vocation for creation and the cultivation and appreciation of art;

(g) creation and investigation in science are free. The state encourages and makes possible investigation and gives priority to that which is aimed at solving the problems related to the interest of the society and the wellbeing of the people;

(h) the state makes it possible for the workers to engage in scientific work and to contribute to the development of science;

(i) the state promotes, foments and develops physical education and sports in all their forms as a means of education and of contribution to the integral development of the citizens;

(j) the state sees to the conservation of the nation's cultural heritage and artistic and historic wealth. The state protects national monuments and places known for their natural beauty or their artistic or historic value;

(k) the state promotes the participation of the citizens, through the country's social and mass organizations, in the development of its educational and cultural policy.

ARTICLE 39. The education of young people and children in the spirit of communism is the duty of all society.

The state and society give special protection to the young people and children. It is the duty of the family, the schools, the state agencies and the social and mass organizations to pay special attention to the integral development of young people and children.

CHAPTER V. EQUALITY

ARTICLE 40. All citizens have equal rights and are subject to equal duties.

ARTICLE 41. Discrimination because of race, color, sex or national origin is forbidden and will be punished by law.

The institutions of the state educate everyone, from the earliest possible age, in the principle of equality among human beings.

ARTICLE 42. The state consecrates the right achieved by the Revolution that all citizens, regardless of race, color or national origin:

—have access, in keeping with their merits and abilities, to all positions and state and administrative jobs and of production and services;
—can reach any rank of the Revolutionary Armed Forces, in keeping with their merits and abilities;
—be given equal pay for equal work;
—have a right to education at all national educational institutions, ranking from elementary schools to the universities, which are the same for all;
—be given medical care in all medical institutions;
—be given medical care in all hospitals;
—live in any sector, zone or area and stay in any hotel;
—be served at all restaurants and other public service establishments;

—use, without any separations, all means of transportation by sea, land and air;

—enjoy the same resorts, beaches, parks, social centers and other centers of culture, sports, recreation and rest.

ARTICLE 43. Women have the same rights as men in the economic, political and social fields and as far as the family goes.

In order to assure the exercise of those rights and especially the incorporation of women into socially organized work, the state sees to it that they are given jobs in keeping with their physical makeup; they are given paid maternity leave before and after giving birth; the state organizes institutions like children's daycare centers and boarding schools and it strives to create all the conditions which help to make real the principle of equality.

CHAPTER VI. FUNDAMENTAL RIGHTS, DUTIES AND GUARANTEES

ARTICLE 44. Work in a socialist society is a right and duty and a course of pride for every citizen.

Work is remunerated according to its quality and quantity; when it is provided, the needs of the economy and of society, the decision of the worker and his skill and ability will be taken into account; this is assured by the socialist economic development, without crises, and has thus eliminated unemployment and the dead season.

Every citizen has the duty to faithfully carry out tasks corresponding to him at his job.

ARTICLE 45. All those who work have the right to rest, which is guaranteed by the eight-hour work day, a weekly rest period and annual paid vacations.

The state contributes to the development of vacation plans and installations.

ARTICLE 46. By means of the Social Security System the state assures adequate protection to every worker who is unable to work because of age, illness or incapacity.

If the worker dies this protection will be extended to his family.

ARTICLE 47. The state protects by means of social aid aged persons who do not have financial resources or anyone who is unable to work and has no relatives who can help him.

ARTICLE 48. The state guarantees the right to protection, security and hygiene on the job by means of the adoption of adequate measures for the prevention of accidents at work and occupational diseases.

He who suffers an accident on the job or is affected by an occupational disease has the right to medical care and subsidy or retirement in those cases when a temporary or permanent incapacity for work ensues.

ARTICLE 49. Everybody has the right to have his or her health protected and cared for. The state guarantees this right:

—by providing free medical and hospital care by means of the installations of the rural medical service network, polyclinics, hospitals, prophylactic and specialized treatment centers;

—by providing free dental care;

—by promoting the health publicity campaigns, regular medical examinations, general vaccinations and other measures to prevent the outbreak of disease. All the population cooperates in these activities and plans by means of the social and mass organizations.

ARTICLE 50. Everyone has the right to an education. This right is assured by the free and far-reaching system of schools, boarding schools and scholarships of all kinds and at all levels of education, and because of the fact that all educational material is provided free of charge, which provides all children and young people, regardless of their family's economic position, with the opportunity to study in keeping with one's abiilty, social demands and the needs of socioeconomic development.

Adults also have this right assured and education for them is also free of charge with the specific facilities outlined by the law, by means of the worker-farmer education program, technological and professional education, training courses in state agencies and enterprises and the advanced courses for workers.

ARTICLE 51. Everyone has the right to physical education, sports and recreation.

Enjoyment of this right is assured by including the teaching and practice of physical education and sports in the study programs of the national educational system; and by the broad nature of the means and the teaching placed at the service of the people, which makes possible the practice of sports and recreation on a mass basis.

ARTICLE 52. Citizens have freedom of speech and of the press in keeping with the objectives of socialist society. Material conditions for the exercise of that right are provided by the fact that the press, radio, television and other organs of the mass media are state or social property and can never be private property. This assures their use at the exclusive service of the working people and in the interests of society.

The law regulates the exercise of these freedoms.

ARTICLE 53. The rights to assembly, demonstration and association are exercised by manual and intellectual workers in the city and in the countryside, and they have the necessary means for this. The social and mass organizations have all the facilities they need to carry out those activities in which the members have full freedom of speech and opinion based on the unlimited right of initiative and criticism.

ARTICLE 54. The socialist state, which bases its activity and educates the people in a scientific materialist concept of the universe, recognizes and guarantees freedom of conscience and the right of everyone to profess any religious belief and to practice, within the framework of respect for the law, the belief of his preference.

The law regulates the activities of religious institutions.

It is illegal and punishable by law to oppose one's faith or religious belief to the Revolution, education or the fulfillment of the duty to work, defend the homeland with arms, show reverence for its symbols and other duties established by the Constitution.

ARTICLE 55. The home is inviolable. Nobody can enter the home of another against his will, except in those cases foreseen by law.

ARTICLE 56. Mail is inviolable. It can only be seized, opened and examined in cases prescribed by law. Secrecy is maintained on matters other than those which led to the examination.

The same principle is to be applied in the case of cable, telegraph and telephone communication.

ARTICLE 57. Freedom and inviolability of persons is assured to all those who live in the country.

Nobody can be arrested, except in the manner, with the guarantees and in the cases indicated by law.

The person who has been arrested or the prisoner is inviolable in his personal integrity.

ARTICLE 58. Nobody can be tried or sentenced except by the competent tribunal by virtue of laws which existed prior to the crime and with the formalities and guarantees that the law establishes.

Every accused person has the right to a defense.

No violence or pressure of any kind can be used against people to force them to testify.

All statements obtained in violation of the above precept are null and void and those responsible for the violation will be punished as outlined by the law.

ARTICLE 59. Confiscation of property is only applied as a punishment by the authorities in the cases and by the methods determined by law.

ARTICLE 60. Penal laws are retroactive when they benefit the accused or person who has been sentenced. Other laws are not to be retroactive unless the contrary is decided for reasons of social interest or because it is useful for public purposes.

ARTICLE 61. None of the freedoms which are recognized for citizens can be exercised contrary to what is established in the Constitution and the law or contrary to the existence and objectives of the socialist state, or contrary to the decision of the Cuban people to build socialism and communism. Violations of this principle can be punished by law.

ARTICLE 62. Every citizen has the right to file complaints with and send petitions to the authorities and to be given the pertinent response or attention in keeping with the law.

ARTICLE 63. Strict fulfillment of the Constitution and the laws is an inexcusable duty of all.

ARTICLE 64. Every citizen has the duty of caring for public and social property, accepting work discipline, respecting the rights of others, observing standards of socialist living and fulfilling civic and social duties.

ARTICLE 65. Defense of the socialist homeland is the greatest honor and the supreme duty of every citizen.

The law regulates the military service which Cubans must do.

Treason against one's country is the most serious of crimes; those who commit it are subject to the most severe penalties.

CHAPTER VII. PRINCIPLES OF ORGANIZATION AND FUNCTIONING OF THE ORGANS

ARTICLE 66. State organs are set up, function and carry out their activity based on the principles of socialist democracy, unity of power and democratic centralism, which are manifested in the following forms:

(a) all organs of People's Power, its executive organs and all the courts are formed by members who are elected and subject to recall at regular intervals;

(b) the masses of workers control the activity of the state agencies, their delegates and officials;

(c) those elected must render an account of their work to their electors and they have the right to revoke them when they are not worthy of the trust placed on them;

(d) every state organ develops in a far-reaching manner, within its jurisdiction, initiatives aimed at taking advantage of the resources and possibilities which exist on a local level and to include the social and mass organizations in their work;

(e) decisions of superior state organs are compulsory for inferior ones;

(f) inferior state organs are responsible to superior ones and must render accounts of their work;

(g) in the activity of local administrative and executive organs there is a system of double subordination: subordination to the corresponding organ of People's Power and subordination to the superior level which handles the administrative matters which are also under the jurisdiction of the local organ;

(h) freedom of discussion, criticism and self-criticism and subordination of the minority to the majority prevail in all collegiate state organs.

CHAPTER VIII. SUPREME ORGANS OF PEOPLE'S POWER

ARTICLE 67. The National Assembly of People's Power is the supreme organ of state power and represents and expresses the sovereign will of all the working people.

ARTICLE 68. The National Assembly of People's Power is the only organ in the Republic invested with constituent and legislative authority.

ARTICLE 69. The National Assembly of People's Power elects, from among its deputies, the Council of State, which consists of one President, one First Vice-President, five Vice-Presidents and 24 other members.

The President of the Council of State is, at the same time, the Head of Government.

The Council of State is accountable for its action to the National Assembly of People's Power, to which it must render accounts of all its activities.

ARTICLE 70. The National Assembly of People's Power is invested with the following powers:

(a) deciding on reforms to the Constitution according to that established in Article 141;

(b) approving, modifying and annulling laws;

(c) deciding on the constitutionality of laws, decree-laws, decrees and all other general provisions;

(ch) revoking in toto or in part the decree-laws issued by the Council of State;

(d) discussing and approving the national plans for economic and social development;

(e) discussing and approving the state budget;

(f) approving the principles of the system for planning and the management of the national economy;

(g) approving the monetary and credit system;
(h) approving the general outlines of foreign and domestic policy;
(i) ratifying and denouncing international treaties;
(j) declaring a state of war in the event of military aggression and approving peace treaties;
(k) establishing and modifying the politico-administrative division of the country pursuant to that established in Article 100;
(l) electing the President, the First Vice-President, the Vice-Presidents and the other members of the Council of State;
(ll) electing the President, Vice-President and Secretary of the National Assembly;
(m) appointing, at the initiative of the President of the Council of State, the members of the Council of Ministers;
(n) electing the President, Vice-President and other judges of the People's Supreme Court;
(ñ) electing the attorney general and the deputy attorney general of the Republic;
(o) appointing permanent and temporary commissions;
(p) revoking the election or appointment of those persons elected or appointed by it;
(q) exercising the highest supervision over the organs of state and government;
(r) keeping informed on, evaluating and adopting pertinent decisions on the reports on the rendering of accounts submitted by the Council of State, the Council of Ministers, the People's Supreme Court, the Office of the Attorney General of the Republic and the Provinical Assemblies;
(s) revoking those provisions or decrees by the Council of Ministers which are contrary to the Constitution or the law or the decree-laws of the Council of State;
(t) annulling or modifying those resolutions or provisions of the local organs of People's Power which encroach on the Constitution, the laws, the decree-laws, the decrees and other provisions issued by a superior organ, or those which are detrimental to the interests of other localities or the general interests of the nation;
(u) granting amnesty;
(v) calling for the holding of a referendum in those cases provided by the Constitution and others which the Assembly considers pertinent;
(w) establishing its rules and regulations; and
(x) all other powers invested by this Constitution.

ARTICLE 71. All laws and resolutions of the National Assembly of People's Power, barring those in relation to reforms in the Constitution, are adopted by a simple majority of votes.

ARTICLE 72. All laws approved by the National Assembly of People's Power go into effect on the date determined by those laws in each case.

Laws are published in the Official Gazette of the Republic.

ARTICLE 73. The National Assembly of People's Power is composed of deputies elected according to the way and number established by the law.

ARTICLE 74. The National Assembly of People's Power is elected for a period of five years.

This period can only be extended by virtue of a resolution of the Assembly itself in the event of war or in the case of other exceptional circumstances that may impede the normal holding of elections and while such circumstances exist.

ARTICLE 75. Thirty days after all the deputies to the National Assembly of People's Power are elected, the Assembly meets on its own right, under the presidency of the oldest deputy assisted by the two youngest deputies acting as secretaries.

The session includes the verification of the validity of the election of the deputies, the swearing in of the deputies and the election by the deputies of the President, the Vice-President and Secretary of the National Assembly of People's Power, who proceed to assume their posts immediately.

Next, the Assembly proceeds to elect the Council of State.

ARTICLE 76. The National Assembly of People's Power holds two ordinary sessions a year and a special session when request by one third of the membership or when called by the Council of State.

ARTICLE 77. More than half of the total number of delegates must be present for a session of the National Assembly of People's Power to be held.

ARTICLE 78. All sessions of the National Assembly of People's Power are public, excepting in the case that the Assembly resolves to hold a closed-door session by reasons of state interest.

ARTICLE 79. The President of the National Assembly of People's Power is invested with the power to:

(a) preside over the session of the National Assembly and see to it that its regulations are put into effect;

(b) call the ordinary sessions of the National Assembly;

(c) propose the draft agenda for the sessions of the National Assembly;

(d) sign and order the publication in the Official Gazzete of the Republic of the laws and resolutions adopted by the National Assembly;

(e) organize the international relations of the National Assembly;

(f) conduct and organize the work of those permanent and temporary commissions appointed by the National Assembly;

(g) attend the meetings of the Council of State;

(h) all other powers assigned to him by this Constitution or the Assembly.

ARTICLE 80. The status of deputy does not entail personal privileges or economic benefits of any kind.

The deputies to the National Assembly of People's Power combine their activities as such with their duties and their regular everyday tasks.

To the extent that their work as deputies demands, they are given leave without pay and receive a daily allowance equivalent to their salary and whatever additional expenses they may incur in the exercise of their duties.

ARTICLE 81. No deputy to the National Assembly of People's Power may be arrested or placed on trial without the authorization of either the Assembly or the Council of State, except in the case of flagrant delict.

ARTICLE 82. It is the duty of the deputies to the National Assembly of People's Power to exercise their duties in the benefit of the people's interests, stay in contact with their electors, listen to their grievances, suggestions and criticism, explain the policy of the state to them and periodically render account to them of the results of their activities. Likewise, it is the deputies' duty to render account of their activities to the Assembly any time the Assembly deems it necessary.

ARTICLE 83. The deputies to the National Assembly of People's Power may be revoked by their electors at any time in the ways and means prescribed by the law.

ARTICLE 84. The deputies to the National Assembly of People's Power have the right to make inquiries to the Council of State, the Council of Ministers or the members of either and to have these inquiries answered during the course of the same session or at the next session.

ARTICLE 85. It is the duty of all state organs and enterprises to provide all the necessary collaboration of the deputies in the discharge of their duties.

ARTICLE 86. The proposal of laws falls on:

(a) the deputies to the National Assembly of People's Power;

(b) the Council of State;

(c) the Council of Ministers;

(d) the commissions of the National Assembly of People's Power;

(e) the Central Organization of Cuban Trade Unions and the national offices of the other social and mass organizations;

(f) the People's Supreme Court, in matters related to the administration of justice;

(g) the Office of the Attorney General of the Republic, in matters within its jurisdiction:

(h) the citizens. In this case it is an indispensable prerequisite that the proposal be made by at least 10,000 citizens who are eligible to vote.

ARTICLE 87. The Council of State is the National Assembly of People's Power's organ that represents it in the period between sessions, puts its resolutions into effect and complies with all the other duties assigned by the Constitution. It has a collegiate character and for national and international purposes it is the highest representative of the Cuban state.

ARTICLE 88. The Council of State is invested with the power to:

(a) summon special sessions of the National Assembly of People's Power;

(b) set the date for the elections for the periodic renovation of the National Assembly of People's Power;

(c) issue decree-laws in the period between the sessions of the National Assembly of People's Power;

(d) give existing laws a general and obligatory interpretation whenever necessary;

(e) exert legislative initiative;

(f) make all the necessary arrangements for the holding of referendums called for by the Assembly;

(g) decree general mobilization whenever the defense of the country makes it necessary and assume the authority to declare war in the event of aggression or to approve peace treaties—duties which the Constitution assigns to the National Assembly of People's Power—when the Assembly is in recess and cannot be called to session with the necessary security and urgency.

(h) replace, at the initiative of its President, the members of the Council of Ministers in the period between the sessions of the National Assembly of People's Power;

(i) issue general instructions to the courts through the Council of Government of the People's Supreme Court;

(j) issue instructions to the Office of the Attorney General of the Republic;

(k) appoint and remove, at the initiative of its President, the plenipotentiary representatives of Cuba in other states;

(l) grant decorations and honorary titles;

(ll) name commissions;

(m) grant pardons;

(n) denounce international treaties;

(ñ) grant or refuse recognition to diplomatic representatives of other states who present their credentials to the Republic;

(o) suspend those provisions of the Council of Ministers which do not adjust to the Constitution or laws, reporting on this action to the National Assembly of People's Power in the first session held following the adoption of the measure;

(p) revoke those resolutions and provisions of the Executive Committees of the local organs of People's Power which infringe the Constitution, the laws, the decree-laws, the decrees and other provisions issued by an organ of superior rank or when they are detrimental to the interests of other localities or to the general interests of the nation;

(q) approve its rules and regulations.

ARTICLE 89. All the decisions of the Council of State are adopted through the favorable vote of a simple majority of its members.

ARTICLE 90. The mandate entrusted to the Council of State by the National Assembly of People's Power expires at the time of the establishment of a new Assembly by virtue of the periodic renovations of the Assembly.

ARTICLE 91. The President of the Council of State is Head of State and Head of Government and is invested with the power to:

(a) represent the state and the government and conduct their general policy;

(b) organize, conduct the activities of, call for the holding of and preside over the sessions of the Council of State and the Council of Ministers;

(c) control and supervise the development of the activities of the ministries and other central agencies of the ministries and other central agencies of the administration;

(d) assume the leadership of any ministry or central agency of the administration;

(e) propose to the National Assembly of People's Power, once elected by the latter, the members of the Council of Ministers;

(f) accept the resignation of the members of the Council of Ministers or propose either to the National Assembly of People's Power or the Council of State the removal of any of those members and, in both cases, to propose the corresponding substitutes;

(g) receive the letters of credence of the heads of foreign diplomatic missions;

(h) assume the supreme command of the Revolutionary Armed Forces;

(i) assume all other duties assigned it by the Constitution or the Assembly.

The function assigned in clause (g) may be delegated to one of the vice-presidents of the Council of State.

ARTICLE 92. In case of the absence, illness or death of the President of the Council of State, the First Vice-President assumes the President's duties.

ARTICLE 93. The Council of Ministers is the highest-ranking executive and administrative organ and constitutes the Government of the Republic.

The number, denomination and functions of the ministries and central agencies making up the Council of Ministers are determined by the law.

ARTICLE 94. The Council of Ministers is composed of the Head of State and Government, as its President, the First Vice-President, the Vice-Presidents, the Ministers, the President of the Central Planning Board and the other members that the law determines.

ARTICLE 95. The President, the First Vice-President and the Vice-Presidents of the Council of Ministers constitute its Executive Committee.

ARTICLE 96. The Council of Ministers is invested with the power to:

(a) organize and conduct the political, economic, cultural, scientific, social and defense activities outlined by the National Assembly of People's Power;

(b) propose the projects for the general plans for the socioeconomic development of the state and, after these are approved by the National Assembly of People's Power, organize, and conduct and supervise their implementation.

(c) conduct the foreign policy of the Republic and the relations with other governments;

(d) arrange international treaties and submit them to ratification by the National Assembly of People's Power;

(e) direct and control foreign trade;

(f) draw up the draft for the state budget and once it is approved to see to its implementations;

(g) adopt measures aimed at strengthening the monetary and credit system;

(h) draw up bills and submit them to the consideration of the National Assembly of People's Power or the Council of State, accordingly;

(i) see to national defense, the maintenance of order and security at home, the protection of citizens' rights and the protection of lives and property in the event of natural disasters.

(j) conduct the administration of the state. unifying, coordinating and supervising the activities of the ministries and other central agencies of the administration;

(k) implement the laws and resolutions of the National Assembly of People's Power and the decree-laws and provisions issued by the Council of State and, if necessary, dictating the corresponding regulations;

(l) issue decrees and provisions on the basis of and pursuant to the existing laws and supervise their implementation;

(ll) grant asylum;

(m) determine the general organization of the Revolutionary Armed Forces;

(n) assume the direction and the methodological and technical supervision of the administrative functions of the local organs of People's Power through the corresponding ministries and other central agencies.

(ñ) revoke or annul those provisions issued by ministers, heads of central agencies and the administrative bodies of the local organs of People's Power which are contrary to the instructions issued from a higher level and whose fulfillment is compulsory;

(o) propose to the National Assembly of People's Power the annulment of, or to the Council of State the suspension of those resolutions and provisions issued by the Assemblies of the local organs of People's Power which infringe existing laws and other provisions or are detrimental to the interests of other communities or the general interests of the nation;

(p) name the commissions it deems necessary to facilitate the fulfillment of the tasks assigned to it;

(q) appoint and remove officials in keeping with the powers it invested with by the law;

(r) assume any duty assigned to it by the National Assembly of People's Powers or the Council of State.

ARTICLE 97. The Council of Ministers is accountable to and renders account of its activities periodically to the National Assembly of People's Power.

ARTICLE 98. The members of the Council of Ministers are invested with the power to:

(a) conduct the affairs and tasks of the ministry or agency under their care, issuing the necessary resolutions and provisions to that effect;

(b) dictate, in the case this is not the specific duty of another state organ, the necessary regulations to make possible the implementation of those laws which concern them;

(c) attend the session of the Council of Ministers, with the authority to speak and vote, and submit to the consideration of the Council whatever bill, decree-law, decree, resolution or any other proposal it considers advisable;

(d) name, according to the law, the officials it is entitled to.

ARTICLE 99. The General Secretary of the Central Organization of Cuban Trade Unions has the right to participate in the sessions of the Council of Ministers and of its Executive Committee.

CHAPTER IX. LOCAL ORGANS OF PEOPLE'S POWER

ARTICLE 100. For political-administrative purposes the country is divided into provinces and municipalities; their number, boundaries and name are determined by law.

The law can also give rise to other divisions.

ARTICLE 101. The Assemblies of Delegates of People's Power setup in the political and administrative divisions into which the country is divided by law, are the superior local organs of state power.

ARTICLE 102. The Assemblies of Delegates of People's Power are invested with the highest local authority for the exercise of their state functions in the area under their jurisdiction. To this effect, they govern in all that concerns them and, by means of the organs which they establish, direct economic, production and service units which are directly subordinated to them and carry out the activities required in order to meet the needs of care, economic, cultural, educational and recreational services of the collective in the territory under the jurisdiction of each.

They also aid in the development of activities and the fulfillment of plans of those units in their territory which are not subordinated to them.

ARTICLE 103. For the exercise of their functions the Assemblies of People's Power are backed up by the initiative and the broad participation of the population and they act in close coordination with the social and mass organizations.

ARTICLE 104. The local organs of People's Power, to the corresponding extent and in keeping with the law, participate in the preparation and implementation of the Uniform Socioeconomic Plan adopted by the state.

ARTICLE 105. In the limits of their jurisdiction, the Assemblies of People's Power:

(a) obey and help to enforce the laws and regulations of a general nature which come from the superior organs of the state;

(b) adopt agreements and enact measures;

(c) suspend, annul or modify, whatever the case may be, the resolutions and measures of the organs subordinated to them which are contrary to the Constitution or the laws, degree-laws, decrees, regulations or resolutions enacted by the superior organs of state power, or those which affect the interests of other communities or the general interest of the country;

(d) elect their Executive Committee and determine its organization, functioning and task, in keeping with the law;

(e) revoke the mandate of the members of the respective Executive Committees.

(f) determine the organization, functioning and tasks of the administrative leadership in the different branches of socioeconomic activity.

(g) designate, substitute or dismiss the heads of their administrative departments;

(h) set up and dissolve work commissions;

(i) elect and revoke, in keeping with the provisions of the law, the judges of the People's Courts in the area under their respective jurisdictions;

(j) study and evaluate the rendering of accounts reports presented by their Executive Committees, judicial organs and assemblies which are their immediate subordinates and adopt the pertinent decisions regarding those reports;

(k) protect and defend the rights of citizens and socialist property;

(l) cooperate in the strengthening of socialist legality, upholding internal order and strengthening the country's defensive capability;

(11) carry out the other functions assigned by the Constitution and the law.

ARTICLE 106. On the second Sunday following the election of all the delegates to the Municipal Assembly of People's Power, it meets by right under the presidency of the oldest delegate in order to confirm the validity of the election of the delegates and once this has been done it will elect the Executive Committee and the delegates to the superior local assemblies. The two youngest delegates act as secretaries.

The other local assemblies are set up in the same way and on the occasion stipulated by the law.

ARTICLE 107. The ordinary sessions and the extraordinary sessions of the Assemblies of People's Power are public. Only when state secrets or the dignity of persons are involved will this not be the case.

ARTICLE 108. In order for agreements of the Assemblies of People's Power to be valid more than half the total number of members must be present. Agreements are adopted by simple majority.

ARTICLE 109. The administrative departments are subordinated to their respective assembly, its Executive Committee and the superior organ of the corresponding administrative branch.

ARTICLE 110. The permanent work commissions organized by branches of production and services aid the Assemblies and their Executive Committees in their respective activities and in controlling the administrative leaderships.

The commissions of a temporary nature fulfill specific tasks assigned within the time limits that are indicated.

ARTICLE 111. The Assemblies are renovated every two and a half years which is the period of the mandate of a delegate. This term can only be extended by means of a decision by the National Assembly of People's Power, in the cases mentioned in Article 74.

ARTICLE 112. The mandate of the delegates can only be revoked by their electors who can do so at any time, by means of the method outlined by the law. The law also outlines the cases and the method for replacing delegates when they are no longer able to perform their duties.

ARTICLE 113. The delegates fulfill the mandate of their electors in the interests of all the community and they must:

(a) make the opinions, needs and problems expressed by their electors known to the Assembly;

(b) report to their electors on the policy of the Assembly and the measures adopted in order to solve the problems posed by the population or outline the reasons why they have not been solved;

(c) render account of their work on a regular basis and in a personal manner to their electors and to the Assembly to which they belong.

ARTICLE 114. The Executive Committee is the collegiate organ elected by the Assembly of People's Power to fulfill the functions outlined by the Constitution and assigned by law as well as the tasks it is given by the Assembly.

The Executive Committee is made up of the number of members determined by the law and they elect, with the ratification of the Assembly, a President, a Vice-President and a Secretary who also hold those posts in the Assembly.

ARTICLE 115. The election of the members of the Executive Committees of the Municipal Assemblies takes place from among the ranks of assembly delegates.

In the Local Assemblies of a superior ranking those who are not members of the Assembly can be elected to the Executive Committee but once this has been done they become delegates to the Assembly itself.

In all cases the election takes place by virtue of candidacies proposed in the manner outlined by the law.

The President of every Executive Committee is also, by right, a delegate to the immediate superior Assembly.

ARTICLE 116. The Executive Committee has the authority to:

(a) summon ordinary and special sessions of the Assembly;

(b) publish and implement the agreements adopted by the Assembly;

(c) suspend the implementation of any measure enacted by the immediate subordinate Executive Committee, when it is unconstitutional, illegal or otherwise contradictory to the measures enacted by the superior organs of state power, or those which affect the interests of other communities or the general interests of the country;

(d) study, evaluate and adopt the pertinent decisions regarding the rendering of accounts reports presented by the immediate subordinate Executive Committee;
(e) direct and control the administrative leaderships;
(f) designated officials of the administrative leaderships;
(g) adopt the pertinent measures to aid in the development of the activities and the fulfillment of the plans of the units established in the territory of the respective assemblies which are not subordinated to it.

ARTICLE 117. In the periods between assembly sessions, the Executive Committee assumes its functions which are outlined in clauses (a), (b), (k) and (l) of Article 105.

The agreements and general measures adopted by the Executive Committee in exercise of those powers must be ratified, modified or annulled by the Assembly in the first meeting it holds afterward.

ARTICLE 118. The Executive Committee periodically renders an account of its work to the Assembly and to the immediate superior Executive Committee.

ARTICLE 119. The mandate given to every Executive Committee ceases when a new Assembly of Delegates to People's Power is set up.

ARTICLE 120. The President of the Executive Committee has the power to:
(a) summon and preside over the sessions of the Assembly;
(b) see to it that the regulations of the Assemblies are enforced;
(c) summon and preside over the meetings of the Executive Committee;
(d) organize the activity of the Executive Committee.

The President may delegate some of these functions on the Vice-President.

CHAPTER X. THE COURTS AND THE OFFICE OF THE ATTORNEY GENERAL

ARTICLE 121. The function of administering justice springs from the people and is carried out on its behalf by the People's Supreme Court and the other tribunals and courts which the law establishes.

The jurisdiction of the courts in their different levels is adjusted to the political-administrative division of the country and the needs of the judicial function.

The law regulates the organization of the courts; the authority and the form of exercising it; the standards that judges must meet; the manner in which they must be elected; the period of time they are to serve in their respective positions and the method for revoking them.

ARTICLE 122. The courts constitute a system of state organs which are set up with functional independence from any other and they are only subordinated to the National Assembly of People's Power.

ARTICLE 123. The main objectives of the activities of the court are:
(a) maintain and strengthen socialist legality;
(b) safeguarding the economic, social and political regime established in this Constitution;
(c) protecting socialist property, the personal property of citizens and other forms which this Constitution recognizes;
(d) safeguard the rights and legitimate interests of state agencies and those of economic and social institutions;
(e) protect the life, freedom, dignity, honor, property, family relations and other legitimate rights and interests of citizens;
(f) prevent violations of the law and antisocial conduct, restrain and reeducate those who are guilty of such violations or conduct and reestablish the dominant position of legal standards when demands are made in protest against their violation;
(g) increase awareness as to the need for strictly observing the law, making timely comments in their decisions aimed at educating citizens in the conscious and voluntary fulfillment of their duty of loyalty to the homeland, the cause of socialism and the norms of socialist living.

ARTICLE 124. The People's Supreme Court is the foremost judicial authority and its decisions in this field are definitive.

Through its Council of Government it can propose laws and issue regulations; makes decisions and enacts norms whose fulfillment is compulsory for all people's courts and, based on their experience, it issues instruction which are also compulsory in order to establish a uniform judicial practice in the interpretation and application of the law.

ARTICLE. 125. The judges, in their function of administering justice, are independent and only owe obedience to the law.

ARTICLE 126. The sentences and other decisions of the courts, pronounced or enacted within the limits of their jurisdiction, must be obeyed and implemented by state agencies, economic and social institutions and citizens, by those directly affected and by those who do not have a direct interest in their implementation but have the duty to participate in it.

ARTICLE 127. All courts function in a collegiate form.

Professional and lay judges participate in the administration of justice with equal duties and rights.

ARTICLE 128. Courts render an account of their work to electors at least once a year.

ARTICLE 129. Revoking a judge can only be done by the organ which elected him.

ARTICLE 130. It falls within the jurisdiction of the Office of the Attorney General of the Republic, as its main objective, to control socialist legality by seeing to it that the law and other legal regulations are obeyed by state agencies, economic and social institutions and citizens.

The law determines the form, duration and occasion in which the Attorney General exercises those powers.

ARTICLE 131. The Office of the Attorney General of the Republic constitutes an organic unit which is only subordinated to the National Assembly of People's Power and the Council of State.

The Attorney General of the Republic is given instructions directly from the Council of State.

The Attorney General of the Republic will handle the leadership and control of all the work done by his office all over the country.

The Attorney General of the Republic is a member of the Council of Government of the People's Supreme Court.

The organs of the Office of the Attorney General are organized in a vertical manner all over the country. They are independent of the Local Assemblies of People's Power and subordinate only to the Attorney General of the Republic.

ARTICLE 132. The Attorney General of the Republic and the assistant attorney generals are elected and subject to recall by the National Assembly of People's Power. The law stipulates the length of time they are to serve.

ARTICLE 133. The Attorney General of the Republic renders an account of his work to the National Assembly of People's Power at least once a year.

Chapter XI. Electoral System

ARTICLE 134. In all elections and in referendums, voting is free, equal and secret.

ARTICLE 135. In elections for deputies to the National Assembly and those for delegates to the Municipal Assembly, and in referendums, all Cubans who are more than 16 years of age, men and women alike, have the right to vote except those who:

(a) are mentally incapacitated and have been declared so by a court;

(b) those who have committed a crime and because of this lost the right to vote.

ARTICLE 136. Members of the Revolutionary Armed Forces and other military institutions of the nation have the right to elect and be elected, just like any other citizen.

ARTICLE 137. All Cuban citizens, men and women alike, who have full political rights can be elected.

If the election is for deputies of the National Assemblies of People's Power they must be more than 18 years old.

ARTICLE 138. The law determines the number of delegates that make up each of the assemblies in proportion to the number of people who live in each of the political-administrative regions into which the country is divided; it also regulates the form and manner of the election.

The delegates to the Municipal Assemblies are elected by previously determined electoral circumscriptions.

ARTICLE 139. The Municipal Assemblies elect from among their own ranks and by means of secret balloting, the delegates to the superior Local Assemblies.

ARTICLE 140. In order for a delegate to be considered elected he must get more than half the number of votes cast in the circumscription.

If this does not happen the law stipulates the manner in which new elections will be held in order to decide who is elected from among those with the most votes.

CHAPTER XII. CONSTITUTIONAL REFORMS

ARTICLE 141. This Constitution can only be totally or partially modified by the National Assembly of People's Power by means of resolutions adopted by nominal voting by a majority of no less than two thirds of the total number of members.

If the modification is total or has to do with the integration and authority of the National Assembly of People's Power or the Council of State or the rights and duties contained in the Constitution, the approval of the majority of citizens with the right to vote is required via a referendum organized for this purpose by the Assembly.

Cuban Situation: U.S. Overview

Arthur T. Downey, U.S. deputy assistant secretary of commerce for East-West trade, presented this overview of the Cuban situation June 11, 1975 in testimony before two subcommittees of the House Committee on International Relations (abridged):

I. A REVIEW OF CUBA'S PRE-REVOLUTIONARY ECONOMIC HISTORY, 1902–1958

Cuba—A Sugar Based Economy

Like most island economies, Cuba was, and is today, heavily foreign-trade oriented. Between the mid-1950's and the 1960's annual imports equaled from 22 to 32 percent of GNP. (See Table 1.) In the years prior to the 1959 revolution, U.S. investment in Cuba was large and this, coupled with close geographical proximity, made the U.S. the number one trading partner of Cuba, with the U.S. regularly accounting for 60 to 70 percent of both Cuban exports and imports. (See Tables 2 and 3.)

Cuba's trading welfare is now and has been in the past, very much tied to sugar. The economy is heavily impacted both by the level of its sugar production and

TABLE 1.—CUBA: RELATION OF GROSS NATIONAL PRODUCT TO FOREIGN TRADE [1]

[Dollar amounts in millions of U.S. dollars]

Year	GNP	As percent of GNP—	
		Exports	Imports
1956	$2.36	31.0	31.1
1957	2.80	28.8	32.0
1958	2.67	24.9	32.2
1961	2.7	23.2	23.7
1962	2.8	18.6	27.1
1963	3.2	17.0	27.1
1964	3.9	18.3	26.1
1965	3.8	18.0	22.8
1966	3.7	16.0	25.2

[1] Gross domestic product utilized 1956–58 and gross material product for 1961–66.

world market sugar prices. In 1958, sugar accounted for 79 percent of Cuba's dollar value of exports and in 1972, even before the large rise in prices, sugar exports provided nearly 74 percent of export income.

Consequently, much of Cuba's economic development has been influenced by international sugar prices and other economic factors outside its control.

Cuban Trade Links with the U.S. 1902–1930

For more than 50 years after U.S. troops departed Cuba in 1902 at the close of the Spanish-American War, the U.S. maintained a special economic relationship with its island neighbor.

Encouraged by the political stability underwritten by the Platt Amendment to the Cuban Constitution, U.S. commercial interests expanded to dominate the economy from 1901 to 1934.

U.S. direct investment increased substantially and by 1927, fully one-half of the sugar industry was U.S. controlled. The balance of U.S. ownership was in the railways, other public services and land. Twenty-two percent of all Cuban

TABLE 2.—CUBAN TRADE WITH THE UNITED STATES

[Selected years in millions of U.S. dollars]

Year	Cuban exports	Percent total exports	Cuban imports	Percent of total imports
1902	49.5	76.9	25.2	41.7
1909	109.4	87.7	46.3	50.7
1919	439.8	76.8	271.1	76.1
1927	256.1	79.0	159.1	61.8
1935	111.5	79.3	55.7	58.3
1940	104.9	82.4	81.0	76.7
1948	366.4	51.6	420.5	79.7
1956	457.1	68.6	19.8	80.1
1957	481.9	59.7	518.6	67.1
1958	527.8	71.1	546.9	63.6
1959	474.3	74.4	435.8	64.7
1960	357.3	57.8	223.7	38.5
1961	35.2	5.6	13.7	2.1
1962	6.8	1.3	13.4	1.8

TABLE 3

	1958	1959	1960	1961	1962	1971	1972	1973	1974
CUBAN EXPORTS (FOB)									
Other IW [1]	167.3	107.2	92.4	58.6	69.0	210	229	341.5	656
United States	498.0	440.0	325.0	30.0	15.8				
Other CPE's [2]	4.0	.2	43.7	156.0	183.0	251	202	315.0	550
U.S.S.R.	14.1	12.9	103.5	300.9	220.3	304	244	575.0	935
Other	59.0	77.7	43.0	79.0	33.0	95	162	148.5	604
Total	742.0	637.0	608.0	625.0	521.0	860	837	1,380.0	2,745
CUBAN IMPORTS (CIF)									
Other IW [1]	136.0	156.0	98.0	116.0	59.0	318	257	411.0	655
United States	581.0	500.0	300.0	26.0	14.0				
Other CPE's [2]	2.0	2.0	44.0	199.0	217.0	238	218	275.0	350
U.S.S.R.			88.0	294.0	411.0	731	778	950.0	1,100
Other	139.0	82.0	108.0	67.0	58.0	100	44	64.0	145
Total	858.0	740.0	638.0	702.0	759.0	1,387	1,297	1,700.0	2,250

[1] Austria, Belgium-Luxembourg, Canada, Denmark, France, Italy, Japan, Netherlands, Norway, Sweden, Switzerland, United Kingdom, West Germany.
[2] Albania, Bulgaria, Czechoslovakia, East Germany, Hungary, Poland, Romania, China, Mongolia, North Korea, North Vietnam.

land and 90 percent of its electrical generating capacity was owned by U.S. companies in the early 1930's.

Sugar and the Economy 1930–58

Sugar, always the lifeblood of the Cuban economy, has been a commodity heavily affected by U.S. legislation and international agreements. Cuba was long dependent on the U.S. as a market for its sugar and it supplied a major portion of total U.S. sugar consumption. (See Table 4.)

The 1937 International Sugar Agreement established a world sugar export market of 3.62 million tons with Cuba's share of the world market at 26 percent. However, the International Sugar Council defined the world market to exclude trade movements between special areas such as the U.S. and Cuba. The U.S. Sugar Acts of 1934 and 1937 allocated 29 percent of total U.S. sugar consumption to Cuban suppliers. Cuba's quota was raised to 42 percent of U.S. imports by a new Sugar Act in 1953.

However, political events and not legal documents were the determining factors in the actual composition of sugar trade during the period. European and Pacific hostilities during World War II left Cuba virtually the sole supply of free world sugar and Cuba actually supplied an average of 45 percent of the U.S. market from 1942–47.

Other Pre-Revolution Economic Developments

The 1940 Cuban Constitution provided an institutional basis for democracy, and an interim of political stability. Beginning in 1941, the Cuban economy exhibited remarkable growth. Several factors were responsible for the growth including the fact that World War II made Cuba the basic free world source of sugar. The sugar industry prospered and by 1947 Cuba's international monetary reserves had increased to $601 million. As a result of a government policy of "Cubanization of the sugar industry," Cuban-owned capacity accounted for 22 percent of production in 1939, but that share had risen to 62 percent by 1958, at which time the Cuban economy had arrived at a high point in its development.

Cuba also began to follow a new international economic policy based largely on bilateral trade agreements (11 of which were concluded by 1958), even though multilateralism had been established as the guiding principal of world trade with the signing of the GATT in 1947. Both Cuba and the U.S. were signatories but they maintained their bilateral tariff preference system by enacting an exclusive supplementary agreement to the GATT in that same year.

Additional positive factors included the establishment of the National Bank of Cuba as the country's first central bank in 1950. The Cuban population shared generally in the increasing level of prosperity as per capita national income rose from 91 pesos in 1940 to 344 pesos in 1951.

Nevertheless, Fulgencia Batista abolished the 1940 Constitution in a 1952 coup d'etat. Batista's economic policy resulted in a decline in sugar production, while the non-sugar industries and tourism continued to prosper, aided by an infusion of U.S. capital. However, the rate of increase in per capita national income slowed

TABLE 4.—CUBAN SHARE OF U.S. SUGAR MARKET SELECTED YEARS

Year	Total deliveries for consumption (million tons)	Percentage supplied by Cuba
1928	6.643	47.0
1930	6.710	43.9
1932	6.249	28.2
1934	6.154	26.6
1947	6.861	31.4
1940	6.443	27.1
1943	6.466	44.2
1948	7.080	41.3
1950	8.249	39.6
1953	8.298	33.4
1956	8.995	34.4
1958	9.087	37.9

to less than 1.5 percent per annum during the years 1951–57, a sharp decline from the average annual increase of 8.3 percent achieved from 1945–51.

An increasingly unstable domestic political situation culminated in the establishment of a revolutionary provisional government by Dr. Fidel Castro, who assumed the post of Prime Minister in January 1959.

U.S. commercial involvement with Cuba had reached a pervasive level by the time the revolution occurred. In 1958, U.S.-Cuba trade totaled more than $1 billion. The U.S. accounted for 71 percent of Cuba's total exports and 64 percent of its imports. Also in that year, Cuba supplied 38 percent of total U.S. sugar consumption, an amount equal to 58 percent of Cuba's total sugar exports. U.S. foreign direct investment in the island controlled ⅓ of the public utilities.[1] U.S. interests controlled more than 30 percent of the sugar industry and exerted major influence in the mining and manufacturing sectors where sales by U.S.-owned firms in Cuba exceeded ¼ of Cuba's GNP.

II. DEVELOPMENT OF A CENTRALLY PLANNED CUBAN ECONOMY 1959 TO PRESENT

The Centralization of Economic Decision Making

From January 1959 to February 1961, Cuba underwent a rapid transformation from a capitalist, market economy to a centrally planned, socialist economy.

Initially, the most important economic institution (resulting from the Agrarian Reform Law of May 1959) was the Institute for Agrarian Reform (INRA). Economic decisions came to be increasingly implemented by departments of the INRA.

The Marxist-Leninist character of the new government was clearly demonstrated when a noted communist, Ernesto (Che) Guevara was appointed President of the National Bank of Cuba in November 1959. Immediately, dollar transfer payments to British and U.S. petroleum suppliers were suspended and imports of crude oil from the U.S.S.R. began to replace traditional suppliers. The Western companies operating the Cuban refineries refused to process the Soviet crude and, in August 1960, these firms were nationalized. The U.S. responded by reducing Cuba's sugar import quota. Cuba then expropriated all U.S. assets and in October 1960 the U.S. established a partial embargo allowing only food and medicine exports to Cuba. U.S.-Cuba trade was thus reduced to negligible amounts. A complete embargo was imposed in 1962, followed by the freezing of Cuban assets in the U.S. and a prohibition on dollar transactions with Cuba in mid-1963. The embargo was made multilateral by the OAS in 1964.

The appraised value of U.S. owned assets expropriated by the Cubans was

---

[1] Estimates of U.S. direct foreign investment in Cuba vary due to methodological differences, e.g., use of historic book value rather than depreciated book value.

TABLE 5.—CUBAN FOREIGN TRADE

Year	By amounts (U.S. million)				By percentages		
	Total	Exports	Imports	Balance	Socialist	Of which U.S.S.R.	Non-Socialist States
1959	$1,377	$637	$740	−$103	30.6	NA	69.4
1960	1,246	608	638	−20	23.4	NA	76.6
1961	1,327	625	702	−77	75.9	44.6	24.1
1962	1,280	521	759	−238	82.9	49.4	17.1
1963	1,411	544	867	−323	74.4	44.3	21.6
1964	1,733	714	1,019	−305	63.1	39.5	36.9
1965	1,552	686	866	−180	69.9	48.4	30.1
1966	1,518	592	926	−334	80.4	52.4	19.6
1967	1,709	711	998	−287	75.8	54.1	24.2
1968	1,740	651	1,089	−438	76.5	51.5	23.5
1969	1,832	664	1,168	−504	72.1	46.7	27.9
1970	2,357	1,046	1,311	−265	71.6	49.2	28.4
1971	2,244	859	1,385	−526	70.7	44.1	29.3
1972	1,928	739	1,189	−450	67.9	47.9	32.1
1973	3,080	1,380	1,700	−320	68.4	49.2	31.6
1974	4,995	2,745	2,250	+495	58.8	40.7	41.2

$1.8 billion, while the U.S. impounded Cuban assets of approximately $30 million. Completing the transition to a state trading nation, a Ministry of Foreign Trade was established as the "only administrative center authorized to conduct Cuba's foreign trade." The National Bank was reorganized in February 1961 and placed in complete control of all internal and external banking, financial and credit activities.

Having nationalized most of the economy by the end of 1961, Castro announced a four-year plan for economic development which projected an annual growth rate of 13 percent for the economy as a whole. By March 1962 the unrealistic growth assumptions of the plan were apparent and stringent rationing of all types of foodstuffs and consumables was decreed.

The Cuban Agrarian Reform Law of 1959 was finally consolidated in October 1963. By early 1964, 76 percent of the agricultural land had been nationalized under the control of the INRA, with 24 percent remaining in the private hands of the members of the Association of Small Farmers. During this transition period sugar production declined to 3.8 million tons in 1963—from 5.9 million in 1959. Overall, the Cuban economy maintained perhaps a 2 percent per annum real growth rate throughout the 1960's, a rate not exceeding population growth.

Shortages were acute and Castro exchanged Bay of Pigs prisoners for $48 million in medicine, food, and tractors from the U.S. in 1962–1963. By October 1965, rationing had been expanded to include sugar and clothing.

Impact of the Move to Socialism on Cuban's Foreign Trade

The impact of domestic political events on Cuba's international economic relations was direct and pronounced. A permit system was established in 1959 to control the flow of imports. Total trade turnover for 1959 fell to $1.38 billion from a 1958 level of $1.6 billion, a 14 percent drop.

The 1958 level of Cuban total trade was not consistently reached again until 1967, although 1964 trade did total $1.7 billion. 1959 imports totaled $672 million and exports $740 million, with the U.S. maintaining its dominant share of 68 and 69 percent respectively. (See Table 5.)

The Decline in U.S.-Cuba Trade

Maintenance of the paramount U.S. position in Cuban trade was to prove only temporary, however, as relations between the U.S. and Cuba continued to de-

TABLE 6.—CUBA: EXPORTS BY MAJOR COMMODITY

[In millions of U.S. dollars]

	1958	1961	1963	1965	1967	1969	1971	1972	1973	1974
Sugar	587	540	473	591	599	503	657	616	1,110	2,470
Raw sugar	496	495	389	511	520	408)	634	596	1,090	2,445
Refined sugar	61	37	70	68	65	80)				
Molasses	30	8	14	12	14	15	23	20	20	25
Minerals	37	36	35	50	54	92	135	125	165	165
Nickel	28	29	32	40	44	86	135	124	164	164
Other	9	7	3	10	10	6	0	1	1	1
Tobacco	49	38	22	33	30	42	32	40	42	35
Raw	37	32	15	19	11	14	14	15	13	10
Manufactures	12	6	7	14	19	28	18	25	29	25
Foodstuffs	22	4	4	5	10	28	36	52	58	70
Of which:										
Fish and shellfish	4	1	1	3	5	13	21	28	42	50
Fruit	2	1	1	1	1	2	3	5	12	15
Rum	1	1	(¹)	1	2	3	1	3	4	5
Other	47	8	13	12	14	6	0	4	5	5
Total	742	626	545	691	705	671	860	837	1,380	2,745

¹ Negligible.

teriorate. Castro chose not to participate in trade negotiations offered during his unofficial visit to the U.S. in 1959.

The redirection of Cuban foreign trade away from the U.S. took a decisive turn in February 1960 when Castro and Soviet Prime Minister Mikoyan signed a Bilateral Trade and Payments Agreement. The two countries exchanged mutual MFN status and the U.S.S.R. committed itself to annual purchases of at least one million tons of raw sugar through 1964. It also agreed not to re-export any of its Cuban sugar purchases. Payment was to be 20 percent in dollars and 80 percent in merchandise. Furthermore, a permanent bilateral clearing arrangement was established between the National Bank of Cuba and the Soviet Foreign Trade Bank, allowing two-way trade without the use of convertible currencies. Such agreements are a common trade settlement mechanism among socialist countries. The Russians also agreed to provide a $100 million, 12 year credit with repayment in sugar and other exports.

The Soviet commitment to one million tons of annual purchases of Cuban sugar, compared with a U.S. purchase of 3.24 million tons in 1958, substantially reduced Cuban dependence on sales to the U.S. The decline in the U.S. share of Cuban trade begun in 1959 now accelerated. (See Table 2.) By 1962, two-way trade between the two countries had dropped from a 1958 high of $1.07 billion to only $20 million.

The Increase in Socialist Country-Cuba Trade

Conversely, trade with the socialist countries increased sharply in 1961. Previously, Cuba traded on a regular basis only with Czechoslovakia, which, as an original GATT member, had non-discriminatory tariff status. The U.S.S.R. had received significant Cuban sugar exports only occasionally.

However, following the 1960 Cuban-U.S.S.R. agreement, the orientation of Cuba's trade swiftly changed towards the socialist countries. (See Tables 3 and 5.)

TABLE 7.—CUBA: IMPORTS OF SELECTED COMMODITIES

[1,000 metric tons]

	1958 [1]	1961	1963	1965	1967	1969	1971	1972	1973	1974
Foodstuffs:										
Corn	NA	NA	NA	NA	NA	112	153	172	112	250
Rice (milled)	194	NA	190	282	157	186	280	256	[2] 220	[2] 225
Legumes	73	NA	64	62	76	81	83	90	NA	NA
Wheat flour	86	[3] 100	248	231	285	290	346	308	335	265
Lard	82	NA	48	39	41	23	26	20	NA	NA
Canned milk	7	NA	17	22	19	17	19	19	20	NA
Raw materials and intermediate goods:										
Wheat	139	[3] 192	278	265	300	343	401	476	426	335
Raw cotton	9	[3] 15	8	23	17	20	19	19	19	NA
Crude vegetable oil	6	NA	36	47	51	56	66	54	NA	NA
Industrial tallow	13	NA	18	10	19	2	NA	NA	NA	NA
Woodpulp	30	NA	52	18	35	30	39	31	NA	NA
Rubber (natural, regenerated, synthetic)	6	NA	6	6	9	9	7	6	NA	NA
Sulfur	11	[3] 64	46	68	105	124	179	123	120	125
Caustic soda	16	[3] 14	23	23	29	36	33	19	38	24
Pig iron	3	[3] 45	25	32	45	81	79	96	NA	NA
Tin plate	22	NA	30	23	43	44	40	39	44	48
Coke	41	[3] 10	28	37	46	52	75	88	NA	NA
Fertilizer	181	NA	331	432	1,250	862	614	652	NA	NA
Malt	18	NA	19	15	20	0	NA	NA	NA	NA
Cotton cloth [4]	NA	NA	NA	81	50	63	57	53	NA	NA
Fuel:										
Crude petroleum	3,500	2,980	3,709	3,483	3,713	4,156	4,757	4,749	NA	NA
Fuel oil	260	835	159	791	975	995	1,409	1,315	NA	NA
Gasoline	125	90	199	120	60	10	86	13	NA	NA
Transportation equipment [5]:										
Locomotives	35	NA	2	NA	NA	66	7	1	NA	NA
Automobiles	16,064	NA	1,457	NA	NA	747	2,037	1,085	NA	NA
Trucks	3,195	NA	3,354	2,928	2,942	1,712	5,274	3,264	NA	NA
Buses	76	NA	712	430	315	62	998	191	NA	NA
Tractors		NA	3,443	6,574	6,249	8,828	7,042	3,024	NA	NA

[1] Provisional. [2] Estimated. [3] Imports from the U.S.S.R. only. [4] Million square meters. [5] Units.

Thus, by 1962, socialist countries had assumed an 82.9 percent share of Cuba's total trade turnover and thus replaced the U.S. as Cuba's dominant trade partner. The U.S. share, 69 percent of 1959 turnover, fell to only 1 percent in 1962.

While the direction of Cuba's trade was dramatically altered after the revolution, the composition of its exports did not change significantly. Sugar accounted for 74 percent of total exports in 1959 and 84.5 percent in 1965. (See Table 6.) Typically, nickel and tobacco together made up another 10 percent, with fish and fruit adding less than 5 percent.

Data on the value composition of Cuban imports in the early years of the Castro government are not available for comparison purposes. However, we do have quantity statistics for some commodity imports. (See Table 7.) Major components of Cuban imports were petroleum and derivative products, since Cuba has little domestic supplies of petroleum.

Fertilizer, rice and wheat were also imported in substantial quantities. Autos, trucks and tractors comprised most of the manufactured goods imports from socialist suppliers. Following the characteristic of other socialist, centrally planned economies, in the early 1960's Cuba reoriented its imports away from consumable goods and put heavy emphasis on importation of capital goods.

As always, however, sugar continued during the 1960's to be the key indicator for Cuban foreign trade. The Soviets became the main sugar purchasers of Cuban sugar as the U.S. withdrew its quota in 1960. The Soviets purchased almost 50 percent of total Cuban production in 1961. Their purchases have fluctuated with the size of the Cuban and Soviet crops (see Table 8) and usually have been at subsidized prices, often substantially greater than existing world market prices. The value of this subsidy was greatest in 1966 when the U.S.S.R. purchased 38 percent of the Cuban crop at 6.11 cents per pound when the world market price was 1.86 cents per pound, equivalent to a subsidy of $140.0 million in that year alone.[2]

Integration of Cuba into the Socialist Community 1970 to Present

The close association of Cuba with the socialist economies in general, and with the Soviet Union in particular, was institutionalized when the Soviet-Cuban Joint Commission for Economic, Scientific and Technological Cooperation was formed in 1970. The Commission has met five times since its inception, beginning in September 1971, and these meetings have set the pace for current involvement of the Soviet Union in the Cuban economy. The first session reportedly

[2] A large portion of world sugar trade is under bilateral preference arrangements at prices greater than the world market price, therefore, the actual Soviet subsidy may have been less than this estimate.

TABLE 8.—CUBAN AND SOVIET RAW SUGAR TRADE

Year	Total Cuban sugar production (metric tons)	Exports to the U.S.S.R. (metric tons)	Soviet share of total production (percent)	Soviet price paid (U.S. cents per pound)	Average world price (U.S. cents per pound)	Total value of Soviet imports (U.S. millions)
1953	5.0	0.011	0.2	3.46	3.41	$0.763
1954	4.746	.012	.2	3.3	3.26	.800
1955	4.394	.561	12.8	3.24	3.24	36.4
1956	4.660	.204	4.4	2.48	3.48	14.2
1957	5.504	.145	2.6	5.14	5.16	14.9
1958	5.610	.201	3.6	3.5	3.5	14.1
1959	5.964	.274	4.6	2.9	2.97	16.3
1960	5.862	1.467	25.0	3.21	3.14	94.2
1961	6.767	3.345	49.4	4.00	2.91	267.6
1962	4.815	2.333	46.4	4.13	2.98	184.5
1963	3.821	0.996	26.1	6.22	8.5	136.8
1964	4.589	1.859	40.5	6.00	5.87	247.3
1965	6.082	2.330	38.3	6.00	2.12	363.7
1966	4.866	1.841	37.8	6.11	1.86	250.8
1967	6.236	2.479	39.9	6.11	1.99	335.9
1968	5.164	1.832	32.9	6.11	1.98	236.3
1969	4.459	1.332	30.0	6.11	3.37	179.3
1970	8.538	3.105	35.2	6.11	3.75	404.8
1971	5.925	1.581	25.1	6.11	4.52	206.2
1972	4.4	1.101	25.8	6.55	7.43	158.6
1973	5.5	1.603	29.1	12.83	9.61	436.6
1974	5.8	1.856	32.8	19.80	29.99	806.2

discussed cooperation in various fields including nickel production, irrigation, fishing, port modernization, civil aircraft and computers.

Between the second and third meetings, Cuba converted its observer status into full membership in the Council for Mutual Economic Assistance (CMEA) in July 1972. CMEA, also known as COMECON, was originally formed in 1949 as a socialist country economic union in response to the Marshall Plan. The scope of its activities has expanded over time to include coordination of the economic plans of member countries, technological cooperation, financial and technical development assistance and the facilitation of intra-CMEA trade. Among the operating CMEA institutions are the International Bank for Economic Cooperation (IBEC), created in 1963 as a trade account clearing bank, and the International Investment Bank (IIB), formed in 1971 to provide financial credits to members for development projects.

Currently, 9 countries are members of CMEA [3] with Cuba unique in that it is the only member not geographically contiguous to the rest of the group and, of course, the only member in the Western Hemisphere.

In joining CMEA, Cuba further institutionalized its close economic ties not only with the U.S.S.R. but also with the other socialist countries. It is generally recognized in the West that CMEA functions and organs have not operated as designed, and that CMEA has not been a major economic instrument. However, to the extent that CMEA is effective, Cuba may benefit from IIB development financial assistance and from an ability to trade multilaterally within CMEA without the necessity of parting with convertible currencies by utilizing the IBEC clearing mechanism.

Several areas of possible CMEA assistance to Cuba have been discussed, including further development of nickel, citrus fruits and paper production from sugar cane waste. Cuba's recent trade with CMEA members other than the Soviet Union has averaged about $300 million since 1970. (See Table 9 for details.) Generally, 75 percent of Cuba's exports to CMEA consist of sugar.

In December 1972, five bilateral economic agreements were concluded between the Soviet Union and Cuba providing for:

---

[3] CMEA members are: U.S.S.R., Poland, German Democratic Republic, Romania, Czechoslovakia, Hungary, Bulgaria, Mongolia, and Cuba. Yugoslavia has observer status and Finland has associated status.

TABLE 9.—CUBA'S TRADE WITH INDIVIDUAL CMEA MEMBERS, EXCLUSIVE OF U.S.S.R.

[In millions of U.S. dollars]

	1968	1969	1970	1971	1972 [1]
East Germany, total	71.1	75.5	114.3	97.6	80
Exports to	35.1	35.4	52.5	48.5	35
Imports from	36.0	40.1	61.8	49.1	45
Balance	−.1	−4.7	−9.3	−.6	−10
Czechoslovakia, total	87.4	70.5	73.7	77.6	70
Exports to	44.6	37.2	56.6	45.5	35
Imports from	42.8	33.3	27.1	32.1	35
Balance	+1.8	+3.9	+29.5	+13.4	0
Bulgaria, total	48.7	48.3	54.9	55.0	55
Exports to	27.9	25.6	31.2	31.0	25
Imports from	20.8	22.7	23.7	24.0	30
Balance	+7.1	+2.9	+7.5	+7.0	−5
Romania, total	23.0	39.2	27.7	25.4	
Exports to	7.4	9.8	13.0	14.8	
Imports from	15.6	29.4	14.7	10.6	
Balance	−8.2	−19.6	−1.7	+4.2	
Poland, total	10.4	11.4	6.6	10.7	
Exports to	6.2	7.8	3.6	8.8	
Imports from	4.2	3.6	3.0	1.9	
Balance	+2.0	+4.2	+.6	+6.9	
Hungary, total	7.0	8.2	10.6	24.4	
Exports to	3.9	4.6	5.6	15.6	
Imports from	3.1	3.6	5.0	8.8	
Balance	+.8	+1.0	+.6	+6.8	

[1] New York Times, Oct. 6, 1974.

Source: The Economic Intelligence Unit, "Quarterly Economic Review, Cuba, Dominican Republic, Haiti, Puerto Rico, Annual Supplement," London, 1974, pp. 14–15.

(1) A restructuring of Cuban debts, i.e., those accumulated prior to 1973 would now fall due in 1986, with repayments in interest-free installments over 25 years.
(2) A line of credit to finance Cuba's balance of payments deficits during 1973-75, with repayment commencing in 1986.
(3) A long-term trade agreement between the two countries, with actual volumes to be negotiated annually. (This bilateral process continues today.)
(4) Technical cooperation and a "low interest" credit of $360 million to construct two new and refurbish seven old textile mills, remodel two nickel plants and improve the auto, electric power and cane harvesting industries.
(5) Establish a new price of 12 cents per pound for Cuban sugar exports and $5,450 per ton for nickel, both subsidized levels; since existing world market prices were then 7.4 cents and $3,500 respectively.

A fourth Commission meeting was held in December 1973 in Moscow, with the only apparent result being a beginning of negotiations between JUCEPLAN, the Cuban State Planning Organization, and the Soviet State Planning Committee (GOSPLAN) on coordination of five year economic plans for 1976-80.

The Soviets have demonstrated interest in assisting Cuba to diversify its basically one commodity economy, by efforts to increase nickel production. A protocol was signed in September 1974 implementing a cooperation program to reconstruct the Moa and Nicaro production facilities and to build a large mining complex at Punta Gorda. A total investment of $600 million is projected, possibly with International Investment Bank participation. Plans call for increasing Cuba's current annual nickel output from 36 thousand to 65 thousand tons by 1980.

The fifth meeting of the Commission occurred in December 1974 amidst little publicity. Havana Radio announced only that "important agreements" on future cooperation were reached.

The composition of Soviet exports to Cuba has remained rather consistent

TABLE 10.—MAJOR SOVIET EXPORTS TO CUBA

[In millions of rubles]

	1968	1969	1970	1971	1972	1973
Machines, equipment, means of transport	205.2	214.0	205.2	176.0	164.4	177.8
Of which:						
Generating equipment	3.3	2.5	7.9	5.3	4.5	8.1
Hoisting gear	7.4	8.2	9.0	10.1	7.0	10.0
Road-building equipment	10.3	12.0	12.6	13.8	9.9	9.5
Tractors, agriculture machinery	24.1	37.9	31.0	31.3	29.8	37.2
Trucks and parts	36.8	31.7	30.2	33.9	32.3	34.8
Aircraft	13.0	5.7	10.2	7.0	7.9	4.3
Oil and oil products	62.6	66.7	69.2	73.5	92.2	114.2
Rolled ferrous metals	13.1	11.3	17.5	15.9	15.1	16.7
Rolled nonferrous metals	9.9	8.8	9.3	8.9	8.2	7.6
Chemical products	9.6	7.8	9.4	13.6	11.9	11.0
Nitrogen fertilizers	9.2	5.9	6.1	4.9	4.6	5.0
Sawn lumber	11.3	10.4	13.1	17.3	12.2	13.3
Cotton fiber	11.7	8.0	10.2	12.0	10.1	10.6
Grain (except groats)	26.9	28.1	28.4	31.9	30.1	30.0
Canned meat	14.7	11.8	12.6	15.4	13.6	15.6
Milk products	6.8	6.3	6.6	6.4	7.8	9.7
Fish and fish products	8.2	8.7	9.2	10.4	11.3	17.5
Flour	27.1	25.9	22.4	24.8	24.8	24.4
Vegetable oils (edible)	9.9	10.2	12.2	15.8	20.3	11.8
Consumer goods	6.9	8.1	12.4	15.6	22.8	27.5
Total (including other items):						
Million rubles	561.8	561.6	580.0	602.0	616.2	679.2
Million dollars [1]	624.2	624.0	644.4	668.9	743.3	922.8

[1] 1971: 0.9 rubles = $1 ; 1972: 0.829 rubles = $1; 1973: 0.736 rubles = $1.

Source: "Vneshniaia Torgovlia SSSR za 1969, 1971, 1973", "Mezhdunarednye Otnosheniia", Moscow, 1970, 1972, 1974

since 1968 with a few interesting exceptions. The portion of machines and equipment in total exports declined from 36.5 percent in 1968 to 26.2 percent in 1973. Consumer goods have increased from 1.2 percent to 4.1 percent of total exports, but actual dollar amounts of consumer goods imports remain small, e.g., about $37 million in 1973. Nitrogen fertilizer has declined from 1.6 percent to 0.7 percent of the total Soviet exports to Cuba (for a more complete composition see Table 10).

The major Soviet export to Cuba is, of course, petroleum. In 1956 Cuban domestic crude production was only 57 thousand metric tons and consumption in 1958 was about 3.1 million tons. Consequently, Cuba has always been dependent on imported petroleum sources, the U.S. and Venezuela being its primary preembargo supplier. Soviet oil supplies have increased substantially from about $70 million in 1968 to $155 million in 1973. As with sugar and nickel, Cuba has benefited from a subsidized price here as well, since Soviet imports in 1974, for example, were priced at about one-half world levels and, although increased in 1975, are still probably near the subsidized price of about $7.50 a barrel charged other CMEA members. Utilizing Soviet figures for the value of oil exports to Cuba and assuming the price equaled 50 percent of the world price on average, the resultant cumulative subsidy totaled about $175 million from 1972–74. In late 1974, a multilateral arrangement was begun which, if expanded, could marginally reduce the Soviet burden in supplying Cuba's oil requirements. A small amount of crude deliveries from Mexico to Cuba are being made on Soviet account. The Cuban-Soviet partners, therefore, save the cost differential between transporting crude oil to Cuba from Mexico as compared to shipping to Cuba from the U.S.S.R. However, the U.S.S.R. still absorbs the margin between the Mexican (world) price and the subsidized price of Soviet deliveries to Cuba.

III. CURRENT CUBAN FOREIGN TRADE

Administration of Foreign Trade

Like other centrally planned economies, Cuba conducts virtually all its foreign trade through a central Ministry. Trade financing is exclusively arranged by

TABLE 11.—CUBA: TRADING ENTERPRISES

[Ministry of foreign trade—Minister: Mancelo Fernandez Font, First Vice Minister: Ricardo Cabrisas Ruiz, Vice Minister for Commercial Policies with: Capitalist Countries: Richardo Cabrisas Ruiz, Socialist Countries: Herninio Garcia Lazo, The U.S.S.R.: German Amado-Balanco Fernandez]

Enterprise	Director	Responsibilities
IMPORT		
Alimport	Ricardo Espino Martinez	Foodstuffs, livestock.
Aviaimport	Eduardo Martinez Valdez	Aircraft, navigation equipment.
Construimport	Olegario Cartelles	Construction equipment.
Consumimport	Jose Luis Mestre Roca	Consumer durables.
Cubacontrol	Eddy Ramos Lopez	Controls, supervises, and inspects exports and imports.
Cubahidraulica	Antonio Riambau Martinez	Irrigation equipment.
Cubametales	Dionisio Arranz Tremols	All metals, wire, fuel.
Cubapesca	Rolando Alvarez Alvarez	Fishing equipment.
Cubatex	Isaac Abascal Coalla	Textiles, cordage, leather.
EduCuba	Benito Fernandez Gashassin-Lafitte	Educational equipment.
Fecuimport	Portirio Mederos	Railway equipment.
Ferrimport	Carlos Rodriguez Benitez	Hardware supplies.
Maprinter	Justo Armesto Pons	Raw materials and intermediate goods.
Maqimport	Jose de la Fuente Menendez	Machinery and equipment.
Technoimport	Jose Enrique Quesada	Technology.
Tractoimport	Guido Valiente Romero	Agricultural machinery.
Transimport	Antonio Vinagre Roca	Automotive and transportation equipment.
USIE	Roberto Rodriguez Llompart	Mining and drilling equipment.
EXPORT		
Cubazucar	Emiliano Lezcano Viqueira	Sugar and sugarcane byproducts.
Cubaniquel	Osmani Martinez Vasquez	Nickel ore.
Cubaexport	Tirso Luis Janicot	Foodstuffs and miscellaneous products.
Cubatabaco	Alberto Ramos Suco	Tobacco and tobacco products.

DOCUMENTS 195

the National Bank of Cuba in accordance with the policies of the Ministry of Foreign Trade.

Foreign trade enterprises have been established to conduct all trade in specific product lines. There are 20 such enterprises for imports and 6 for exports. A complete listing together with current directors, appears in Table 11.

Total Trade

The value of Cuba's total trade increased dramatically from $3,080 million in 1973 to $5,195 million in 1974, an increase of 68 percent. Dollar value of total exports nearly doubled to about $2.7 billion, as a result of a nearly tripled world sugar price. This increased Cuba's import capacity and total imports thus rose by 42 percent. The resulting surplus in Cuba's balance of trade of almost $300 million was the first since the Castro takeover in 1959.

Largely by reason of price increases on that portion of its sugar sold to the West, the socialist countries' share of the total dollar value of trade declined rather sharply from 68.4 percent in 1973 to 58.8 percent in 1974, while the Industrialized Western countries and other non-socialist countries' shares were about one-fifth respectively. Consequently, hard currency earnings nearly tripled to about $1.4 billion. (See Tables 3 and 5 for details.)

Export Composition

As usual, sugar dominated the composition of Cuban exports, accounting for 90 percent of the 1974 total, or $2.4 billion. The steady increase in exports of shellfish grew by 25 percent in 1974, to $53 million. Other exports, such as nickel, tobacco and citrus fruits maintained their approximate 1973 levels. The composition of Cuban exports appears in Table 6.

Import Composition

Data on the composition of 1974 imports is not yet available but it is unlikely that it has changed materially since 1973. Table 9 presents the composition of Soviet exports to Cuba for the years 1968 to 1973 and is a reasonable indicator of the kinds of imports for which Cuba has a demand, e.g., oil and related products, transportation equipment, agricultural machinery, grain, flour, chemicals and some consumer goods.

Cuban Dependence on the U.S.S.R.

Although the Soviet Union's share of total Cuban trade in dollar value terms declined sharply from 51.6 percent to 38.7 percent in 1974, Cuba remains substantially dependent on the U.S.S.R. Almost all of its petroleum imports and a major portion of its machinery and foodstuffs come from the Soviet Union. The Soviets have purchased sugar from Cuba at subsidized prices which have provided Cuba with equivalence of about $825 million since 1961. Also, Cuba continues to receive substantial financial assistance in the form of credits, with the Soviets providing about $200 million in 1974. The amount of Soviet assistance in the form of loans arranged since 1961 totals approximately $4.4 billion, with sugar subsidies adding another $825 million. (See Table 12 for details.) Little is known about the repayment structure of the debt to the Soviets. However, maturities are beyond 1986 and could constrain Cuba's capacity to import from the West in the long term, since although hard currency repayment presumably is not required, Cuba will be required to commit to the Soviets a substantial portion of its exports in order to effect repayment in kind.

Recent Developments in Cuban Trade

There are some recent signs of a further shift of Cuban trade to the West that have received wide publicity. Canadian and Mexican trade missions early this year recorded $21 million and $32 million in export sales negotiated.

Argentinian subsidiaries of U.S., Italian and German transportation equipment manufacturers recorded about $300 million in railway and vehicle sales between August 1973 and August 1974.

Western nations that are competitors of the U.S. in world trade have, since early 1973, offered trade financing credits to Cuba totaling about $3.324 billion. Since these credits must be used to finance exports from the grantor, and since each has some specific time period during which the credits can be used, it remains to be seen to what extent the credits will be utilized. Nevertheless, as

TABLE 12.—CUBA: ECONOMIC ASSISTANCE FROM THE U.S.S.R.

[In millions U.S. dollars]

	1961	1962	1963	1964	1965	1966	1967	1968	1969	1970	1971	1972	1973 [1]	1974 [2]
Trade deficit	−9	189	297	135	105	247	216	382	436	162	427	534	460	−165
Cuban exports (f.o.b.)	304	222	164	275	323	274	366	290	233	529	304	244	565	935
Cuban imports (c.i.f.)	295	411	461	410	428	521	582	672	669	691	731	778	1,025	1,100
Interest charges	0	Negl	Negl	6	14	18	21	28	34	45	57	69	[3] 0	[3] 0
Other invisibles	18	22	25	23	20	23	23	22	24	24	25	28	33	33
Total payments deficit	9	211	322	143	139	388	260	432	494	231	509	631	493	−198
Cumulative debt	9	220	542	685	824	1,112	1,372	1,804	2,298	2,529	3,038	3,669	4,162	4,360
Sugar subsidy payments [4]	90	71	9	−66	176	138	214	150	86	150	56	−22	95	−345
Total cumulative aid	99	381	712	789	1,104	1,530	2,004	2,586	3,166	3,547	4,112	4,721	5,309	5,162

[1] Provisional.
[2] Preliminary.
[3] A Cuban-Soviet bilateral agreement of December 1972 exempts Cuban debt from further interest charges.
[4] The annual value of sugar subsidy payments is estimated as the difference between the value of sugar exports to the U.S.S.R. and the value of these exports computed at the average price for Cuban sugar sold on the world market. It is considered a grant and not subject to repayment.

indicated below, the volume of Western credit offerings is very large vis-a-vis the size of the Cuban economy, since the latest available [4] Gross Material Product figure for 1966 was only $3.7 billion.

Offers of trade financing credits since August 1973

	U.S. millions
Argentina	[1] $1,200.0
France	350.0
Canada	134.0
Euromarkets	138.0
U.K.	596.5
Japan	5.6
Spain	900.0
Total	3,324.1

[1] $200 million a year for 6 years. Deadline for utilization of other credits shown is unknown.

Other recent developments include a multilateral shipping concern that is in the process of being established among a number of Latin American and Caribbean nations, including Cuba. The corporation, Flota Mercante Del Carib, is to have initial capitalization of $30 million and five vessels. Member countries include Columbia, Costa Rica, Cuba, Venezuela, Panama, Nicaragua, Mexico, Jamaica and possibly others.

Also, early in 1975 three major trading nations established diplomatic relations with the Castro government. Iran, Venezuela and West Germany, because of their economic and trading capabilities, could develop into very important trading partners. Thus, there are signs, not yet fully reflected in trade data, of a significant Cuban expansion of its trading relations with the West and new indications of Western willingness to trade with Cuba.

IV. CURRENT STATUS OF U.S.-CUBAN TRADE

Commerce Department Involvement

The legal foundation of the U.S. embargo on trade with Cuba is essentially contained in three statutes; the Foreign Assistance Act of 1961, as amended, the Trading With the Enemy Act of 1917, as amended, and the Export Administration Act of 1969, as amended. The first two statutes provided the legal authority for the promulgation of the Cuban Assets Control Regulations, 31 C.F.R. Part 515, which prohibit virtually all commercial and financial transactions with Cuba or Cuban nationals, absent specific authorization therefore from the Secretary of the Treasury or his designee. These regulations are currently being administered by the Office of Foreign Assets Control in the Department of Treasury, and will be reviewed with you by representatives of that agency.

The third statute, the Export Administration Act of 1969, as amended 50 U.S.C. App. § 2401 *et seq.*, empowers the Department of Commerce to control exports to achieve three policy objectives; to protect the domestic economy from the excessive drain of scarce materials and to reduce the serious inflationary impact of foreign demand, to further significantly the foreign policy of the United States and to fulfill its international responsibilities, and to protect the national security of the United States. On February 3, 1962,[5] the President issued Proclamation 3347 which established an embargo on U.S. trade with Cuba. Responsibility for administration of the embargo was delegated to the Departments of Treasury and Commerce. This Department's implementing regulations provide that prior approval from the Commerce Department is required to export or reexport virtually any U.S. origin commodity or technical data to Cuba.

Export Licensing to Cuba, 1971–June 1975

Relatively few exceptions to the embargo have been granted by this Depart-

[4] Pat Holt, of the Senate Foreign Relations Committee recently quoted an estimated Cuban 1973 GNP of $15.1 billion.

[5] The Export Administration Act of 1969, as amended, is a successor to the Export Control Act of 1949, which contributed authority to the 1962 embargo.

ment. The following table shows export licensing to Cuba during the last few years for two categories of authorizations, (1) gift parcels shipped in bulk and (2) other exceptions to the general embargo (the figures in parentheses show the number of applications approved).

LICENSED SHIPMENTS TO CUBA, BULK GIFT PARCEL AND OTHER EXCEPTIONS, 1971-75

Year	Bulk gift parcels		Other exceptions	
	Amount	Number of applications	Amount	Number of applications
1971	$79,200	(21)	$50,322	(21)
1972	6,300,000	(254)	51,956	(38)
1973	3,600,000	(32)	112,660	(24)
1974	4,566,300	(21)	541,610	(34)
1975 (January-May)	3,075,000	(5)	27,744	(14)

Under the "Other exceptions" category, a few individual commercial shipments of unique anti-cancer medicines have been approved over the years. Shipments for the Pan American Health Organization and supplies for foreign diplomats in Cuba constitute the bulk of the remaining authorizations and since 1970 have ranged from about $50 to $60 thousand per year. In 1973, such authorizations total $112,660 because of very large shipments for the Health Organization.

Otherwise, most exceptions have involved sales by U.S. subsidiaries in third countries, and have been approved only when U.S. foreign policy considerations have been paramount.

Effectiveness of the U.S. Embargo

The trade embargo with Cuba was particularly effective in the early years, that is during most of the 1960's, since it denied the Cuban economy badly needed spare and replacement parts for a wide range of machinery and vehicles which were predominantly of U.S. origin. In recent years, Cuba has been able to switch to other capital goods suppliers, and thus has become less dependent on U.S. equipment. Accordingly, the adverse effect of the embargo on Cuba has lessened. However, Cuba continues to show interest in selected U.S. products and appears to have a particular preference for such U.S. items as automotive vehicles, video equipment, food processing and air conditioning equipment, rice, *et alia*.

The success of the embargo over U.S. goods was due to an energetic enforcement program by the USG and cooperation on the part of many U.S. firms and their subsidiaries abroad. Numerous reports at attempted diversions of U.S. goods were received by the USG and were investigated. Commerce issued at least 45 denial orders [6] in the 1960's against firms and individuals for transacting, or attempting to transact, sales of U.S. origin commodities for ultimate destination to Cuba. In such instances, foreign firms purchased U.S. goods for use, ostensibly, in their countries; the actual intent, however, was to divert or transship such goods to Cuba. In the majority of cases, the individuals or firms who were charged with violations of the Export Control Regulations were foreign; in some, involving conspiracy, U.S. firms or individuals were also involved. Since, Cuba's primary requirements were for replacement parts and spares for its mining, transportation, sugar mill, power industries, etc., which had been developed with U.S. equipment, the sources of supply for replacements and spares were the original U.S. manufacturers. A close rapport between these manufacturers and Commerce enforcement personnel enabled Commerce to thwart many proposed exports to West European countries after establishing that illegal diversions to Cuba were planned. The combined Commerce and Treasury controls governing the supply of such goods or foreign-made equivalents by U.S. subsidiaries abroad are also believed to have been similarly successful in preventing shipments to Cuba during the 1960's. USG monitoring of Cuban requests for certain special items of U.S. manufacture is, of course, being maintained and whenever relevant information is obtained, appropriate action is initiated to ensure that such exports are not made.

---

[6] Denial of U.S. export privileges pursuant to administrative compliance proceedings.

The restrictions imposed by the Department of Commerce on trade with Cuba have been part of overall U.S. policy. There is, however, one aspect of Commerce's role vis-a-vis Cuba that is more positive. Over the past 20 years, the U.S. National Weather Service of the NOAA, has consistently maintained telecommunications contact between its Miami office and the Havana Weather Service. This network serves the humanitarian purpose of supplying essential data on hurricane activity in the Caribbean and South Atlantic areas. The service is leased from a U.S. firm and, rental fees are paid by the Cubans and NOAA, in alternate six-month periods.

In addition to the telecommunications link, U.S. Hurricane Hunter aircraft operate over Cuba several times a year. Flight clearance, both inside and outside the commercial overflight corridor are obtained via the Swiss Embassy and both military (U.S. Navy) and NOAA civilian aircraft are utilized.

V. POTENTIAL ECONOMIC BENEFITS FROM A RESUMPTION OF U.S.-CUBA TRADE

Costs of Continuing the Embargo

Whenever natural trading patterns between two trading partners are distorted or broken, there are losses to both sides. Cuba and the U.S., by reason of their geographical proximity and the complementary nature of their production, were natural trading partners and could be again in the future if conditions were to permit.

So long as the other industrialized nations of the West and Western Hemisphere nations participated with the U.S. in the embargo of Cuba, there was a significant cost in lost trading opportunities to Cuba and its Soviet sponsor bore a heavy subsidy burden to keep the Cuban economy afloat.

The economic opportunities lost to the U.S. through participation in the embargo were minimized by alternative sources for the products that Cuba could supply and the relatively small import potential of Cuba stemming from its poor hard currency position. However, other nations outside the CMEA bloc are increasing their commerce with Cuba as higher sugar prices make Cuba a more attractive trading partner. This, unilateral continuation of the Cuba embargo now becomes a bit more costly to the U.S. though that economic cost is still relatively small.

Cuba as an Exporter to the U.S.

Sugar.—Currently, sugar imports can no longer be used as an active instrument of U.S. foreign policy since the U.S. Sugar Act expired at the end of 1974.

Essentially, the U.S. now participates in a world free market, except that the embargo forecloses Cuban sources. Cuban sugar could, if the embargo is lifted, compete with other foreign and domestic sources for the U.S. market.

In general, American sugar consumers and producers would probably not be greatly affected by a resumption of U.S.-Cuban trade in sugar. This derives from the fact that the world sugar price is set by free market forces—i.e., world marketing of sugar and free market demand for sugar. We do not think that either would be significantly influenced by a redirection of Cuban sugar exports.

Of course, there could be *marginal benefits* derived from reopening the U.S. market to Cuban sugar. The transport costs would obviously be lower, than from the Philippines for example.

On the other hand, sugar imports from Cuba would be subject to Column 2 tariff rates even if the embargo were lifted immediately. Most Favored Nation treatment would be made available only under the provisions of the Trade Act of 1974 and this would require Cuba to meet the freedom of emigration provisions as well as to enter into a complex bilateral commercial agreement with the U.S.

The tariff differential (Column 2–Column 1) for sugar is approximately 1.2 cents per pound. Under free market conditions, one would expect that this differential would impede U.S.-Cuban sugar trade to some extent. Just how much would depend on a variety of issues—some of which we can enumerate but which are too complex to analyze completely. They include: Cuban incentives to recapture part of the U.S. sugar market both for political and longer-run economic motivations; the relationship between world sugar market prices and the prices that Cuba might achieve through bilateral large scale contracts if they can negotiate them, the size of transport savings; and any premium American companies may be willing to pay to regain access to Cuban sugar.

There are however, other constraints on the exports of Cuban sugar to the U.S.

There is a question of what amount of Cuban sugar is not already earmarked for the Soviet, Eastern European and Japanese markets. Cuban sugar export patterns for selected years are shown in Tables 14 and 15. Actual delivery volumes are established in annual bilateral negotiations with these countries. Therefore, only rough estimates of potential U.S. supplies are feasible.

Since 1971, total Cuban sugar production has averaged 5.4 million tons and 25 to 35 percent has been exported to the Soviet Union. In addition, the remaining members of CMEA have consistently received 750 to 850 thousand tons of Cuban sugar while exports to North Korea, North Vietnam and the PRC usually total 550 thousand tons. Finally, since 1971, Japan has annually taken from 900 thousand to 1 million tons. Therefore, the amount of Cuban sugar saleable on the world market can be expected, on average, to be about 2 million tons, all of

TABLE 14.—CUBA: EXPORTS OF SUGAR AND MAJOR RECIPIENTS

[In millions of U.S. dollars]

	1958	1972	1973	1974
Total	557	596	1,090	2,445
U.S.S.R.	14	156	445	830
Other CPE's [1]	4	163	242	505
Japan	47	149	182	440
Other	127	128	221	670
United States	365			

[1] Albania, Bulgaria, Czechoslovakia, East Germany, Hungary, Poland, Romania, China, Mongolia, North Korea, North Vietnam.

TABLE 15.—CUBA: EXPORTS OF SUGAR AND MAJOR RECIPIENTS BY QUANTITY

	1958		1972		1973		1974	
	1,000 metric tons	Percent of total	1,000 metric tons	Percent of total	1,000 metric tons	Percent of total	1,000 metric tons	Percent of total
Total	5,632	100.0	4,140	100.0	4,797.0	100.0	5,370	100.0
U.S.S.R.	188	3.3	1,097	26.5	1,661	34.6	1,900	35.4
Other CPE's [1]	61	1.1	1,197	28.9	1,351	28.2	1,370	25.5
Japan	556	9.9	909	22.0	985	20.5	1,200	22.3
Other	1,587	28.2	937	22.6	800	16.7	900	16.8
United States	3,240	57.5						

[1] Albania, Bulgaria, Czechoslovakia, East Germany, Hungary, Poland, Romania, China, Mongolia, North Korea, North Vietnam.

TABLE 16

[In millions of U.S. dollars]

	1972	1973	1974
CUBA: EXPORTS OF NICKEL			
Total	124.0	164	164
U.S. IMPORTS OF NICKEL AND MAJOR SOURCES			
Total	350.0	376	494
Canada	264.0	242	307
Norway	46.0	44	57
United Kingdom	19.0	35	40
U.S.S.R.	.3	11	40
Australia		11	19

which could theoretically be purchased by the U.S. since there are no long-term agreements with non-communist countries. Another constraint is legal. Absent a claims settlement, any imports of Cuban sugar could result in U.S. court action based on attachment of the sugar by former owners of the plantations.

Nickel.—Nickel is another U.S. import item produced by Cuba on which a transportation cost advantage from trade with Cuba might exist. U.S. nickel imports and recent Cuban exports are shown in Table 16.

Cuba annually produces about 35 thousand tons of nickel sulfide slurry and nickel oxide, 50 percent of which was exported to the Soviet Union in 1972. As noted above, Cuba's capacity is to be expanded to 65 thousand tons by 1980, which would make Cuba a major world source; Canada, the present largest producer, averages about 270 thousand tons annually. The $169 million of exports in 1974 could increase still further, both by reason of increased production and a recent uptrend on price.

Of course, much of this new capacity may be committed to CMEA members as product payback for loans and technical assistance, but a portion could be available to U.S. buyers. Cuban nickel exports for selected years appear in Table 16.

Other Products.—Only 15 percent of Cuban cigars and rum were exported to the U.S.S.R. in 1972. The Soviets also purchased 33 percent of the citrus crop in that year. Cuba does not export fish to the Soviet Union although it does market substantial quantities elsewhere.

In sum, the U.S. can expect that Cuban sugar, nickel, tobacco, rum and fish will be available if the embargo is lifted. However, it should be noted that a lack of non-discriminatory tariff status could seriously impede some of these imports.

The Potential for U.S. Exports to Cuba

The most significant potential U.S. loss from continuation of the embargo, however, lies in the possibility of lost job-creating export sales. Unless the U.S. economy is at full employment without exports to Cuba, the embargo on Cuba eliminates exports to that country. It therefore decreases total U.S. export volumes, with consequent unfavorable impact on the balance of payments and domestic employment levels. Of course, the volume of potential exports to Cuba and the opportunity cost of failure to trade is, at its largest, very small relative to the size of the U.S. economy.

Any assessment of the potential Cuban market for U.S. exports depends on several factors. (1) Whether or not Cuba is attempting to diversify its sources for imports to relieve present dependence on socialist sources, (2) Whether the substantial savings in transport costs will actually influence Cuba's purchasing decisions, (3) Whether U.S. trade financing credits will be available and competitive terms, (4) The extent of any competitive edge from technical and quality superiority, that accrues to U.S. goods, and (5) Cuban hard currency capabilities, largely the product of sugar and nickel prices.

If such factors are, in fact, positive influences, U.S. sales could be expected in some of the product areas currently supplied by Soviet and Western sources. One could anticipate sales of know-how and equipment in such areas as transportation equipment (especially autos and trucks), sugar cane processing equipment, merchant marine and port equipment, railway and communications systems, housing construction and computers. Further, Cuba may be a large market for U.S. agricultural commodities such as wheat, flour, rice, corn, vegetable oil, protein livestock feeds, and for fertilizers.

Additionally, a substantial market for U.S. rice may exist in Cuba. Cuba is one of the largest per capita rice consumers in the Western Hemisphere and, before the revolution, the U.S. annually supplied an average of about 187 thousand tons (about $35 million per year at then current prices) during 1956-59. Recently, Cuba has obtained most of its rice from the Peoples' Republic of China, importing an estimated 225 thousand tons in 1974. Since political ties between the PRC and Cuba are not particularly strong, in a normalized trade situation the U.S. might be able to capture most of that market, especially when the transportation advantage is considered.

Given that the Cuban people have continued to be exposed to U.S. products and tastes via Florida media broadcasts, it is possible that the U.S. could some day supply a major share of Cuban consumer goods imports. However, while a severe suppressed demand exists as a result of years of rationing, the size of the consumer goods import market depends on the Cuban government policy choice between capital investment and consumption. Indications are that the 1976–80 five-year plan is not likely to move Cuba far in the direction of a consumer society. The current market for U.S. consumer goods exports is thus probably very small (1974 imports of consumer goods from the Soviet Union were only about $37 million).

There is also an impossible-to-quantify market for spare parts for U.S. equipment installed in Cuba before 1960. No specific figure is available and the Cubans are reported to have replaced U.S. equipment in some instances with Soviet and other Western technology. Nevertheless, a potentially significant instant market could still exist.

Cuba's capacity to import, of course, varies directly and dramatically with the world price of sugar. For example, from 1961–74, Cuban sugar exports to nonsocialist buyers averaged 1,850 thousand metric tons, which, at the high 1974 average world price of 29.99 cents per pound, would have earned about $1,109 million. However, that same export volume at the 1958 world average price of 3.5 cents per pound, would have earned Cuba only $129 million. Since the Cuban revolution, world sugar prices have ranged from a yearly average in 1966 of 1.86 cents to an all time high of more than 50 cents at the end of 1974.

Cuban Gains From Trade

Other witnesses before these proceedings have indicated that, to be justified, U.S. trade with socialist Cuba must benefit the general populace of both countries. Although difficult to assess, such would seem to be the likely case in Cuba. Access to the U.S. market expands the potential hard currency market for sales of Cuban sugar, nickel, tobacco, fish and rum, providing there is production capacity not already committed to the CMEA bloc countries. Increased hard currency earnings would expand Cuba's capacity to import high quality equipment and consumer goods from Western markets, including the U.S., rather than from CMEA, with substantial savings in transport costs and an easing of resupply constraints and servicing problems.

Trade with the U.S. might result in efficiency improvements in the Cuban sugar industry from an infusion of U.S. agribusiness technology and equipment, fertilizers and agriculture chemicals. Superb natural growing conditions have allowed Cuba to pursue a policy of extensive rather than intensive sugar production, resulting in neglect of the agronomy side of their sugar industry, while concentrating on the harvesting and mill processing side. A lack of purchasing power and insufficient domestic production, limited the use of pesticides and fertilizer, both routine means toward higher yields in the U.S. cane industry. Thus, although Cuba is consistently a top world sugar producer, ranking third after the U.S.S.R. and Brazil [7] in 1975 (see table 18) substantial under-utilized production potential exists.

---

[7] Table 18 illustrates the dramatic growth of Brazilian raw sugar production (from 2.84 million tons in 1958 to 7.4 million tons for the 1975 crop year) compared to Cuban production of 5.6 million tons in 1958 and 5.5 for 1975.

TABLE 18.—CUBAN RAW SUGAR PRODUCTION COMPARISON WITH OTHER WORLD PRODUCERS

[Millions of tons]

	1958 [1]	1959	1960	1961	1962	1971	1972	1973	1974	1975	Percent of 1975 total
Cuba	5.6	5.96	5.86	6.77	4.80	5.90	4.40	5.2	5.80	5.5	6.92
Brazil	2.84	3.45	3.26	3.45	3.62	5.1	5.4	6.3	6.9	7.4	9.31
U.S.S.R.	NA	NA	NA	NA	NA	8.9	8.0	8.5	9.5	8.5	10.69
Philippines	1.37	1.53	1.63	1.5	1.62	2.06	2.55	2.54	2.91	2.7	3.4
United States	4.50	4.99	5.07	5.5	5.59	6.27	6.66	6.02	5.9	5.4	6.79
All other	30.29	33.57	33.08	37.38	36.7	42.27	43.59	46.74	49.5	50.0	62.9
World production	44.6	49.5	48.9	54.6	51.8	70.5	70.6	75.3	80.5	79.5	100.0

[1] Indicates end of crop year, e.g., 1958 for crop year 1957–58.

Only 19 percent of the 1974 crop was mechanically harvested. About 1,000 harvesters were in use and these were obtained mainly from Australia, the U.S.S.R. and domestic sources. Cuba is making slow but steady progress in mechanizing the harvest and further modernization would release labor for other uses.

Similar gains could result from the assistance of U.S. know-how in the tourist industry, another potential source for hard currency income. Prior to the revolution, the Cuban tourist industry was a major hard currency source. In the late 1950's, annual foreign visitors numbered about 350 thousand and Cuba had a surplus on its balance of tourist account of $20 million in 1958. At that time, Cuba ranked third after Mexico and Panama, among Latin American countries in net tourism earnings. There are many factors which render the late 50's inappropriate for projections of tourism in the late 70's, but some potential for this industry probably does exist, should Cuba choose to develop the necessary services and facilities.

VI. IMPEDIMENTS TO A RESUMPTION OF U.S.-CUBA TRADE

The resumption of U.S.-Cuban trade depends on the degree and pace with which the existing barriers are reduced and removed. In summary, these barriers are: (1) the U.S. embargo, (2) U.S. legislation and regulations that in one way or another prohibit or adversely affect trade, and (3) the problem of business facilitation, given the radically different institutional framework that faces American traders in dealing with a non-market economy like the Republic of Cuba.

1. The Embargo

A relaxation of the trade embargo can be effected under existing legislation; it can be accomplished by revisions of the Cuban Assets Control Regulations administered by the Treasury Department and the Export Administration Regulations administered by the Department of Commerce. The relaxation can be a complete lifting of the embargo accomplished in a single action, or a gradual step-by-step process, substantially the same as that employed previously in the relaxation of the embargo on trade with the Peoples' Republic of China. The relaxation should, of course, be undertaken in such a manner as to continue the authority of the Commerce Department to regulate exports to Cuba for purposes of national security, short supply, and foreign policy.

A determination would have to be made as to whether U.S. exports to Cuba should be treated in essentially the same way as those of the Soviet Union, most Eastern European countries, and the Peoples' Republic of China, or in a different manner. At a minimum, Cuba's present close relationship with the Soviet Union would require maintaining some controls over the export of U.S. strategic commodities and technology whose unrestricted acquisition or diversion to communist countries might prove detrimental to U.S. national security interests.

TABLE 19—AWARDS OF THE FOREIGN CLAIMS SETTLEMENT COMMISSION TO CLAIMANTS AGAINST CUBA

Type of claimant	Filed	Awarded	Denied	Amount awarded	Amount denied
Corporate	1,146	898	248	$1,578,498,839.55	$1,277,494,373.14
Individual	7,670	5,013	947	221,049,729.14	269,363,329.53
Total	8,816	5,911	1,195	1,799,548,568.69	1,546,857,702.67

10 highest certifications of loss:

Claimant—	Validated award
1. Cuban Electric Co	$267,568,413.62
2. International Telephone & Telegraph, and International Telephone & Telegraph as trustee	130,679,758.02
3. North American Sugar Industries, Inc., et al	108,975,063.13
4. Moa Bay Mining Co	88,349,000.00
5. United Fruit Sugar Co	85,110,147.09
6. West Indies Sugar Co	84,880,957.55
7. American Sugar Co	81,011,249.24
8. Standard Oil Co	71,611,002.90
9. Bangor Punta Corp., et al	53,379,123.06
10. Texaco, Inc	50,081,109.67

2. Other U.S. Legal Restrictions to the Normalization of Relations

A. The Castro government has expropriated or nationalized American private property worth about $1.8 billion as determined by the Cuban Assets Claims Commission. A partial listing of major claims appears in Table 19. As long as these claims are outstanding, normal banking and shipping relationships cannot be restored, since Cuban assets in the U.S. would be subject to possible attachment. Moreover, Congress has passed legislation preventing Cuba from receiving "any benefit" until the President determines that Cuba has taken appropriate steps to settle the outstanding claims for Cuba's taking of property at least 50 percent owned by U.S. citizens.

B. MFN and the Trade Act of 1974—Cuban exports to the United States would be subject to Column 2 tariff rates unless the conditions of Title IV of the Trade Act concerning emigration are met. Moreover, granting MFN treatment would require the U.S. and Cuba to enter into a bilateral trade agreement. The lack of MFN could seriously hamper Cuban ability to export to the U.S. Cuba would be ineligible for generalized preferences as a communist country under Section 502(B)(1) and as an expropriator of U.S.-owned property under Section 502(b)(4).

C. Financial—as noted above, Cuba is now heavily in debt to the Soviet Union and has accepted substantial lines of credit from Canada among others. At present, Eximbank credits and guarantees could be made available only if the President finds that such action is in the national interest and, furthermore, that Cuba is complying with Sections 402 and 409 of the Trade Act of 1974 concerning freedom of emigration.

It is possible that Cuba will be found to be in default on obligations to the U.S. Government and therefore subject to the provisions of the Johnson Act. If so, private citizens would be unable to make general, all-purpose loans or buy Cuban Bonds. The prohibition has been interpreted inapplicable to extension of normal commercial credit, as part of a specific export transaction.

3. Business Facilitation and Interfacing With a Non-Market Economy

Should the trade embargo be lifted and American businessmen become free to pursue Cuban trade, they will be faced with a very different economy and a radically changed institutional framework from that in existence prior to 1959. State monopolies control all of Cuba's trade; no foreign investment is allowed. While Cuban exports have not changed greatly, their import demands shifted after the revolution toward a greater emphasis on machinery, and equipment and away from consumer goods.

Businessmen who want to do business with Cuba will generally not deal with the end-users of their products, but rather with foreign trade enterprises. Moreover, information on the Cuban economy is very limited.

Cuban Situation: A More Sympathetic View

Fidel Castro's own views were presented to Americans in filmed interviews conducted in July and October 1974 by Frank Mankiewicz and Kirby Jones with film producer Saul Landau. Among excerpts from the film:

QUESTIONER. What are the Cuban conditions for re-establishing relations with the United States?

CASTRO. I would say that number one is the lifting of the economic blockade. Because the economic blockade is an act of force, an act of coercion which the United States exerts against us, because it employs all its international influence, all its political strength and all its economic power trying to asphyxiate the Cuban economy, and this policy has affected us for many years and we regard this as an extremely hostile act against us. And therefore we have established our position that we are not disposed to negotiate under conditions of economic blockade. And in order to start discussing all the differences and all the problems as one would like, it is necessary to meet one condition: that the economic blockade is stopped. When the economic blockade is ended, we shall be in a condition to speak under conditions of equality: the United States and ourselves.

The United States not only refuses to trade with us, but it takes punitive measures against the ships that come to Cuba, against the countries that trade with Cuba. Now, here you have a recent example: for example, Bangladesh. A small country with 50 million inhabitants that has suffered a great natural catastrophe, enormous floodings, which is in need of food. Then the United States, in order to grant Bangladesh certain shipments of foodstuffs—I believe 100,000 tons of wheat and some other foodstuffs—it set as condition to Bangladesh that it break its commercial relations with Cuba. Actually, it is a great shame that in order to be able to extend a certain assistance to a country very much in need of it, you impose on it a harsh condition, a humiliating condition.

Once the blockade stops, then we can start discussing all the other problems, as may be desired. Because there are problems that are of interest to us. There is the Guantanamo Base—it is one of the problems to be discussed.

Guantanamo is a piece of the national territory of Cuba. It is occupied by the United States, but we do not say that in order to start discussion, they must withdraw from Guantanamo; rather we have posed a single condition: that the economic blockade be stopped.

QUESTIONER. In 1963 were there some overtures toward better relations between the United States and Cuba?

CASTRO. You can't call it even a single step—before Kennedy was assassinated. What happened was very interesting, and that is, that a French journalist, Jean Daniel, who later wrote about this several versions, writing after many years, not always the truth, of course, but in general sticking pretty much to the truth. Jean Daniel went through Washington prior to coming to Cuba and he talked to Kennedy, with President Kennedy, and when Daniel told him he was coming to Cuba, Kennedy was very interested in his trip. And he suggested several topics to Daniel, so that Daniel could bring them up in his conversations with me, and Kennedy asked him to report back to him on his return to Washington. Then, Jean Daniel arrived in Cuba and we talked. I went with him to Varadero and he was explaining to me all the details of his conversations with Kennedy, the topics Kennedy had suggested and his interest in my reply to some of these questions. In my opinion, this was a definite gesture on Kennedy's part to try to establish contact, an exchange with us, and as I was listening to everything he was telling me about his conversation with Kennedy, the news broke over the radio that an attempt had been carried out against Kennedy's life. It really seemed such a shame, such a tragic, painful ending to Kennedy's life.

We understood what the implications were, and we were concerned about the possibility that an attempt would be made to blame Cuba for what had happened, but this was not our only concern. We were disgusted, because although we were in conflict with Kennedy politically, we held nothing personal against him as revolutionaries, and there was no reason to wish him personal harm. Besides, Kennedy could be followed by someone worse, and I always used to say that at least we knew Kennedy, that we had fought against him during the Bay of Pigs incident, the missile crisis, and all that. He was a known enemy, but let me add also that the Kennedy who was assassinated in Dallas was a much more experienced man than the Kennedy who had assumed the presidency two years before. Because then, Kennedy lacked experience, he had talent, but lacked maturity and experience when he assumed the presidency. He learned a lot from those first two years. I have no doubt about that. They exerted considerable influence on his outlook on international problems.

I have no doubts that Kennedy would someday have reconsidered his policy toward Cuba. Unfortunately, the only indication we had of this was the interview with Jean Daniel, and the message he sent us through him. The same day we were receiving the message, Kennedy was assassinated.

QUESTIONER. Some say that you have traded dependency on the U.S. for a new, even stronger dependency on the Soviet Union.

CASTRO. I know that the Soviet politicians are consistent in their ideas about the necessity of international detente and about peaceful coexistence, and we, on the other hand, have unlimited trust in them.

We have complete confidence in the loyalty of the Soviet leadership towards the Cuban revolution and we have never had any concern whatsoever to this effect. We know that the Soviets are absolutely loyal in their relations with Cuba, and we have never had the slightest worry, because we have faith in them—this is the truth.

Of course, to us the solidarity of the Soviet Union has been of very great importance. We have received from the Soviet Union large-scale aid in every respect, which has been decisive for us in this struggle against the blockade. You only have to look, for example, at the very problem of fuel supplies, which has been a very serious problem for many countries. We had no energy crisis. We had no blockade of fuel supplies, and during these 15 years our country continued to receive from the Soviet Union all the fuel it consumes, year in, year out. During all these years, our country received from the Soviet Union the wheat it consumes, it received a lot of transportation equipment, agricultural equipment, industrial equipment.

All the development of our electric power supply has been carried out essentially with Soviet equipment, and today we produce three times as much electrical power as we did before the triumph of the revolution. Our mechanical industry has also been developing with the assistance of the Soviet Union, and in addition, food supplies, many food products, we receive fertilizers, raw materials, and a whole series of essential products. So that for us, the aid given by the Soviet Union during these years of blockade and of crisis has been decisive.

While we were subjected to aggression from the United States during these 15 years, from them we received aid. We have had insuperable proof of the spirit of friendship and of solidarity on the part of the Soviet Union.

How can our relations with the Soviet Union be compared with the relations that existed with the United States?

The Soviet Union has extended to us payment facilities, it has granted us large credits and whenever the circumstances of a financial order required it, it has always displayed the best attitude towards us.

The United States owned our mines. The United States was the owner of our electric power plants, of our telephone companies, of the main transportation companies, of the principal industries, of the best lands, of the largest sugar mills. They owned our banks, they owned our foreign trade. In a few words, they owned the Cuban economy.

The Soviets do not own a single mine in Cuba, not a single factory, not a single sugar mill, not one hectare of land, not a single bank, not a single business, not a single public utility. So, then, all the natural resources, all the industries, and all the means of production belong to our country and before the revolution they were under the ownership of another country. They were properties of a foreign business.

It was really fortunate for us that a country with resources, such as the Soviet Union, would have the inclination and the will to help us. Otherwise, we could not have made it through those so very difficult years.

QUESTIONER. What is the situation of political prisoners?

CASTRO. At present, in Cuba, there remain about 20 percent of the counterrevolutionary prisoners that we had in the first years of the revolution. 80 percent have been released through various plans, we freed them. We released 80 percent, we did not put any conditions on anyone to release them. We believed they could be released; there is a part that we do not believe can be released as yet. It is a moral issue, a question of justice, not a question of negotiation.

QUESTIONER. What will be the role of the Party?

CASTRO. The Party gives the direction to the state and to the whole society. It holds the supreme political command. This will be the role, the function of the Party, which will be recognized in the constitution itself. This will be included in the constitutional precepts of the country; the Party's role, that is. Because the Party will play a political role, a role of uniting the people, of educating the people, of guiding the people and including the guiding of the state.

It is true that we are trying to maintain, trying to enable the individual to feel the greatest freedom possible. Of course, we are opposed to the criterion of interfering in the personal life of people, even though the revolution assigns many tasks to everyone, and gives a lot of work to all, because the students have a lot of work. For example, they work in production, they study, participate in cultural, artistic and sports activities, in brief, they have not a minute free during the day.

Women do a great deal of work as workers, as members of the Federation of Women, as housewives, and besides they are members of the CDR's, and if they are also active members of the Party, they have a lot of activities. Besides, they also belong to the trade unions. I hear that people are complaining, for example, that the teachers have a lot of work—in the schools, with the programs, the teachers' union, the women, many meetings, so I must say, in truth, that everyone here has many social obligations and many political obligations.

But this is also bringing about that everyone feels he is a part, is a participant, that no one feels alienated from the process, that no one feels indifferent to the state. Everyone here identifies with the revolutionary state and with the tasks of the state. Today, each Cuban citizen can say as Louis XIV said, "L'etat—c'est moi" (I am the State). And this identification between the citizen and the power is decisive, without it the revolution could not have maintained itself.

QUESTIONER. Would you allow an opposition newspaper to publish?

CASTRO. No, in reality not.

QUESTIONER. Why not, really?

CASTRO. We are starting with one idea—that the newspapers here belong to the workers. We are starting out with the idea that there is a social order that holds office coercively in the name of the majority, and in reality in our concepts we do not allow, we do not allow, the existence of press organs of class enemies of the Revolution to publish against the Revolution. This is our concept. I don't ask that you agree because we understand that these newspapers are weapons which we do not make available to the enemies of the Revolution. We certainly think so. I don't ask that you agree with out manner of thinking, but we have nothing to conceal and nothing to keep secret. We conceived the Revolution theoretically as a process of the dictatorship of the exploited against the exploiters.

QUESTIONER. Would you allow opposition to exist?

CASTRO. It is so that there exists no opposition in the known classical sense, to which you are referring. There can be opposition. It is acted out within the Party, within the Party. It can be acted out within its mass organization, it can be acted out within the factories—but not as a nationally organized party representing one class. There is the right to give an opinion, there is the right to disagree, but when the majority agrees on a specific decision, the minority must submit to the decision of the majority.

Saul Landau, producer of the film from which the above was excerpted and an associate fellow of the Institute for Policy Studies, took at least 10 trips to Cuba since the Castro revolution and made five films about Cuba. He testified May 20, 1975 at the hearings of the House subcommittees on international relations and told the members that since 1959, "Cuba has built an entirely new country." He noted three "striking" things about Cuba: (1) "If you just look at the physical environment of roads, buildings, schools, factories, dams, hospitals, nursery schools, and apartment buildings now, you will see a transformed physical environment." (2) "What strikes you is the youth of the population. By 1980 the great majority of Cubans will have no living memory of life under any different kind of social order." (3) "The third thing that strikes one . . . is the amount of political involvement of the average Cuban citizen. . . . The average Cuban citizen spends enormous amounts of his waking hours at meetings before work, during lunch, after work. He or she may have two or three meetings a day and almost every sector of society is discussing policies, laws, which they are now enacting, and the various problems that they are facing in the work situations." Landau said in his prepared statement:

I have seen the results of the U.S. embargo policy on Cuba, from the Cuban point of view and from our own, and after making ten visits to Cuba since 1960 and talking for hours, and on one occasion days, with Prime Minister Castro, I have concluded that the embargo policy not only failed to achieve its objective, but caused deep hatred and bitterness against the United States government.

Most of my visits to Cuba were made for journalistic or filmmaking purposes. I travelled to every Province many times, and to the Isle of Pines. I spoke at length on and off camera to peasants in the remotest rural villages and to workers in the most congested urban centers. I have talked with government leaders and professionals, loyal supporters and some who remain critical of the Castro led government.

From my experience and reflection, I would say that we have not isolated the Cuban Revolution or the Cuban people. We have forced them to seek and make new friends on new terms, or to reevaluate their old friends with new criteria. And in sixteen and one-half years the Revolution has sunk deep-roots with adults and with those who have grown up knowing the Revolution from birth.

These young people have received from the Revolution their education, uniforms and books, a daily liter of milk and often times all bed and board. They know also that the United States has given them nothing but shortages, hostility, and, has at times sent Cuban nationals on mysterious CIA-connected missions.

What Cuban youth read about in their newspapers and listen to on radio and TV is U.S. "imperialist" action in Indochina, and each one of them is taught and believes that if our troops had not been tied up in Vietnam, they could have been used against the Cubans. On the other hand the Soviets have offered Cuba enormous amounts of aid and have required little in return. . . .

It is time to change our myopic policy, and what Cuba asks as a demonstration of U.S. good faith costs us little. Castro has demanded of the U.S. that the embargo be lifted as a necessary first step toward beginning negotiation of the many points of conflict between our country and Cuba—and only the food and medicine embargo. By our lifting the embargo, argue opponents of detente with Cuba, we would be legitimizing a dictator and giving into his demands. The fact is that Castro's legitimacy, after sixteen consecutive years in command, is no longer open to question in the world of nations, and his demands are hardly excessive. Our embargo was designed to strangle and isolate the Cuban Revolution, and it has not worked. Each year Cuba's foreign trade and relations expand. The provocations that caused the U.S. to act against Cuba no longer weigh heavily with most of our body politic. We enjoy formal relations with the Soviets and Chinese and other Communist nations.

In addition to the many economic reasons for lowering the blockade, a more important reason in my opinion derives from analyzing some simple statistics. More than 50% of the people in Cuba today have never lived under or have a memory of a different social order, and most of Cuba's physical wealth, her schools, hospitals, roads, resorts, factories, have been built since the Revolution. In short, Cuba in 1975 is a new country, with a new population and a new man-made environment. The language, many customs, and the palm trees remain the same, but to the sixteen year old Cuban today the Cold War policy that the U.S. has pursued against Cuba only makes him or her feel angry and deprived.

For example, Cubans learn from reading their newspapers and listening to their radios and to Castro's speeches that many of their shortages and deprivations stem directly from the U.S. economic blockade. Rationing, by the way, which some critics select as a point of attack, was adopted as a result of the U.S. blockade to insure that the scarce resources were equally shared, and that income difference would not mean differences in the amount of food or clothing that an individual could buy. . . .

A favorite charge against Castro is the "export of revolution." When we asked him about this charge Castro replied that Cuba had indeed exported much sugar, but revolution was not a comparable commodity and therefore could not be exported. He has admitted aiding other revolutionary movements (with material, men and ideas) without success in the past in Latin America. He said that if one calculated the amount that the United States spent on counter revolution, the entire Cuban effort would barely show on a statistical chart. It is now recognized by his friends and enemies alike that Cuba is not participating in Latin American violence. The reports of guerrilla training camps in Cuba have not been confirmed by any reliable source. One need only look at Cuba's improved relations with Peru, Panama, Venezuela, Columbia, Argentina, Mexico, Honduras and several of the Caribbean countries to deduce that Castro's policy has changed. A majority of OAS countries recognized this. . . .

Critics of Cuba have made numerous charges ranging from their disagreement or dislike for particular Castro policies, to their fear that Castro has turned Cuba into a Soviet puppet state, with police everywhere and large sectors of the population starving and impoverished.

No responsible journalist or recent visitor has seen evidence of police state behavior, or indeed any signs of the extreme poverty found in most Latin American countries. In fact Castro has indeed aided other countries that could not help him materially, such as Chile under Allende, South Yemen, Peru, and Honduras when they suffered natural catastrophes. This would appear to indicate growing prosperity rather than the reverse.

We have heard about lower sugar production for most years due to a labor shortage while at the same time Castro is accused of using forced labor. In sixteen years, Cuba's school population has more than quintupled and her teacher population has more than quintupled. Most Cuban doctors fled to the U.S. in the early years of the Revolution and Cuba now has graduated an equal number from her medical school, while the nursing population has grown by geometric proportions. All social services have grown and the entire labor force was reordered. It is much harder today to find surplus labor for part time work in Cuba—like cane cutting.

The two Cubas of 1958 and 1975 are not comparable in many ways, just as it would be both unfair and unwise to compare the U.S. with Cuba. We are the major developed power; Cuba is a small developing nation. We have relations today with many countries of different levels of growth and social systems, many of them authoritarian and dictatorial, in which political prisons and torture are routine and everyday phenomenon.

Cuba does have political prisoners, as Castro himself admitted. In 1967 and 1968, as a TV journalist, I interviewed groups of prisoners in Cuba, one group at a so-called rehabilitation farm. The people I talked with said they had been convicted of crimes ranging from conspiracy against the state to illegal money changing. Their conditions, compared to U.S. prisons, were clean and acceptable. Adequate food, bedding and shelter were combined with family visiting cottages. But it was prison. In July, 1967, members of the press were shown weapons seized from Cuban nationals in Cuba, some of whom said they were paid by the CIA, which ranged from booby traps to rifles with sniper scopes and potassium cyanide bullets. All of these prisoners denied that their missions included anything more than bringing people in or out of the island. They had no explanation for the weapons.

One reason for the existence of political prisoners and committees for defense of the Revolution has been U.S. policy of selective sabotage, infiltration and perhaps assassination. In any case, political prisoners exist in many countries, some of whom are close allies of the U.S. Castro say that he hopes that soon all remaining political prisoners will be ready for rehabilitation, and he claims that the political prisoner population has been reduced by some 80%. If the U.S. dropped its embargo and hostile policies, I believe Cuba could relax its internal vigilance.

The claims that Cuba has 100,000 political prisoners, and of wide scale torture and poor conditions in Cuban prisons have had no verification by responsible sources. Thousands of foreigners now visit Cuba each month, including many journalists. Nowhere have I seen reporting which documents these claims.

It is impossible to answer some of the exaggerated criticism of Castro's revolutionary policies. I hope to put Cuba into a light with which Americans who have not been there can see with some insight the process of this revolution, 90 miles from Florida.

Cuba is a socialist country. The means of production, except for some small farms, belong to the state. The state represents the people, it claims, and the state is directed by the Communist party. The Party speaks with only one voice. This all sounds very grim until we look at the everyday details. Millions of Cubans attend meetings of every variety where they discuss and debate every issue of social and political life. At union and workshop meetings, women's group and block meetings, and finally at Party and Party youth meetings, Cubans formally discuss their politics. On busses and street corners, beauty parlors and bars Cubans talk politics informally. But this discussion is limited by the context that the Revolution, through its leaders, have established.

The Revolution is seen by Cubans as a dictatorship, designed to bring about rule by one class over another. Workers are the dictators and they are represented as a class. Those who previously had rights to employ workers or exact rents or profits, no longer have representation as a class. This is by design and no one tries to hide it. It is a standard communist theory. And I reiterate it so that when we criticize Cubans for not having many opinions represented in their newspaper we understand that they don't want many opinions. They are not a capitalist democracy like we are. They think that capitalism was tried and failed to provide for the needs of their people.

Journalists like James Reston of the New York Times, Laurence Stern and Terry Shaw of the Washington Post, Dan Rather of CBS, plus countless others have all come back with positive impressions from travelling throughout Cuba. The overwhelming majority of Cubans inside Cuba support with enthusiasm their leader Fidel Castro and the Revolution he leads.

At the same time many Cubans blame the United States for their shortages and hardships over the past 16 years. They do not feel themselves under Russian control. Only Soviet aid is noticeable, not Soviet military or technical personnel; although they are present, mostly in Havana.

I think we must face the obvious: the Cuban Revolution has survived the U.S. policy designed to hurt and kill it. Now it is beginning to prosper. The French Minister of Trade met with Castro last week in Cuba after concluding expanded trade deals. Soon after, a Cuban trade delegation, led by the important Carlos Rafael Rodriguez, went to London. Cuban trade expands. As we endure recession ironically, the majority of Cubans have never had it better. But life in Cuba today, as Cubans enjoy the consumer goods recently bought with sugar profits, cannot be compared with life before the Revolution.

A qualitative change has occurred in Cuba and in her relations with other countries. Tourists pour in from Europe, Canada and even Mexico and Venezuela. Castro, however, was very cautious when we asked him about American tourists, and said "we must think very carefully before we bring Americans back to Cuba." I think it is our turn to show to a small and old historic neighbor and friend that we have the broad vision that is in keeping with our size, power and historic ideals.

The Cubans made a Revolution because they faced one kind of dictatorship, a corrupt, gangster-ridden society where the rich prospered and the poor suffered. Now they have changed that. The new dictatorship sees the poor dividing the wealth much more evenly and those who possessed great wealth no longer have it. This includes American property.

Sixteen years have gone by since Castro and his bearded band marched into Havana after overthrowing the Batista dictatorship. In those sixteen years Cuba has been transformed by Revolution. It probably will never return to the shabby past, where Havana was known as a playground for rich Americans, where beggars and prostitutes patrolled the streets. We did little to change the Batista society. We accepted it for all of its injustices.

It think it's time we accepted the Cuban Revolution whether or not we agree with it. It has taken away property and jailed those who oppose it actively.

But it also has brought a new life to the poor and to the young. By 1980 the young, those born since the Revolution will compose the great majority of the Cuban people, living in a society built since 1959. That is the Cuba to which we will relate.

Repression & Political Prisoners

The charges of political repression and political imprisonment in Cuba come largely from leaders of the Cuban exiles—numbering hundreds of thousands—who have fled Castro's Cuba. Cuban-born Frank Calzon, educated in the U.S. after leaving Cuba in 1960, testified July 9, 1975 before the House subcommittees on international relations. He said in his prepared statement:

Very few contemporary political developments have produced as many essays, symposia, controversies, articles and studies as the present revolution in Cuba.[1] Extensive as it is, the literature on the Castroite revolution has nevertheless dealt rather superficially with a number of topics, among them the human rights issue and its byproducts: repression and the political prisoners in the island.

One obvious reason for the lack of an extended study on the matter has to do with the availability and reliability of data on the subject. To the usual difficulties associated with Cuban data [2] it must be added that this is not a topic which would receive the enthusiastic support of the Foreign Ministry authorities in charge of showing the friendly visitors the achievements of the revolution.

Another, is that political realities exclude the possibility of independent surveys, interviewing, sampling and *in situ* inspections which could provide much of the research input for such a study.[3]

Cuba, however, is not unique in this respect; the researcher with a minimum familiarity with current methodology in comparative social studies has found that brief guided tours are no substitute for systematic, critical research.

For this short typology I have relied on a variety of sources: books and articles in both the Cuban and foreign press; denunciation presented to various international bodies; letters smuggled out of prison; taped telephone conversations—one surprisingly by the mother of a murdered student leader who denounced the crime from Havana; letters from friends and relatives; statements by Premier Fidel Castro; acknowledgements from various public figures and international organizations; interviews with former political prisoners; and official reports and statements from international organizations such as the International Red Cross, the Inter-American Commission on Human Rights, Amnesty International, the International Rescue Committee and the International Commission of Jurists.

"Soviet-Cuban collaboration," explained Soviet leader Brezhnev during his 1974 visit to the island, "embraces today the most varied spheres of life. It includes metallurgy, agriculture, the fishing fleet, scientific research and art. From

---

[1] See Nelson P. Valdés and Edwin Lieuwen's *The Cuban Revolution: A Research Study Guide (1959–1969)* (Albuquerque: University of New Mexico Press, 1971) Bibliography contains almost 4,000 entries. For more recent publications see *Cuban Studies Newsletter* (Pittsburgh, Penn: University of Pittsburgh Center for Latin American Studies). Published biannually since 1970.

[2] See Carmelo Mesa Lago's "Availability and Reliability of Statistics in Cuba," *Latin American Research Review* (1969). Interestingly, Cuban Premier Fidel Castro has acknowledged that the Cuban government has released false statistics to confuse the enemies of the revolution. *Granma*, Official organ of the Central Committee of the Communist Party of Cuba (January 2, 1965).

[3] For an examppple of Cuba's refusal to allow visits by independent academicians with a solid reputation for serious research see Lowry Nelson's *Cuba: The Measure of a Revolution* (Minneapolis: University of Minnesota Press, 1972) pp. VII–VIII.

a simple form such as commerce it reaches to include cooperation in production and the coordination of the national economic plans."

Breshnev's statement, emphasizing the wide spectrum of Soviet-Cuban cooperation, failed to mention however, that the Soviet Union provides much needed technical guidance and support in two key areas: foreign intelligence [4] and domestic control; two areas which in the Soviet Union are under the direct control of what is usually referred to as the KGB.

Thus, from April 25 to 27, 1974 the DGEP (General Directorate of Penal Establishments) sponsored the First National Reunion of Penal Establishment Specialists *who had studied in the Soviet Union.*

In Cuba, as in the Soviet Union, the government has extended the meaning of "political crimes" to include almost every area of human activity.[5] This politization of the penal code is a major departure from the position traditionally taken by dictatorial governments in Cuba and elsewhere in Latin America where political crimes are usually defined as engaging in armed opposition, sabotage, criticisms of the regime, general strikes, writing or distributing pamphlets, or similar activities which fall clearly in the context of an open opposition to the government.

In Cuba today the situation is quite different. At least partially due to the dogmatic character of the regime, thousands of individuals without overt political aims have been sent to prison to join the thousands who have opposed the regime within the traditional political context.

In spite of the promises made by Fidel Castro during the insurrectionary period (restoration of the 1940 Constitution, general elections within a year after achieving power, "absolute guarantee" of freedom of the press and political and individual rights, etc.)[6] the Cuban government continues to demand immediate obedience to its every whim. Sixteen years after the triumph of the revolution Cuba continues to be governed by decree without an independent judiciary or a legislative branch.[7]

The government decrees rely not on the consent of the governed but on the type of coercion and terror a regime which is unaccountable to anyone grows to demand as indispensable for its own survival.

The politization of the legal code has taken a heavy toll on Cuban society: for every arbitrary program and every coercive measure of the regime an opposition has erupted. The outcome has been that every official government goal has been followed by a new decree and new directives defining new "crimes" and new penalties. What this really means is that almost every government program has brought in its wake an influx of Cubans into the prisons of the island. The penal system has no parallel in the history of the country and can be compared on an equal footing with the Stalinist period in the Soviet Union.[8]

Estimates of the number of prisoners are hard to come by, and no official statistics are available. It could be stated safely, however, that "tens of thousands are held in jails, concentration camps and rehabilitation or forced labor establishments." [9]

In mid 1965 Premier Castro acknowledged that there were close to twenty thousand prisoners;[10] and Lee Lockwood, an apologist for the Cuban Premier, indicated that the number was "still growing ... in spite of the fact that

---

[4] On the coupling of Cuba's DGI (General Directorate for Intelligence) and the Soviet KGB see Brian Crozier's *Soviet Pressures in the Caribbean* (London: Institute for the Study of Conflict; 1973); James D. Theberge (Edit.) *Russia in the Caribbean* (Washington: Georgetown University Center for Strategic Studies: 1973) pp. 43–47; and Leon Gouré and Morris Rothemberg's *Soviet Penetration of Latin America* (Coral Gables, Florida: University of Miami Center for Advanced International Studies, 1975).
[5] Thus apolitical activities are suspected. Those who are not enthusiastically in favor of the new order are assumed to be against it.
[6] For a documented account of the impact of Castro's refusal to implement his promises see Theodore Draper, *Castro's Revolution: Myths and Realities* (N.Y.: Praeger; 1962) pp. 16–20.
[7] For an initial account see *Cuba and the Rule of Law* (*International Commission of Jurists*; 1962). Also Hugh Thomas *Cuba: The pursuit of Freedom* (New York: Harper and Row; 1971) pp. 1458–1462.
[8] See K. S. Karol *Guerrillas in Power* (N.Y.: Hill and Wang, 1970) and René Dumont. *Is It Socialism* (Paris, 1970). Both authors are well known Marxists who had earlier sided with the Cuban experiment. Both books give ample evidence of the arbitrary and personalistic character of the regime.
[9] Philip W. Bonsal, *Cuba, Castro and the United States* (University of Pittsburgh Press; 1971) p. 190. Mr. Bonsal, a career diplomat was the last U.S. ambassador in Havana.
[10] Lee Lockwood, *Castro's Cuba, Cuba's Fidel* (New York: The MacMillan Co.; 1967) pp. 210–211.

counterrevolutionary activity has been slackening gradually since the Missile Crisis."[11]

Exile sources have published larger estimates. José Alvarez Diaz quotes a source offering a list of 93,631 names in 1962.[12] And Mario Lazo in *Dagger in the Heart* reports seeing an official list containing 69,315 prisoners in 1967.[13] During that same year *The New York Times* estimated that there were 40,000 political prisoners.[14] And also in 1967 Marino de Medici, an Italian journalist, estimated that there were 50,000 prisoners in the regular prisons of the island. De Medici's estimate is closer to the *Times*', yet at the same time he reported there were an additional 80,000 in the UMAP (Military Units for Aid to Production) forced labor camps.[15]

The Journal de Geneve, writing on the latest meetings of the United Nations Commission on Human Rights reported a 50,000 estimate.[16] And as recent as last June 1, a sympathetic writer to the Cuban regime wrote in the *Washington Post* that "estimates vary from 25,000 to 50,000 prisoners."[17]

The Association of Former Cuban Political Prisoners estimated this last June that there are 60,000 men and women in the regular political prisons of the island without counting people in work-camps and various other similar official programs.[18]

Whatever the exact figure, the evidence strongly indicates that after more than fifteen years of revolutionary government extensive discontent persists, and the regime's continuing reliance on harsh penalties and new efforts to attain greater control since 1970 strongly suggest that dissatisfaction is on the increase.

In view of the Cuban government's repeated denials to various international organizations who have requested to visit the prisons in Cuba,[19] the only ones who could give an exact figure are the Cuban officials or their Soviet advisers.

What can be stated without doubt is that Premier Castro's penal code has affected every stratum of Cuban society. The political prisoners are far from a homogenous group: there are relatively few who remained incarcerated accused of crimes related to the old regime; there are also the old revolutionaries, former allies of Fidel Castro who felt betrayed at the radicalization of the process; there are the rebellious youths who refuse to incorporate themselves into the government plans; and the small farmers who provoked the government wrath by hiding part of their crops for private consumption; those who have been caught writing a Cuban version of Samizdav; others like the Jehovah Witnesses who challenge the regime by refusing to participate in political activities; and others yet who have attempted to leave in small boats without the proper official permits.

The question of free immigration is a particularly painful one: there are thousands of Cubans who are "legally" not permitted to leave the country. Those who are caught trying to flee are given lengthy prison terms; those who apply for exist visas are immediately fired from their jobs and are then "permitted" to earn a living "working in agriculture." It takes a minimum of two years from the time a person applies to leave to the time when he is issued an exit visa. In the meantime, regardless of physical condition, profession or other factors they are to work in the fields.

If a person applies for an exit visa and after he is fired from his job refuses to "work in agriculture" then he is charged with "vagrancy" and sentenced to a work camp.

---

[11] *Ibid*. Lockwood's book is based on an interview with Premier Castro. He submitted his material to the Cuban Premier before publishing to insure its accuracy.
[12] José Alvarez Diaz, *Cuba: Geópolitica y Pensamiento Económico* (Miami: Editorial Universal) p. 382.
[13] Mario Lazo, *Dagger in the Heart* (Funk & Wagnall; 1970) pp. 410–411.
[14] *New York Times*, "Havana relocating political prisoners," Sept. 24, 1967.
[15] Quoted by L. Nelson: already cited (p. 223).
[16] *Journal de Geneve*, Mar. 7, 1975.
[17] Terri Shaw. "Cuban Prisoners Said 'Resentenced' Before Terms End," *The Washington Post*, June 1, 1975.
[18] My interview with Ms. Gloria Solano, Washington. June 19, 1975.
[19] See among others the Inter-American Commission on Human Rights' *Report Regarding the Situation of Human Rights in Cuba* (June 13, 1967) p. 25, Appendix No. 2; also Letter dated Aug. 1, 1974, from the President of the International Red Cross.

In spite of these difficulties, including the fact that their homes and personal possessions are confiscated by the state, "over seven hundred thousand people have emigrated from Cuba since Castro came to power."[20] And they are not, as Professor Ernst Halperin has pointed out confined to the upper classes: "among more recent immigrants, there is a steadily rising proportion of persons from the lower sector, workers and peasants; these are as antagonistic to the regime as the dispossessed members of the upper class."[21] ...

In order to attempt to understand why roughly 10% of the population has made the decision to pay those penalties and go into exile, we must now turn to a brief history of the various stages that marked the development of the political prison in Cuba.

The old regime crumbles; the first prisoners

Upon the revolutionary victory during the first few days of 1959, a preponderant majority of the Cubans, and most sectors in Cuban society supported the revolution. During that first stage, however, the first inklings of what would develop into a full fledged police-state began to appear.

Fulgencio Batista, it must be remembered had fled the night of December 31, 1958, while the bulk of the revolutionary army—including Fidel Castro—was still at the other end of the island in the Oriente mountains. Thus, most of the major individuals involved in the old regime had made it out of Cuba even before the rebels had really established that Batista had fled.

Left, however, were a handful of army officers and others who were often not the main culprits, but who had been caught in the preceding civil war. Many were charged and tried. There were procedural arbitrarities, the writ of habeas corpus had been suspended, and the atmosphere as one individual charged with "war crimes" pointed out, was more that of a Roman circus, than that of a court room.[22]

In another notorious case, a group of former pilots in the Cuban airforce were tried and found innocent of having committed war crimes. Fidel Castro was not happy with the decision. He had them retried and condemned.[23]

The irregular proceedings and the obvious injustices that were being committed were usually explained away in terms of the confusion of the times and the emotionally charged character of the revolutionary victory.

Many of those men, some innocent, some not—tried under unusual circumstances during the first few months of 1959 were often executed. Most of those who were not became the first group of political prisoners in post-revolutionary Cuba.

The shift to the left: revolutionaries in prison

If during the first few months of 1959 the officers of the old armed forces were being tried, during the last months of the year an unexplainable development was happening: after Fidel Castro refused to make good his democratic promises, many of his former friends, men who had fought for the revolution in the mountains and in the urban underground were being taken to trial.

The period extends roughly from mid 1959 until the Bay of Pigs fiasco. It was characterized by Castro's disavowal of his democratic promises, and his growing reliance on the Communist cadres, who had played an insignificant role during the insurrectionary period.

Many significant figures in the revolutionary government expressed their opposition: the head of the Air Force fled to Florida and denounced the presence of members of the Cuban Communist Party (PSP) in key positions; the Minister of Agriculture and author of the Agrarian Reform Law was executed; the Revolutionary President, hand-chosen by Mr. Castro, was forced to resign and

---

[20] P. Bonsal; previously quoted. (P. 190).
[21] Ernst Halperin, "The Cuban Revolution in 1968." *Current History* (January 1969) p. 46. Professor Halperin was at the time with the Political Science Department of the Massachusetts Institute of Technology.
[22] Thomas; previously cited (p. 1088).
[23] Thomas; previously quoted, p. 1202.

eventually sought asylum in a foreign embassy; the General Secretary of the Cuban Confederation of Workers was sent to prison; and many ministers and key people in the revolutionary process went into exile.

The president of the Federation of University Students at the Universidad Central (Las Villas province) was executed, as well as various other groups from the University of Havana.

In one famous case, the military commander of Camaguey province, Rebel Army Major Huber Matos, resigned his post in a personal letter to Castro in which he alluded to the Communist influence in the government. Castro had him arrested. The head of the Rebel Army disappeared mysteriously on a flight from Camaguey to Havana; and in the trial that followed the Cuban Premier accused Matos of slandering the revolution (since the revolution "was not Communist") and sentenced him to 20 years for treason.

Many of those who opposed the betrayal of the revolution remain in prison to this day. Matos has been severely beaten. He has not been allowed to receive visitors during the last 5 years, and has been denied medical attention. Amnesty International asked its members last March to write to Fidel Castro on his behalf.[24]

Another well known case was that of Pedro Luis Boitel, a student leader at the University of Havana who had been a member of the urban underground against Batista. Boitel opposed the "statization" of the University and the Federation of Students and was sentenced to 10 years in prison. At the end of his term the regime refused to release him. He participated in several hunger strikes, and after a severe beating in the Principe Castle he died without receiving medical assistance. He was buried in secret.[25]

Boitel was in prison until his death in May 1972. He belonged to a particular group of prisoners, those with impressive revolutionary records who took a stand early in the process. To this day many of them are kept incommunicado from other prisoners.

The farm sector

Although initially the revolution had the support of most of the rural population, by 1962 the government had discarded its original promises of making the farmers owners of their small farms. The government was instead collectivizing the land into state farms along the Soviet pattern. Rural associations such as the "Colonos" and "Hacendados" had been dissolved by January of 1961.

The ANAP, or National Association of Small Farmers was created more as an instrument of government policy than anything else: not even its president is elected by the members of the organization. Farmers are forbidden to slaughter their own animals and are required to sell their crops to the government. They "own" their farms for life, i.e. they cannot be sold or inherited. Since the nationalization of all small businesses (barbershops, bars, news-stands, etc.) in 1968, the small farmers are the only private entrepeneurs remaining in Cuba.[26]

A French Marxist, René Dumont reported in 1970 that Cuban agriculture was being militarized: "The military in charge of work crews carry revolvers which is understandable (sabotage) but makes me uneasy . . . In the South of Central America one recognizes the boss on a plantation, whether he be the owner or manager, by the fact that he carries a revolver, whereas his workers have machetes . . ."[27]

The effort to control the rural population had began somewhat earlier. Lee Lockwood, an acknowledged admirer of the regime had pointed out that "the majority of the internees are not, as one might assume, men of urban backgrounds, but campesinos—peasants from the mountains and the outlying rural areas. Most are serving terms ranging from two to twenty years . . ."[28]

---

[24] See "Cuban Prisoners Said 'Resentenced' Before Terms End." *The Washington Post*, June 1, 1975. *Denounciation to the Human Rights Commission of the United Nations;* March 1975.
[25] Inter-American Commission on Human Rights, *Resolution on Case 1604;* April 27, 1973. National Catholic News Service, "Jailed Student Leader Dies in Cuba from Torture." June 5, 1972. Also *Appeal from Clara Abrahan de Boitel to save her son.* To Paul VI.
[26] J. Sucklicki, *Cuba, Castro and Revolution* (U. of Miami Press: 1972) p. 57.
[27] R. Dumont, "The militarization of Fidelismo," *Dissent* (Sept. 1970) p. 417.
[28] Lee Lockwood, previously cited. P. 210.

Since then, the revolutionary leadership has tightened its controls. At the Second Farmers Congress (ANAP) in 1971, the organization approved a resolution calling for the eradication of "every remaining vestige of class and private ownership of the means of production." Thus in fact calling for its own eradication. The farmers however had demonstrated some interest in finding ways that would allow them to sell some of their crops. Fidel Castro was very clear on that point: Those individuals who engage in black market operations should be made the object of political work. And the incorrigible ones should be deprived of all their rights and be treated as class enemies . . .[29]

Thus in the rural sector the government programs have encountered enough resistance, which is often translated into low production, to make it necessary for the Cuban Premier to raise the specter of "class enemies." More than half of the political prisoners in today's Cuba continue to come from rural backgrounds.

The labor front

Paralleling its farm policy, after its initial wide spread support, the regime decided to acquire absolute control of the unions so that they would in fact become instruments of government policy. Raul Castro put it bluntly in 1963: "Previously, it was necessary for trade union leaders to constantly struggle for advantages, for obtaining more profits from the capitalist magnates. Today the great task of the CTC–R (National Workers Union) and of the trade unions compressing it, is to increase production, activate voluntary workers, augment discipline at work, increase yield, and improve the quality of what is produced . . ."[30]

To this day, some of the union leaders who opposed the total abdication of union rights continue in prison. Among them, David Salvador, former Secretary General of the Revolutionary Confederation of Cuban Workers.

Beginning in 1970, the regime has enacted a series of new decrees punishing "absentism," "loafing," and introducing the "workers biography," which is a complete file of his behavior, attitudes, etc. to be kept at his labor center. Entries are to be made for such things as "activities that negatively affect production, disturb labor discipline, and show a low level of consciousness." Failure to meet production quotas is also to be indicated.

Absenteeism from work is defined by decree as "the crime of loafing" and carries penalties ranging from house arrest to imprisonment in workcamps forced labor) for one to two years.[31]

The Cuban prison system, it must be noted, is a huge source of slave labor along the Stalinist model. Prisoners that are considered dangerous are kept in maximum security prisons which are nevertheless a small section of the total prison system with various specialized jails, work-camps, rehabilitation centers, etc.

In every province the government also has various "open fronts" composed by traveling brigades. In Havana alone there are 8 fronts. Prisoners are thus used for most construction projects, often working many additional hours of "voluntary work" each week. Most of the country schools, roads, etc. have been built by prisoners, which in many cases end up receiving thirty or fourty pesos a month, which are sent to their families.

Ironically, some of the "revolutionary showcases" which are part of the official guided tours have been built by slave labor.

Often during the sugar crop the official Cuban press reports the movement of "brigades from the Ministry of the Interior." Those brigades are composed for the most part by dissidents and political prisoners.

Building the New Man: Repression of the youth sector

One of the main constants in revolutionary policy has been its preoccupation with the younger generations. The New Man, however, has not as yet traveled down the old streets of Old Havana, as a 24 year old poet has explained it in a poem which has circulated among student groups in Cuba.

The poet, Miguel Sales, is now serving his second sentence in the political prison at La Cabaña Fortress in Havana. His "crime" having returned to the island to pick up his wife and two year old daughter.[32]

---

[29] *Granma* (Official Organ of the Cuban Communist Party) Jan. 9. 1972.
[30] *Revolución*, January 23. 1963. p. 4. *Revolución* was the official newspaper in Cuba during the first years of the revolutionary government.
[31] Law No. 1231. Mar. 16. 1971; *Granma*, Mar. 28. 1971.
[32] "Exiles Get 30 Years in Jail," *The Miami Herald*, Nov. 14. 1974. See also letters and

According to Cuban official sources 60% of those in the 16 year old group were neither studying nor working in 1971; 79% of those who entered elementary school in 1965 did not complete the 6th grade, and 86% of those who went to high school quit before graduation.[33]

Castro has put the blame for the high rate of juvenile delinquency on "leniency of the existing (pre-revolutionary) Cuban criminal code with respect to offenses committed by youths under 18 years of age."[34]

The official youth publications have decried "eccentric appearance, long hair and tight pants." After condemning as "men of a bankrupt universe" those youths who like modern music and dance their "epileptic dances with the great shamelessness," the Minister of Education called for greater discipline to control the rebellious youths.

Fidel Castro explained the government's position: "The Minister of Education tried persuasion, tried persuasion, tried reasoning with some of these youngsters, tried to advise them. Very well. But of course, advice alone is not sufficient. If they don't understand persuasion, then they will have to understand another kind of procedure . . . Those youngsters will be educated or reeducated; those cases will be treated the way they should be treated. . . ."[35]

The "other type of procedure" was to send out the Army trucks to pick up several hundred Cuban teenagers in downtown Havana and send them to workcamps in Camaguey province.

Significantly, the regime has also decreed that Cuban males between the ages of 17 and 29 cannot leave the country.

In view of these restrictions and of the hard line approach the regime chooses to use in regard to its most pampered group, there is very little that remains untried in their efforts to control other "unorthodox" minorities.

The drive for total conformity: Representation of Afro-Cuban sects, intellectuals, the Jehovah's Witnesses, homosexuals, and others

Since the mid 1960's special units, at one time called UMAP (Military Units for Aid to Production) were created ". . . to include only young men of draft age whose moral outlook did not in the eye of the authorities, make them fit for regular military duty. The units became a catchall for homosexuals and other undesirables and in fact functioned as prison camps."[36]

The First National Congress on Education and Culture (1971) passed various resolutions against the Afro-Cuban sects,[37] the Jehovah's Witnesses, homosexuals and dissident intellectuals among others: ". . . the pathological character of homosexual deviations was recognized . . . all manifestations are to be firmly rejected . . . and it is not to be tolerated for notorious homosexuals to have influence in the formation of our youth on the basis of their "artistic ability'."[38]

They were also barred from performing abroad.[39]

These measures cannot be minimized, as some have attempted to do outside the island by blaming them to the "machismo mentality." The fact is that in spite of social pressures there was never a systematic massive repression of homosexuals in the Island.

In regard to the intellectuals, the revolutionary policy has been that they are able to write freely, as long as they are subservient to the revolution. Castro said: "In behalf of the Revolution everything; against the Revolution nothing at all. . . "[40]

---

[33] Prensa Latina (Cuba's official news and propaganda agency) *Direct fom Cuba*, "Cuba's Second Educational Revolution," Havana. Aug. 15, 1973) No. 81, ES2814. See also Carmelo Mesa Lago, "Castro's Domestic Course," *Problems of Communism*, (September 1973) p. 35.
[34] Ibid.
[35] Quoted in "Generation Gap Cuban Style," *Dissent*, January 1970.
[36] Jose Yglesias, "The Case of Herberto Padilla," *New York Review of Books*, June 3, 1971. Until the regime's overt repression of the Cuban intellectual community, Yglesias had written very favorably about the revolution.
[37] In regard to *ñañigo* and *abacuás*, the Afro-Cuban sects, the issue seems to be at least in part that they are secret societies.
[38] *Granma*, official organ of the Communist Party of Cuba, May 9, 1971.
[39] Ibid.
[40] Fidel Casto, *Words to the Intellectuals* (Publications of the Ministry of Foreign Relations), June 1961.

In spite of various crises, including the ordering of various writers into the UMAP camps, the situation remained somewhat fluid until 1971, when Heberto Padilla, a Cuban poet internationally recognized, was imprisoned. Padilla had the temerity of attempting to have his poems smuggled out of the island to be published abroad.

Padilla had said in one of his poems:
Don't tell me that there are crimes more or less beautiful
because there are no beautiful crimes.
There are no degrees in crime.
Don't attempt to convince me that every hope
has to be for a time in the hands of executioners . . .[41]

After more than a month of strict confinement, the regime's security police "persuaded" Padilla to recant and to confess publicly that he had committed the errors attributed to him.

Padilla's "confession" prompted a letter signed by more than sixty European and Latin American intellectuals. The group which included some of the most well-known leftist intellectuals: J. P. Sartre, Susan Sontag, Octavio Paz, Simone de Beauvoir, and others, addressed the Cuban Premier: "We believe it our duty to communicate to you our shame and anger. The pitiful text of the confession that Heberto Padilla has signed could have only been obtained by means of methods which are the negation of legality and revolutionary justice . . ."[42]

Referring to the proceedings as recalling "the most sordid moments of Stalinist times, its prefabricated judgments and witch huntings," they pleaded with the Cuban Premier "to spare Cuba from the dogmatic obscurantism, and cultural xenophobia, and the repressive system that Stalinism imposed in socialist countries . . ."[43]

On April 30, 1971 Fidel Castro delivered his reply while addressing the First National Congress on Education and Culture in Havana. He said: "Now you know it, bourgeois intellectuals and bourgeois libelants, agents of the CIA . . . you will not be allowed to come to Cuba just as UPI (United Press International) and AP (Associated Press) are not allowed to come. Our doors will never again give them the chance to come here as jury members . . . in order to win an award, whether national or international, he must be a true revolutionary, a true poet, a true revolutionary."[44]

Since then, the Cuban intellectuals are required total obedience to the official guidelines. The result has been a growing number of intellectuals who refuse to write for the approved publications. Some have been sent to work-camps, and a Cuban variant of the Soviet Samizdav is published, albeit irregularly in the island.

Conclusion

The penal population in the political prisons in Cuba is a representation of Cuban society. Every major group: labor, farmers, youth; minorities such as the Jehovah's Witnesses and others are represented. They are imprisoned due to specific policies against them by the regime.

Although specific figures are not available, there seems to be a consensus among most sources that there are around 50,000 political prisoners in Cuba.

Aside from the prisoners who are serving sentences for strictly political crimes, there are thousands of others who are sent to prison as a systematic way of handling pressures in Cuban society.

Numerous international organizations have called attention to the problem. The International League for the Rights of Men is presenting a separate report here today. Amnesty International asked its members this March to write to the Cuban Premier. In some of its *Yearbooks* and in a letter dated August 1, 1974, the president of the International Red Cross acknowledged its inability "to achieve any practical results."

---

[41] *Poetry and Politics Selected Poems of Herberto Padilla.* (F. Calzon, L. Ymayo, M. L. Alvarez, editors) Washington: Georgetown University Cuban Series/G.U.C.S.A.; 1974) p. 57.
[42] "Sixty Western Intellectuals Berate Castro." *The New York Times,* May 22, 1971. See also *Le Monde,* Apr. 29, 1971, and *Le Nouvel Observateur,* Mar. 8, 1971.
[43] *The New York Times,* May 22, 1971. Front page.
[44] *Granma,* May 9, 1971.

The International Commission of Jurists, the International Rescue Committee, the World Office of the Jehovah's Witnesses have also made efforts in regard to the prisoners in Cuba.

As late as May 29th, the Inter-American Commission on Human Rights passed two resolutions denouncing violations of the rights "to life, liberty, and personal security; equality before the law, fair trial, protection from arbitrary arrest and due process of law."

Earlier the Commission had reported that:

". . . there are many persons in Cuba, including women and children, who have been jailed for political reasons and executed without prior trial or after a trial in which the accused did not enjoy the guarantees of due process.

". . . That the situation of the political prisoner in Cuba sentenced to imprisonment after having been arbitrarily arrested and subjected to trials in which the guarantees of due process have not been observed, continues to have extremely serious characteristics incompatible with the principles set forth in the Charter of the Organization of American States, the American Convention of Human Rights, the American Declaration of Human Rights and Duties of Man, and the Universal Declaration of Human Rights."

Specific characteristics of the prison system that have received considerable attention by the above mentioned international organizations are the following:

Murders;
Nakedness, body searches, beatings;
Illegal reimposition of sentences;
Lack of medical attention;
Inadequate food;
Lack of visits, sometimes for years.

During various recent trips to the island, several members of Congress were given several names and addresses of prisoners and relatives, who in spite of the consequences, would be willing to talk to members of the U.S. Congress in Cuba.

Unfortunately, Sen. McGovern and others have taken the position that they go to Cuba to see *only* the achievements of the revolution.

The prisoners and their families are not usually listed as part of those achievements, and therefore they are not included in the official tours given by the Foreign Ministry.

The following are some of the Cubans we have alluded to:

Major Huber Matos, La Cabaña Prison, Havana.
Miguel Sales, La Cabaña Prison, Havana.
Ana Lazara Rodriguez, America Libre Prison Camp, Guajay, Havana.
Mrs. Clara Abrahan de Boitel, Jovellar 155, apto. 5, Havana Cuba. (Mrs. Boitel son, Pedro Luis, was murdered in prison.)
Mrs. Marta Socarras de Sales, Calle 21 #3418, entre 34 y 36, Marianao, Havana. (Mrs. Sales husband has been sentenced to 30 years for attempting to bring her and their daughter to the United States. Mrs. Sales has been fired from her job.)

These names could be classified as some of the "revolutionary failures." The purpose of Congressional hearings and of foreign trips is usually to find out enough facts on a subject for possible legislation. To do so requires an analysis of both "achievements" and failures. It is rather unfortunate that the recent visits by members of this Congress to the island have been perceived as attempts by freely elected representatives of a free people to befriend a sadistic tyranny.

The Church in Castro's Cuba

Dr. Jose I. Lasaga, Cuban-born psychologist currently serving as director of psychological training at Crownsville (Md.) Hospital Center, testified before the House International Relations subcommittees July 9, 1975 on the situation of the church under Castro. Dr. Lasaga, who had been active in Catholic lay movements in Cuba before his departure from Cuba in 1961, said in his prepared statement:

Since all Marxist socialist states are political systems based on a well defined philosophical theory, an adequate understanding of their theoretical background will shed a great deal of light on the purpose and meaning of their decisions in relation to the different religious faiths.

In Marxism Leninism all religions are seen as a hindrance to human progress, because of their emphasis on a transcendental reality. They are expected to fade out in a socialist regime, but, as in other areas of social change, the state has an important role to play in the acceleration of the process. Lenin had clearly postulated: "We should fight against religion. This is the ABC of all materialism, and therefore of Marxism".[1] And in 1963 the Ilitchev Report to the Ideological Commission of the Communist Party stated that "officially the church" (that is, the Orthodox Church) "is loyal to the Soviet regime", but "we should not allow the church people and the sectarians to take advantage of any means of access to the souls".[2] ...

Although the picture of the situation of religious groups in Marxist socialist countries is rather dark, we must mention as a positive sign: (a) the exchange of ideas that have taken place in different parts of Europe between Christian and Marxist intellectuals, for instance the socialist thinkers Roger Garaudy from France and Milan Prucha from Czechoslovakia, (b) the fact that during the Hungarian uprising of 1956 and the Prague Spring of 1968 there were honest, sincere and promising contacts between state and religious leaders. However, it is necessary to emphasize: (a) that the dialogue between intellectuals has always taken place on a strictly personal level, (b) that some of those Marxist thinkers are considered as unorthodox by the communist parties of their respective countries, and (c) that the two great political movements mentioned before, the Hungarian Revolution and the Prague Spring, were militarily crushed by the Soviet Government because of their "revisionistic" tendencies.

II. HISTORICAL BACKGROUND

A. Church and social class: the Catholic church in Cuba before Castro

How was the Catholic church seen by the Cuban people before 1959? Some important points have to be made in order to make an objective appraisal of a rather complex picture:

1. In a very careful survey of public opinion which was conducted in Cuba in 1954, it was found that, although 99% of members of the high socio-economic class called themselves Catholic, this figure came down to 88% for the middle class and to 67% for the low income groups.[3]

---

[1] Lenin, V. I. "Actitud del Partido Obrero ante la Religión." In Lenin V. I. "La Ideologia y la Cultura Socialistas". Moscow: Ediciones en Lenguas Extranjeras, no date.
[2] Informaciones Católicas Internacionales (Mexico City), March 7. 1964.
[3] Lasaga, José I, "Responsabilidades de los laicos en la América Latina", address to the II World Congress for the Lay Apostolate, Rome, October 5–13, 1957. (The figures for the whole sample were as follows: Catholics, 72.5%; Protestants, 6%; Spiritualism, "santeria" and African faiths, 1.5%; Jews. 0.5%; Freemasons who considered freemasonry as a religion, 0.5%; no religious affiliation, 19%. These figures were taken from a public opinion survey carried out by the Agrupación Católica Universitaria in 1954. Its results were published in the same year in a mimeographed book called "Encuesta Nacional sobre el Sentimiento Religioso del Pueblo de Cuba". Although all the interviewers were practising Catholics, they operated under very strict instructions in order to guarantee a maximum of objectivity for the data.

2. At that time the Cuban bishops were not so much concerned with the need for social change as many Catholic bishops in Latin America are today, but some very influential priests were continuously preaching the necessity of a more just social order, like the future auxiliary bishop of Havana, Eduardo Boza, now in exile; the founder of the Movement for a Christian Social Democracy, Fr. Manual Foyaca, S.J., also later exiled; and the director of the most important Catholic publication in Cuba, the magazine "La Quincena", Fr. Ignacio Biain, who stayed in the country until his death, and for many years tried to improve the relations between the Catholics and the Revolution.

3. Although using an approach that could be called "paternalistic" according to our post-Council standards, an extremely large number of priests and religious were heavily involved in the service of the poor. In the survey of public opinion which was mentioned before, 3,360 subjects, belonging to all socio-economic classes, were asked how they felt about the role of the church in relation to the rich and the poor, and the results were the following: 31% considered that the church was more interested ("se ocupa más") in the poor than in the rich, 50% considered that it was equally interested in both, and only 19% considered that it was more interested in the rich.[4] The classical Marxist image of the church as allied to the rich against the poor was obviously not very popular in Cuba.

B. *Church and politics: The Batista regime*

The political picture of the relations between the Catholic church and the state after Batista's military coup in 1952, is even more complex than the description of the social situation. It is, therefore, important to analyze it from different points of view:

1. The church had complete religious freedom during the Batista regime, and although many Catholics died in the struggle between Batista and the opposition, and some of them were assassinated by the Army or the police, it was because of their personal involvement in the Anti-Batista movements and not because of their religious convictions. The relations between Batista and the Catholic organizations at times became extremely tense, but there was no overt confrontation in those years between church and state.

2. Batista's coup was highly unpopular among the younger generations and large number of Catholic young men and women sooner or later became involved in the opposition movement, especially in Castro's "Movimiento 26 de Julio." During the Sierra Maestra period of the Revolution many distinguished Catholics and Protestants actively cooperated with Castro and gave him all kinds of personal and logistic support. The general strike of April 1958 counted a large number of former leaders of the Catholic Young Workers among its most dedicated activists. At a given moment during the civil war between Castro and Batista, the most important leaders of the underground in the two largest cities of the country were: a fervent Catholic, "El Curita" (The little priest), in Havana, and a dedicated protestant, Frank Pais, in Santiago de Cuba.[5]

3. For humanitarian reasons the Catholic bishops and the Papal Nunico made many personal interventions at different times to save the lives of leaders in the Castro movement who were being persecuted by the regime. After the attack on the Moncada headquarters in 1953, the Archbishop of Santiago de Cuba, at the request of Castro's family, obtained from Batista the necessary guarantees for this leader's personal safety in case he wanted to surrender after the failure of the uprising. Having made contact with Castro, the Archbishop himself accompanied him to Santiago in order to protect his life from any possible assassination attempt on the part of Batista's troops. Later, in the Sierra Maestra years, many leaders of the "26th of July Movement" saved their lives by finding political aslyum in a Latin American Embassy thanks to the personal efforts of the Papal Nuncio at that time Mgr. Luigi Centoz. We may mention,

---

[4] Agrupación Católica Universitaria, B.I.P.: Encuesta sobre el Sentimiento Religioso del Pueblo de Cuba, a mimeographed booklet, Havana, 1954. A summary of the conclusions of the survey was later published as a brochure: Agrupación Católica Universitaria, B.I.P.: "Encuesta: Cómo piensa el pueblo de Cuba sobre la existencia de Dios, la Virgen, divorcio, supersticiones", Havana, no date.

[5] Cubillas, Vicente: "El aporte de la Igesia Evangélica a la causa redentora", Bohemia, Havana, Feb. 1, 1959.

among others, the names of those who a short time later were designated mayor of Havana, Secretary at the Presidency and the Minister of Education.

4. During the war against Batista many priests, at different times, left their pastoral assignments in the cities in order to become chaplains of the guerrillas. In contrast to the case of Camilo Torres in Colombia, all those priests joined the guerrilla movement with the explicit and official blessings of their respective bishops.

A few days after the end of the war, in the section "Inside Cuba" of "Bohemia", the most widely read Cuban magazine, it was said: "In the hour of victory Castro has acknowledged: Cuban Catholics have given their most determined support to the cause of freedom." [6]

C. Church and politics: 1959 and thereafter

In the first months of 1959 Castro presented himself to the people as a nationalistic leader who was in favor of strong changes in the social structure of the country, but who was planing to carry them out with the necessary respect for all democratic freedoms. During this period Castro enjoyed the full support of the majority of the Catholic population, and many Catholic leaders willingly cooperated with the government at various levels of the administration. When the first proposals of a land reform were made public, some bishops made explicit declarations in favor of the idea, and some priests openly expressed their solidarity with the Revolution or their sympathy for it.

However, since the beginning of the new regime certain anti-religious and pro-Marxist moves became more and more apparent. With the exception of Fr. Sardiñas, no other guerrilla chaplains were allowed to have any further contact with the Rebel Army. Three months after Castro's victory, all books dealing with social matters in the library of the training center of the Army, in Campamento de Columbia, were taken out from the shelves and substituted by strictly Marxist-Leninist texts, most of them printed in Russia.

The good relations between the Catholic Church and the Revolution did not last very long. Sooner or later, bishops, priests and lay leaders became convinced that Castro's purpose was not to carry out a democratic social revolution, but to establish a dictatorship according to Marxist principles. By the end of 1960 many Catholic leaders (including a large number of those who had previously fought against Batista) started joining the different underground movements, and some of them came to the States to participate in what was called the "*Brigade 2506*", later to be known in this country as the "Bay of Pigs invasion brigade"

The bishops officially protested on different occasions some anti-religious governmental measures, but gave very definite instructions to the priests and religious not to participate in any political movement against the regime. However, some priests and religious, who felt that their duty was to prevent a communist takeover in Cuba, cooperated in many different ways with the underground movements, although no one was ever involved in any strictly military act.

Castro's victory on April 17, 1961 opens a period of increasing limitation of the rights of the church and overt persecution of religious and priests. The Bay of Pigs invasion gave him the opportunity that he needed in order to justify a measure that is inevitable in all communist countries, that is, the nationalization of all private schools. At different times during the year 1961, and using different types of pressure, hundreds of priests and religious were forced to leave the country. Most orders of expulsion were communicated verbally, so that it could be said later that the persons involved were leaving of their own accord.

In the months that preceded the Bay of Pigs invasion and in the months that followed it, all the activities of the church were, step by step, reduced to religious services inside the walls of the temples. The Catholic press disappeared, all Catholic radio and television programs were closed, all Catholic organizations were prevented from having outdoor demonstrations or even indoor meetings, and some of their buildings were occupied by the militias or the army and eventually nationalized by the regime. A similar process took place in relation to all Protestant churches.

---

[6] (Anonymous) "La Cruz y el Diablo", in the section called "En Cuba". **Bohemia**, Havana, Jan. 18–25, 1959.

III. THE PRESENT SITUATION

A. *The changes in the policies of the Catholic Church after Pope John XXIII*

The Catholic Church has taught for centuries that any person or group may cooperate with a regime which is guided by a philosophy that is alien to the Catholic faith if this cooperation is a "licit act" by itself, is immediately geared to the service of the nation, and has more positive than negative effects. But for a long time all communist parties and all communist regimes were explicitly excluded from the application of this principle, because Pius XI and Pius XII considered that cooperating with a communist party or regime was always a disservice to the people. This situation changed dramatically after the advent of Pope John XXIII to the highest position of the Catholic Church. In his encyclical letter "Pacem in Terris" (April, 1963), the pope encouraged the cooperation of Catholics with other groups whose philosophy was different from the Christian conception of life, and did not exclude any party or regime from this principle. This decision was the result of the pope's policy of "dialogue" with all non-Catholic faiths and philosophies.

Another important change has also taken place in the policies of the Vatican during the pontificates of Pope John and Pope Paul, and it is what might be called "the rule of noncondemnation". Pope John said in a famous speech that the guiding principle of the church in our days should be "the medicine of mercy, not that of severity".[7] According to it, the strong condemnations of all regimes that encroached the church's rights which characterized the pontificate of Pius XII have been superseded by some general declarations of the difficulties that the church is experiencing in our time. This policy of "noncondemnation" has been openly contested by many distinguished Catholic leaders, such as Cardinal Mindszenty of Esztergom (Hungary), Cardinal Slipyj of Lwow (Ukraine) and Cardinal Wyszynski of Warsaw (Poland), but it is still the prevailing attitude of the Vatican in relation to the persecutions that the church is experiencing at the present time in numerous European, African, Asian and American countries, either with communist or with noncommunist regimes. Taking into account the existence of this policy, it is obvious that the silence of the Vatican at the present time does not mean that the church is not being deprived of its rights in any specific country in any part of the world.

In Cuba the possibility of a collaboration of Catholic priests and lay men and women with the Revolution, whenever they think that a certain measure is geared to the benefit of the people, has already been explicitly stated by the directives of the Catholic bishops. In April, 1969 the Episcopate protested against the embargo of trade by the OAS,[8] and in April, 1974 it encouraged a more active participation of the faithful in the present social context of Cuba.[9]

Those documents have been coldly or angrily received by some Catholics, both in Cuba and in the circles of exiles, but at the other end of the political spectrum we may also mention the existence of a small but influential group of Cuban Catholics who consider that the church is still unduly tied by what they call "a false apoliticism". Like the Pax priests in Eastern Europe they would like to see the church taking a more militant position in favor of the Revolution both in Cuba and in the rest of Latin America.[10]

The Council of Evangelical Churches, composed by the official leaders of many of the most important Protestant denominations in Cuba, is also in favor of a positive cooperation with the regime, and the Director of the interdenominational Evangelical Seminary of Matanzas has published many articles trying to find a theological foundation for a Christian commitment to the Revolution.[11] This obviously does not necessarily mean that their opinions are shared by all Protestant ministers living in Cuba at the present time.

---

[7] Pope John XXIII: opening address, II Vatican Council, Rome, October 11, 1963.
[8] Cuban Bishops: Carta Pastoral Colectiva, April 10, 1969.
[9] Cuban Bishops: Exhortacion del Episcopado Cubano a los sacerdotes, religiosas, religiosos y fieles, April 30, 1974.

[10] Raúl Gómez Treto and others: Al Venerable Sínodo Episcopal de nuestra Santa Iglesia Católica, Havana, September 11, 1974.
[11] Arce, Sergio: "¿Es posible un teología de la Revolución?", and "Misión de la Iglesia en una sociedad socialista", in Hageman, Alice L. and Wheaton, Philip E.: "Cuba: La Religión en la Revolución". Buenos Aires: Granica, 1974.

B. Verbal and social "détente"

In the last few years the violent declamations against the Catholic Church that characterized Castro's TV presentations in the early sixties have completely disappeared from his speeches, and in his meetings with different groups of Latin American Catholics he has frequently expressed his hope for a close cooperation of Christians, as individual persons, with Marxist revolutions. This attitude of "rapprochement" to the Catholic Church was specially ostensible during his visit to Chile in 1971.[12]

At the social level this new approach has been apparent in Castro's personal courtesies toward the Superior General of the Jesuits and toward the representative of the Secretary of State of the Vatican, Mgr. Casaroli, during their respective visits to Cuba. . . .

C. Facts

It is a well known fact, attested by all observers who have visited Cuba, that *the churches are open* and that, in general, *religious services* are performed in them without any obvious interference from the Cuban authorities. The practice of religious ceremonies, "with due respect for the law," is also guaranteed by the state in the project of a new constitution which was made public last April.[13]

The most serious violation of the freedom of worship which has taken place in recent years was the legal resolution of July, 1974, outlawing the religious denomination called Jehovah's Witnesses. The decision was based on their refusal to honor the national emblems in the customary ways, because of their fear of idolatry, and on their pacifist philosophy of conscientious objectors. The words used by the project of constitution in relation to both subjects, in the article that defines the freedom of worship, makes clear that this denomination is not going to be allowed to function in Cuba in the future except in the improbable case of a change in their religious beliefs.[14] In fact, in the last few years many Jehovah's Witnesses have been accused of illegal activities and sent to labor camps because of their remaining loyal to their faith.

It is also a fact that the members of some Catholic religious congregations have been allowed to continue their *charitable work in certain institutions under* state management, like the leprosarium, the homes for the aged, etc.

The freedom of worship and the possibility of working in a few governmental agencies for the benefit of the sick, the old and the poor represent the positive side of the coin from the point of view of the Catholic church.

On the negative side we must point to the following facts:

1. *Freedom of worship does not mean freedom of speech inside the churches.—* All priests and ministers are under continuous surveillance by the Committees for the Defense of the Revolution in their respective communities, and no one will dare to overtly express any disagreement with any important governmental decision even inside the walls of a church. Cardinal Wyszynski's courageous statements about human rights in Poland would not be tolerated in Cuba.

2. The *number of Catholic priests and religious is in a process of progressive decline.—*These are the figures for priests (both diocesan and religious):

Before Castro:
1945	518
1950	539
1955	693

After Castro (before the 1961 crisis):
1960	723
1965	220
1970	215
1974	195

These figures will become even more impressive if the normal increase of the population is taken into account. In 1974 there was only one priest for every

---

[12] Assmann, Hugo (ed.): "Habla Fidel Castro sobre los cristianos revolucionarios'". Montevideo: Tierra Nueva, 1972.
[13] Anteproyecto de Constitución, art 54, *Granma,* Havana, April 10, 1975.
[14] Anteproyecto de Constitución, art. 54, paragraph No. 3.

46,000 inhabitants (roughly one per 33,000 Catholics) which is the lowest figure for all Latin America.[15]

The main reason for the shortage of priests is the extreme difficulty that the church is experiencing in replacing those who die, retire or are forced to leave the country. The number of young men who are ordained every year is very small in relation to the needs of the whole nation, and it is *unbelievably difficult for any priest who is living abroad, be it Cuban or alien, to obtain the necessary permissions to work in Cuba on a permanent basis.*

It has been said by some reliable sources that one of the purposes of the visits to Havana of Fr. Arrupe, on behalf of the Jesuit Order, and Mgr. Casaroli, on behalf of the Vatican, was to obtain the necessary permissions to send some priestly replacements to Cuba. But, in spite of the courteous atmosphere of the official meetings, the bureaucratic excuses that prevent a large number of priests to enter the country have remained essentially unaltered.[16]

3. *There is no freedom of establishing religious schools.*—All Catholic and Protestant schools were closed in 1961 and there is no hope for their existence in the future, since all teaching is a function of the state.[17] The only exception to this rule are the seminaries for the formation of priests and ministers, which, as in Russia, are still accepted by the regime.

4. *There is no freedom of communication.*—The churches have no means of making their ideas or opinions known to the masses, since all information media are owned and controlled by the government or by government dominated institutions. There are no Catholic journals or magazines, no radio or television programs. The only means of communication which has been left to the Catholic Church are a few extremely modest local newsletters.

5. *The rights of assembly and association are extremely limited.*—Workshops and seminars may be acceptable if they deal either with purely dogmatic matters or with some moral or social principles which do not openly disagree with the avowed purposes of the Revolution. But the formerly powerful national Catholic lay organizations are all practically dead. And anybody trying to start any religious organization with a group of young men or women is immediately advised that his activity will be considered as both useless and counterrevolutionary, since all youngsters who want to do something for the benefit of the poor, the community or the nation, have a much better alternative, which is to join the Union of Young Communists. In fact a few priests who have been "overzealous" in their pastoral activities have had serious difficulties with the regime, and some of them have been forced to leave the country against their will.[18]

6. *Freedom of movement is not a universal right in Cuba.*—Some aliens who want to visit the country obtain their visas rather easily. Others do not, for different reasons. It is a fact that many superiors of religious orders have not been able at all to obtain a visa in order to visit their fellow members in Cuba, and some others have been able to travel to that country only after months or years of interminable administrative procedures. Once in Cuba, some visitors are granted a relative freedom of movement throughout the country; others are subject to highly sophisticated forms of control and surveillance, like an Italian priest who visited Cuba in 1970 and was able to move freely for almost two weeks, until some governmental authorities decided that, as a friendly gesture to a distinguished visitor, he should be provided with a car, a chauffeur and a guide.[19]

7. *Political and religious discrimination against students* is a reality at the highest levels of education, especially in nontechnical schools. In 1965 a very severe purge of students who were not politically reliable took place in all universities. Students were subject to a thorough investigation of their political and religious beliefs either by a group of professors or a group of fellow students, and

---

[15] Figures taken from Annuario Pontificio (Pontifical Yearbook). In Fernández,. Manuel: "La Iglesia de Cuba ante nuevas perspectivas". *La Religión*, Caracas, July 17, 1974.

[16] Fernández Manuel: "La Iglesia de Cuba ante nuevas perspectivas", op. cit.

[17] Anteproyecto de Constitución, art. 38–b.

[18] Fonseca, Jaime: "A look at Cuba under Castro: Church and Marxism face-to-face". *The Catholic Review,* Baltimore, April 18, 1969.

[19] Gheddo, Piero: "Un mese con la rivoluzione cubana". *Mondo e Missione,* Milan, Feb. 1971.

those considered as "unreliable" were not allowed to continue their education.[20] In February 1970 these policies were publicly justified by Radio Habana-Cuba on the basis that the money of the people should not be used to train potential enemies of the Revolution. Even today political and religious discrimination of students is a reality in Cuba, although the elimination of "undesirables" is taking place in less dramatic ways than in 1965.[21]

8. *There is an obvious job discrimination against dedicated religious persons*, especially in the teaching profession. Within this profession, the discrimination is more severe against teachers of history, philosophy, literature, etc. than against teachers of purely scientific subjects, like mathematics or physics. Elementary school teachers who are active church goers are frequently advised by some of their colleagues or supervisors that there is an unacceptable contradiction between being a dedicated member of a church and being a teacher in a country whose official philosophy is atheistic and materialistic.[22]

9. *Political discrimination against religious persons* is a necessary part of all communist regimes and Cuba is not an exception. "The communist party is the supreme leading force of society and state",[23] and no religious person can have any important position in it without admitting the materialistic and atheistic philosophy of Marxism Leninism. This means, in fact, that no religious person has been or will ever be able to play the role of an important decision-maker in Cuba.[24] Some collaboration at lower levels (like technical jobs in the ministeries, responsible positions in hospitals, some diplomatic jobs like the embassy at the Vatican, etc.) has already been possible to some selected religious persons. It is not impossible that a historical evolution of some communist parties might eventually lead to a humanistic revision of their conceptions of society, but at present there are no indications of any change of this type in the foreseeable future.

10. *There is no freedom from forced indoctrination.* The old concept of the establishment of a given religion has reappeared in all communist countries in the form of the establishment of an anti-religion. "The socialist state . . . (says the project of the constitution) bases its activity and educates the people in the materialistic scientific conception of the universe".[25] This means that education at all levels is supposed to respond to a materialistic and atheistic conception of the world. All theoretical courses offered at the universities and high schools have to agree with the basic principles of Marxism Leninism. The atheistic and materialistic indoctrination starts at the elementary school level, and in some cases at the kindergarten level, and children from religious families are thus subject to a continuous conflict between what they learn at home and what they are taught at school.

11. *The efforts to control the soul of the people, and especially of the young generation, are not limited to the materialistic and atheistic indoctrination that takes place in all schools.* In a rather frank statement of the purposes of the regime, the First National Congress of Culture and Education recognized the existence of a conflict between church and state, and recommended "the programming of extracurricular activities, and the attention to children and youngsters in the use of their *free time and recreation*" as a way of preventing them from being attracted to the church. A more striking example of the strategies used by the regime in order to minimize the influence of the churches even with adults is the decision made by Castro in 1965 of establishing "the Giron week", geared

---

[20] Information obtained by the author from students who were living in Cuba in the sixties. See also: "Detalles de la depuración en la Universidad de la Habana", *Diario de las Américas*, Miami, April 10, 1965.
[21] Brauning, Robert: "Cuban church small but strong in spite of pressure, priest says" (an interview with Fr. H. Boon, head of the Communications Division of the National Council of Missions of the Belgian Bishops' Conference), *NC News Service*, Washington, July 12, 1974.
[22] Information obtained by the author from teachers who were living in Cuba until 1972. See also: "Prohiben a los maestros públicos toda profesión de fe religiosa bajo castigo", *Diaria de las Américas*, Miami, Jan. 1, 1972. Also: "Christians survive in hope, journalists report", *N.C. News Service*, Washington, April 4, 1973.
[23] Anteproyecto de Constitución, art. 5.
[24] See Interview with Fr. P. Richard, *NC News Service*, Washington, March 3, 1972.
[25] Anteproyecto de Constitución, art. 54. See also art. 38-a ("the state bases its educational and cultural policies on the scientific conception of the world as established and developed by Marxism Leninism") and art. 39 ("It is the duty of all society to educate the youth in the spirit of Communism").

to the celebration of his victory against "American imperialism", and then making it a movable event which will necessarily coincide with the days when most Christian churches are commemorating the passion and death of Chirst.

It seems therefore evident, from the information presented in the preceding paragraphs, that in his dealing with the churches, as in many other aspects of the Cuban life, Castro is following the *Russian model*.

We may now answer in an objective way the most disputed question about the presence or absence of religious freedom in Cuba.

If the Soviet definition of religious freedom is used, that is the right to worship within the walls of a church, it may be said, with some reservations (like in the case of Jehovah's Winesses), that there is religious freedom in Cuba.

However, a more widely accepted definition of freedom may also be used, that which implies that all members of a religious body are able to enjoy, as individuals and as a group, all the basic human rights that are guaranteed by all democratic constitutions. According to this definition, which is the one that coincides with the principles embodied in the bill of rights of the United States, we will be forced to acknowledge that *there is no religious freedom in Cuba.*

Index

A

ABOUREZK, Sen. James (D, S.D.)—135
ADETT Zamora, Mario—52
AEROLINEAS Argentina—18
AFARS & Issas, French Territory of the (Djibouti)—122, 125
AFRICA—63, 115-26, 127-31. Castro tour—120. Cuban troops—103, 116, 121-3, 127-34, 139, 162. Military aid—122-3, 126. See also specific country
AGEE, Philip—91-2
AGRARIAN Reform Law—188
AGRICULTURE—56-7, 107, 193-4
 African slave trade—5-6.
Agrarian reform—142, 188-9
 Coffee—6, 165. Collectivization & state farms—215-6. Corn purchase—74
  Drought—66-7, 164
  Farm production—110. See also specific commodity
  Labor developments—67
  Mechanization—203
  Sugar & sugar production—5-6, 8, 33-7, 40, 45, 47, 49, 57, 62-7, 77, 86, 107, 110, 160, 164-5, 185-8, 191-2, 199-200, 202-3, 210. Swine epidemic—67
  Tobacco production—65, 67. Tractor & other machinery purchase—74
AIRCRAFT—44, 193-4. Bombings: airline offices—137, 149, 155; Cuban jet—148-51. Cuban refueling stops—117-8, 158. Flights to Cuba—56, 61, 77, 137. Hijackings—See under 'H.' Soviet-Cuban developments—44, 102. U.S. airlift ends—107
ALARCON de Quesada, Ricardo—14, 30, 75, 78-9
ALBANIA: Trade—186, 200
ALGERIA—103. Cuban military aides—130. U.S. military aid—122
ALLEGHENY Airlines—19
ALLENDE Gossens, Salvador—32, 55-9, 75-6, 84. CIA activities—93, 99
ALLENDE Fernandez, Beatriz—154-5
ALMEYDA, Clodomiro—60
ALPHA 66 (militant anti-Castro group)—23-5
ALTAMIRANO, Carlos—77
ALVAREZ, Sebastian—151
AMADOR, Fonseca—20
AMARO Salup, Raul—108
AMERICA Libra Prison Camp—218
AMERICAN Air-Line Pilots Association—49
AMERICAN Airlines—21
AMERICAN Institute for Free Labor Development (AIFLD)—158
AMERICAN Sugar Co.—203
AMNESTY International—156-7
AN American Company: The Tragedy of United Fruit (book)—160
ANDERSON, Jack—95
ANGEL de la Flor, Miguel—81
ANGOLA: Cuban intervention & relations—1, 115-29, 130-4, 162; troop withdrawal set—121-3. U.S. aid—117, 122; Young on Cuban role—126-7
ARAB Nations—103-4. See also specific country
ARAFAT, Yasir—103

229

ARAGONES Navarro, Emilio—74
ARAWAK Indians—5
ARAZOZA Rodriguez, Hector—162
ARELLANO, Osvaldo Lopez—54
ARGENTINA: Air hijackings—18, 32. Armed forces—111. Cuban trade & relations—48, 74-5, 195; auto export licensing—81; financing credits—197; OAS & trade sanctions—81, 85, 90-1
ARGUELLES, Rafael—55
ARMAMENTS: Aircraft—44. Cuban military aid—54. Submarine base & missiles—41-4, 122. U.S.-African aid—122-3
ARMED Communist League (Mexican guerrilla group)—22
ARMED Forces of National Liberation (FALN) (Venezuelan guerrilla group)—51
ARMY of National Liberation (ELN)—(Colombian guerrilla group)—53
ASPIN, Rep. Les (D, Wis.)—135-6
ASSASSINATIONS—53, 107, 147-8, 152, 155. Castro plots—25, 91-100, 152. JFK—147-8, 158-9. Letelier murder—148. See also TERRORISTS & Terrorism under 'T.'
ATOMIC Energy—80, 161, 166
AUSTRALIA: Cuban trade—107, 200, 203
AUSTRIA: Trade—186
AUTOMOBILES & Other Vehicles—62, 74, 81, 194
AVIATION—See AIRCRAFT
AYERS, Bradley—92
AZORES Islands—117-8

B

BABUN Sr., Santiago—29-30
BABUN Jr., Santiago—30
BABUN, Teofilo—29-30
BAHAMAS—31, 86
BAKER, Sen. Howard (R, Tenn.)—139
BANANAS—110
BANGOR Punta Corp.—203
BANZER Suarez, Col. Hugo—52
BARBADOS—48, 62, 91. Terrorism—149, 152
BARTCH, Carl—42-3
BASEBALL—115
BATISTA y Zaldivar, Fulgencio—1, 9-11, 164, 187, 214
BAY of Pigs Invasion—11, 160
BAY of Pigs Veterans' Association—148
BAZAN, Raul—76
BEANS—110
BELGIUM—186

BELL, Rep. Alphonzo (R, Calif.)—47
BENIN—130
BIESTER, Rep. Edward G. (R, Pa.)—47
BINGHAM, Rep. Jonathan (D, N.Y.)—106, 132, 134
BINH, Mrs. Nguyen Thi—46
BISSELL, Richard—97-100
BLACK Panthers (U.S.)—45
BLANCO, Amado—33
BOITEL, Pedro Luis—70, 215
BOLIVIA—33, 62. Cuban relations—48. 'Export of revolution'—52-3. Kidnappings & hijackings—20. OAS & trade sanctions—90-1
BOMBINGS—25-6, 86, 137, 148-51, 157. See also TERRORISTS & Terrorism
BOSCH, Juan—89
BOSCH, Orlando—150-2
BOTI, Regino—36
BOTTINI, Federico—105
BOUMEDIENNE, Houari—103, 120
BOURGUIBA, Habib—104
BOYNTON, Thomas James—18
BRANCH, Taylor—150
BRAS, Juan Mari—50
BRAVO, Douglas—51
BRAVO Pardo, Maj. Flavio—68
BRAY 3d, Charles W.—16
BRAZIL: Armed forces—111. Cuban relations—48. 'Export of revolution'—54. Hijackings—17-9. OAS & Cuban sanctions—85, 90-1. Sugar production—202
BRIGADE 2506 (organization of veterans of the Bay of Pigs invasion)—153
BRIGADE Veteran Association—155-6
BRITISH Steel Corp.—63
BRITISH West Indian Airways—18, 149
BREZHNEV, Leonid—101-2
BROOKE, Gen. John—7
BROWN, Frederick Z.—150
BUCHANAN, E. W.—21
BUCKLEY, Sen. James (R-Conservative, N.Y.)—84
BUDGET—164
BUFKIN, David—161-2
BULGARIA: Cuba & Angola—120. Trade—186, 192, 200
BUNDY, McGeorge—95
BURGENER, Rep. Clair W. (R, Calif.)—139
BURMA—160
BURNHAM, Forbes—150, 158-9

C

CAAMANO, Claudis—51-2, 82
CALE, Melvin C.—22-3

INDEX

231

CALZON, Frank—211-9
CAMACHO Omiste, Edgardo—59
CAMBODIA—135
CAMEROON—116
CAMPILLO Sainz, Jose—89
CAMPORA, Hector Jose—74
CANADA: Cuban relations & trade—33, 49, 77-8, 158, 161-2, 186, 200. Exiles' air route cut—27. Financing credits—197. Fishing boats seized—160-1. Spies deported—161-2. Terrorism—25-6, 31-2
CANADIAN International Development Agency—77
CAPE Verde—130
CARBONNEAU, Marc—32
CARDONA, Jose Miro—11
'CARLOS' (Ilich Ramirez Sanchez)—107
CARLSON, Sten—28
CARRION, Jose Luis—21
CARTER, Jimmy: Cuban military role in Africa—127, 130-2. Other Cuban relations—131-6, 147
CASADO, Manfredo—89
CASAROLI, Archbishop Agostino—108
CASAS, Maj. Zenen—69
CASTILLA Mas, Maj. Belarmino—65, 68
CASTREJON Diez, Dr. Jaime—32-3
CASTRO, Juana—86
CASTRO Coto, Isabel—10
CASTRO Diaz-Balart, Mirta—10
CASTRO Ruz, Fidel:
 Assassination plots—88-9, 91-100, 152
 Background—1, 9-12
 Economy & sugar harvests—64-6, 163-4. Exiles & exile actions—23, 25
 Foreign relations: African policy—120, 123, 125-6, 130-1; Angola—115-26, (troop withdrawal statement)—123; Arab nations—103-4; see also specific country. Bolivia—52. Chile—57, 75-6; Allende & coup involvement—58-9, 75-6. China & 'peaceful coexistence' problems—101-3. Communism & Communist-bloc nations—11-2, 101-4, 120. 'Export of revolution'—51-2, 57-8, 77, 121-2, 126, 130-1. Jamaica—162-3. Nonaligned nations—103-4.
OAS—58-9, 79, 84, 86. Panama & canal treaty—157. Soviet relations & aid—38-41, 46, 101-4, 165-6, 205-6. U.S. policy—45-6, 58-9, 79, 84, 204-5; anti-hijacking pact—148-9; CIA assassination plots—88-9, 91-100; efforts to renew ties—82-4, 86, 132, 143, 146-7; Kennedy assassination—88, 94, 205; '62 missile crisis—114; trade embargo issue—113. Venezuela—82, 84, 86
 Government reorganization—163
 Interviews—204-7
 Nuclear energy—161
 Photograph—4. Post-revolution developments—216-7; executions—214; intellectuals & other dissidents—217-8. Political prisoners & arrests—11, 29, 69-70, 156, 206, 212. Press & censorship—207
 Vagrancy laws—71
CASTRO Ruz, Raul—11, 68, 96, 102, 216
CASTRO Ruz Gonzalez, Lina—9
CASTRO y Argis, Angel—9
CASTRO'S Cuba, Cuba's Fidel (book)—212
CASTRO'S Revolution: Myths and Realities (book)—212
CATHOLIC Church, Roman—105, 108, 159. Batista regime & politics—221-2. Decline in priests—224-5. Historical background—220-1. Religious guarantees—224-7
CATHOLIC University (Chile)—56
CEAUSESCU, Nicolae—102
CENTRAL Intelligence Agency (CIA) (U.S.)—29-30, 107, 145-7, 209. Assassination plots—88-9, 91-100. Bay of Pigs invasion—160. Cuban jet bombing—148-50. Kennedy probe—93-6. Letelier assassination—153. Organized crime involvement—92, 94-100. Swine fever plot—131-2
CHEVECO Hernandez, Lt. Cmdr. Angel—68
CHILE: CIA & Allende coup—93, 99. Cuban relations—48-9, 75-7, 101-3; Allende coup role—75-6; Cuban ships & cargo detained—77; guerrilla training & terrorism—52, 153; Letelier murder—148; Schneider assassination—97-8; OAS & trade sanctions—85, 90-1
CHILES, Sen. Lawton (D, Fla.)—79
CHINA, People's Republic of (Communist)—35, 44. Cuban trade pact—41, 186, 200. Cuban-Soviet relations—101-3. Export of revolution—158
CHINESE Population—5
CHRYSLER Corp.—74, 81
CHURCH, Sen. Frank (D, Ida.)—96-7, 144-5
CIENFUEGOS harbor—42-4
CITROEN (French firm)—74
CIVIL Aeronautics Institute (Cuban)—102

CLISSOLD, Stephen—37
COAL—80
COFFEE—6, 64, 110, 165
COLBY, William E.—91
COLOMBIA: Cuban relations & trade—48, 51, 62, 86, 158. 'Export of revolution'—53. Hijackings & anti-hijack pact—18, 105. OAS & trade sanctions—81-2, 86, 90-1. Terrorism—152
COLUMBUS, Christopher—5
COLUMBUS, Diego—5
COMECON—49, 161, 186, 192-4, 200, 202
COMMENTARY (magazine)—34
COMMISSION on U.S.-Latin American Relations (U.S.)—84-5
COMMUNICATIONS—41, 56-7
COMMUNISTS & Communism—41, 68-9, 101-4, 108, 110, 120, 161, 163-4, 206-7
CONGO Republic—116, 130
CONSTRUCTION Industry—67
CONSTITUTION—164, 167-85, 187
COPELAND, Miles—91
COPPER—57
CORN—190
COSSETTE-Trudel, Jacques—32
COSSETTE-Trudel, Louise—32
COSTA Rica: CIA activities—93. Cuban relations & trade sanctions—62, 82, 85, 90-1. Hijackings—19-20
COTO, Isabel—10
COTTON—190, 193
COUNCIL for Mutual Economic Assistance (CMEA, or COMECON)—49, 161, 186, 192-4, 200, 202
COURTS & Judicial System—108, 183-4
CRIME—108. Organized crime—92, 94-100
CRIOLLOS—3, 5-6
CROSS, James R.—31-2
CROWE, Judge Guthrie—77
CUBA
    Agriculture—See under 'A.' Armaments—See under 'A.' Arrests, trials & executions—214-5. Athletes defect—55. Atomic energy—80, 161, 166. Aviation—See AIRCRAFT
    Budget—164
    Cabinet changes & reorganization—68-69. Catholic Church & religious freedom—218-27. Communications—See under 'C.' Constitution—108-10, 164, 167-85, 187
    Disasters—54-5, 67, 70-1. Drugs & narcotics—See under 'D'
    Early rebel movement—1, 10-1.

Economy—64-8, 107, 110, 185-8; five-year plan—163-4; foreign debt—40, 64; GNP—185, 197; industrialization—36-7, 67, 74, 101; rationing—66-7, 165, 208-9; sugar prices & economic problems—165-6; tourism—203, 210. Education—111, 164, 172-3, 208. Elections & electoral system—7, 108-9, 164, 177, 184-5. Energy developments—66-7, 79-80, 165-6; see also specific energy source, e.g., ATOMIC Energy, HYDROELECTRICITY, OIL, THERMOELECTRICITY. Exiles—See under 'E.' 'Export of revolution'—See under 'E.' Exports & imports—See TRADE Developments. Expropriation & nationalization—203-4, 215
    Family Codes—109. Fishing industry—See under 'F.' Foreign relations & aid—See under 'F.' Free speech laws—69, 109
    Health program—72. Historical background—3, 5-9
    Intellectuals, homosexuality & other dissidents—217-8
    Jehovah's Witness jailed—67. Judicial system—108, 183-4
    Labor developments—207, 209-10, 216-7; absenteeism & vagrancy laws—71-2; CTC union election—66; trade union organized—66-7; women, status of—67; worker productivity—65-8, 71-2. Letelier slaying & related developments—153-5
    Metals & mining—See under 'M.' Military defense—111
    National Assembly of People's Power—164-5, 176-81, 184-5
    Population & language—3, 5. Press & censorship—62. Prisoners—See under 'P' Reorganization—164-5
    Social & political system—206-10. Sports—55, 115, 133-6. Sugar—See under 'S.'
    Terrorists & terrorism—See under 'T.' Trade developments—See under 'T'
    Women—67-8, 109
    Youth—216-7
CUBA, Castro and Revolution (book)—215
CUBA, Castro and the United States (book)—212
CUBA and the Rule of Law (book)—212
CUBA: The Measure of a Revolution, The (book)—211

INDEX

CUBA: The Pursuit of Freedom (book)—212
CUBA: Ten Years of the Revolution (book)—37
CUBA, the U.S. & Russia 1960-63 (book)—11
CUBAN Broadcasting Institute—56
CUBAN Electric Co.—203
CUBAN Labor Confederation (CTC)—66
CUBAN Liberation Front—25
CUBAN Nationalist Movement—153
CUBAN National Liberation Front—148
CUBAN Revolution: A Research Study Guide (1959-69), The (book)—211
CUBAN Trade Commission—25
CUBAN Women's Federation—68
CUBAN Workers Federation (CTC)—110-1
CZECHOSLOVAKIA—41, 102. Trade—186, 190, 192, 200

D

DAIRY Production—65
DANIEL, Jean—205
DAVIS, Angela—46-7
DAYAN, Moshe—103
De ALMEIDA, Luis—121
De BEAUVOIS, Simone—69, 218
De BOITEL, Clara Abrahan—218
De CARVALHO, Otelo—124
De CESPEDES, Carlos Manuel—6, 9
DECOLONIZATION Committee (U.N.)—114-5
De la TORRIENTE, Jose—107
DELLENBACK, Rep. John (R, Ore.)—47
DELLUMS, Rep. Ronald (D, Calif.)—128, 140
DELTA Airlines—18-20
DEMOCRATIC Party (U.S.)—46, 159
DEMONSTRATIONS—24, 61-2, 69
De NASCIMENTO, Lopo—121
DENMARK—186
De SALES, Marta Socarras—218
DEVELOPING Countries & Nonaligned Nations Conference—103-4
De VINCENTI, Mrs. Julia Rivera—51
DGI (Cuban secret police)—153-4
DIAZ, Raul J.—152
DIAZ-Balart, Mirta—10
DIAZ Ordaz, Gustavo—91
DIAZ Rovirosa, Aristides—101
DIEM, Ngo Dinh—97-8
DILLON, C. Douglas—93
DINA (Chilean secret police)—153
DISASTERS & Accidents—54-5, 70-1
DIVORCE—109, 172
DIXON, Richard Frederick—21

DJIBOUTI, Republic of (formerly French Territory of Afars & Issas)—122, 125
DOLE, Sen. Robert (R, Kan.)—138-9
DOMINGUEZ Benitez, Jesus—23
DOMINICAN Republic—10, 48, 51-2, 89-90. CIA assassination plot—91-3, 97-100. Guerrilla & Cuban infiltration—51-2, 89-90. Hijacking incident—18. OAS & Cuban sanctions—85, 90-1
DONG, Pham Van—103
DORTICOS, Osvaldo—11, 40, 66, 68, 75, 114, 121, 164
DOWNEY, Arthur T.—185-8
DROUGHT—66-7, 165
DRUGS & Narcotics—29, 144
DRURY, C. M.—25-6
DULLES, Allen—96
DULLES, John Foster—96
DUMONT, Rene—215
DUTCH Antilles Airways—17

E

EARTHQUAKE—54-5
EASTERN Air Lines—17-21
EASTLAND, Sen. James O. (D, Miss.)—45
EATON, Cyrus—80
ECHEVERRIA Alvarez, Luis—91, 104-5
ECHO 2 (missile)—44
ECUADOR—48, 62. CIA activities—91. OAS & Cuban sanctions—85-6, 90-1
EDELMAN, Peter B.—92
EDELSTAM, Harold—76
EDUCATION & Illiteracy—111, 164, 172-3, 208, 217
EDWARDS, Col. Sheffield—98
EFIK language—5
EGYPT—122
EISENHOWER, Dwight D.—96-7, 99-100
ELECTIONS & Electoral System—108-10, 164, 177, 184-5
ELECTRICITY—67, 101, 160, 165-6, 206
EL SALVADOR—85, 90-1
EMMICK, Frank—145-6
ENERGY Developments—206
EQUATORIAL Guinea—116. Cuban troops—130
ERVIN Jr., Lorenzo Edward—18-9
ESCALONA, Enrique—68
ESCH, Rep. Marvin (R, Mich.)—47
ESCOBAR, Romulo—30
ESPIONAGE: Cuban spies deported—161-2. Letelier accused—153-5. See also 'Espionage & terrorism' under EXILES & Exiles Activities

ESTABA Moreno, Judge Delia—150
ESTRADA Palma, Tomas—8
ETHIOPIA: Cuban troops & advisers—125-6, 128-30
EUROMARKETS—197

EXILES & Exiles Activities:
  Bombings—25-6, 86, 137, 153, 155, 157; Cuban jet bombing—148-51
  Castro regime, arrests & executions—23. Chilean regime support—153. CORU activities—148-9, 152-3. Cuban fishing boats attacked—31, 149. Cuban official defects—27
  Espionage & terrorism: Anti-Castro plots—25, 152; CIA assassination plots—92-3; U.S.-based activities—152, 155-6, 160; Letelier murder link—148, 152-3
  International network—152. Invasion attempt—23-5
  Leader slain—155
  Political prisoners—See under 'P'
  Repatriation routes—12, 26-7
  Soviet subs & arms report—43-4
  U.S. asylum—12; U.S. informs on exiles—146
  See also specific group and individual names
EXPORT Administration Act of 1969 (U.S.)—197
EXPORT of Revolution (Cuban):
  Africa, troops & advisers—103, 116, 121-3, 127-34, 139, 162; Angolan intervention—1, 115-27, 130-4, 139, 162; (Cuban aircraft refueling stop)—158-9; (Garcia report on Cuban role)—123-5; (troop withdrawal set)—121-3. Cameroon—116; Canadian deportation of spies—161-2; Castro's policy—77, 126, 130-1, 209; Congo Republic—116; Cuban-Soviet military build-up—122, 127-8; Ethiopia—128-30; Equatorial Guinea—116; Gabon—116; Guinea-Bissau—116, 122; Malawi—116; Mozambique—116, 130; Sao Tome e Principe—130; Sierra Leone—116, 130; Somalia—116, 122; Tanzania—116; Zaire—127-8; Zambian revolt & Cuban aid—129
  Latin America—51-4, 75-6, 82, 88-90, 119, 158-9; Bolivia—52-3; Brazil—54; Chile & Allende coup involvement—75-6; Dominican Republic invasion—51-2, 89-90; Guatemala—53; Guyana—119, 158; Nicaragua—161; OAS condemnation—53; Uruguay—54; Venezuela—52-3, 82, 119
  Oman—122
  Portugal—63
  South Yemen—103, 116, 122.
  Syria—103
  U.S. views on—52-4, 114-22, 126-7, 130
EPROPRIATION & Nationalization—11, 136, 139, 141-3, 188-9, 203-4

F

FACIO, Gonzalo—82, 85
FALN (Fuerzas Armadas de Liberacion Nacional, Puerto Rican terrorist group)—154
FAMILY Laws—172
FAR (Fuerzas Armadas de Revolucion, Guatemalan guerrilla group)—53
FASCELL, Rep. Dante B. (D, Fla.)—140
FEDERAL Bureau of Investigation (FBI)—94, 147-8, 150, 152-3
FEDERATION of Women—207
FERNANDEZ, Marcelo—73, 107, 110, 133, 146
FERNANDEZ Rodriguez, Capt. Serafin—68
FERRE, Gov. Luis A. (P.R.)—50-1
FERREIRA, Joaquim Camara—18
FERREYRA, Jose Carlos—61
FIGUERES, Jose—20, 62, 93
FIGUEROA, Agapito—66-7
FIGUEROA Cordero, Angel—147
FINNEY, Michael R.—21
FISCHLE, Alfred—20
FISHING INDUSTRY—28-9, 31, 62-3, 110, 134, 137, 189, 191, 194-5, 202. Cuban boats seized—160-1. Bombing & other attacks—29-31, 149. Trade agreement—158. 200-mile limit—160-1
FITCHLI, Alfred—24
FITZGERALD, Desmond—98
FLOODS & Storms—67
FLORIDA—28
FLOUR—33
FOLGAR, Hildo—150
FON language—5
FONSECA Amador, Carlos—24
FORD, Gerald R.—106, 113-4, 116-7, 119-20, 139. CIA assassination plots—91, 93
FORD Motor Co.—74, 81
FOREIGN Assistance Act of 1961 (U.S.)—197
FOREIGN Relations (Cuban) (including aid):
  Africa—63, 120, 123, 125-6.

INDEX

Angola—115-26. See also Angolan conflict under 'EXPORT of Revolution.' Arab nations—103-4, 108; see also specific country. Argentina—74-5, 197
    Bahamas—86. Barbados—48, 62. Bolivia—52. British credits—63, 107, 197
    Canada—157-8, 197. Caribbean—62. Chile—48-9, 55-60; Allende & coup involvement—58-9, 75-7. China & 'peaceful coexistence' problems—35, 41, 101-3. Comecon—161. Communist bloc countries—11-2, 41, 101-4, 120, 161, 192-3
    Developing countries & nonaligned nations conference—103-4
    Ethiopian-Somali conflict—125-6 France—197
    Guyana—48, 62
    Hijackings & anti-hijacking agreements—See under 'H'
    Jamaica—48, 62, 162-3. Japan—63, 197
    Latin America—48-9, 62-3, 78-80, 103-4, 106, 209; see also specific country
    Mexico—13, 73-4, 89, 104-5
    OAS—12, 47-50, 55, 59-61; readmission developments—56, 78-9, 81-2, 85-6, 90, 160; trade sanctions—34, 47-8, 55, 73, 81, 90-1
    Panama—157. Peru—48-9; 54-5. Polish credit pact—102
    SELA—104. South Korea travel ban lifted—64. Soviet aid & trade—38-44, 46, 84, 101-4, 164-6, 192, 196, 205-6, 210, 212; arms, missiles & submarine missile base—1, 11, 41-4; communications net agreement—41; financing credits—105-6; industrialization program—36-7, 66; thermoelectric deal—101. Spain—107, 197. Sweden & economic aid—64; embassy siege—76
    Trinidad & Tobago—48, 62
    U.S.—11, 45-6, 86, 106, 136-8, 159, 204-5; CIA plots—88-9, 91-100, 131-2; Congressional policies—132, 139-43, 159; currency restrictions eased—135; diplomat exchange—138-9; efforts to improve relations—82-4, 86, 131-44, 146-7, 159-60; expropriation issue—11, 136, 139, 141-3, 188-9; fishing developments—28, 134, 137, 160-1; hijacking agreement—132, 136, 139 (see also HIJACKINGS under 'H'); 'interest' offices open—143-4; JFK assassination probe—147-8; political prisoners & human rights issue—132-4, 137, 139-41, 144-7; P.R. independence—114-5; Senators & others visit—135-7, 147, 159-160; sports—115, 133-6; State Dept. informs on exile activities—146; travel restrictions end—87, 132-3, 135-7; visas denied—80
    Vatican—108. Vietnam economic aid—41, 103
    West Germany—108
FOSTER, William (Soviet freighter)—77
FOX, Francis—162
FRANCE—107. Trade & financing credits—186, 197
FRASER, Rep. Donald M. (D, Minn.)—140
FREEMASONS—220
FREIDHEIM, Jerry W.—41
FRENZEL, Rep. William (R, Minn.)—47
FRIAS, Maj. Guillermo Garcia—68
FROMETA Ilva, Nora—68
FRONT de Liberation du Quebec (FLQ) (Quebec terrorists group)—32
FRUIT—190-1
FULBRIGHT, Sen. J. William (D, Ark.)—42, 60, 82
FUNSETH, Robert—88

G

GABON—116
GALL, Norman—34
GARCIA Landaetta, Ivan Gustavo—20
GARCIA Marquez, Gabriel—123-4
GARI Camany, Pablo—30
GAZMURI, Jaime—56
GENERAL Directorate of Penal Establishments (DGEP)—212
GENERAL Motors Corp.—74, 81
GEOGRAPHY—3
GERINE-Lajoie, Paul—77-8
GERMAN Democratic Republic (East Germany): Cuban trade—186, 192, 220. Military aid to Africa—126
GERMANY, Federal Republic of (West Germany)—108, 186
GIANCANA, Sam—94-6
GIL, Pedro—146
GOLDWATER, Sen. Barry (R, Ariz.)—84
GOLENDORF, Pierre—70
GOLF Two (Soviet submarine)—44
GOMEZ, Maximo—6
GONZALEZ, Antonio—152
GOODWIN, Robert L.—21
GOULART, Joao—54
GOURE, Leon—34-8
GRABER, Pierre—24

GRAIN—193, 195
GRANMA (yacht)—10
GRANT, Gerald—20
GRAUSAN Martin, Ramon—9
GREAT BRITAIN: Cuban trade—49, 62-3, 186, 200. Cubans expelled—101. Diplomat kidnapped—31-2. Financing credits—197. Hijackings incident—18. Seven Year's War—5-6
GREATER Minneapolis Chamber of Commerce—137
GREGORY, Dick—93-4
GRENADA: Trade sanctions—91
GUAM—7
GUANTANAMO Bay—8, 139
GUANTANAMO Naval Base—39, 47
GUATEMALA: Anti-Castro demonstration—61-2. Cuba & the 'export of revolution'—53. OAS & Cuban sanctions—85, 90-1
GUERRILLAS in Power (book)—36, 212
GUEVARA, Ernesto "Che"—10, 36, 123, 188
GUILLERMO, Ignacio—152-3
GUINEA: Cuban troops & 'export of revolution'—122, 130. U.S. military aid—122
GUINEA, Equitorial—See EQUATORIAL Guinea
GUINEA-Bissau, Republic of—116. Cuban troops—130
GURNEY, Sen. Edward J. (R, Fla.)—52-4
GUTIERREZ Alea, Tomas—80
GUYANA—77, 119. Cuban relations—48, 62; air agreement—77; military training—158; terrorism—152

H

HAAS, Capt. William R.—23
HAITI—62. Cuban relations—48. Trade sanctions—85, 90-1
HANSEN, Michael Lynn—22
HANSEN, Rep. Orval (R, Idaho)—47
HARVEY, William—98, 100
HASSAN II, King (Morocco)—128
HEALTH Program—72
HEINZ III, Rep. John H. (R, Pa.)—47
HELMS, Sen. Jesse (R, N.C.)—137
HELMS, Richard—92-3, 97-9
HEREDIA Cabieses, Joaquin—62
HERMAN Perez, Hamlet—51-2
HERNANDEZ, Plutarco—20
HERNANDEZ Cuesta, Raul—162
HERRERA Reyes, Ernesto—107
HERTER, Christian—96
HIJACKINGS & Anti-hijacking Developments: Air hijackings—17-23, 32; hijackers given asylum—32. Cuban-Colombian anti-hijacking pact—105. Mexico—16. Ship hijacking—27. U.S.-Cuban anti-hijacking agreement developments—13-7, 47, 49, 105-6, 136, 139, 148-9. Venezuela—17, 105
HILL, Charles—21
HINO Motors (Japan)—63
HOLT, Pat M.—82-3
HOMOSEXUALITY—217
HONDA Bay—8
HONDURAS: Cuban trade sanctions—85, 90-1. Cuban military aid—54
HONECKER, Erich—102
HOOVER, J. Edgar—147
HORTON, Rep. Frank (R, N.Y.)—47
HUERTA, Rear Adm. Ismael—75-6, 81
HUGHES, Howard R.—95-6
HUMAN Rights Abuses—See PRISONERS & Prisons
HUMBERTO Reyes, Manuel—156
HUMPHREY, Sen. Hubert H. (D, Minn.)—44
HUNDLEY, William—94
HUNGARY: Cuban trade—186, 192, 200
HUNT Jr., E. Howard—94
HUNZIKER, Karl—24
HURWITCH, Robert A.—42
HUSAK, Gustav—102
HYDROELECTRICITY—80

I

IBARRA Vasquez, Carlos—156
ILLITERACY—111. See also EDUCATION & Illiteracy
IMIAS (Cuban freighter)—77
IMMIGRATION—213-4
INDIANS—5
INGERSOLL, Robert S.—85
INSIDE the Company: CIA Diary (book)—91-2
INSTITUTE for Policy Studies—207
INTER-American Press Association (IAPA)—62, 70
INTERNATIONAL Air Transport Association—14
INTERNATIONAL Bank for Economic Cooperation (ICEC)—192
INTERNATIONAL Investment Bank (IIB)—192
INTERNATIONAL Sugar Agreement (1937)—187
INTERNATIONAL Sugar Organization—36
INTERNATIONAL Telephone & Telegraph Co.—203
INTERSPUTNIK (Communist communications organization)—41

INDEX

IRAN—108
IRON—40
ISAACS, Allan—86
IS It Socialism (book)—212
ISLA de Pinos (Isle of Pines)—3, 8
ISRAEL—103–4
ITALY: Cuban trade—186

J

JABLONSKI, Henry—102
JACKSON, Henry D.—22–3
JAGODA, Barry—115
JAMAICA: Cuban relations & aid—48, 62, 162–3. Terrorism—149. Trade sanctions—86, 91
JANOS, Lee—94
JAPAN: Cuban trade & aid—49, 63, 186, 197. Hijacking incident—22
JAVIER Alejo, Francisco—73
JAVITS, Sen. Jacob (R, N.Y.)—82–4, 138
JEHOVAH'S Witnesses—67, 217–8
JENKINS, Kempton B.—87
JEWS & Judaism—5, 220
JOCELYN C (vessel)—28
JOHNNY Express (Panamanian freighter)—29–31
JOHNSON, Billy H.—23
JOHNSON, Lyndon B.—94, 97, 99–100
JOHN XXIII, Pope—223–4
JONES, Gilbert—19
JONES, Kirby—204
JOSEPH, Cuthbert—81
JUCEPLAN (Junta Central de Planification)—36

K

KAROL, K. S.—36
KENDALL, Donald—81–2
KENNEDY, Sen. Edward M. (D, Mass.)—87–8, 96, 156
KENNEDY, John F.—42, 88, 205. Assassination probe—93–4, 159. CIA activities—92–6, 98–100. '62 missile crisis—114
KENNEDY, Robert F.: Bay of Pigs invasion—160. CIA assassination plots—92, 94–6
KENYA: U.S. military aid—122–3
KESSLER, Murray—25
KGB (Soviet secret police)—94
KHARLAMOV, Mikhail—121
KIDNAPPINGS—21–2, 149. Bolivia—20. Brazil—54. British aide in Canada—31–2. Mexican prisoner exchange—32–3. Nicaraguan terrorists—105. See also TERRORISTS & Terrorism under 'T'
KIRBO; Charles—133
KISSINGER, Henry A.—80–1, 93, 114. Cuba & Angola—115, 117, 121–2. 'Export of revolution charge'—115, 117–21
KLM Dutch Antillean Airways—18
KOREA, Peoples Republic of (North Korea)—135. Cuban trade—186, 200
KOREA, Republic of (South Korea)—64
KOSYGIN, Aleksei N.—38
KUHN, Bowie—115, 133
KUWAIT—103
KUZMIN, Mikhail—33

L

LABADIE, Robert—14
La CABANA Prison—218
LAGO, Carmelo Mesa—211
LANCTOT, Jacques—32
LANDAU, Saul—155, 204, 207–11
LANGUAGE—5
LANSDALE, Maj. Gen. Edward G.—95–6, 100
LAROTTA, Antonio—53
LASAGA, Dr. Jose I.—218
LATIN America—48–9. Allende overthrow—93, 99. CIA activities—91. Communist leaders meet—103. Cuba joins group talks at U.N.—78. Energy group formed—79–80. Opposition to Cuban embargo—82, 90–1. SELA formation—104. See also specific organization (e.g., ORGANIZATION of American States), topic (e.g., TERRORISTS & Terrorism) or country
LATIN American Economic System (SELA)—104
LATIN American Energy Organization (OLADE)—79–80
LAWYERS—108
LAZARA Rodriguez, Ana—218
LEASE, Russell—70
LECHIN, Juan—53
LEGUMES—190
LEIVA, Reynaldo Naranjo—20–1
LEO, Joseph—150
LESCAZE, Lee—155
LETELIER, Isabel—155
LETELIER, Orlando—148, 152–3
LIBYA—104. Cuban military advisers—130. U.S. military aid—122
LIEUWEN, Edwin—211
LIEVANO, Indalecio—86
LIMA, Turcios—53
LIQUOR—202
LITTLE War (1880)—6
LITTON Industries, Inc.—87

LIVESTOCK—194, 201
LOCKWOOD, Lee—215
LOPEZ Mateos, Adolfo—91
LOPEZ Muino, Fernando—80
LOPEZ Portillo, Jose—134
LOWENTHTAL, Abraham—154
LUGO, Freddy—148, 151
LUGO, Jose Luis—21
LUMUMBA, Patrice—92, 97-8
LUSSIER, Arthur—25
LUSSON, Maj. Antonio Enrique—68, 70-1
LUVALU, Pascal—121
LUZARDO Garcia, Manuel—68
LYLA Express (Panamanian freighter)—29-31
LYONS, Lt. Thomas—152

M

MACEO, Antonio—7
MACHADO, Gerardo—8-9
MACHADO Ventura, Jose R.—69
MACHIN, Jose Maria—82
MAGOON, Charles—8
MAHEU, Robert—95-6
MAINE (U.S. warship)—7
MALAGASY Republic (Madagascar)—130
MALAWI—116
MALDONADO, Victor Alfonso—16
MALI: U.S. military aid—122
MANKIEWICZ, Frank—204-7
MANLEY, Michael—162-3
MAP—2
MAPU-OC (Chilean Marxist-Leninist organization)—154
MARBLE Island (Cuban vessel)—77
MARCHAIS, Georges—163
MARI Bras, Juan—89
MARIEL port—43
MARIGHELLA, Carlos—54
MARIN, Rufo—20
MARTI, Jose—6
MARTIN, Americo—51
MARTINEZ Marquez, Guillermo—25
MASEFIELD, John—21
MASNATA, Silvio—16
MATANZAS Province—108-9
MATOS, Huber—215, 219
MAZZUKA, Joseph—25
McCANN, Thomas P.—160
McCLOSKEY, Rep. Paul (R, Calif.)—47
McCLOSKEY, Robert—26-7, 43, 56
McCONE, John A.—95-6, 98-100
McDONALD, Rep. Larry (D, Ga.)—153-5
McGEE, Sen. Gale (D, Wyo.)—84, 87

McGOVERN, Sen. George (D, S.D.)—88-9, 97, 114, 135-6, 138
McKINLEY, William—7
McKINNEY, Rep. Stewart B. (R, Conn.)—47
McNAMARA, Robert S.—95
MEANS, Marianne—94
MEAT (beef & pork)—65, 67, 110
MEDICINE—198
MEDRANO Caballero, Jorge Tulio—17
MEIN, John Gordon—53
MEMORIES of Underdevelopment (film)—80
MENDEX, Vicente—24
MENGISTU Haile Mariam, Lt. Col.—125
MESTIZOS—3
METALS & Mining—40-1, 49, 57, 73, 77, 158, 189, 191, 193-4, 200-2
MEXICO: CIA activities—91. Cuban relations—12, 48, 61, 80, 134; air service canceled—13; hijack pact—16; trade & trade sanctions—73-4, 82, 85, 90-1. Hijacking incident—19-20, 22. Oil—89. Terrorism—149 Tourism—203
MEYER, Charles—55
MIAMI, Fla.—152, 155, 160
MIDDLE East—103-4, 122. See also specific country
MILES, Jennifer—63
MILITARY Units for Aid to Production (UMAP)—217
MILLER, James M.—25
MILLS, Don—78
MIR (Movement of the Revolutionary Left, Chilean guerrilla group)—154
MIR (Movement of the Revolutionary Left, Venezuelan guerrilla group)—51
MIRET Prieto, Maj. Pedro—68
MISSILES—1, 41-4, 114, 122. See also specific type of missile
MLW-Worthington, Ltd. (Canada)—77-8
MOA Bay Mining Co.—203
MOBUTU Sese Seko—118, 128
MOEC (Colombian guerrilla group)—53
MONDALE, Sen. Walter (D, Minn.)—97, 133
MONGOLIA: Cuban trade—186, 200
MONTIEL Arguello, Alejandro—105
MOORE, Lewis D.—22-3
MORALES Navarrete, Ricardo—150
MORENO, Rafael—56
MOSHER, Rep. Charles S. (R, Ohio)—47
MOSS, Robert—124-5
MOTION Pictures—80
MOUSSET, Andre—107

INDEX

MOVEMENT of the Revolutionary Left (MIR) (Chilean guerrilla group)—154
MOVEMENT of the Revolutionary Left (MIR) (Venezuelan guerrilla group)—51
MOZAMBIQUE—116. Cuban military advisers—130. U.S. military aid—122
MR-13 (Guatemalan guerrilla group)—53
MTS Daphne (U.S. cruise ship)—137

N

NAKAOKA, Tatsuji—22
NATIONAL Airlines—18–21
NATIONAL Assembly of People's Power—164–5, 176–81, 184–5
NATIONAL Association of Small Farmers—215
NATIONAL Bank of Cuba—188
NATIONAL Front for the Liberation of Angola (FNLA)—115, 117–8, 124, 162
NATIONAL Front for the Liberation of the Congo (FNLC)—127
NATIONAL Revolutionary Council of the Congo—123
NATIONAL Society of Film Critics (N.Y.)—80
NATIONAL Union for the Total Independence of Angola (Unita)—115–8, 123–4
NATIONAL Westminister Bank (Great Britain)—63, 107
NAZAR, Miguel—105
NELSON, Lowry—211
NESSEN, Ron—113–4
NETHERLANDS: Cuban trade—186. Hijacking incident—17
NETO, Agostinho—115, 123, 126
NEWSWEEK (magazine)—95
NEW York Times (newspaper)—94
NICARAGUA: Cuban guerrilla training—161. Hijacking incident—19–20. Terrorism—105. Trade sanctions—85, 90–1
NICKEL—49–1, 49, 73, 189, 191, 193–4, 200–2
NIGERIA—122
NIPE Bay (Oriente Province)—44
NIXON, Richard M.—16, 47–8, 98
NOLAN, Rep. Richard (D, Minn.)—146
NORTH American Sugar Industries, Inc.—203
NORTH Atlantic Treaty Organization (NATO)—122
NORTH Korea—44
NORTH Vietnam—41, 44
NORTHWEST Airlines—20
NORWAY: Cuban trade—186, 200
NOSENKO, Lt. Col. Yuri I.—94
NOVIKOV, Vladimir—33
NOVO, Guillermo—152–3

O

OCEANOGRAPHY—45–6
OIL (& oil products)—33–5, 53, 73, 164–6, 188, 190–1, 193–4, 206. Cuban oil prices & production—67, 84. Four-nation oil deal—89. Fuel consumption—66. Imports—146–7, 158
OMAN—122
ORDOQUI Mesa, Joaquin—110
ORIENTE Province—9, 11, 44
ORGANIZATION of African Unity (OAU)—117–8
ORGANIZATION of American States (OAS)—12, 59–61. Argentine-U.S. auto export licensing—81. Cuban prisons & human rights abuses—156. Cuban relations & readmission developments—47–8, 78–9, 82, 85–6, 90; Castro rejects readmission—86, 160. Embargo developments—34, 56, 81, 104–5, 188; 'Exporting revolution' condemned—53. Sanctions listed—73, 90–1. U.S. influence—79
ORTEGA, Humberto—20
OSWALD, Lee Harvey—94, 147–8, 159
OTERO, Rolando—152
OVANDO Candia, Alfredo—52
OVANDO y Bravo, Msgr. Miguel—105

P

PACIFIC Southwest Airlines—21
PADILLA, Heberto—69, 218
PADRON, Francisco—65
PALESTINE Liberation Organization (PLO)—103, 154
PALMARES Armed Revolutionary Vanguard (Brazilian terrorist group)—17
PALOMARES Duque, Lema—107
PAN American Airways—19–20
PAN-American Games—45, 55
PANAMA—48, 62. Cuban relations & aid—157. Freighter attack—29–31. Hijackings—17. OAS & trade sanctions—85, 90–1. Ships & cargo detained—77. Terrorism—149, 152. Tourism—203
PAPER & Textiles—158
PARAGUAY—48. OAS & trade sanctions—85, 90–1
PASTRANA Borrero, Misael—82
PAUL VI, Pope—159
PAZ, Octavio—218
PELL, Sen. Claiborne (D, R.I.)—82–4

PENA, Lazaro—110-1
PENA Jaquez, Toribio—89
PEOPLE'S Liberation Army (Colombian guerrilla group)—53
PEPSICo Inc.—160
PERAZA, Gerardo—101
PERCY, Sen. Charles (R, Ill.)—89
PEREZ, Carlos Andres—104, 151
PEREZ Marcano, Hector—51
PERUYERO, Juan Jose—155
PERU: Cuban ties & trade resumed—48-9, 62. OAS & trade sanctions opposed—81, 85, 90-1. Quake aid—54-5. Terrorist bombing—106-7
PHILIPPINES—7, 202
PHILLIPS, David A.—93
PHIPPS, Frank—162
PHOTOGRAPH—4
PLATT Amendment (U.S.)—7-8
PLAYA Larga (Cuban vessel)—77
PLAZA, Galo—55, 60
POETS—217-8
POLAND—102. Cuban trade—186, 192, 200
POLLACK, Michael B.—25
POPES: John XXIII—223-4. Paul VI—159
POPULAR Democratic Party (Puerto Rico)—70
POPULAR Movement for the Liberation of Angola (MPLA)—115-9, 121, 122-5
POPULATION—3
PORTUGAL—117-8. Cuban trade—160
POSADA, Luis—148-52
POWELL, Jody—138-9
PRENDES Gutierrez, Orlando—63
PRESBYTERIAN Church (U.S.)—46
PRESS & Censorship—62, 70, 207, 222
PRIO Socarras, Carlos—9, 86
PRISONERS & PRISONS—156-7, 206, 209-10, 212-3, 218. American prisoners—88; Americans & families freed—28-9, 137, 144-7; drug charges—29. Bolivian escapees—33. Colombian sailors released—86. Exiled commandos freed—156-7. Hijackers & terrorists given asylum—31-3. Imprisonment, arrests & executions—69-70, 150-1; post-revolution—214-5. Labor camps—213. Mexican prisoners released—32-3. Panamanian freighter captain & crew held—29-31. Prison conditions & abuses—70, 209, 156-7, 215-6, 218; AI report—157. Prisoner exchange—28-9. UMAP (special prison camps)—217. U.S., political repression & other human rights issues—132-4, 139-41, 156-7, 209-19

PROTESTANTS—220, 222
PROUTY, L. Fletcher—92-3
PUERTO Ricans—89, 154
PUERTO Rican Socialist Party (parent organization of FALN)—154
PUERTO Rico—7, 50-1. Independence issue—79, 114-5, 154

Q

QADDAFI, Muammar el-—104, 125
QUESADA, Alarcon—50-1
QUESADA Fernandez, Jose Antonio—23

R

RABASA, Emilio—73, 82
RADIO—57
RAILROADS—77-8, 195
RAMIREZ Sanchez, Ilich ('Carlos')—107
RAMON Fernandez, Jose—111
RAMPHAL, Shridath—81
RANKIN, J. Lee—147
RED Sea-Persian Gulf region—121
REED, Walter—7
REFUGEES—76, 107. See also EXILES & Exile Activities
RELIGION—5, 67, 108, 217-27. See also CATHOLIC Church, Roman and other groups
REPUBLICAN Party (U.S.)—46, 139-43, 159
RESUMEN (Venezuelan magazine)—158
REVOLUTIONARY Armed Forces (FARC) (Colombian guerrilla group)—53
REYES, Dr. Manolo—43-4
RHODES, Lawrence M.—17
RHODESIA: Cuban guerrilla training—161-2
RICARDO, Herman—148-151
RICE—110, 190, 201
RICHMOND, Rep. Frederick W. (D, N.Y.)—146
RIO Treaty (1948)—20
RISQUET, Jorge—65
RIVERO Milan, Fernando E.—162
RIVERS, Rep. L. Mendel (D, S.C.)—42
ROA Garcia, Raul—14, 16, 24, 33, 57, 60-1, 76, 82
ROCA, Blas—109
ROCKEFELLER Commission (U.S.)—93-6
RODRIGUEZ, Carlos Rafael—13, 33, 106, 117, 124-5
RODRIGUEZ, Julio Israel—66
RODRIGUEZ, Capt. Pedro—63
RODRIGUEZ Lopez, Rogelio—63

INDEX 241

RODRIGUEZ Verdes, Jesus—162
ROGERS, William P.—15-6, 27, 59, 61, 106
ROMANIA (Rumania): Cuban trade—102, 186, 192, 200
ROSS, Robert—152
ROSSELLI, John—92, 94-8
ROYAL Canadian Mounted Police (RCMP)—32, 162
RUBBER—190
RUIZ, Maria del Carmen—147
RUM—73, 201-2
RUMANIA—See ROMANIA
RUMSFELD, Donald—122-3
RUSK, Dean—95
RUSSIA in the Caribbean (book)—212
RUTH, Steve—70

S

SAEZ Merida, Simon—51
SAINZ Rodriguez, Raul—107
SALAZAR, Albaida—107
SALES, Mrs. Marta Socarrasde—219
SALES, Miguel—216, 219
SALVADOR, David—216
SANDINIST National Liberation Front (Nicaraguan terrorist group)—20, 105, 161
SAO Tome e Principe—130
SARGEN, Andres Nazario—23
SARTRE, Jean-Paul—69, 218
SAVIMBI, Jonas—115-6, 118
SCALI, John—75
SCHACHI, Efrain—85
SCHATZ, Dr. Albert—72
SCHLESINGER, James R.—91, 93
SCHOOR, Daniel—91-2
SCIENTISTS—45-6
SCRANTON, William—121
SEAL, Barry—25
SECOND Front of the Escambray (exile group)—23
SELA (Latin American Economic System)—104
SENDIC, Raul—54
SEQUIN, Pierre—32
SERAFIN, Aldo Vera—152
'SERB' missile—44
SEVEN Years' War (1756-63)—5
SEVILLA Sacasa, Guillermo—105
'SHADDOCK' missile—44
SHAMP, David—28
SHIPS & Shipping Industry, Cuban—27-31. Fishing developments—See FISH & Fishing Industry. Ship bombings & other attacks—29-31, 149; cargo detained—77, 160-1; fishing boats—31, 149. Ship purchases & modernization—62-3, 75, 102, 160; link-up—73; missile-firing patrol boats—44; Soviet aid—84. Territorial waters—See WATERS, Territorial
SIERRA Leone—116. Cuban advisers—130
SIGMUND, Paul. E—75
SINDERMANN, Horst—102
SOMALIA—116. Cuban relations—63, 125, 129-30; military build-up & troops—122. Ethiopian conflict—125-6. Soviet relations—129-30; military buildup—122
SOMOZA, Anastasio—24
SONTAG, Susan—69, 218
SOURANDER, Bo—76
SOURANDER, Margarethe—76
SOUTHERN Airways—105-6
SOUTH Africa—121
SOUTH-West Africa People's Organization (SWAPO)—123
SOVIET Penetration of Latin America (book)—212
SOVIET Pressures in the Caribbean (book)—212
SOVIET Relations with Latin America, 1918-1968 (book)—37
SPAIN—5-7. Cuban relations & problems—63-4; financing credits—107, 197; terrorism—155; trade—107, 162
SPANISH-American War (1898)—7
SPARKMAN, Sen. John J. (D, Ala.)—87, 105-6
SPECTATOR (British magazine)—91
SPIRITUALISM—220
SPORTS—45, 55, 115, 133-6
SPRANDEL, Fritz—28-9
STANDARD Oil Co.—203
STEEL—57, 158
STEWART, Dr. Harris B.—46
STUBBS, Clemmie—18
STUDENTS for a Democratic Scoiety (SDS)—45
STURGIS, Frank—94
SUAREZ de la Paz, Ismael—27
SUAREZ Esquivel, Dionisio—153
SUDAN—122
SUGAR—5-6, 8, 33-7, 40, 45, 47, 49, 57, 62-7, 77, 86, 107, 110, 160, 162, 164-5, 185-8, 191-2, 194-5, 199-200, 202-3, 210
SUGAR Acts of 1934 (U.S.)—187, 199
SUNOL Ricardo, Maj. Eddy—68
SUSLOV, Mikhail—163
SWEDEN—64. Cuban trade—186
SWITZERLAND—24. Cuban trade—186
SYRIA: Cuban troops report—103

T

TAFT, William Howard—8
TANZANIA—116, 130
TELLER Amendment (U.S.)—7
TENASSEE, Patrick—158
TEN Years' War (1868-78)—6
TERRITORIAL Waters—See WATERS, Territorial
TERRORISTS & Terrorism:
    Assassinations—53, 149; Castro plots—25, 91-100, 152; Cuban exile leader—155; ex-Cuban official—107, 152; JFK—147-8, 158-9; Letelier—148, 152-3
    Bolivia—20, 53. Bombings—25-6, 86, 106-7, 137, 148-151, 153, 155, 157. Brazil—54
    Canadians given asylum—31-2. Colombia—53. Cuban exiles—See EXILES & Exile Activities
    Dominican Republic invasion—51-2, 80-90
    GREAT Britain—31-2. Guatemala—53
    Hijackings—See under 'H' International network—107, 152-5; see also specific terrorist group
    Kidnappings—20-2, 31-3, 54, 105, 149
    Latin guerrillas, Castro ties—51-3
    Mexico—32-3, 149
    Nicaragua—105
    Other guerrilla activity—See EXPORT of Revolution
    Spain—155
    Venezuela—52-3
TEXACO, Inc.—203
TEXTILES—194
THERMOELECTRICITY—101
TIME (magazine)—92, 95
TOBACCO—64-5, 67, 110, 189, 191, 194, 202
TODMAN, Terence—137
TORONTO Globe & Mail (newspaper)—124-5
TORRALBA Gonzalez, Maj. Diocles—68
TORRES, Gen. Juan Jose—52
TORRES Rizo, Julian—154
TORRIJOS, Brig. Gen. Omar—17, 157
TOURE, Ahmed Sekou—120
TOURISM & Travel Restrictions—45, 64, 80, 86-7, 159-60, 187, 203, 210
TRADE Developments, Cuban:
    Argentina—74-5, 195. Australia—107. Austria—186
    British trade & credits deal—49, 62-3, 186
    Canada—77-8, 158, 186. Caribbean—62. Chile—56-7, 75; Cuban ships & cargo detained—77. China, Communist—35, 41, 186. Colombia—158. Communist bloc nations—49, 110, 186, 200; see also specific country; COMECON—49. Corn—74. Cuban trading enterprises—194-5
    Denmark—186
    Euromarkets—197; see also specific country
    Financing credits—62-3, 195-7. Fishing industry exports—110, 158, 189, 191, 194-5. Foodstuffs—189, 194. France—186
    Germany, East—186, 192. Grains—195
    Italy—186
    Japan—49, 63, 186, 200
    Metals—73, 158, 195, 200-1. Mexico—61, 73-4
    Netherlands—186. Nickel—195, 200-1. Norway—186
    Oil & oil products—33-4, 40, 89, 146-7, 165-6, 188, 190-1, 193-4. OAS & trade sanctions—56-7, 104-5, 188; Sanctions lifted—62-3, 73
    Paper & textiles—158. Peru—62. Poland—192. Portugal—160
    Shipping purchases—62-3, 75. Slavery—5-6. Spain—64, 107, 162. Steel—158. Sugar—33-5, 40-1, 65-7, 107, 110, 162, 165-6, 185-92, 194-6, 185-92, 194-6, 199-204; Latin cartel—86. Sweden—186. Switzerland—186
    Tobacco—189, 191, 194, 201. Trade gains & export commodities—200-3; deficits—40, 64, 107, 193, 195-6
    U.S.S.R.: sugar sales & other commodities—33, 35, 40-1, 64, 158, 165-6, 186, 188, 190-1, 195-6, 200; deficit problems—40, 64. U.S.-Cuban trade—133, 136-8, 186-91, 200; auto firms—74-5; embargo developments—44-51, 59-60, 81, 87-9, 106, 113-4, 133, 136-8, 188, 197-8, 204, 208; export licensing—197-8; pre-revolutionary trade—185-8; resumption benefits—199-201, 203-4; sanctions eased—44, 113-4, 137-8; trade curbs effectiveness—198-9
    Vehicle, tractor & machinery purchases—63, 74-5, 77-8, 190, 193-5
TRADE Reform Act (U.S.)—104
TRADING With the Enemy Act (1917-74) U.S.—77-8, 80, 197
TRANS Caribbean Airways—19

TRANSPORTATION—63, 70–1, 74, 77–8, 107, 190, 193–5
TRANS World Airlines—19, 21
TRAVEL Restrictions—See TOURISM & Travel Restrictions
TREATY of Paris (1763)—5; (1898)—7
TREATY of Zanjon (1878)—6
TRINIDAD & Tobago—48, 55, 62, 148. OAS & trade sanctions—62, 81, 85, 90–1. Terrorism—152
TRUDEAU, Pierre Elliott—78, 157–8
TRUJILLO, Rafael—91–3, 97–100
TSHOMBE, Moise—123
TULLER, Charles A.—22
TUNISIA—104
TUPAMARUS (Uruguayan guerrilla group)—54
26th of July Movement—27

U

UGANDA—122. Cuban advisers—130
UNION of Soviet Socialist Republics (U.S.S.R.):
Angolan conflict—116–7
Cuban relations & aid—1, 33–44, 66, 101–4, 165–6, 196, 203, 205–6, 210, 212; deepwater port built—84; industrialization program—36–7; military aid—41–44; oil—67, 89, 188; sugar trade & other products—33, 65, 67, 110, 186, 188, 190–1, 193–4, 200, 202; trade dependency—195–6
KGB & Kennedy assassination—94
Letelier—153–5
Middle East Military role—12
Nonaligned nations denounce imperialism—103–4
Somalia—129–30
U.S.-Cuban confrontation—30; aircraft patrol coast—44
Defense, Department of—42, 44, 87, 103. Diplomat exchange agreement—138–9. Drugs & narcotics—See under 'D'
Economic overview of Cuba—185–204. Exiles & anti-Castro plots—25, 146. 'Export of Revolution'—See under 'E.' Expropriation issue—114, 136, 139, 141–3, 188–9; claims settlement awards—203–4; see also specific firm
Fishing developments—134, 137; ships seized—28–9, 77
Guantanamo naval base—39
Hijackings—See under 'H'
'Interest' offices open—143–4
Journalist deportation—149–50.

Justice, Department of—25, 94–5
Kissinger—81, 86–7
Missile crisis (1962)—1, 11, 114
Party platforms—46, 159; Platt Amendment—7–8. Political prisoners & human rights issues—114, 132–4, 139–41, 156–7, 209–19; Americans—137, 144–7. Puerto Rican independence—114–5
Refugees: airlift ended—107; leader slain—107
Zairian invasion role—127–8
UNITED Air Lines—18–9
UNITED Brands Co. (U.S.)—160
UNITED Front of Revolutionary Action (FUAR) (Colombian guerrilla group)—53
UNITED Fruit Sugar Co. (U.S.)—203
UNITED Nations:
Air hijacking resolution—14. Angolan conflict—121. Anti-Castro demonstration—69; bombing—149
Chilean-Cuban relations—75–6. Commission for Trade & Development—49. Cuban aides ousted—63
Intergovernmental Oceanographic Commission—46
Latin Group talks—78. Law of the Sea Conference—78
PLO—103. Puerto Rican independence—50–1, 79, 114–5
U.S.-Cuban confrontation—30
UNITED Revolutionary Organization (CORU)—148–9, 155
UNITED States:
African military aid—122–3. Agriculture, Department of—36. Aides to Cuba ousted—63. Angolan conflict & aid—117; Cuban troops—121–3, 130–4
Bay of Pigs invasion—11, 160
CIA activities—88–9, 91–100, 131–2, 148–50, 153, 160; FBI involvement—94; JFK probe—93–6, 147–8; organized crime—92, 94–100. Commerce, Department of—46, 197–9, 185–204. Congressional views on rapprochement—47–54, 60, 79, 83–4, 114, 128, 132, 134–43, 159, 211–9; House Interamerican Affairs Subcommittee—44; Republican opposition—139–43; Senate Foreign Relations Committee—81–4, 132, 137–8; Senators & others visit—72, 82–4, 88–9, 135–7, 147; trade sanctions—87–9, 106, 137–8. Congress (other developments): Select Committee on Intelligence Operations—94, 96–100, 185–8, 207–8, 211–27; Subcommittee on Internal Security—45, 152. Currency restrictions—135

Spanish-American War (1898)—7. Sports—133-6. State, Department of—13-6, 21, 23, 26-7, 30, 42-6, 56, 74, 80-6, 88, 113-5, 118, 126-30, 132, 135, 144-6, 150, 153, 156. Sugar production—202
Trade developments—See under 'T.' Travel restrictions eased—45-6, 87, 132-3, 135-7; visas denied—80
U.S.-Cuban population—70
URUGUAY—58. CIA activities—91. Cuban 'export of revolution'—54. OAS & Cuban sanctions—85, 90-1

V

VAGRANTS & Vagrancy Laws—71-2
VALDES, Juan Gabriel—154
VALDES, Maj. Ramiro—68
VALDES, Nelson P.—211
VALENZUELA Acebal, Rene—162
VANCE, Cyrus—126, 132-3
VARIG Airline (Brazilian)—18
VASQUEZ Carrizosa, Alberto—81
VATICAN—108, 223
VAZQUEZ Rojas, Genaro—33
VEIGA Gonzalez, Roberto—111
VENCEREMOS (We Shall Win) Brigade—45
VENEZUELA: Cuban relations—48, 84, 86; trade sanctions—82, 90-1. Hijackings & anti-hijacking accord—17, 105. Oil—89. SELA formation—104. Terrorists & terrorism—51, 53; Cubans—51, 119, 148-53. U.S. journalists deported—149-50
VEST, George S.—80
VIACAO Aerea de Sao Paulo (VASP) (Brazilian airline)—18
VIETNAM—135
VIETNAM, Democratic Republic of (North Vietnam)—163. Cuban relations & aid—103; trade—186, 200
VIETNAM, Republic of (South Vietnam)—97-8
VIGNES, Alberto—81
VILLA, Jose—29-31
VOLSKII, V. V.—37

W

WALINSKY, Adam—92
WARREN, Earl—159
WARREN Commission—93-4, 159
WASHINGTON Post (newspaper)—91-2, 123
WATERS, Territorial—28-31, 86, 134, 137. Law of the Sea Conference (U.N.)—78
WATKINS, Augustus—19
WEATHER Underground (U.S. terrorist group)—154
WEINKLE, Julian—34-8
WESTERN Airlines—22
WEST Indies Sugar Co.—203
WEYLER, Gen. Valeriano—7
WHALEN Jr., Rep. Charles W. (R, Ohio)—47
WHEAT—190
WHITLAM, Gough—107
WILLIAMS, Eric—55
WILLS, Frederick—158
WILSON, Jorge—55
WOMEN—67-8, 109, 172-4, 207
WOOD, Gen. Leonard E.—7
WORLD War I—8
WRIGHT, Burke—160

Y

YELIN, Saul—80
YEMEN, People's Democratic Republic of (formerly Southern Yemen)—103, 122, 125
YORUBA language—5
YOUNG, Andrew—126-7, 130-1
YOUNG Cubans (exile group)—25
YOUTH—216-7
YUGOSLAVIA—102, 120

Z

ZAIRE: Angolan war—117-8. Lumumba assassination—92, 97-8. Shaba (Katanga) invasion—127-8. U.S. military aid—122-3
ZAMBIA: Cuba—63, 129
ZAMORA, Pedro—107
ZERO Point (People's Revolutionary Army) (guerrilla group)—105
ZHIVKOV, Todor—163
ZIEGLER, Ronald L.—30
ZINC—77